# THE WRITINGS OF
# RABASH
## ASSORTED NOTES
### Volume Seven

LAITMAN
KABBALAH
PUBLISHERS

Rav Baruch Shalom HaLevi Ashlag

The Writings of RABASH
Volume Seven—Assorted Notes

Copyright © 2023 by Michael Laitman All rights reserved
Published by Laitman Kabbalah Publishers

Contact Information
E-mail: info@kabbalah.info
Website: www.kabbalah.info
Toll free in USA and Canada: 1-866-LAITMAN

1057 Steeles Avenue West, Suite 532, Toronto, ON, M2R 3X1, Canada

No part of this book may be used or reproduced in any manner without written permission of the publisher, except in the case of brief quotations embodied in critical articles or reviews.

ISBN: 978-1-77228-144-6

Translation: Rinah Shalom, Chaim Ratz
Translation Assistance: Mickey Cohen, Moshe Eisenberg
Content Editing: Noga Bar Noye
Editing and Proofreading: Mary Pennock, Mary Miesem, Joseph Donnelly, Michael Kellogg, Debbie Wood
Internal Design: Gill Zahavi
Cover Design: Baruch Khovov/Inna Smirnova
Executive Editor: Chaim Ratz
Printing and Post Production: Uri Laitman

SEDOND EDITION: SEPTEMBER 2023

# Table of Contents

501- The Quality of Truth – 1 .................................................................15
502- If Man Wins, the Creator Is Happy ..............................................16
503- Partnership.......................................................................................17
504- The Secret of the Lord Is to Those Who Fear Him.......................18
505- True Mercy ......................................................................................19
506- Saved Us from the Hand of the Shepherds...................................20
507- What Is Joy?.....................................................................................22
508- The Ascent of *Malchut* to *Bina* ......................................................23
509- The Revelation of the Love of the Creator....................................25
510- Concealed and Revealed ................................................................26
511- The Middle Line..............................................................................27
512- He Who Disputes Peace.................................................................27
513- Gathering Wood .............................................................................27
514- Welcoming Guests – 2 ....................................................................27
515- Concerning the surrounding lights ...............................................28
516- A Shoe .............................................................................................28
517- The Constitution of the Torah ......................................................29
518- He Who Comes to Defile ...............................................................30
519- Concerning the *Tzimtzum* [Restriction] .......................................31
520- Water Will Flow from His Buckets................................................31
521- The Mind [Reason] that Governs Man.........................................32
522- "Right" Means Wholeness..............................................................33
523- What It Means to Bear a Son and a Daughter in the Work ..........33
524- What Is, He Swallowed *Maror* [Bitter Herb],
    He Will Not Come Out, in the work? ...........................................34
525- Three Lines – 3 ................................................................................35
526- With All Your Heart.......................................................................36
527- The God of Israel............................................................................36
528- Prayer..............................................................................................37
529- I Will Give You My Blessing..........................................................37
530- Movement Due to Shame ..............................................................38
531- The Essence of the Correction ......................................................38
532- The Main Choice............................................................................40
533- The Creator Pulls the Man Close..................................................41
534- Concerning the Groom ..................................................................42
535- A Cup of *Kiddush* ..........................................................................43
536- You Shall Tithe ...............................................................................44
537- This Month Is to You.....................................................................45

538- I Give Him My Covenant of Peace .................................................. 47
539- Questions about "Return O Israel" ............................................... 48
540- Nourishment ....................................................................................... 48
541- When the Lord Favors Man's Ways ............................................. 49
542- Return, O Israel – 2 .......................................................................... 49
543- Tell the Children of Israel .............................................................. 50
544- Man Is Born a Wild Ass [Donkey] ............................................... 52
545- Laboring and Finding ..................................................................... 53
546- He Made Everything Good in Its Time ...................................... 55
547- The Attribute of Caution ................................................................ 56
548- Doing and Hearing .......................................................................... 56
549- Feeling the Lack ................................................................................ 57
550- If You Seek Her as Silver ................................................................ 58
551- The Torah as a Spice ....................................................................... 58
552- He Who Comes to Purify Is Aided – 1 ....................................... 59
553- The Difference between Concealed and Revealed ................... 61
554- The Power of Thought .................................................................... 62
555- The Exile of the *Shechina* [Divinity] ............................................ 63
556- The Torah, from the Words "Shot Through" ............................ 64
557- Concerning *Ohr Hozer* [Reflected Light] .................................. 65
558- Desire for Spirituality ..................................................................... 67
559- One Hundred Blessings .................................................................. 67
560- Generations ....................................................................................... 71
561- The Soul of Israel ............................................................................. 72
562- Wisdom and Prayer ......................................................................... 74
563- Definitions – 2 ................................................................................... 75
564- Fire, Wind, Water, Dust .................................................................. 77
565- To Do Them Today .......................................................................... 80
566- Cast Their Seed Among the Nations ........................................... 81
567- The Quality of Truth – 2 ................................................................. 82
568- The Meaning of "Right" and "Left" .............................................. 83
569- The Meaning of the Offering ......................................................... 84
570- General Attainment and Personal Attainment .......................... 85
571- He Is One and His Name, One ..................................................... 87
572- Two Labors ........................................................................................ 88
573- They Shall Fear You ........................................................................ 90
574- If You Come ....................................................................................... 91
575- The Purity of the Work ................................................................... 92
576- A Shabbat Dish ................................................................................. 94
577- Concerning the Goal ....................................................................... 97
578- Half a *Shekel* – 2 .............................................................................. 99
579- I Will Remove the Stony Heart ................................................... 100
580- A Good Neighbor and a Bad Neighbor .................................... 101

581- The Act Is What Decides ................................................................. 102
582- One Whose Wife Provides for Him ............................................... 103
583- Righteous and Wicked ..................................................................... 104
584- The Face of the Lord Is in Evildoers ............................................. 105
585- The Kingship and the Governance to The One Who Lives Forever .. 106
586- Which Is the Straight Path ............................................................. 107
587- The Upper One Scrutinizes for the Purpose of the Lower One ... 108
588- *Malchut* of the Upper One Becomes *Keter* to the Lower One ...... 109
589- God Did Not Guide Them .............................................................. 111
590- Those Who Walk to the Land of Israel ......................................... 112
591- Renewed Work .................................................................................. 115
592- The Names of *Malchut* ..................................................................... 116
593- One Should Not Appease One's Neighbor When He Is Angry ... 117
594- The Commandment of Repentance .............................................. 118
595- The Measure of the Greatness of the Creator ............................ 119
596- Nothing New Under the Sun ......................................................... 119
597- A Generation Goes and a Generation Comes
 and the Earth Forever Stands ......................................................... 119
598- What It Means that Shabbat Is Called "Guest" in the Work ....... 120
599- Arise, O God ...................................................................................... 121
600- From the Depth I Called You, Lord – 1 ....................................... 121
601- Prayer and Request ......................................................................... 122
602- One Should Not Be Ashamed of the Mockers ........................... 123
603- There Is *Shechina* in the Wall ......................................................... 123
604- Why He Waited until the War Against Amalek .......................... 124
605- And Jethro Heard ............................................................................. 124
606- Those of Little Faith ........................................................................ 125
607- Remember that You Were a Slave ................................................ 126
608- Not because You Were Many ......................................................... 126
609- God Is More Terrible than Your Sanctifiers ................................ 127
610- Buying a Woman .............................................................................. 127
611- Capital and Fruits ............................................................................ 128
612- Concerning This World and the Next World – 2 ....................... 129
613- When a Woman Inseminates ......................................................... 129
614- Bitter Herb ........................................................................................ 130
615- The Reward for the Work ............................................................... 130
616- The Governance of *Malchut* ........................................................... 130
617- Peace at Home .................................................................................. 131
618- Awakening – 2 .................................................................................. 131
619- King of the Nations ......................................................................... 131
620- Concerning a Blessing .................................................................... 133
621- A Minor *Mitzva* [Commandment] ................................................. 135

622- Overcoming ............................................................................................136
623- Purify Our Hearts ..................................................................................137
624- *Ushpizin* [Sukkot Guests] .....................................................................138
625- The *Mitzva* of *Sukkah* ........................................................................138
626- Anything that the Merciful One Does, He Does for the Best ......139
627- Law and Judgment - 1 ..........................................................................140
628- The Qualities of "Idol-Worshippers" and "Israel" ...................... 141
629- One Who Despises a Wise Disciple ..................................................142
630- And There Was Evening and There Was Morning......................143
631- *Kedusha* [Holiness] and *Tahara* [Purity] ..........................................143
632- I Will Always Yearn.............................................................................144
633- Revealing a Portion and Covering Two Portions - 2 .....................145
634- Fear of Heaven .....................................................................................146
635- This World and the Next World - 1 .................................................147
636- The Need for Flavors of Torah .........................................................148
637- Four States in the Work .....................................................................149
638- Man's Inclination ................................................................................150
639- This Is the Making of the *Menorah* [Temple Lamp] - 2 ................151
640- A Blessing and a Curse .......................................................................153
641- Inheritance of the Land .....................................................................154
642- Justice, Justice You Shall Pursue ......................................................156
643- Supporters of the Torah ....................................................................157
644- Passing the Dead before the Bride...................................................158
645- By Your Actions, We Know You ......................................................159
646- The Generations of Jacob Joseph ..................................................... 161
647- A Prayer Requires a Deficiency........................................................163
648- The Joy of the Giver............................................................................164
649- Preparation for the Light ..................................................................164
650- Criticism on Bestowal.........................................................................165
651- Day and Night .....................................................................................165
652- If Any Man of You Brings an Offering...........................................165
653- Concerning Threshing........................................................................166
654- Who Despises the Day of Smallness ...............................................167
655- Shoots Like an Arrow ........................................................................167
656- For the Iniquity of the Amorite Is Not Complete........................167
657- What Is Reality and What Is Imagination.....................................168
658- This World and the Next World - 2 ................................................169
659- What Are Torah and Work? ..............................................................169
660- How Did They Sin?.............................................................................170
661- Branch and Root .................................................................................170
662- Four Discernments in the Desire ..................................................... 171
663- If He Is Rewarded, His Work Is Done by Others ......................... 171
664- Feeling the Sin Increases the Light..................................................172

665- Counsels against the Inclination .................................................... 172
666- He Who Comes to Purify Is Aided - 2 ......................................... 173
667- A Descent and Ascent in the Work............................................... 173
668- In a Place Where Repentants Stand.............................................. 174
669- The Good Inclination and the Evil Inclination.......................... 174
670- You Shall Give Him His Wages On His Day............................... 174
671- Sorting Food and Waste................................................................. 175
672- The Creator Craves the Prayer of the Righteous........................ 175
673- The Death of a Righteous.............................................................. 175
674- To Admonish Another ................................................................... 176
675- The Quality of Joseph .................................................................... 176
676- Being Privileged.............................................................................. 177
677- Why *Matza* Is Called "Bread of Poverty" .................................... 177
678- Male and Female ............................................................................ 178
679- Signs of the Son of David .............................................................. 178
680- Annulment—the Baal Shem Tov Way......................................... 179
681- When a Woman Inseminates - 2 .................................................180
682- Exit and Entry in the Work...........................................................180
683- A Wise Sees the Future.................................................................. 181
684- The Quality of Moses .................................................................... 181
685- The Creator Complements the Desire ....................................... 181
686- The Most Important Is the Right ................................................182
687- Make for Yourself an Ark..............................................................182
688- Raise a Contribution for Me - 2 ..................................................183
689- The Matter of Father and Son......................................................184
690- This World and the Future...........................................................186
691- The Torah Was Given in Secret.................................................... 187
692- The Torah Is Called *Tushiya* - 1 ................................................... 188
693- The Torah Is Called *Tushiya* - 2 ................................................... 189
694- Great Is a Transgression that Is *Lishma* ....................................192
695- And They Shall Take to You Pure Olive Oil ............................... 195
696- Your Strength to the Torah...........................................................196
697- And You Shall Honor It, Not Doing Your Ways........................197
698- Two Kinds of Internality...............................................................198
699- The End of Correction ..................................................................198
700- Covering and Revealing ................................................................198
701- Confidence......................................................................................199
702- From the Depths I Have Called You, Lord - 2 ...........................199
703- *Miketz* [After].................................................................................. 200
704- Why Was the Torah Given to Israel ............................................201
705- Impudence ...................................................................................... 202
706- By the Sweat of Your Brow .......................................................... 203
707- A Treasure of Fear of Heaven ...................................................... 204

708- The Prayer of the Righteous .................................................. 205
709- Education ............................................................................. 205
710- Three Generations, Three Lines ....................................... 206
711- There Has Never Risen a Prophet Like Moses .............. 206
712- Desire and Intellect ............................................................. 207
713- One Who Walks along the Way ....................................... 208
714- Torah of *Hesed* [Mercy/Grace] ......................................... 208
715- Concerning Preparation for a Fast .................................. 209
716- Concerning Pride ............................................................... 210
717- Voice and Speech ............................................................... 210
718- Anyone Who Mourns Jerusalem ..................................... 211
719- And Judah Approached Him - 2 ...................................... 211
720- He Who Adds Knowledge, Adds Pain ............................ 212
721- The *Segula* of Torah and *Mitzvot* ..................................... 214
722- Action and Thought ........................................................... 215
723- *Tzimtzum* ............................................................................. 216
724- Balak Saw ............................................................................. 216
725- Man's Soul Will Teach Him .............................................. 217
726- Going on the Road ............................................................. 217
727- The Most Important Is the Environment ...................... 218
728- Faith - 2 ................................................................................ 218
729- This World Is Sanctified by Man ..................................... 219
730- Nicer than Gold .................................................................. 219
731- Charity for the Poor .......................................................... 220
732- Before the Face of the *Menorah* ...................................... 222
733- In Its Time, I Will Hasten It ............................................. 224
734- The Western Candle .......................................................... 225
735- On the Day When the Tabernacle Was Established .... 226
736- The Diminution of the Moon .......................................... 227
737- A Eulogy .............................................................................. 229
738- A Covenant of Salt ............................................................. 231
739- Two Types of Attire ........................................................... 231
740- Three Gifts .......................................................................... 232
741- To Cleanse the People ....................................................... 233
742- The Lord's Revenge Against Midian .............................. 238
743- The Journeys of the Children of Israel .......................... 238
744- Abraham's Gemstones ...................................................... 239
745- When the Creator Came ................................................... 240
746- Concerning the Fetus ........................................................ 241
747- In the Heat of the Day ...................................................... 242
748- To Renew the Reason ........................................................ 242
749- The Commandment of the Upper One .......................... 244
750- How Terrible Is This Place ............................................... 245

751- Anyone in Whom There Is Fear of Heaven – 2 .............................. 245
752- Before I Was Circumcised – 2 ..................................................... 246
753- Concerning the Evil Inclination ................................................... 247
754- The Complaint of the Angels ...................................................... 248
755- To Enjoy in Order to Bestow ....................................................... 249
756- A Deficiency from the Light ....................................................... 249
757- Toil ............................................................................................. 249
758- The Measure of Overcoming ...................................................... 250
759- Man as a Whole .......................................................................... 250
760- The Material of the Soul ............................................................. 252
761- Two Discernments in the *Kelim* .................................................. 253
762- Degrees of *Aviut* ......................................................................... 253
763- Inverse Relation between Lights and Vessels .............................. 254
764- The View of *Kedusha* .................................................................. 255
765- He Who Learns Torah in Poverty ................................................ 256
766- The Ability to Receive ................................................................ 257
767- You Shall Make Holy Garments ................................................. 257
768- The Suckling of the *Klipot* .......................................................... 258
769- Merging of the Body ................................................................... 259
770- The Difference between the Soul and the Body .......................... 260
771- Walking ...................................................................................... 260
772- Writing a Book of Torah ............................................................. 261
773- The Difference between Torah and Ethics .................................. 261
774- It Is Good to Thank the Creator .................................................. 262
775- The Thoughts of a Gentile and Those of Israel ........................... 262
776- Still of *Kedusha* .......................................................................... 263
777- A Prayer for the Exile of the *Shechina* ........................................ 263
778- Pleasure Cancels the Mind .......................................................... 265
779- Bless the Fruit of Your Womb .................................................... 265
780- And You, Write .......................................................................... 266
781- The Way of the Baal Shem Tov .................................................. 266
782- How Great Is Your Name ........................................................... 268
783- A Ransom for His Soul ............................................................... 268
784- The Meaning of Shabbat ............................................................. 269
785- Law and Judgment – 2 ................................................................ 269
786- The Lord Came from Sinai ......................................................... 270
787- ABYA in the Work ..................................................................... 271
788- He Raises the Poor from the Dust – 1 ......................................... 272
789- From the *Peh* and Above, It Is Not Considered a *Kli* .................. 273
790- Be Careful with What Comes Out from Your Lips ..................... 274
791- Demand and Receive Reward ..................................................... 274
792- A Stubborn and Rebellious Son .................................................. 275
793- Write Them on the Tablet of Your Heart .................................... 276

794- The Place of Attainment ................................................................... 277
795- Hear, My Son, Your Father's Morals – 2 ........................................ 277
796- The Real State .................................................................................. 278
797- A Gift ................................................................................................ 279
798- The Merit of the Little One ............................................................ 280
799- The Birth of the Moon .................................................................... 282
800- A Broken Heart – 2 ......................................................................... 283
801- The *Klipa* of Ishmael ...................................................................... 284
802- If Any Man of You Brings an Offering – 2 ................................... 285
803- The Order of Conveying the Wisdom ......................................... 286
804- Raises the Poor from the Dust – 2 ................................................ 287
805- Concerning Joy ............................................................................... 288
806- Esau's Head Is Holy ....................................................................... 288
807- Fire Is Called "Judgments" ............................................................ 289
808- Wholeness and Deficiency – 2 ...................................................... 289
809- Wholeness in Life ........................................................................... 290
810- He Who Fears Me ........................................................................... 291
811- Returning to One's Origin ............................................................. 292
812- Turn Away from Evil and Do Good – 3 ....................................... 293
813- The Desire to Bestow – 2 ............................................................... 294
814- Times in the Work .......................................................................... 295
815- *Bo* [Come] ........................................................................................ 297
816- Observed and Received .................................................................. 299
817- The Meaning of "Poor" ................................................................... 299
818- Happy Are They Who Keep Judgment ........................................ 301
819- Borrowing Vessels .......................................................................... 302
820- The Discernment of "In Everything" ............................................ 304
821- We Will Do and We Will Hear – 2 ................................................ 306
822- A Handmaid Who Is Heir to Her Mistress .................................. 307
823- The Name *Shadai* ........................................................................... 308
824- Internality and Externality ............................................................ 308
825- Choice .............................................................................................. 309
826- A Messenger to Circumcise .......................................................... 311
827- The Godliness Made the Concealment ........................................ 311
828- A Lot ................................................................................................ 312
829- The Basis of Learning the Revealed ............................................. 312
830- The Need for Gentiles .................................................................... 313
831- The Need for the Torah ................................................................. 313
832- Dead Fish ........................................................................................ 314
833- Turn Away from Evil and Do Good – 4 ....................................... 314
834- "Grow!" ............................................................................................ 315
835- Gird Your Sword ............................................................................ 315
836- Servant and Son .............................................................................. 317

837- Adhere to His Attributes .................................................................. 317
838- The Trueness of Providence ............................................................318
839- A *Kosher* Woman ............................................................................ 319
840- Quick Nearing ..................................................................................319
841- Coerced ............................................................................................ 320
842- The Work in General ...................................................................... 320
843- The Work Is the Reward ..................................................................321
844- Labor Is the Reward ........................................................................321
845- None as Holy as the Lord ............................................................... 322
846- Faith Is the Quality of *Malchut* .................................................... 323
847- Willows of the Brook ...................................................................... 323
848- The Days of the Messiah ................................................................ 323
849- A Condition for Marrying a Woman ............................................324
850- A Proselyte Who Converted ..........................................................324
851- A Desire for Levirate Marriage ......................................................324
852- Two Kinds of Scrutinies ................................................................. 325
853- The Need to Recognize the Greatness of the Creator ................ 326
854- Takes His Part and the Part of His Friend ...................................327
855- Wood and Stone .............................................................................. 328
856- Man's Nature ................................................................................... 328
857- The Need for a *Kli* without Light .................................................. 329
858- Moses Assembled ........................................................................... 330
859- You Shall Increase Their Inheritance ........................................... 330
860- With What to Aid? ..........................................................................331
861- The Work of the Lines ....................................................................331
862- Will Give Wisdom to the Wise ...................................................... 332
863- Korah's Complaint ......................................................................... 332
864- See Life ............................................................................................. 333
865- Wholeness Is One Hundred ........................................................... 333
866- Peace to the Far and to the Near ...................................................334
867- The Governance of Peace ..............................................................334
868- The Reason that Obligates .............................................................334
869- Matrimony ...................................................................................... 335
870- *Adam HaRishon* Was a Heretic ................................................... 335
871- A Scorpion and a Snake ................................................................. 336
872- Who Makes a Way through the Sea ............................................. 336
873- *Ibur* [Conception] – 2 ....................................................................343
874- Rest and Joy, Light to the Jews ..................................................... 344
875- Three Lines .....................................................................................351
876- The Creator Created the Evil Inclination,
     He Created for It the Torah as a Spice ........................................ 359
877- Three Prayers .................................................................................. 364
878- Their Leg Was a Straight Leg ........................................................370

## Rosh Hashanah

879- Good Writing and Signing ................................................. 373
880- Judgments ...................................................................... 374
881- *Rosh Hashanah* and *Yom Kippur* ...................................... 375
882- *Rosh Hashanah* ............................................................... 375
883- For Man Is the Tree of the Field ........................................ 377
884- The *Rosh Hashanah* Prayer ............................................... 379
885- With a *Shofar* You Will Renew .......................................... 381
886- *Malchuiot*, Memories, and *Shofarot* ................................. 383
887- I Do Swear ...................................................................... 385
888- Good Days ...................................................................... 386
889- The Quality of Mercy ........................................................ 386

## Yom Kippur

890- The Sorrow of the *Shechina* – 2 ........................................ 387
891- The Meaning of *Yom Kippur* ............................................. 388

## Sukkot

892- An Article for *Sukkot* ...................................................... 389
893- The Fruit of a Citrus Tree ................................................. 391

## Simchat Torah [The Joy of Torah]

894- *Simchat Torah* [The Joy of Torah] ..................................... 392

## Hanukkah

895- The Meaning of Hanukkah ................................................ 393
896- Repel Admon in the Shadow of Tzalmon ............................ 397
897- What Is Hanukkah ........................................................... 399
898- What Is the Miracle of Hanukkah ..................................... 401
899- *Hanu-KoH* ..................................................................... 402
900- Two Degrees ................................................................... 403

# The 15th of *Shevat*

901- *Rosh Hashanah* for the Trees .................................................... 405
902- Israel Are Compared to an Olive Tree ........................................ 406
903- Concerning the Fifteenth of *Shevat* ............................................407
904- Man Is the Tree of the Field ....................................................... 409
905- *Daveh* [Afflicted] or *Hod* [Glory/Majesty] ................................. 411

# Shabbat [Sabbath] *Zachor* [Remember]

906- The Meaning of Amalek ..............................................................413
907- When He Let His Hand Down, Amalek Prevailed ..................... 414
908- Blotting Out Amalek ...................................................................415

# Purim

909- Revealing the Concealment ........................................................ 417
910- Until He Does Not Know ...........................................................419
911- The Meal of a Wicked One .........................................................419
912- What Is Purim ............................................................................ 420
913- His Law He Contemplates .........................................................421

# Passover

914- Two Opposites ............................................................................ 428
915- I and Not a Messenger ............................................................... 429
916- The Day after Shabbat [Sabbath] ............................................... 429
917- A Kept *Matza* [Passover Bread] ................................................ 430
918- Concerning Passover ................................................................. 430
919- Concerning the Environment ....................................................431
920- The Torah Spoke Regarding Four Sons ..................................... 433
921- The Need for an Act from Below ................................................434
922- The More One Speaks of the Exodus from Egypt ..................... 435
923- And he said, "When You Deliver the Hebrew Women" ............ 436
924- And God Spoke to Moses .......................................................... 439
925- And I Will Take You as My People ............................................ 440
926- Come unto Pharaoh ................................................................... 442
927- Concerning *Hametz* and *Matza* ................................................ 445
928- Behold, a People Has Come Out of Egypt ................................. 448
929- The Passover Offering ................................................................ 448
930- Concerning the Beginning of the Month ................................... 449

931- *Peh-Sah* [speaking mouth] .......................................................... 450
932- The First Innovation.................................................................... 450
933- Concerning the Exodus from Egypt ............................................ 451
934- The Duty to Tell the Story of the Exodus from Egypt ................ 452
935- Concerning the *Matza* [Unleavened Bread] ................................ 453
936- The Time of Redemption ........................................................... 453
937- Questions for the Exodus from Egypt ........................................ 455

## The Omer Count

938- Considering the *Omer* [Count] .....................................................457

## Shavuot [Feast of Weeks]

939- The Exodus from Egypt and the Giving of the Torah ................. 459
940- The Point in the Heart ............................................................... 460
941- Mount Sinai ................................................................................461
942- Concerning the Mind Controlling the Heart ............................. 462
943- Three Discernments in the Torah .............................................. 463
944- The Giving of the Torah Is with Two Eyes................................. 464

## The Ninth of *Av*

945- The Ninth of *Av*.......................................................................... 466

Explanation of the Article, "Preface to the Wisdom of Kabbalah" ......467

# 501- The Quality of Truth – 1

"'These are the generations of Jacob Joseph.' Anyone who looked at Joseph's face would say that he is Jacob. Come and see that in all the sons of Jacob it is not written 'These are the generations of Jacob Reuben son of Joseph,' for his face looks like the face of his father."

To understand the above, Jacob's form was truth, as it is written, "You will give truth to Jacob," and Joseph's form is *Yesod*, a covenant, for he is regarded as righteous, *Yesod*, such as the test with Potiphar's wife.

Also, regarding the verse "Go onto Joseph; do all that he will tell you," it was interpreted in the *Midrash* that Joseph told them, "My God does not feed the uncircumcised, go and circumcise yourselves and I will give you."

We need to understand what is the quality of "truth" and what is the quality of "covenant." "Truth will grow from the earth." This means that the growth of truth is by being placed in the earth. And what is found on the face of the earth? Nothing but lies. Yet, precisely this is the state of truth. Thus, "truth" is regarded as "beneficial."

Therefore, if a lie helps then it is the truth, meaning that in fact we must tell a lie now, and precisely by this, the true goal will be revealed, as in "From *Lo Lishma* [not for Her sake] we come to *Lishma* [for Her sake]." For this reason, during the descent, a person should still be happy and say, "This state that I feel now is the best state for me."

This is what is presented in *Midrash Shmuel*, and it is common knowledge that truth is heavy; hence, its carriers are few. That is, it is hard to say that what I feel now is true Providence in the manner of good and doing good, and I must accept the situation gladly and lovingly.

This is the meaning of "Buy truth," through labor, "and do not sell," meaning that you cannot find anyone who will want to buy, for it is work that one must buy by himself and no one can help him and sell him the truth, for every person has truth according to his own degree. This is *Emet* [truth], from the words *Amat HaBinyan* [cubit], which is a unit of which each has his own measurement, and the clothing of one does not fit the size of another.

# 502- If Man Wins, the Creator Is Happy

"He who sells sadness, etc., but the Creator is happy."

The question is, How is this similar to a seller? After all, the seller does not keep the object, while the Creator, even though He gave the Torah to the people of Israel, the Torah still remains with Him. The Torah is not something corporeal, where we can say that if He gives it to the created beings, the Torah does not remain with Him.

Some want to interpret that this refers to the verse that we say about the Torah, "It is not in heaven," that it was given to the people of Israel to determine the rules.

We should interpret that we understand the Torah in two ways: 1) The quality of the Torah, whose light reforms him, as in "I have created the Torah as a spice," to mitigate the evil inclination. 2) The quality of the Torah called "The eye has not seen."

The intention of the Emanator is for the lower ones to receive pleasure. Yet, man uses the Torah in the opposite manner, wanting the Creator to receive pleasure. He receives this power from the Torah, from that spice. It follows that he is fighting with the Creator, meaning that the Creator wants man to receive pleasure, and man wants the Creator to receive pleasure.

Thus, he uses the Torah in the opposite direction from the seller. It was said about this that the Creator says, "My sons defeated Me." That is, they fight against the will to receive that the Creator imprinted in their hearts, where if the man wins, the Creator is happy.

It follows that the Torah of the Creator is according to the purpose of creation, and "His Torah" is when man uses the Torah with the aim of the spice, when he takes the Torah in order to please the Creator. This is why the Torah is named after man.

The Torah is named after its use: If a person wants to receive the Torah with the Creator's intention—to do good to His creations—so the creatures will enjoy, it is called "the Torah of the Creator," when the Torah follows the line of the Creator. If a person takes the Torah so as to have the power to bestow, this is regarded as man's intention, where man wants to bestow contentment upon his Maker, and then it is regarded as his Torah.

# 503- Partnership

"This day the Lord your God commands you to do." The writing says, "Come let us bow and kneel and bless the Lord, our Maker." But kneeling is included in bowing, and bowing is included in kneeling, so what is it trying to say by "let us bow and kneel and bless"?

Moses looked into the spirit of holiness and saw that the Temple was destined to be ruined and the bringing of the first fruit was destined to be stopped. He stood and determined for Israel that they will pray three times a day, since the Creator favors prayer more than all the good deeds and offerings, as it is written, "May my prayer be counted as incense before You; the lifting up of my hands as the evening offering."

"And you shall do them with all your heart and with all your soul." The writing warns Israel and tells them: "When you pray before the Creator, you shall not have two hearts, one before the Creator and one for other things" (*Midrash Tanchuma, Ki Tavo*).

We should ask, If a person engages in commerce and sustenance, his mind must be full of thoughts. How is it possible that he will be able to free himself for some time from all the thoughts with which he was preoccupied?

However, the people of Israel are as one body. As the body has a head and hands and legs, and each one has its special role, and what the mind thinks, meaning if there are good thoughts in the mind, then all the organs are happy, and if the mind is troubled, so is the mood in all the organs. It is like a partnership, where if each one does his job, everyone is happy, as it is written, "which God has created to do," for there is nothing without labor.

Hence, the husband toils and brings money, and his wife takes the money and toils with it, buying groceries and cooking, and seeing that the food is tasty, and then both are happy.

If the woman cooks well, her husband will have good appetite and will then have strength to go to work and bring in money. Likewise, if the feet walk and the hands buy and give the food to the brain, the brain has the strength to think.

Likewise, since the people of Israel are one body, if those who engage in commerce and toil and support wise disciples, who are called "heads of the congregation," the wise disciples impart the pleasure in what they toiled all day and acquired the taste of Torah and *Mitzvot* [commandments]. They can impart this flavor to the supporters. Likewise, during prayer, they will feel the taste of the prayer.

Thus, naturally, where there is pleasure, the body is accustomed to become free of other thoughts.

# 504- The Secret of the Lord Is to Those Who Fear Him

There is the power of faith that our forefathers extended, that through faith we can draw the upper pleasures, and then the body, too, enjoys them.

"The secret of the Lord is to those who fear Him." Before the time of the Messiah, only those who had complete fear of the Creator were rewarded with the secret, meaning the upper pleasure that not just anyone could hear and feel, and which is called "a secret."

But at the time of the Messiah, which is the time near the end of correction, it will not be a secret. Rather, "They shall all know Me, from the least of them to the greatest of them." Hence, now, when it is near that time, one who engages in Torah and Mitzvot [commandments] can already draw and feel the sublime pleasures that were thus far concealed.

Hence, with each and every Mitzva [commandment], we must aim to draw upper vitality and pleasure until the body, too, enjoys it. Afterward begins the work of the righteous in the manner of in order to bestow and not receive for oneself.

## 505- True Mercy

Tevet, December-January

It is written in the Shabbat [Sabbath] song, *Anyone Who Sanctifies*, "Raise your hands to the holiness and say unto God, 'Blessed is the Lord who gave rest to His people, Israel.'"

"And he called his son, Joseph, and said to him, ... 'Do with me mercy and truth.'" RASHI interpreted that true mercy means that he does not expect a payment in return. He asked why he called only Joseph. He replied that it was because he had the ability. "And he commanded Joseph saying, 'Before his death, your father commanded, 'Thus shall you say to Joseph, 'Please bear the crime of your brothers.'''" RASHI interpreted that they changed the words because of the peace, since Jacob did not command this.

"And I will give you one portion more than to your brothers." RASHI interpreted, "Because you trouble yourself with my burial." Thus, there is no true mercy here; it would be better that if he wanted him to keep it, he would pay him, if he wanted to give him.

However, this is the meaning of calling specifically Joseph to do a true mercy, because of the intention that he would go in this way. The intention was concerning the brothers, that he would not avenge them if he walks by a path that is not of mercy and truth. This is what they implied by "Before his death, your father commanded."

# 506- Saved Us from the Hand of the Shepherds

After Shabbat, *Shemot*, *Tav-Shin-Lamed-Het*, December 31, 1977

"Moses said ... 'And they will say to me, 'What is His name?' What shall I say to them?' And God said to Moses, 'I will be who I will be.' He said, 'Thus shall you say to the children of Israel, 'I will be' sent me to you.'" RASHI interpreted, "I will be" with them in this trouble, and I will be with them in the enslavement of the rest of the kings.

He said to Him, "Master of the world, why am I reminding them of another trouble? This trouble is enough for them." He told him, "Well said, thus shall you say to the children of Israel, 'I will be' sent me to you." RASHI interpreted that the Creator reiterated what He had said earlier to Moses alone, and said "I will be" twice, while to Israel, he said "I will be" only once (*Berachot* 9).

"And they said, 'An Egyptian man saved us from the hand of the shepherds.'" There is an allegory in the Midrash about a man who was bitten by a donkey, and he ran to put his feet in the water. He put it in the river and saw an infant sinking in the water, so he stretched out his hand and saved him. The infant said to him, "Were it not for you, I would have been dead." He replied to the infant, "It was not I who saved you, but the donkey, which bit me and I ran from it. He is the one who saved you." This is why they said to their father, "An Egyptian man saved us from the hands of the shepherds." But who caused the Egyptian man to come to us? The Egyptian man that he had killed.

What does this tell us? We can interpret this by intimation. Moses was to come to the general public of Israel and tell them that the Creator will deliver them from exile. Therefore, He told him only once, "I will be," meaning that they would have exile only in that Israel are in exile among the nations of the world.

In other words, we should discern between the gentile in Israel—who is in exile among the nations, when one wants what the nations want, meaning every corporeal thing, and the gentiles do not give them what they want. When the gentiles of the nations of the world rule over the gentiles of the people of Israel, this is called "corporeal exile."

But exile is primarily in the quality of Israel in a person, when he should observe the Torah and *Mitzvot* [commandments] and the gentiles within him do not give him the freedom to do what he wants. At that time, one feels that he is in exile within his own body. Before one emerges from this exile, from corporeal lusts, he cannot feel spiritual pleasures from Torah and *Mitzvot*.

Then, the body is made to understand that it is better for it to relinquish corporeal lusts, for by this he will be rewarded with real pleasures. And when he begins to relinquish corporeal lusts, the body wants to show its governance and resists his actions. This is the meaning of the words, "Ever since I came to Pharaoh to speak in Your name, he has done harm to this people, and You did not save Your people at all."

That is, before we begin to speak with the body, called "wicked Pharaoh," "to speak in Your name," meaning relinquish everything for sake of the Creator, we see the lowliness of the body and begin to feel the exile. This is one "I will be," meaning in this trouble. This pertains to the general public of Israel.

However, there is work called "the quality of Moses," which is the Torah. This is the second trouble. That is, when one has been rewarded with spiritual pleasures, there is the trouble that at that time he cannot aim in order to bestow, meaning to decide that if not for the purpose of *Mitzva* [commandment], he relinquishes the spiritual pleasures. This is harder than relinquishing corporeal pleasures because the greater the pleasure, the harder it is to relinquish it.

This is regarded as the second "I will be," meaning a second trouble. However, this pertains only to those who learn Torah, called "the quality of Moses." This is (not) for the whole of Israel to learn, but to learners of Torah, who must know that it is forbidden to receive spiritual pleasures for oneself, as well, but rather only in order to bestow, called *Masach* [screen] and *Aviut* [thickness].

The Creator promised Moses that He would deliver them from both the first and second troubles. However, we must know that emerging from the first trouble is mainly emergence from corporeal lusts, and that without it, it is impossible to achieve spiritual pleasures.

This is the allegory in the Midrash, "An Egyptian man saved us from the hands of the shepherds." That is, the fact that he killed the Egyptian, meaning the first reason, we must also remember, even afterward, when we come to the second state, which is the exile over spiritual pleasures, that we must receive them in order to bestow, and the body disagrees. That is, killing the Egyptian refers to corporeal lusts, called "Egyptian."

Conversely, the second trouble is the quality of Israel, meaning that he has spiritual pleasures, and yet he is in trouble because he must overcome in order to bestow and needs the Creator to deliver him also from this trouble.

# 507- What Is Joy?

It is known that joy is not an entity but an offshoot and a result of something. If one has some pleasure, that pleasure yields excitement that is called "joy." Accordingly, we understand that one who has no pleasure in his life is unable to have joy because he lacks the cause and the reason that will engender this offshoot called "joy."

We see that little children are always happy. The reason is that because of the smallness of their minds, they can enjoy anything. They do not evaluate or calculate, and find delight and pleasure in every little thing, which gives them a reason to be happy.

But when a person grows up he becomes limited in receiving pleasure according to the measure of his maturity, since his maturity prevents him from being excited over everything. Naturally, he cannot enjoy just anything.

This is the meaning of "Adding knowledge, adding pain," for one who is knowledgeable is spoiled and not every food you give him can delight him. This is so on purpose, so that man will see that of all the pleasures in this world, nothing gives him pleasure or can delight him in a way that he can be happy with it, since these pleasures are suitable only for those with small minds.

Therefore, this gives a person the ability to emerge from the lusts of this world and begin to derive pleasure only from things that are more important than corporeality, so he can derive delight and pleasure from spiritual things and enjoy only this, and only such pleasures will bring him joy.

Hence, when he looks at someone whose pleasure is nothing more than enjoying eating and drinking and respect and so forth, he sees him as a little boy who enjoys playing with toys.

It follows that one who sees he has no joy the way other people have, it is because he is at a higher degree. Therefore, he should know that the Creator is giving him a chance to begin to engage in Torah and work, and this will bring him the real joy called "the joy of *Mitzva* [commandment]."

# 508- The Ascent of *Malchut* to *Bina*

It is explained in the "Preface to the Wisdom of Kabbalah" that if man had been extended only from *Malchut*, which is the will to receive only for oneself, he would be utterly unable to perform any act of bestowal.

Only through the mixing of *Malchut* with *Bina* there are sparks of bestowal in *Bina*, too, and from this, man becomes able to perform acts of bestowal. This is also what caused *Tzimtzum Bet* [the second restriction] by which man can come to perform acts of bestowal.

To understand this in the work, we should interpret that we see that there is a big distance between reception and bestowal. The quality that connects the two is bestowal in order to receive, where reception has been mixed into *Bina*, so that in *Bina*, called the "desire to bestow," there is a mixture of reception.

It therefore follows that when one performs an act of bestowal, the will to receive is involved there. Hence, even then it is forbidden to extend abundance because he will blemish it with the will to receive within him.

But at the same time, the body already agrees to work because there is a mixture there of the body's interest, since when one wants to work only in order to bestow, the body comes and asks, "What is this work?" meaning what will I gain from this?

Sometimes a person can work only in order to bestow upon the general public, for when he feels the affliction of the public, the body has the power to annul his own interest before the well-being of the general public.

However, this is explicitly when he is certain that by annulling his self, the general public will be saved. At that time, the individual is annulled before the general public, since there is a nature that the smaller one can annul before the bigger one.

However, when the saving of the general public is uncertain, he will not have the strength to annul before the general public because doubt does not take precedence over certainty, for losing his life is certain, but saving the public is doubtful.

Also, if a person does not see that by engaging in Torah and *Mitzvot* [commandments] in utter devotion he will derive pleasure for the sake of the body, and he begins to work so that this would be for the sake of the Creator, it is doubtful in his eyes, for who knows if the Creator will enjoy his work. Therefore, he is doubtful about it, and doubt does not take precedence over certainty, since he needs faith in order to believe that there is contentment above from his work.

Since the body does not have such powers, before a person is rewarded with faith, he must work in *Lo Lishma* [not for Her sake], which comes to a person by the mixing of *Malchut* with *Bina*, as said above.

Thus, a person cannot work *Lishma* [for Her sake] until he has faith. For this reason, if a person wants to work *Lishma*, he must focus all his energy only on this point: to pray to the Creator to send him the light of faith, for only then will he be rewarded with engaging in Torah and *Mitzvot Lishma*.

# 509- *The Revelation of the Love of the Creator*

"And shone on them from Seir." This means that from what the children of Seir said, that they do not want to receive, from this it shone for Israel and added to them much light and love. "Appeared from Mount Paran." From what the children of Paran said, that they do not want to receive, much love and illumination was properly added to Israel (*The Zohar, Hukat*).

We should ask why the love of Israel was contingent upon the nations of the world not wanting to receive the Torah. This implies that had the nations of the world received the Torah, there would have been no room for the love of Israel. Can it be that if one loves another and wants to show his love for him, he expresses it in a way that because his friend does not wish to obey him, this is why he loves him? Is this a praise or condemnation, since he stipulates the love on his friend; he is the cause, while for himself, he has no love for him.

The thing is that the children of Seir and the children of Paran are within each and every one. The evil in man has many names according to its actions. There is love for the people of Israel in that man's evil does not want to accept the Torah and *Mitzvot* [commandments], and man overcomes the evil.

From this, the illuminations extend to the people of Israel, for in truth, the Creator wants to give to the created beings more than they want to receive. Only because of the bread of shame there is a correction that man must first show his choice. But as soon as one shows the choice, His love for him is immediately revealed.

The matter of choice pertains specifically when the bad in him reveals its power, meaning that it objects to his engagement in Torah and *Mitzvot*. Naturally, you find that precisely when the nations of the world in man show the power of resistance, there is room for choice.

Hence, precisely by the children of Paran not wanting to receive the Torah, this is the place where the Creator can show His love for him because the man has already discovered His power.

But if they do not object to him, he has no room to show his choice, and the Creator cannot reveal His love, for if He were to reveal His love for man, there would be no possibility for choice.

# 510- *Concealed and Revealed*

The concealed—a spiritual flavor that is hidden from us. The revealed—the taste of corporeality is revealed to us. When we can receive the taste of corporeality in order to bestow, the Creator reveals to us the flavor of the concealed, meaning the flavor that was concealed in spirituality becomes revealed.

## 511- The Middle Line

The middle line: There is an allegory about two people who wanted to make a meal. One said that he would provide everything but salt, vinegar, garlic, and the rest of the spices. The other one was to provide the spices. In the end, they had a dispute and each one made his meal alone: One served flour, fish, meat, and herring, and the other one made a meal and served all the spices.

Of the guests in the two meals, who could enjoy? It is impossible to eat the spices by themselves. Who can eat only salt, or garlic, or onion, or black pepper, or a hot green? Also, who can eat meat or fish without salt?

Thus, they had no choice but to make peace, and then they held both meals and they were tasty.

## 512- He Who Disputes Peace

Korah went for dispute, and one who disputes peace, disputes His holy name, since the name of the Creator is "peace."

## 513- Gathering Wood

Shadow of Fear disputed the Shabbat [Sabbath], for he was gathering wood. *Mekoshesh* [gathering], from the word *Hekish* [knocked] on trees, to see which one was bigger.

## 514- Welcoming Guests – 2

"Welcoming guests is greater than welcoming the *Shechina* [Divinity]." Why is welcoming guests great? Through it, we are rewarded with welcoming the *Shechina*, as in, "Great is the learning that leads to action."

# 515- Concerning the surrounding lights

When beginning the work, it comes from the surrounding light, which shines. However, when we want to receive inner light, it becomes dark because the surrounding lights shine even when one still has no *Kelim* [vessels] suitable for reception in order to bestow, while the internality comes specifically in vessels of bestowal, which he does not have. Therefore, when he goes under the *Tzimtzum* [restriction], the importance of the work departs from him.

# 516- A Shoe

A shoe is something by which one buys a possession. The shoe is placed on the leg, and *Raglaim* [legs] are regarded as *Meraglim* [spies]. The shoe is placed on the feet, and then the legs do not hurt when they want to hold a person up, for legs mean that the person stands on his legs.

What does it mean that the legs on which a person stands will not be harmed? Also, why was it said about Moses, "Take your shoes off your feet," if a shoe means that he is wearing the argument of the spies? And accordingly, what will be the meaning of "Take off your shoes"?

We should say that *Raglecha* [your legs] comes from the word *Reglilut* [habit/custom], meaning that which comes to a person by education. In order not to lose his education, he needs a *Naal* [shoe] from the word *Man'ul* [lock], meaning to close. However, with the quality of Moses, who is the Torah, it is the opposite, from the word *Min'al* [shoe/footwear], meaning that there we must throw away the shoes and accept everything in the way of the Torah.

# 517- The Constitution of the Torah

What is the prohibition on teaching Torah to idol-worshippers? "This is the constitution of the Torah [law]."

This means that one who wants to be rewarded with the Torah, he must take upon himself the kingdom of heaven above reason. This means that if the body comes to ask him Pharaoh's question, "Who is the Lord that I should obey His voice?" and the wicked one's question, "What is the work?" he should not give any intellectual reasoning, meaning search for excuses and rationalize them. Rather, we must reply, "I mindlessly take upon myself the kingdom of heaven as a law."

By taking upon himself the kingdom of heaven as a law, he is called "Israel," meaning he emerges from the control of idol-worshippers, which is what the body demands—that everything will be in the external mind, that the body will understand. He emerges from this control, and at that time he is regarded as "Israel."

At that time, he is worthy of receiving the light of Torah, which is called that the Torah exists, and this is the meaning of the prohibition to teach Torah to idol-worshippers, as was said, "He did not do so to any nation and they did not know the ordinances."

This is the meaning of what our sages said, "The world exists only on those who restrain themselves at a time of quarrel, as was said, 'The earth hangs on nothing.'" "Restraining" means that he does not reply when the body begins to fight with the person with the arguments of "Who" and "What." He does not provide any answer to this, and this is called "restraining." By this there is existence to the world. The rest with which one should be rewarded in the world is only through "nothing," when he has no foundation but only because it is a law.

"This is the constitution of the Torah." *Malchut* is called "constitution" and comes from ZA, who is called "Torah." It is not that the Torah itself is ZA; rather, it is only the judgment of the Torah, the decree of the Torah, which is *Malchut*.

# 518- *He Who Comes to Defile*

It is written in *The Zohar* (*BeHaalotcha*, Item 66): "He who comes to defile, meaning to see that he is impure, is defiled. That is, he is shown from above the dumbness of the heart, that the heart is impure, dead, as in 'The wicked in their lives are called "dead."'"

Conversely, one who regards oneself as whole and does not criticize one's actions is righteous according to his understanding and belongs to the general public, whose work is in a manner of reward and punishment.

"Until they gain knowledge and acquire much wisdom," while they are in a state of "still" and are searching for the truth, "they are shown that secret" of the meaning of *Lishma* [for Her sake]. Who reveals it to them? It comes from above. This is called "He who comes to purify is aided."

It follows that one who is impure, who understands that he is impure, dead, as in "The wicked in their lives are called 'dead,'" this is the first discernment. This is when he is on a "far away road," namely he is shown from above that he is far from the path of truth and wants to escape the campaign until he invokes mercy. Hence, on First Passover, he is still not pure.

Passover is "left line," meaning he is shown the secrets of Torah. "Right" is called "pure," which is the state of *Hesed* [mercy/grace], when his work is in order to bestow. However, on Second Passover he repents, purifies himself with *Hesed*, meaning to bestow. At that time, he can be rewarded with Passover, which is the left line, *Hochma*.

## 519- Concerning the Tzimtzum [Restriction]

Since Malchut received all the light that the Emanator wanted to give, which is called "filling all of reality," and wanted to receive more pleasure, and since, with respect to the reception of the light there is nothing to add, she awoke to receive pleasure by being a giver.

As the Creator is the source of the pleasures and has joy from bestowing upon the worlds, as it is written, "There has never been joy before Him as on the day when heaven and earth were created," for this reason, once Malchut received everything in the manner of filling all of reality, a thought came before Him that she would receive pleasure from giving to the Creator. Hence, she said, "I do not want in order to receive, but I will receive only in order to bestow."

## 520- Water Will Flow from His Buckets

"Water will flow from his buckets." It is known that "water" is called "Torah." "From his Dlayim [buckets]" comes from the word Dal [poor/meager].

When a person regards himself as poor, meaning in lowliness, and says, "Since I am a poor and lowly person, I do not deserve to have a clue about the work of the Creator more than regular people," who follow only what they received from education, and who have no need to understand the Torah and Mitzvot [commandments]. Rather, everything that they received by education when they were little children, they settle for it and engage in Torah and Mitzvot as much as they can, and do not say they have a deficiency for the aim to bestow, etc. Rather, they settle for little.

Likewise, after each time a person works in the left, he sees that he is deficient and is not progressing in the work of the Creator. That is, he does not know more than other people who work in one line.

By a person shifting to the right line, saying that he is not more important than those who are on a single line, and whatever grip on *Kedusha* [holiness] he has, he appreciates it more than any aspect of meager [*Dal*], and the *Dal* becomes a *Dli* [bucket] with which to pump out the water of Torah, this is the meaning of "Water will flow from his buckets."

# 521- The Mind [Reason] that Governs Man

"Anyone who is proud," says the Creator, "he and I cannot dwell in the same abode."

"Reason" is the primary governor in man. Yet, what reason [mind] governs a person? It is precisely the mind, when he understands that through this act, the body will enjoy. That is, if the mind does not think that it will bring him pleasure, he does not have the power to relinquish the pleasure. We should ask why a person should relinquish the pleasure.

It can be that by this act, he harms others, and others will later take revenge on him, and for this reason he must relinquish. Sometimes, when he is biased by the pleasure, he cannot see the truth—that afterward he will suffer because of it.

## 522- "Right" Means Wholeness

*The Zohar* (*VaYikra*): "Right" means wholeness, where even if he has nothing and he only remembers that there is spirituality, although he does not have it, he is still happy with what he has and says that there are many people in the world, including himself, who often do not even remember that there is the matter of serving the Creator in the world. But now he does remember it, and he is happy and thanks the Creator for rewarding him. This is called "one door."

The other door is the "left," meaning criticism about the work, namely that if spirituality is really so important, why is he not yearning for the wisdom of the Torah? At that time, a person falls into a descent because he is still unable to work with great labor. Thus, he receives a descent from the "left."

We need a "right" so as to be whole and be able to receive the abundance. However, they do not have *Kelim* [vessels]. From the left they receive the *Kelim*, meaning the deficiencies. During the deficiency, they part. This is similar to receiving in order to bestow. From the "left," only the *Kelim* are made.

## 523- What It Means to Bear a Son and a Daughter in the Work

"A man who does not want to complete the holy name, meaning to bear a son and a daughter ... it is better for him if he were not created" (*The Zohar*, *VaYikra*, Item 95).

We should understand the meaning of son and daughter and that if one does not have them, it is better if he were not created. "Father" and "Son" are "cause" and "consequence." Hence, when a person takes upon himself the kingdom of heaven, called "faith," this faith should engender in a person a son and a daughter.

"Son" means a male, which is *Hassadim*, vessels of bestowal. This is why ZA is called "male," since his quality is *Hassadim*. *Malchut* is called "daughter," "female," who uses the vessels of reception in order to bestow. For this reason, *Hochma* is attributed to *Malchut*.

Hence, a person must achieve the wholeness of above, meaning *Hassadim*, male, and *Hochma*, female. Therefore, the faith that a person receives should engender in a person a son, called "light of *Hassadim*," as well as a daughter, who is regarded as *Hochma*.

Otherwise, the Name is incomplete, since the holy name is The Good Who Does Good, good for himself and good for others. We can interpret "himself" as the good inclination and "others" as the evil inclination, meaning *Hochma* and *Hassadim*.

By this we can interpret "Rewarded, his work is done by others." When a person is rewarded, his work is done by others. Who are the "others" within man? It is the evil inclination, for then "with all your heart, with both your inclinations" will come true. It follows that "others," too, meaning the evil, do the work of the Creator.

# 524- What Is, He Swallowed Maror [Bitter Herb], He Will Not Come Out, in the work?

The meaning of *Maror* [bitter herb] is as it is written, "And they made their lives bitter with hard work," by asking "Who?" and "What?" These questions caused them labor, for by wanting to overcome, yet not being able to, they tasted a bitter taste.

But we should explain their questions within reason, and naturally not feel bitterness in the work. He says that what the evil inclination asks is not questions, so he does not feel bitterness. It follows that he does not have *Maror* in the work, making him have to go above reason.

Now we can understand what our sages said, "If he swallows" the *Maror* "he will not come out." The ARI says about this that *Maror* has the *Gematria* of *Mavet* [death], which is judgments. We should ask what it implies that *Maror* has the *Gematria* of *Mavet*. The thing is that the *Maror* we eat is a reminder that they made their lives bitter with hard work.

We should say that in the work, "hard work" means that it is difficult to overcome and emerge from self-benefit, and that he wants to work only for his own benefit. This is called "wicked," who asks, "What is this work" of bestowal "for you?" What will you gain out of it? But it is known that "The wicked in their lives are called 'dead.'"

It follows that hard work is called *Maror*, when a person tastes bitterness in having to work for his own sake. This is the intimation that *Maror* has the *Gematria* of *Mavet* and judgments, since there was a judgment on self-benefit that it is forbidden to use this *Kli* [vessel], and this is why there are restrictions and concealment there.

Now we will explain why we must chew—since we must feel the taste of bitterness.

# 525- Three Lines – 3

"Right" is regarded as the essence of the *Sefirot*, similar to seeing, hearing, smell, and speech.

"Left" is *Masach* [screen] and *Aviut* [thickness], namely the will to receive and the *Masach*.

Afterward, when the middle line comes, it determines that the seeing, hearing, smell, and speech will not shine with light of *Hochma*, called GAR, but with *Hassadim*.

The middle line is called *Daat*. When it decides between *Hochma* and *Bina*, which are called "edges," and each edge is called GAR, and each middle line is called VAK because it is what decides between them and what sustains the illumination of both of them, it is like a compromise between them.

For this reason, *Hochma* illuminates *Hochma* and has no need for *Hassadim*, and *Bina* illuminates *Hassadim* and has no need for *Hochma*, unlike *Daat*, which extends illumination of *Hochma*. It follows that on one hand, *Hochma* is extended, but it is only illumination of *Hochma*, which is in *Zeir Anpin*, and *Bina* receives *Hochma* only in *Zeir Anpin*. It turns out that this is called "deciding," as though both are pleased with this compromise. Thus, *Daat* is only VAK.

# 526- With All Your Heart

If one is rewarded, his work is done by others, for "When the Lord favors man's ways, his enemies, too, make peace with him." This means that the evil in him also returns to the good, and then the words "with all your heart—with both your inclinations" come true in him. It follows that others, too, meaning the bad, do the work of the Creator.

# 527- The God of Israel

"The God of Israel," meaning importance, when a person appreciates the work while he is Israel.

"King of the Nations" means what measure of importance one attributes to spirituality during a descent, when the quality of nations within him governs him.

## 528- Prayer

A prayer: When a person learns Torah, he wants to know the connection between the Torah that he is learning, since when he learns rules it is clear that he needs judgments. But when a person learns Torah, and the Torah does not speak of judgments, so what is the connection between this Torah and the person?

If he wants to know and asks the Creator to understand the connection, this is called a "prayer." This is a great and very important thing, since he has a connection with the Creator because he wants something from Him.

## 529- I Will Give You My Blessing

"What is the connection between *Shmita* [remission every 7th year] and Mt. Sinai?" Answer: *Shmita* is called *Malchut*, which should be for the sake of the Creator, meaning not to receive anything. In this regard, a question arises, "If you say, 'What will we eat on the seventh year,'" meaning if we do not want anything in return for the labor in Torah and *Mitzvot* [commandments], from where will there be nourishment? It is written about this, "And I will give you My blessing."

We should ask why it is written, "If you say, 'What will we eat on the seventh year?'" if we accept the *Malchut* above reason, meaning that we get no provision from this, that it sustains us, but rather everything is for the sake of the Creator. The answer is that the Creator will send the blessing. This is called a "miracle," and we do not rely on miracles, meaning that this, too, is an answer above reason.

By nature, if we work on sustenance, we can obtain sustenance. But if a person works on things that we are told explicitly that there is no payment for the work, from where will they take provision?

It therefore follows that one must not provide answers that come from the intellect in regard to provision, but only believe in the Creator, as it is written, "And will command My blessing on the sixth year," which is regarded as *Yesod Tzadik* [righteous], namely a giver.

In other words, if you work on accepting the kingdom of heaven without reward, called "only in order to bestow," this will be a unification with the *Sefira Yesod*, and *Yesod* will bestow upon *Malchut*. By taking upon yourselves the matter of *Shmita*, meaning accepting the kingdom of heaven without demanding from the earth, meaning *Malchut*, to yield fruit, by this you can be rewarded with the light of Torah.

This is the meaning of "And you shall observe My statutes and … you will live securely on the land." That is, dwelling on *Malchut* will be secured, namely in complete wholeness.

# 530- Movement Due to Shame

Why are we in movement and not like our root? I enjoy rest, and the fact that I am in motion is only due to shame.

Answer: Since our root is at rest, it is because it has nothing to add, as it is in utter wholeness. Conversely, we are in utter deficiency. Therefore, if we enjoy rest, we are considered lazy.

# 531- The Essence of the Correction

Sivan, Tav-Shin-Lamed-Zayin, June 1977

Rabbi Yannai says, "We have neither the tranquility of the wicked nor the afflictions of the righteous" (*Avot*, Chapter 4). We should interpret this similar to what Raba said to our great sages, "I beseech you, do not inherit a double hell" (*Yoma* 72b).

It is known that the matter of the afflictions of the righteous is regarded that he wants to work only in order to bestow. If he does not succeed, this is called "suffering." It is called "recognition of evil," meaning he comes to a clear realization that there is nothing worse in the world than the evil inclination because this is what obstructs from achieving the delight and pleasure that the Creator has prepared for the created beings.

The essence of the correction we should do is to achieve equivalence of form, and on this was the *Tzimtzum* [restriction]. When one comes to feel that only this is the obstructor, he repents, meaning attempts to achieve equivalence. To the extent of the suffering he feels, so he moves away from it.

It was about said it, "Happy is the man whom the Lord afflicts," and also "He whom the Lord loves, He admonishes." In other words, to come to feel this, we need assistance from the Creator.

This is the meaning of what Rabbi Yannai says, that we do not have the tranquility of the wicked. That is, when the wicked satisfy their deficiency, they are at peace and do not need more. But one who wants to walk on the path of truth is not satisfied with this, since he knows that the essence of life is to achieve *Dvekut* [adhesion] with the Creator, which is bestowal.

Thus, when a person receives the satisfaction of his deficiencies, it does not make him tranquil, so it does not awaken him because this is not wholeness. However, he also does not suffer from the fact that the body received satisfactions. Thus, he can remain in the state he is in.

Conversely, if the righteous fall into a state of self-love, they suffer from it and want to run away from the suffering, so they move to the side of *Kedusha* [holiness], while the wicked are to the contrary, now they achieve complete satisfaction.

However, in the middle, he is empty-handed both ways, and this is called "double hell." This is the meaning of what he said, that we do not have the tranquility of the wicked, who are satisfied, or the afflictions of the righteous, for we have not achieved the state of "He whom the Lord loves, He admonishes."

# 532- The Main Choice

The main choice concerns the reason that obligates a person to engage in Torah and *Mitzvot* [commandments]. A person must observe all 613 *Mitzvot*, or he will be punished in this world, since when the Temple existed, there was the conduct of "four deaths of the courthouse," and the commandments to do were imposed. But concerning the reason that obligates a person to observe the Torah and *Mitzvot*, here there is choice, for there cannot be coercion about this.

As it is written in *The Zohar*, there are three reasons: 1) reward and punishment in this world, 2) reward and punishment in the next world, 3) bestowing upon the Creator. That is, since he cannot bestow upon the Creator and observe "As He is merciful, so you are merciful," he engages in Torah and *Mitzvot* as a *Segula* [cure/power] that will bring him to have a desire and yearning to bestow upon the Creator.

This is the meaning of spirituality being above place and time, meaning when we tell the body to observe Torah and *Mitzvot* because of spirituality, meaning to bestow upon the Creator, these words have no place within the body; it does not understand them because the body asks what it will get out of it.

If it is asked, "Will you be able to observe tomorrow because of spirituality?" it answers "Not today, not tomorrow, and not ever!" since there is no room in it where it is possible to engage in spirituality.

This is called "spirituality is above place," meaning that a person must pray to the Creator to help him come to be able to engage with a desire in order to bestow although there is no place or time from the perspective of the human mind that he will ever be able to work in order to bestow.

However, if a person comes to realize that this is the path of truth, he focuses all his work on this point, that the Creator will help him come to be able to take upon himself the true line required of the created beings: the aim to bestow.

# 533- The Creator Pulls the Man Close

*Av, Tav-Shin-Mem-Zayin, August 1987*

"And it came to pass because you hear." RASHI interpreted, "If you obey the minor *Mitzvot* [commandments], which a person tramples with his heels, you will hear." The interpreters asked why it is written only "ordinances" and not "laws," as well.

They explain that "because" contains the laws, and the intimation is in the word "because" (this is how [the book] *Kli Yakar* explains it), since Satan and the nations of the world count on them in the sense that their taste is unknown, and therefore people treat them lightly and trample them with their heels. This is why he mentions them with the word *Ekev* [because, or *Akev* (heel)], and not with the word "laws."

He is referring to the matter of faith, where the nations of the world claim that everything should be with awareness, meaning that when one should observe Torah and *Mitzvot* [commandments] not in order to receive reward, the body does not understand this and asks, "What are these *Mitzvot* and what is the reason for doing them if the body receives no reward for it?"

Hence, the whole world scorns this, which is why the commandment concerning it uses the word *Ekev* [because, similar to *Akev* (heel)]. When a person wants to achieve the goal, he should not mind that the whole world chases after the satisfaction of the desires of the body. Rather, he should try to do the Creator's will, meaning that his only wish will be to bring contentment to the Creator.

If a person says that it is hard to walk on this path, the Torah promises us, "The Lord your God keeps," etc., meaning that the Creator will guard a person who wants to achieve the truth, so he can achieve this.

This is the meaning of "The Lord is near to all who call upon Him in truth." In other words, one who prays to the Creator, who wants to walk on the path of truth, is close to the Creator, meaning that the Creator comes near him. This means that the Creator gives him the power to be in equivalence of form with the Creator.

# 534- Concerning the Groom

*The Zohar, Av, Tav-Shin-Lamed-Zayin, August 1977*

The reason why there is such a requirement to delight the groom is that *Hatan* [groom] comes from word *Nachut* [inferior] in degree, as our sages said, "One who is of inferior degree receives a woman."

All the holy names are not His essence, since "There is no perception or thought in Him whatsoever." Rather, all the names are what they attained, as Maimonides said, "What we do not attain, we do not know by name." Rather, all the names are according to how they attained Him. Thus, one who received *Hochma* [wisdom] from the Creator calls the Creator "Wise," and one who received *Gevura* [strength] from the Creator calls Him "Strong," and so forth.

By this we can understand what our sages said, "Why were they called 'Members of the Great Assembly'? It is because they restored the former glory. That is, Daniel and Jeremiah could not say, 'The Mighty and the Terrible,' and the members of the great assembly did say it," as explained in *Masechet Kidushin*.

Therefore, when we say *Hatan* [groom] in the sense of *Nachut* [inferior] in degree, it is when a person does not feel the greatness of the Creator because he is in a low state. When the person himself is in a state of being on a low degree, he calls the Creator "Groom."

Our sages said, "A disciple in exile, his teacher is exiled with him." Baal HaSulam interpreted that when one is in a state of "exile," meaning that the *Kedusha* [holiness] threw him out from the land of Israel, he says that his teacher is also like him, meaning that his teacher is also in lowliness. Therefore, his teacher cannot help him out of the state he is in.

For this reason, a person must delight the groom, meaning that then, too, a person must serve the Creator with gladness. For this reason, at the end of correction, when everything has been corrected, "The whole earth will be full ... and they shall all know Him, from the least of them to the greatest of them." In other words, even though he was previously on an inferior degree, at that time they will be corrected.

This is the meaning of "Will rejoice over you ... as the groom rejoices over the bride," so even one who is on an inferior degree will be rewarded with joy because everything will be corrected. This is why we are required to increase the joy of the groom, for the corporeal branch implies the spirituality, which is that one should try, specifically when he is on a low degree, to increase the joy as though he were in utter completeness.

# 535- A Cup of *Kiddush*

It is written in *The Zohar*, Pinhas (Item 49): The fifth correction is the cup of "And the heaven and the earth were concluded," meaning a cup of *Kiddush* [lit., "sanctification," a blessing recited over wine to sanctify the Sabbath].

In *Gematria*, a "cup" is "God" [in Hebrew], 86. "Concluded" amounts to *AB* [in *Gematria*], and the bride, who is *Malchut*, includes them, meaning the name "God," and the name *AB*.

This cup, which is *Malchut*, is full of her wine, meaning abundance, illumination of *Hochma* of the Torah, which is *ZA*, called "Torah." This should testify to the work of creation, which is *Bina*, since abundance of illumination of *Hochma* is called *Edut* [testimony], from the word *Eden* [Eden], and *Bina* is the source that gives it. This is the meaning of the need to testify to the work of creation.

By this he can explain that in "concluded," he can testify to the work of creation. But since testimony is only by eyesight, how can one testify by eyesight to the work of creation? After all, one can know what happened just by hearing.

Indeed, testifying to the work of creation means testifying that the intention of creation is to do good to His creations. How does one know? If he is rewarded with the quality of Shabbat [Sabbath], he testifies by eyesight, since he sees that this is the intention of creation because this is what he tasted.

# 536- You Shall Tithe

29 *Av*, *Tav-Shin-Lamed-Zayin*, August 13, 1977

"You shall tithe." It was interpreted, "Give tithing so you will grow rich." But how did our sages explain the commandment in the verse in a way that is *Lo Lishma* [not for Her sake], meaning that the intention is that he would give charity so as to get? It should be said, as was said, "We will do and we will hear," meaning that through the act they will achieve the state of "We will hear," meaning the act affects the intention.

It follows that when a person gives tithing, meaning an act of giving, he should aim "to get rich," meaning to be rewarded with a desire and yearning to give. That is, as the act is giving and not receiving, so he will be rewarded with the thought and intention being only to give and to receive anything in return.

We should also say, "You shall tithe," meaning "tithe" on the action, where if he performs an act of giving, "You will get rich," for then he will be rewarded with his intention also being that of bestowal and not that of reception.

And what happens afterwards? "So you will grow rich," since it is impossible to receive from the Creator the delight and pleasure, called "wealth," before one has equivalence of form. At that time, when he is rewarded with his aim being to bestow, as well, he will be rewarded with the wealth called "so you will grow rich."

## 537- *This Month Is to You*

*Tishrey, Tav-Shin-Lamed-Het, October 1977*

Rabbi Yehuda said, "The Torah should have started from 'This month is to you,' which is the first *Mitzva* [commandment] that Israel were commanded. What is the reason it began with 'In the beginning'? It is because 'He told His people the might of His deeds, to give them the inheritance of the nations.' Thus, if the idol-worshippers would say to Israel, 'You are robbers, for you have conquered the lands of seven nations,' they tell them, 'The whole earth belongs to the Creator; He created it and gave it to whom He pleases. Upon His wish He gave it to them, and upon His wish He took it from them and gave it to us.'"

We should ask why He did not keep the land of Israel for Israel and gave it to them, for which there was a need to make a change in the Torah and not begin the Torah from the place where Rabbi Yehuda says. We should also ask, If the essence of creation is truly because it is called *Resheet* [beginning], why did He give the big countries to the nations of the world and a small country to Israel?

We should say that all that is spoken of is spirituality, but the corporeal branches extend from the upper roots. Therefore, we should say that He created the world in this way in order to do good to His creations, meaning that to begin with, He created the will to receive, which is the *Kli* [vessel] to receive the upper pleasures, and then, in order to have equivalence of form, called "bread of shame," He gave a prohibition that it is forbidden to work with the *Kli* [vessel] called "in order to receive." This quality is called "gentiles" or "nations of the world," or *Sitra Achra* [other side], or *Klipa* [shell/peel].

It is permitted to receive only in order to bestow, and this is regarded as taking all the pleasures that previously belonged to the nations, and giving to Israel, meaning in order to bestow upon the Creator, which is called "Israel." Thus, the will to receive asks, "Why are you robbing, since initially, before the *Tzimtzum* [restriction], it belonged to us?"

The answer to this is that the Creator created it, meaning initially He gave to the gentiles, since this is the heart of creation. Yet, this is called "uncorrected" because there is the bread of shame there. Thus, the doing good to His creations will not be complete. For this reason, He gave it to Israel, meaning that by giving everything in order to bestow, the reception of the pleasures will be complete.

Thus, "He took it from the nations" because here, in order to receive, there will not be the complete pleasure, "and gave it to Israel," meaning to the *Kli* that works in order to bestow, for by this the reception of the pleasures will be complete.

However, it is difficult to correct and make everything be in order to bestow. This is why the land of Israel is called "a small country," whereas the land of in order to receive is a very big country. However, the land of Israel will spread over the entire world, meaning that all the will to receive will be corrected with the aim to bestow.

## 538- I Give Him My Covenant of Peace

*Tammuz, Tav-Shin-Lamed-Bet*, June 1972

It was said, "Behold, I give him My covenant of peace." It is known that to the extent that one allots, so he is allotted, an eye for an eye. But here, Pinhas committed murder when he killed them both, so how does this relate to him deserving to have peace? What "an eye for an eye" is there here?

As it is known, the purpose of creation is to do good to His creations. Yet, due to the disparity of form that separates the Giver from the receiver, the abundance is not drawn out so as not to come to separation. For this reason, each one has complaints and grievances against the Creator.

Likewise, between man and man, when a person has no lack, he does not fight with another, and all the quarrels occur because a person feels a lack within him. Therefore, he has complaints and quarrels with his friend and with the Creator over why the Creator does not complement his wishes that he wants.

Yet, in truth, the thing that prevents the abundance from spreading downward is the lack of equivalence of form, meaning the *Kli* [vessel] that is able to receive, which is the aim for the sake of the Creator. It is known that all the sins come only from reception for oneself. For this reason, since the sin of Zimri spoiled all the *Kelim* [pl. of *Kli*] that were able to receive and blocked the pipelines of abundance from spreading down, by this, disputes between man and man increased, for through the sin they made the vessels of reception for themselves bigger, and also caused disputes between man and the Creator because good abundances stopped coming down.

Hence, when Pinhas killed them, he corrected the *Kelim* so they are able to receive the abundance from above. This made peace between man and the Creator because the Creator gave abundance once again, and this is the meaning of "soothed My wrath," since the Creator's wish is to bestow, and Zimri caused Him to stop bestowing.

Also, peace was made between man and man, since everyone's vessels of reception were corrected, so they had nothing over which to be in dispute with their friends. This is why the verse says, "Therefore, say, 'Behold, I give him My covenant of peace,'" for he caused the peace through what he did.

## 539- Questions about "Return O Israel"

"Return, O Israel, to the Lord your God, for you have failed in your iniquity. Take with you words and return to the Lord."

1) What is "to the Lord"?

2) "You have failed in your iniquity." What is the obstacle that the iniquity caused, since the iniquity itself is the obstacle?

3) What is "Take with you words and return to the Lord"? What are these words, for it implies that he should take with him excuses so he will have a way to excuse himself before the Creator, but are there excuses before the Creator?

## 540- Nourishment

Just like a person would die of starvation without corporeal nourishment, without spiritual nourishment, the nourishment of the soul, he will also have to die and the spiritual soul will depart from him.

As with corporeal nourishment, where one who eats a lot of food becomes strong, with the nourishment of the soul, it, too, becomes stronger and healthier so the impure souls cannot defeat it.

## 541- When the Lord Favors Man's Ways

"When the Lord favors man's ways, his enemies, too, make peace with him." That is, the Sitra Achra [other side], too, receives reward for doing its mission, by which spirit was made above, which caused abundance in all the worlds. For this reason, it, too, makes peace with man, as in the allegory presented in The Zohar about the prince and the prostitute.

## 542- Return, O Israel – 2

"Return, O Israel, to the Lord your God." That is, do not engage in Torah and Mitzvot [commandments] because others tell you that you must engage in Torah and Mitzvot. Rather, one should come to a degree where he feels the existence of the Creator, that "The whole earth is full of His glory," since one who sits at home is unlike one who sits before the King. This is called "your God."

"For you have failed in your iniquity." Do not say that the first generations were better than these, and the iniquities caused us not to be able to feel it. It is written about this, "For you have failed in your iniquity," meaning in your personal inequities. That is, the bad in man wants only to receive for himself and not because of the glory of heaven, and does not want to have faith in the sages that we should learn Lishma [for Her sake], meaning for the sake of the Creator, and not for ourselves.

However, "It is not the uneducated who are pious." Rather, "Take with you words and return to the Lord," for the name HaVaYaH is called "the quality of mercy."

## 543- Tell the Children of Israel

*Shevat, Tav-Shin-Lamed-Het,* January 1978

It is written in *The Zohar* (Item 261 in the *Sulam* [Ladder commentary on *The Zohar*]): "Rabbi Shimon said, '*Koh* [Thus] you shall say to the house of Jacob,' in saying, from the side of judgment. 'And tell the sons of Israel,' as was said, 'And He said to you His covenant.' It is written, 'I have said today unto the Lord your God,' 'to the sons of Israel,' males who come from the side of mercy."

It is explained that "telling" means mercy for Israel, meaning the males, who come from the side of mercy. RASHI says that "the house of Jacob" is the women. "Speak to them with soft words, and tell the sons of Israel punishments and precisions, meaning to the males—words as hard as tendons" (*Mechilta*).

Thus, *The Zohar* implies the opposite—to the women the quality of judgment, and to the males the quality of mercy. But here it is implied that it is soft to the women and as hard as tendons to the males.

There, in *The Zohar* (Item 269 in the *Sulam*), he says, "He said to them: 'Any person should speak with another person according to his ways: with a female according to her ways, with a man according to his ways, and with a mighty man according to his ways. I said to Rabbi Hiya my son, 'As it is written, 'Thus you shall say to the house of Jacob, and tell the sons of Israel.'''"

According to what Maimonides wrote at the end of *Hilchot Teshuva*, "Therefore, when teaching children, women, and uneducated people, they are taught to work out of fear and in order to receive reward. Until they gain knowledge and acquire much wisdom, they are told that secret bit-by-bit and are accustomed to this matter with ease until they attain Him and know Him and serve Him from love."

It therefore follows that "Thus shall you say" is soft words, which is *Lo Lishma* [not for Her sake], meaning for the sake of self-love, which is for the sake of the will to receive, called "the quality of judgment" because there was a *Tzimtzum* [restriction] on that *Kli* [vessel] that it is forbidden to use them. Hence, on one hand, it is soft, since women are those who understand only that which concerns their vessels of reception, which is called "female," meaning the receiving *Kli*, while males are those who can understand the matter of bestowal, that the heart of the correction is equivalence of form, which our sages called "Cling unto His attributes, as He is merciful, so you are merciful." This is the opposite of the vessels of reception, called "the quality of judgment," and this is called "as hard as tendons" because it is hard for the body to accept this work of bestowal.

Thus, on one hand, it is called "merciful" because it is bestowal. And yet, it is as hard for the body as tendons, and the body does not agree to this path in the work of the Creator, the path of truth, which is in order to bestow.

By this we can understand why we need to change the order of the truth, since as it is written in *The Zohar*, we must speak with each one according to his understanding, so he can understand that through this goal it will be worthwhile for him to take upon himself Torah and *Mitzvot* [commandments]. Therefore, we naturally have to change our speech with each one according to his understanding.

It is written in *The Zohar*, Yitro (Item 279 in the *Sulam*): "'You yourselves have seen what I did to the Egyptians, and how I bore you on eagles' wings' with mercy. What are the wings of eagles? Rabbi Yehuda said, 'With mercy' … Rabbi Shimon said, 'The way of the eagle in the sky.' What is 'in the sky'? With mercy. Like an eagle that has mercy over his sons and judgment for others, the Creator has mercy for Israel and judgment for idol-worshipping nations."

We should ask why we must go with the quality of judgment against the nations of the world, why we cannot go with the quality of mercy with them, too. Is there bias in the matter?

We should say that this speaks of the same person, who is regarded as a small world, for man consists of a son, called "My son, My firstborn, Israel," and also with the quality of the nations of the world. In other words, man's vessels of reception are called "the nations of the world," and man's vessels of bestowal are called "a son of the Creator."

Usually, reception is of the utmost importance and bestowal is scorned.

This is the meaning of "I bore you on eagles' wings," meaning that the Creator lifts His son, the *Kli* [vessel] of bestowal, and makes it important to him. Naturally, it will fall, meaning that the vessels of reception will be to him of low importance. This is called "a judgment to the nations of the world." This is called "preparation for the reception of the Torah."

Because the Torah exists only in those who put themselves to death over it, meaning their selves, namely they should put to death the vessels of reception by not feeding them unless it is in order to bestow. Naturally, it falls and is regarded as dead, while the quality of bestowal is regarded as alive.

# 544- Man Is Born a Wild Ass [Donkey]

*6 Iyar, Tav-Shin-Lamed-Zayin*, May 5, 1977

It is written in *The Zohar* (*Emor*, Item 59) about the verse, "When an ox or a sheep or a goat is born," it asks, "It does not say 'a calf or a lamb or a he-goat or a kid [young goat],' but rather 'an ox or a sheep or a goat.' It explains that what she has in the end, she has when she is born."

That is, man is not so: What he has in the end, he does not have in the beginning because "Man is born a wild ass." The reason is that a beast means that it cares only for itself and has no feeling of others. When one is born with the will to receive, he has no passion to change his ways.

Hence, what he has in the end, he also has in the beginning. But man is not so. Although "A man is born a wild ass," in the end he will achieve the degree of "man," meaning with sensation of others. By this he will come to feel Godliness, which is called "Know the God of your father and serve Him."

"It shall remain seven days under its mother." *The Zohar* interprets that it is so that that power will settle in him, which was appointed over him and will exist in him. By what will it exist in him? When one Shabbat [Sabbath] is over him … for there is no existence to people unless in the light of Shabbat, as it is written, "And on the seventh day, God concluded His work, which He had done," and afterward, it is written, "It shall be accepted as a sacrifice of an offering by fire to the Lord." This is what the *Sulam* [Ladder commentary on *The Zohar*] interprets.

Regarding the matter that there is no existence to the six days of action except through the light of Shabbat, it is because Shabbat is called a "similitude of the next world," and "the next world" means "the purpose of creation." As long as it has not been revealed over the work, called "six days of action," regarded as the correction of creation, the wholeness is not apparent on the correction if the purpose of the correction has not been revealed, when a person sees that the purpose is on the correction.

# 545- Laboring and Finding

20 *Iyar, Tav-Shin-Lamed-Zayin,* May 8, 1977, Tiberias

It is written in *Midrash Rabbah*: "Anyone who fears Me and does words of Torah, all the wisdom and all the Torah are in his heart."

We should ask according to what is explained, "I did not labor and found, do not believe," how is it possible to be rewarded with the Torah without labor? According to a common question, How is labor related to finding, since finding comes absentmindedly, so why the word "labor" in regard to finding?

According to the above *Midrash*, we should say that if a person makes an effort in fear, and fear means faith, that one must believe that it is impossible to approach the Creator without equivalence of form in the form of a desire to bestow, and one makes the labor with the desire to bestow, so he is rewarded with finding. In other words, the Creator gives him Torah and wisdom as in the above-mentioned *Midrash*.

Indeed, we should ask why specifically the Torah of the Creator requires labor, while the rest of the teachings can be acquired without labor? After all, we see that nothing can be obtained without labor.

It can be said that what our sages call "labor" by which one achieves the Torah is different from the effort one makes in other teachings. Obtaining other teachings requires intellectual efforts. By exerting to understand the matters, one comes to grasp them, obtaining the teaching being taught.

This is not so with the Torah. The true Torah is called a "gift," and the word "labor" has nothing to do with "gifts," since a gift does not depend on the labor of the receiver but on the view of the giver. If he wishes, he gives gifts to anyone he wants. Thus, how can we speak of labor with regard to the Torah?

Rather, we see that usually when a person wants to give gifts, he gives them to his loved ones. Therefore, if the receiver wants to be given a gift, he cannot ask the giver for a gift. Instead, if the receiver tries to make the giver see that he is among the ones who love the giver, the giver will naturally give him gifts.

It therefore follows that in order to be rewarded with the gift of the Torah, he must exert himself with all kinds of actions so the giver will see that he is among the ones who love him. Then he will give him gifts anyhow.

It is a great effort to make the Creator see that he is among the ones who love the Creator, since a person must try not to want anything, and that his only desire will be to bestow contentment upon the Creator and not for his self-love, but for the love of the

Creator. This is a great effort because it is against the nature with which he was created.

Through this labor, one is made to be among those who love the King, and then the Creator gives it to him as a gift.

This is why there is labor here—to love the Creator and not for self-benefit but in order to bring contentment to the Creator. At that time, "I found," meaning that the Creator gives a person the delight and pleasure as a find, since he exerted himself in the opposite direction—to bestow upon the Creator. Finding means that the Creator bestows delight and pleasure upon the person.

A summary of the above-said:

1) Why can we not acquire Torah without labor, as this implies that the rest of the teachings can be acquired without labor?

2) What is the labor applied specifically with regard to the Torah?

3) Why is Torah called "finding"? If he comes to it absentmindedly, as with a find, how can we speak of labor?

4) The Torah is a gift and not a find.

5) If the Torah is a gift, how can we speak of "labor in order to receive a gift"? After all, the *Kli* [vessel] of a gift is called "love," meaning that we give gifts to those we love.

# 546- He Made Everything Good in Its Time

"He made everything good in its time." That is, at the end of correction, when everything is good because the sins have become as merits, it is obvious that even those who cause the sins will be good.

This is the meaning of "If he is rewarded, he sentences himself and the entire world to the side of merit," meaning that when one repents, he sentences himself, meaning that all his actions have become merits. Likewise, the whole world, to the extent that they cause him the sins, to the extent they caused the sins, now that they have repented, they, too, become merits.

## 547- The Attribute of Caution

"He who is small is big, and he who is big is small."

The reason is that the profits are mainly from the *Milchama* [war], which is regarded as *Lechem* [bread], which one obtains only through plowing, sowing, and harvesting.

Hence, he who is small, who feels small, meaning that he still has room for work, is big, meaning that he has the state of war, he elicits the quality of bread. But one who is big—who does not find any more room for work—is small because he can no longer gain. This is why he is small, since the profits are the most important.

## 548- Doing and Hearing

"Speech" is regarded as action, and "hearing" means I hear, meaning think, which is something that is acceptable to the heart. This is as it is written, "And you shall give to Your servant a heart that hears." This is the meaning of "We will do and we will hear," that it is impossible that hearing will be revealed before a person reveals the action, which is the choice.

In other words, when the hearing is revealed, there is no place for choice. For this reason, the hearing is concealed and when one must engage in Torah and *Mitzvot* [commandments] only in action and not in hearing, there is labor because the heart does not understand if it is worthwhile to engage in Torah and *Mitzvot*, and all its actions are only by accepting the burden, as it is written in the prayer before wearing the *Tefillin* [phylacteries], which is next to the heart, to thereby enslave the lusts and thoughts of our hearts to His work. In the action, there can be enslavement, but in hearing, there is no place for enslavement.

This is as our sages said, "He who comes to purify is aided." It was interpreted in *The Zohar* that he is given a holy soul, which is regarded as hearing.

It therefore follows that the whole concealment of the hearing is only in order to have room for the revelation of the power of choice. This is the meaning of the words that hearing depends on the speech, meaning on the action. This is the meaning of "By the word of the Lord, the heavens were made."

In other words, when a person engages in the word of the Creator, which is Torah, his intention should be toward acting, that he will be rewarded with acting for the sake of the Creator meaning that his actions will be for the sake of the Creator.

It is upon this that the hearing in the sense of acting is revealed, namely that all his actions that are for the sake of the Creator, in them the hearing is revealed. This is as *The Zohar* said, that the hearing depends on the speech.

## 549- *Feeling the Lack*

It is human nature that with any possession, sometimes he appreciates it even though the majority of people do not regard the possession at all. Still, he values it, meaning in a place where he wants to boast before others.

When one wants to add to his possession, then even if most people regard his possession as substantial, he still regards it as nothing and feels lacking. This is so because by nature, man yearns for rest, and only where he feels some deficiency in himself will he take upon himself the burden of labor in order to mend it.

Providence has prepared the two feelings, although they are conflicting, for several reasons: 1) A person feels vitality only from wholeness. 2) A person must praise the Creator, but only on wholeness can one praise the other, for giving him the wholeness.

Feeling the lack leads to movement, which then brings him to prayer, for there is prayer only for a deficiency.

## 550- *If You Seek Her as Silver*

"If you seek her as silver and search for her as treasures, then you will understand the fear of the Lord and discover the knowledge of God" (Proverbs 2:4-5).

We should ask who does not know what is fear of the Creator, and what does the verse, "Then you will understand the fear of the Lord" tell us.

We should say that the verse refers to understanding the quantity and quality of the fear of the Creator, where fear means "faith," and in faith there are already measures.

## 551- *The Torah as a Spice*

"Rabbi said, 'One must not pray for the wicked to be taken away from the world, for had the Creator removed Terah from the world while he was idol-worshipping, Abraham Our Father would not have come to the world, and there would not have been the tribes of Israel, King David, or the Messiah King, and the Torah would not have been given and all those righteous and pious people and the prophets would not have been in the world;" (*The Zohar, VaYera*, 105).

In ethics, when a person has bad qualities and foreign thoughts, he should not pray that the Creator will put them to death. Rather, they must be in the world so as to have room for choice, since the time of choice is called "a time of labor."

This is the meaning of Terah begetting Abraham, for specifically through labor are we rewarded with wholeness, called Abraham. It is likewise with all of the wholeness of the rest of the righteous, since the reward is according to the effort.

Likewise, the Torah was not given because Torah is as our sages said, "I have created the evil inclination; I have created the Torah as a spice." It follows that precisely when there are these wicked in a man, he needs the Torah, as our sages said, "The light in it reforms him."

In this manner, we should interpret the complaint of the angels, who said, "Give Your glory on the heaven," and He replied to them, "Is there evil inclination in you?" We should ask, Is the Torah something limited that cannot be divided between angels and people down below on earth?

We should say that the argument of the angels that the Torah belongs specifically to the angels, since the Torah is sublime, for precisely when he is in a state of "angel," he has connection to the Torah. The Creator replied to them: "Moreover, one who has evil inclination has connection to the Torah, since the Torah is regarded as a spice for the evil inclination. But the angels have no connection to the Torah because they have no vessels of reception."

# 552- He Who Comes to Purify Is Aided – 1

*Heshvan*, September/October

"He who comes to purify is aided." The main purpose of "He who comes to purify" is in the action. "He is aided" refers to the thought, for only on the action can one overcome, but not on the intention.

This is the meaning of "I will bless you in all that you do," since only on action can there be a commandment, while the intention is not within man's hands. It is only in the hand of the Creator to give man the real intention. This is why it is considered that he is aided, meaning that the choice that was given to man was said only about the action but not about the intention.

This is the meaning of "We will do and we will hear." When one observes the action, the Creator gives the intention, regarded as "We will hear." This is the meaning of a prayer without an intention being like a body without a soul.

This is also the meaning of the three partners in man: the Creator, his father, and his mother. The Creator gives the soul, meaning the intention, and the father and mother are regarded as the giving force and the receiving force, where by these two forces, an act is born. In other words, the giving force does the deed, and the receiving force does not let him do the act of bestowal, which is why at that time he has room for choice.

One must increase the "right" over the "left," meaning the giving force over the force of reception. However, this is regarded only as an act, which is tantamount to a prayer without an intention. The intention is called "the soul," and the Creator gives it.

Through these three forces, the man is born. But when he has no room for choice, he does not need assistance from the Creator so he has no soul. It follows that man can be created only through these three forces.

This is the meaning of "Father gives the white, mother the red." "White" means as it is written, "Though your sins be as scarlet, they shall be as white as snow." "White" is when one has yearning for Torah and Mitzvot [commandments]. "Red" is the appellation of sins, as in "Though your sins be as scarlet," the quality of Ima [mother], who is the female quality, meaning the will to receive, has no need or desire to do Mitzvot.

Specifically through those two forces, the quality of "man" emerges, and then the Creator gives him the "soul," meaning the intention called "hearing," as it is written, "In the end, after all is heard, fear God and keep His commandments, for this is the whole of man." Our sages said the whole world was created only for this.

We should understand the meaning of "all is heard." We should interpret that "hearing" means the flavors of Torah and the flavors of *Mitzvot*, and we are rewarded with it specifically by doing. This is the meaning of "We will do and we will hear." Also, this is the meaning of "In the end," meaning that in the end he is rewarded with the quality of "We will hear." We should engage in "fear God," etc., meaning in doing, which is called "fear of heaven."

# 553- The Difference between Concealed and Revealed

"Revealed" means that which another can see, as it is something that is revealed outside. Hence, there is no difference whether a person learns rules or legends or Kabbalah; it is all considered "revealed." "Concealed" is that which another cannot see, as it is hidden from others, and this pertains to the intention.

The sensation about it is that his friend cannot know his aim while performing a *Mitzva* [commandment]. Also, he cannot know what flavor he feels while performing the *Mitzvot* [pl. of *Mitzva*] or while learning the Torah. This is called "concealed."

It was said about this, "The secret things belong to the Lord our God, and the revealed things, to us and to our children," etc., meaning that we are commanded only to acting, which is revealed. This is the meaning of what is written, "The revealed things belong to us and to our children, to do all the words of this Torah [law]."

"And the concealed things belong to the Lord our God," for "concealed" refers to the intention, and hearing is in the hands of the Creator, for only He can give to man, and the man cannot receive it. But on this there is no matter of choice.

# 554- The Power of Thought

When one begins to think a certain thought, he creates that thought. When we say that the Creator made him think the thought, then it is the Creator who creates the man, and the man creates the thought. It follows that the thinking man is an offspring with respect to the Creator, and the thought is an offspring with respect to man.

When the man thinks, he is called "Who." He asks who he is. When he obtains an answer to his question, the answer is called "what." The "what" is regarded as *Hochma* [wisdom], which is regarded as *Koach-Ma* [the power of what]. That is, the "what" dresses in him as a force, which is the power of the thought.

When a person begins to reflect on the wondrous powers within him, he must say that it is a Godly force that is clothed within him performing all those actions without his awareness. Also, the man has no control over himself, over the actions unfolding within him. However, he does have a power that can interfere through corrected actions that he must provide for his body, such as food, which is an element that interferes with the processes of the body.

Man is one part of the whole of creation and must be included in them and receive nourishment from them. By this, he unites with them. In other words, one must receive within him parts of wind, water, and sun, etc., since he is one link in the chain of creation.

We must always be in a state that is regarded as "good," meaning that we are living in a world that is all good, and everything we feel is for the best.

When people harm him for no reason, but only because they are inherently wicked, and this is why they afflict him, he should not think that this is a coincidence. Rather, for all his anger at them, he must not take revenge on them, but he must say that everything comes from Providence.

By having to overcome his inclination and admit all the powers of the anger into *Kedusha* [holiness], it is a test that the Creator wants to test him if he can maintain his wholeness at such a time and love the Creator.

By overcoming, a person becomes powerful.

He must know that the partner is clothed within him.

He must not think or do something that is unbecoming of the partner.

He must think of the exaltedness of the Creator and yearn that there will be light.

# 555- The Exile of the Shechina [Divinity]

The meaning of the exile of the Shechina is that everyone expels her and she has nowhere to dwell in the lower ones, for the lower ones are inviting the Sitra Achra [other side]. When he comes and wants to enter, they close the doors of the mind and heart, meaning that all the matters that are built on the will to receive—thought, speech, and action—are willing to work and toil for them.

But when the Shechina comes, meaning the desire to bestow, whether in mind or in heart, they immediately lose the tools of work and labor. And even if they occasionally do something for her, they are regarded as something redundant in the world, meaning that they would be happier if that quality did not exist in reality.

Sometimes, when a person is in a state of rest and the thought of the desire to bestow comes and knocks and asks for permission to enter, she is told that they have no time because they are busy with the will to receive, and the desire to bestow comes and casts flaws in the pleasures of the will to receive.

This is the meaning of the Shechina coming and knocking on doors, and she is despised the way one despises a poor person knocking on doors. There is a custom among the Sephardic [Jews of Spanish origin] to answer to the poor, "God have mercy," but for now, there is no room for her.

Redemption is for the Redeemer to come and let her into the hearts of the people of Israel. Then she will be the "queen" and the will to receive, the "handmaid." Then, each one will yearn to play with her. But only the Messiah of the Creator can redeem her from her troubles so she does not knock on doors, and only the Messiah of the Creator can reveal her glory and esteem.

# 556- The Torah, from the Words "Shot Through"

"Everything is in the hands of heaven but the fear of heaven," for man can add only fear.

The soul of Israel is regarded as *VAK*, and the soul of Egypt is regarded as *GAR de Haya*. At that time, there was a mixture of *VAK* within *GAR*. This is the meaning of "extracting a nation from within a nation." There are roots in it: 1) potential root, 2) actual root. The potential root is in *Ein Sof* [infinity], and the actual root is different for each one.

By this we will understand what is written, that the root of *Atzilut* begins only at *Nekudot de SAG* due to their descent to *NHY de AK* where they mixed with the *Behina Dalet*. But in the three prior *Partzufim* [pl. of *Partzuf*], there is still no root. We should understand this, since it is explained in several places that all the worlds are rooted in *Ein Sof*, so why does he say that there is no root to *Atzilut* in the first three *Partzufim*?

The thing is that we should always distinguish between potential and actual in the world. In *Ein Sof*, all the worlds were rooted in the discernment of the root. But here we are speaking of the actual, meaning that the root begins in practice specifically from the beginning of the association of the quality of mercy with judgment, which was done specifically in *Nekudot de SAG*.

Prior to the *Nekudot*, only the quality of judgment is used, since what we say, that the world of *Ein Sof* is the root of the worlds, this is only in potential, like a blueprint. There is one who makes a plan for a building and builds the building according to the plan. Then, on one hand, it can be said that with the very plan, the whole building has been completed. On the other hand, the plan is not even the beginning of the building since the building is an actual thing so we need a root for the actuality, and this began only in *Nekudot de SAG*, where the association of the quality of mercy with the quality of judgment was rooted in practice.

# *557- Concerning Ohr Hozer [Reflected Light]*

It is written in *The Study of the Ten Sefirot* (Part 2, Chapter 1, Item 3) that *Ohr Hozer* ascending from the *Masach* [screen] upward is called "connection" because it holds and captures the upper light in the *Igul* [circle] in a way that where the *Ohr Hozer* does not clothe the upper light, that light is regarded as nonexistent from the perspective of the emanated being because he cannot attain it without this attire called *Ohr Hozer*.

By this we should understand why not everyone has the sensation of Godliness, since it is written, "I fill the heaven and the earth," and "The whole earth is full of His glory," and yet we do not feel anything.

The answer is that where there is no clothing called *Ohr Hozer*, the upper light is regarded as nonexistent from the perspective of the emanated being, and because the whole meaning of the *Ohr Hozer* is that he receives only according to the intention to bestow, as long as one has not emerged from self-reception, he does not have this *Ohr Hozer*. Thus, although "The whole earth is full of His glory," it is regarded as nonexistent from the perspective of the lower one.

It follows that the only thing that one must do in order to achieve the goal is to focus all of one's work on one point: to be able to dedicate all of one's free time for the sake of the Creator. This is the meaning of "Everything is in the hand of heaven but the fear of heaven." This means that the Creator gives everything. The upper lights are already prepared for a person, as in "More than the calf wants to suckle, the cow wants to nurse," and all we need is a *Kli* [vessel]. After the *Tzimtzum* [restriction], this *Kli* is called *Masach* and *Ohr Hozer*, and this is what connects the upper with the lower. That is, through it, the lower one connects to the upper one.

When this connector does not exist, the lower one cannot see the upper one, and the upper one is regarded as nonexistent from the perspective of the lower one. Hence, to the extent that one begins to work for the sake of the Creator, to that extent he acquires connection with the upper light. And by the measure of his connection, so is the measure of his attainment.

We should understand the matter of *AHP* of the upper one that fell to *Galgalta ve Eynaim* [*GE*] of the lower one. We should interpret that *GE* and *AHP* reflect *Katnut* [smallness/infancy] and *Gadlut* [greatness/adulthood]. The correction that *Hochma* and *Bina* did for the sake of the sons, for which they are called *Abba* [father] and *Ima* [mother], as explained in several places in *The Study of the Ten Sefirot*, is as in "An exiled disciple, his teacher is exiled with him."

Therefore, when the lower one sees no *Gadlut* in the upper one, the lower one does not even have *Katnut*. This is the meaning of the *AHP* of the upper one, meaning *Gadlut* of the upper one, being placed in the *Katnut* of the lower one. At that time, it means that the lower one still does not have *Katnut*.

Only when the lower one sees that the *AHP* of the upper one have risen, through it, the lower one receives *Katnut*. But prior to this, he does not even have *Katnut*.

It therefore follows that the lower one must first believe that there is an upper one in reality, and that he does not feel the upper one because the lower one does not see the greatness of the upper one. This is called "*Shechina* [Divinity] in exile," meaning that the *Shechina* is for him as dust; he does not feel that there is more than the taste of dust in the upper one.

Hence, when one begins to observe the greatness of the upper one, which is considered that the *AHP* of the upper one have ascended, the lower one also ascends and begins to attain the feeling of Godliness.

This depends on the measure that it pains him that he sees the faults of the upper one. Thus, to that extent, the upper one becomes ascended in him. It follows that this is a correction for the purpose of the lower one.

## 558- Desire for Spirituality

There is will to receive for corporeality.

There is a person who has no will to receive, not even for corporeality. Everything he does is involuntary, meaning that he would be more satisfied if he did not have to eat and drink and so forth.

There is a desire to receive spirituality. Hence, before one has a desire to receive spirituality, he has nothing to relinquish.

## 559- One Hundred Blessings

"And he sowed in that land and found on that year one hundred gates." Through the 355 days in each year, meaning that there are many follies and nonsense, and he saw that he was in a state of "What?" unlike Abraham, who was nonetheless "dust and ashes," but truly a state of "What?" where by wanting to raise all the follies to *Kedusha* [holiness] he came to a state of "What." (Also, perhaps he is in the state of "The wicked will fail and the righteous will walk in it.") When he was in "One hundred gates" in the quality of "doing," he was then rewarded with a blessing, which is "hearing," which is that the *MA* [what] becomes *Me'ah* [one hundred], meaning that he extends the quality of the "Champion of the World" into the *MA* and it becomes *Me'ah* [one hundred] blessings.

Also, we need to understand the meaning of the Written Torah and the Oral Torah. In the Torah, the Written Torah is called *Yod-Hey-Vav*, as was said, "And we are what," where first we must be ones who believe in the words of our sages, and then we are rewarded with *Me'ah*, meaning the bottom *Hey*, so when the bottom *Hey* shines, as well, meaning when we extend the *Yod-Hey-Vav* into the bottom *Hey*, there is wholeness and it is called "One hundred blessings."

This is the meaning of "light," "water," "firmament," which are one hundred blessings that a person should do each day. This is the meaning of "You will also decree a thing, and it will be established for you."

"Light" means that first there was the discernment of light, and then it was restricted and the light became "water." Afterward, it was decreed that a "firmament" would be made between the upper and lower waters, where a person feels that he is under the firmament, that he has become separated, and then he cries. This is the meaning of "Lower water cries."

At that time, he corrects himself and achieves his wholeness. This is the meaning of "It will be established for you," when the word of the Creator comes true. That is, the Creator is felt in all of Creation, and this is the meaning of "one hundred blessings." This is the meaning of "And Isaac dwelled by Be'er-lechai-roi." In other words, he returned all the follies and sorted them out for lechai-roi (which is *LeChai* [the One] who Lives Forever).

This is the meaning of the three wells, meaning three scrutinies:

1) *Oshek* [robbing] means that he saw that the *Klipa* [shell/peel] was robbing the *Kedusha* [holiness] by depicting depictions about the Creator, that He is not "The One whom my soul loves," and saying that she is a depiction of the Creator, as was said about Sarah, "I was despised in her eyes," for she makes depictions and says that she is the form of the *Shechina* [Divinity]. It follows that she robs the real form.

This is the meaning of "This year, slaves." According to the form that the handmaid gives to *Dvekut* [adhesion] with the Creator, "Next year, free," meaning that from this day forth, we are accepting the real form, like sons and not like slaves, who gives the form of free, who becomes liberated from this form.

Afterward, in the second scrutiny, "hatred," as in "You who love the Lord, hate evil."

Precisely through the bad we are rewarded with being beloved friends, where he says that it is not as the form that the *Sitra Achra* [other side] makes in the manner of robbery, but that the real form is in the manner of "beloved friends," as it is written, "Have you seen he who my soul loves? I have sought he who my soul loves; I almost left them until I found he who my soul loves. I held him and I will not let go of him."

3) Then he comes to a well, meaning to a scrutiny called Rehovot because now "The Lord has made room for us, and we will be fruitful in the land." This is the meaning of "Isaac dwelled in Gerar," meaning he was *Nigrar* [following/pulled after] the Creator like a shadow follows a person, as he was rewarded with private Providence.

This is the meaning of "Who is it who rises from the desert like plumes of smoke?" First, it was made out of the frog through the beatings. When he wanted to submit, they proliferated. Finally, he saw a capitol lit up, which are only doubts about the Creator.

"Rising from the desert" means that while a person is still in the desert, meaning among the *Klipot* [shells/peels], "as plumes of smoke," meaning that the "World, Year, Soul" in him are all as plumes of smoke and he cannot stand them and he runs from them, which is the meaning of *Harei Battar* [Mountains of Battar], where *Harei* are bad *Hirhurim* [thoughts], and *Battar* means carcasses, that from this, one becomes dead, separated from the Life of Lives.

This means that the *Shechina* [Divinity] says, "Run my beloved on the mountains of perfumes," where through the *Het* [Hebrew letter], meaning of inferior degree, when he receives everything in the form of doing, he is later rewarded with these mountains becoming perfumes, namely that he raises everything to *Kedusha* [holiness].

This is the meaning of myrrh, where before he felt *Merirut* [bitterness] in all the "world, year, soul," and he is rewarded with *Levona* [incense], the upper *Loven* [whiteness], which is the one hundred blessings, meaning that the [letter] *Het* becomes a *Kof*, meaning blessings.

This is the meaning of the minister of forgetfulness being called "Bad-Mouth," meaning that by gossiping and slandering the Creator, the Creator makes those who mention forget, for it is a great flaw called "robbery," for this form is not real. Rather, He is good and does good, and this is called "My soul's Beloved," and then we can find Him.

Conversely, we cannot find the form of the *Sitra Achra* [other side] because it does not exist in reality.

This is the meaning of "powders of the merchant," where if even the dust of slander stays in the body after slandering, it is still harmful. However, when one takes everything as doing above reason, he is rewarded with great lights, called "scent," which is "and he smelled it in the fear of the Lord," said about the Messiah, that we cannot receive lights unless as a scent that rises from below upward.

This is why as there are entertainments in MAN, so there are entertainments in MAD. In other words, according to the joy one has during the action, so he has joy in MAD, meaning in hearing. The most important is the preparation of the *Kelim*, which is the meaning of the inversion into vessels of bestowal.

# 560- Generations

The work is mainly in the manner of "You are in partnership with Me," since were it not for this, a person might be as that day old fly that is born in the morning and dies in the evening, since from the perspective of the Creator, a person might receive the tower filled with abundance in a single day. Thus, why does one need seventy years, and in each year 355 [in the Hebrew calendar] days? It is because "You are in partnership with Me."

"The greedy, all he gets is irritation." This is the will to receive, which belongs to man, for in Him, there is no such thing. In order for man to turn it into *Kedusha* [holiness], a person uses it each time with the same works; what he did yesterday, he does today, and tomorrow, too, until it becomes loathsome in his eyes and he connects to *Kedusha*.

This is the meaning of "At that time, he tells between a servant of the Creator and one who does not serve Him." That is, both are doing the same things, the same nonsense, but this one brings all the nonsense to *Kedusha*.

This is the meaning of "'Folly of follies,' said Kohelet," meaning that he assembled all those follies into *Kedusha*, and from them come great unifications. The root of all the follies is the frog, but through the beatings, they proliferated, as it is written, "And they came into your home and into your stomach," for the root is knowing everything and doing, which applies both in mind and in heart, for in spirituality, mind and heart are one.

However, in man, they seem as two. This is the meaning of the jokers of the generation saying that Sarah was impregnated by Abimelech, meaning that Isaac is the son of Abimelech, that he is a foreigner and not the son of Abraham, who is the father of faith, but rather that what he does is only in the manner of hearing, which precedes doing.

For this reason, the Creator made Isaac's features similar to Abraham's. That is, "face" is the root of *Bina*, whose basis is only hearing, but it is in order to bestow, so the jokers of the generation would see that Isaac was doing in the manner of reception, meaning in hearing, and there was no distinction between one who works in reception in order to bestow or in reception for himself.

This is why he raised all the follies and nonsense to *Kedusha*, regarded as "You are in partnership with Me," where he first made the doing in completeness.

This is the meaning of "There is no flavor in the elders," meaning that Abraham was only in the manner of "Taste and see that the Lord is good," "And there is no counsel in infants," which is a correction in the form of an advice, as it is written, "And he divided the people into two camps," meaning he divided between the tent of Leah and the tent of Rachel. It follows that there is still no wholeness.

Conversely, Isaac said to put order in all the follies, meaning he raised all the calculations of sleep, roasting, and eating to *Kedusha*. He said about this, "Half is on me and half is on You," meaning that he became a partner in the work of creation.

# 561- The Soul of Israel

"Therefore, man is called 'unique,' to teach you that anyone who destroys one soul from Israel, the text says about him that it is as though he destroyed a whole world. Likewise, anyone who sustains one soul from Israel, the text says about him that it is as though he sustained a whole world" (Sanhedrin 37).

We should say, Why did the writing say this? After all, we have divisions in the Torah between individuals and the collective where the collective takes precedence over the individual, and it also stands to reason that the individual is one, and not many. Thus, what is the reason that the writing says that the individual is like the collective?

Our sages said, "He who performs one *Mitzva* [commandment], happy is he for he has sentenced himself and the entire world to the side of merit" (*Kidushin* 40). Why is this so? After all, we see that there are wicked in the world, and it is known that in each generation, we have righteous, as our sages said, "There is no generation that has none such as Abraham," etc.

Thus, the merit that the righteous caused should have been apparent to the collective. Yet, we see that someone who invents some invention in science, this wisdom that the wise extended is enough for the whole collective. That is, one who wants to delve in the wisdom can benefit from what the wise person extended to the collective. But clearly, one who does not engage in science has no connection to that innovation that the wise person extended.

It is likewise in spirituality: "He who performs one *Mitzva* sentences himself and the entire world to the side of merit." That is, one who engages in the work of the Creator can benefit from the lights he has obtained through his sentencing.

Accordingly, "One who sustains one soul from Israel," who made the sentencing to the side of merit, sustains his soul, since "The wicked in their lives are called 'dead.'" It follows that without sentencing, he is "half and half," like a person hanging between life and death. By sentencing, he becomes alive. It follows that the lights that he drew suffice for the whole collective.

This is the meaning of "The world stands on one righteous," meaning that the light that he extended is as in "A candle for one, a candle for one hundred." Hence, he who loses his soul, by sentencing to the side of fault, loses a whole world, meaning that he denied the revelation of the light that was enough for the entire world. This is the meaning of the words, "One must say, 'The world was created for me.'"

This is why there is the precision, "He who sustains one soul from Israel," meaning that the intention is a soul in the quality of Israel, but not in the nations of the world, since the intention is on the decision toward the quality of Israel, which is called that he has sentenced to the side of merit.

This is why there is the intimation in regard to Israel, "You are called 'man,' and the nations of the world are not called 'man,'" since anything spiritual must have its grip on corporeality. Hence, when sustaining the corporeal soul of Israel, he has the same judgment as keeping the spiritual soul of Israel, since with respect to branch and root, the corporeal soul of Israel implies the spiritual soul. However, we should know that this pertains mainly to the spiritual.

# 562- Wisdom and Prayer

"Hannah was speaking in her heart, and Ali thought that she was drunk." We should ask why not crazy.

It is known that prayer should be in a manner of "And her voice was not heard," meaning not for oneself but in order to bestow. This is the meaning of "I borrowed it from the Lord," for her entire prayer was in the form of "for the Creator" and not for herself. Also, *Hochma* from above downward is regarded as drunkenness.

He thought that her intention was *Hochma* in the manner of from above downward, but her intention was on her heart, meaning that her heart was not fine. This is the meaning of her speaking about her heart not being fine.

Ali means *Al Liba* [on her heart], meaning that *Hochma* does not spread inside the heart, which is called *Hochma* from above downward. Her intention was on her heart, that the heart was not fine, meaning that her prayer was why she deserved such a harsh punishment that the heart would yearn to extend from above downward, while her request was that the Creator would send her a spirit of purity, so the heart would yearn for the manner of from below upward.

# 563- Definitions – 2

Fire as a lion, fire as a dog: Fire is the foundation of the *KLA*, as it is in falling. It is *Hesed*, as strong as a lion. It is also the sense of sight, under which the act becomes established, whether good or bad.

This is a memory in the book: *Sefer* [book] comes from the word *Sof-Ohr* [end of light], as in gatekeepers. It is as the Creator said to Moses, "Write this," etc., for the written word is not always remembered, and the solution is, "And he found it written," since in time, it is forgotten, and through the *Sof-Ohr*, he remembered.

Amalek and the tearing of the Red Sea: These are two opposites. The tearing of the Red Sea is the departure and concealment of fire of a layperson, the last discernment, called "dog." This is the meaning of "But against any of the sons of Israel a dog will not bark." For this reason, "Judah became His holy place," the quality of *AVI*, the sanctity in the fire of the High One, and their leader jumped into the sea and walked as though on land. And the Egyptians, who followed them like a dog from their beginning, since the last discernment has been torn and vanished.

At that time, "Six hundred choice men" were delighted. This is *VAK de Gadlut*, "with officers in all of them," meaning that their *GAR* also appeared to them. This is the meaning of "Egypt was chasing them," in singular form [in Hebrew].

At that time, "The horse and its rider He has hurled into the sea," "like a stone into raging waters," since these waters, in which there was the quality of dog, water of *MIKVEHON* when Israel already stood as a wall, in regard to the tearing. "Did not bark," etc., they were reawakened over the Egyptians and fell into the waves of the sea.

Rephidim: Since they came to Rephidim, that dog, who drowned the officers of Pharaoh, returned. This is the meaning of "And you are tired and weary and not fearing God," for because the last discernment has been torn from them, they were resurrected as *OMETZ*, which is the plundering of the sea. Naturally, they did not have any fear because there was no barking dog. Thus, they tried the Creator again, "Is the Lord among us, or not?" as did the officers of Egypt.

And then they did not have water to drink, like a blocking under the OMETZ, called "dry without water" (and although even inside the sea they came in dryness and were not tired, and a handmaid by the sea saw, etc., and babies in their mothers' wombs sang, it was for that time the reason for the miracle of the salvation from Egypt, and there was no time to be thirsty for water).

Then he struck the rock and water poured out. That is, Moses let down his hand. It is known that when he let it down, Amalek prevailed. Hence, "And Amalek came."

The words of RASHI: There is an allegory about a father, etc., you saw the father: The Creator has already carried him on His shoulders, as in "Like an eagle that stirs up its nest ... will carry him on His wing," as in, a lion. He gave them an object: the plundering of Egypt, and he gave them the plundering of the sea, since they were granted with great possessions from Egypt, as in the woman lending from her neighbor, since when the evil *Klipa* [shell/peel] hangs her stench on the upper one, and they sat on the meat-pots that the Lord had killed, meaning carcasses killed by prey, and not slaughtered by man (from the MIKVEHON) although the matter is known to begin with (that it is a land that is not theirs), that there is nothing wrong here.

And no iron tool was heard, God forbid, for by this disclosure they went out from there, as in "I and not a messenger." And yet, the thieves already had a great many vessels of silver and vessels of gold. This is the meaning of "And every woman shall borrow from her neighbor." It follows that a seed of holiness, who do not possess and who are powerless to understand anything about the work of the *Kelim* [vessels], through the enslavement by the *Klipa* of Egypt against their will, had the right to also borrow into their own possession for some time.

Afterward, "The man Moses was great in the eyes of Pharaoh." They recognized the children of Israel, that they were descendants of holiness, and the matter became known. Nevertheless, they had favor for them and they gave them the *Kelim*.

The plundering of Egypt: This is the disclosure of *Hassadim*, since from the time when they were enslaved by the strewn upper light.

The plundering of the sea: This is the rising, since they came into a dry land. This is the meaning of "The Lord will be king," since "They saw Egypt dead upon the seashore." That is, *HaVaYaH* fought, since the water stood like a wall, from *KLA*, a lion, to their right, and from *MIKVEHON*, a dog, to their left. And they came in the dry land (as in, *Har Horev* [mountain of dryness]) inside the sea. And there they had all the abundance of Egypt in their possession, which they had lent them.

Afterward, when the Egyptians followed them, the upper water from the right returned and covered the chariots, and then the children of Israel were saved and said, "This is my God and I will praise Him," and they did not want to return to the door of the abyss in *MIKVEHON* in the work of the officers. Afterward, they saw them dead by the seashore, meaning that part that was torn off from the sea as that wall to their left; this is what put them to death.

# 564- *Fire, Wind, Water, Dust*
## 17 *Shevat*, January-February

Fire, wind, water, dust, dream, fat, incense, criminals of Israel, sleep, eating, and drinking.

Fire and water are *Yod-Hey*. Wind and dust are *Vav-Hey*, *MA* and *BON*. However, all this is after the association of the quality of mercy with judgment. The water themselves were divided into *Hey* in the upper water and *Hey* in the lower water, which is the main *HaVaYaH de SAG*. There is a division between them because fire, water, and wind are primarily the quality of mercy, and the quality of judgment in *Hitkalelut* [inclusion].

The fire is the vital source (*KLA*). It is the difference between life, which is warm, and death, which is cold. Also, *Chaim* [life] from the word *Chom* [heat/warmth], and man is nourished from it as in the sleep.

Water is primarily the quality of mercy, and the quality of judgment in *Hitkalelut*. Two times *Mi-Mi*, the water basis and the acid basis. Hence, the basis of water is suitable for light and for lighting, and the acid basis, from the words *Hometz-Yayin* [vinegar-wine] *Chom-Etz* [warmth of the tree], since the power of judgment operates there in *Hitkalelut*. Hence, man is nourished by it without effort, since there is no excessive effort in upper *Ima*.

Wind is the pillar that decides between fire and water and ascends up to *Keter*. Hence, it is considered the vital root, in which there is also the fire, as well as water, and it is the rising and adorning together. For this reason, man is nourished by it in a perpetual and never ending *Zivug* [coupling]. There is no effort in its nourishing, but it rather extends by itself.

Dust is primarily the quality of judgment, and the quality of mercy in *Hitkalelut*. Hence, man is not nourished by it directly, as with the water and wind, but by plowing, sowing, and harvesting, and the thirty-nine works, as it is written, "By the sweat of your brow you shall eat bread."

These are the scrutinies in the thought, as in "a work of craftsmanship," since the water and wind are primarily the quality of mercy. Hence, there is no work of craftsmanship there since the scrutinies are done by themselves without effort.

Conversely, in the dust there is very little of the quality of *Ima* and the quality of mercy, and it constantly requires effort to recognize it and sort it.

This is the meaning of eyes, ears, nose, and mouth being the roots, which are called *Hushim* [senses], as it is written, "the sons of

Dan: Hushim" and "Hushai the Archite," and as in "My ear heard and confirmed it; my eye saw and coveted it."

The eyes and the ear are *AB SAG*, *Yod-Hey*, fire and water. Hence, waste that emerges from the eyes are the tears, as in tearing, which is the association that is revealed in the ear, as in living water. The waste of the ear blocks the hearing.

Nose and mouth are *Vav-Hey*, *MA* and *BON*, wind and dust. There are two holes in the nose, *Nukvin de Pardashka*. From one there is life, and from one there is the Life of Lives. The first is the mercy and adornment, and the second is the rising. Waste that emerges from the nose is in plural form, which is not so in the eye and the ear. The mouth is dust, and the *BON*, where the teeth grind the food with great effort, and its waste is more than all of them, and it is the saliva of the mouth.

During sleep, a person closes his eyes and lies completely devoid of any level. This is as in "shuts his eyes from looking upon evil." Hence, at that time he can be nursed from the Highest of High, which is the fire basis (*KLA* in falling). At that time, one of his ribs is taken from him, etc.

*Chalom* [dream], from the words *Chol-Em* [sand-mother], and *Helev* [fat] comes from *Chol-Av* [sand-father]. *Chol-Av* is the *Helbona* [incense] and the prayer from the criminals of Israel who said, "How will we help for we will harm it, and they made a secular Temple, since it emerged from their noses and became loathed."

*Chalom* is the fire basis, which *Lochem* [fights] against the water and makes it boil, and "A foolish son is his mother's woe," for then all the bloods gather together to the heart, and impure and pure are there together. Hence, when he wakes up from his sleep, his end is in pure blood that pours out from the heart to all the organs. This is the meaning of "I awoke for the Lord supports me," as in the *Samech* [Hebrew letter, and also "support"], meaning from upper *Ima*, (since sleep is the final *Mem*, *YESHSUT*).

This is the meaning of "I am asleep but my heart is awake," since "The voice of my beloved knocks, 'Open for me,'" which is the nourishing from the basis of fire. "I arose to open," as in the *Samech*, as said above, for this is why there is no *Nun* in *Ashrey* [happy are they], which is "falling," because of the *Samech* of awakening.

This is the meaning of "liquid myrrh on the handles of the lock," meaning that because the handles of the lock were carved from one of his ribs during sleep, meaning *Ima*, it is now possible for the light to breach and break through the lock that was made, which is the meaning of "putting to death and reviving, and brings forth salvation," for it is impossible anyhow.

This is the meaning of "How fair are your feet in shoes," meaning of *Ima*, similar to Moses' "Take your shoes off your feet," which is the meaning of "For the place on which you stand," the place of Moses, the *Yesod de Abba*, whose place is *Yesod Ima*, and she was certainly a land of holiness.

# 565- To Do Them Today

"To do them today and to receive the reward for them tomorrow," meaning we have to work *Lishma* [for Her sake]. Thus, why should he remember "and to receive the reward for them tomorrow"?

There are two matters here:

1) We should believe that there are endless pleasures in Torah and *Mitzvot* [commandments], that all the pleasures of this world are but a tiny light compared to what is found in a tiny degree in *Kedusha* [holiness], as it is written in *The Zohar* and in the writings of the ARI. Otherwise, he has no respect for Torah and *Mitzvot*. In order for one's intention to be in order to bestow, he must say "and to receive the reward for them tomorrow," meaning he says, "Now I want to make a choice and take upon myself the burden of Torah and *Mitzvot* only for the sake of the Creator."

# 566- Cast Their Seed Among the Nations

"'Then all the congregation lifted up their voices and cried,' as the writing says, 'She raised her voice against me; therefore, I hate her.' That voice that you cried caused you to be hated ... at that time it was decreed that the Temple would be ruined so that Israel would be exiled among the nations, for so the writing says, 'Therefore, He raised His hand to cast them down in the desert, and that He would cast their seed among the nations and scatter them in the lands.' Raising a hand against raising a voice" (*Midrash Rabbah, Shlach*, 16).

To understand all the above in the work, we should interpret the meaning of the Temple. When a person is rewarded with a temporary illumination of *Kedusha* [holiness], it is considered that he has entered the Temple.

The ruin of the Temple is when the illumination is taken away from him. The ruin comes when the person sins, meaning when he uses this illumination in order to enjoy it in his heart, or when he receives from it support in the mind. At that time, it departs from him.

There is the voice of the Creator and there is the voice of the lower one, called "her voice" or "their voice." "The voice of the Creator" is when he speaks only so as to thereby bring contentment above. The voice of the lower one is when the speaking is in order to bring contentment to man, as it is written, "And they raised their voice." Also, "She raised her voice against me," which caused all the ruin.

During the ruin, the Temple does not remain intact, as in the state he had prior to being rewarded with the Temple. Rather, it gets worse, for there is a rule that if a person does not rise, he falls.

Hence, due to the sin, besides taking from him what he was given, he is also punished. This is called being exiled among the nations, when they fall under lusts and desires of the nations of the world. This is the meaning of "He raised his hands to cast them down in the desert," where there is no settlement of the mind of *Kedusha*.

"To cast their seeds among the nations" means that the forces called "their seeds" are for the lusts of the nations, so he cannot do any work unless it gives pleasure to the body, regarded as the nations.

"To scatter them in the lands" means that all their thoughts are scattered, thinking what the uneducated think. This is the meaning of saying, "Raising a hand against raising the voice," that they sinned only in the voice, having a thought about their own benefit, but their desire was to be in *Kedusha*, but against that, the raising of the hand was that they fell lower down, meaning desired only corporeal things.

However, this is so for the purpose of correction. Otherwise, they would not feel the lack, that they must correct their actions. Rather, they would settle for little, meaning for the state they had prior to being rewarded with illumination; they agreed to remain that way.

However, when they fall lower down, there is hope that finally, the living will place it to his heart to make repentance and rebuild the Temple.

## 567- The Quality of Truth – 2

The truth has the power to shine vitality for a person even when the truth is very bitter.

We see that often when a person sees the lowliness of his state, he is still happy about it, meaning that he has vitality. Instead of regretting and feeling the gravity of his state and being bitter, he feels delight and pleasure.

We see that in corporeality, when someone sees that he is bare and indigent while his friends have abundance, he feels bad and has no peace of mind. But in spirituality, when one sees the lowliness of one's state, it gives him peace of mind.

The thing is that in spirituality, everything depends on the quality of truth, since to the extent that one follows falsehood, to that extent he becomes remote from the Creator, as it is written, "He who speaks lies shall not be established before My eyes." Hence, when one sees his true state, that he is bare and indigent in his spiritual state, since this is the truth, the truth shines for him so he will have vitality.

Through the vitality, he obtains a measure of confidence that henceforth he will be able to correct his actions. Based on this, he ascends in the measure of confidence and begins to come into the work of the Creator.

Conversely, when one fools oneself and does not see the truth will remain forever in a state of descent and lowliness, and no one will be able to help him in this because he is not asking for help, since he does not feel that he needs anything in spirituality.

# 568- The Meaning of "Right" and "Left"

15 *Kislev, Tav-Shin-Gimel*, November 24, 1942

The beginning of the work is extending the light. This is called "right." Afterward, we must discover the rejecting force, which is the resistance to clothing, and by this we have *Ohr Hozer* [reflected light], which is a *Kli* [vessel] for reception of the abundance. To the extent that one can maintain the rejecting force, the abundance exists in him.

This is the meaning of "I have given help to one who is mighty." Hence, when the abundance comes to him he should strengthen himself substantially with *Achoraim* [posterior] to reject the abundance. This is the meaning of the *Ohr Yashar* [direct light] and *Ohr Hozer* depending on each other and chasing one another, for when *Bina* is devoid of *Hassadim*, she turns her *Panim* [face] away from *Hochma*.

The reason is that since she lacks the power of bestowal, she cannot receive *Hochma*, called *Haya*, which is the *Hayut* [vitality] of the degree. But after she receives *Ohr Hozer* from *Malchut*, at which time the power of bestowal becomes established in her, she receives *Hochma* once more.

Once she receives *Hochma*, she lacks *Hassadim* once more because now she is busy receiving *Hochma*, so she returns to the state of *Achoraim*, meaning she stops receiving *Hochma* and extends *Hassadim* once more, and so forth repeatedly.

It therefore follows that they are dependent on each other, since when she has *Hassadim*, she receives *Hochma*. Otherwise, she does not receive. Also, they are chasing one another because when she has *Hochma*, she lacks *Hassadim*, and this is called "And the animals were running back and forth," and so is always the order.

This is not so when someone clings to one end. It is said about him, "And crushed the sides of Moab." This is also the meaning of "Israel have swinging; the nations of the world do not have swinging." "Swinging" means moving back and forth, and in this way, they go from strength to strength, like the nature of the light, which moves to and fro, once on the right and once on the left.

# 569- The Meaning of the Offering

We see that an offering must be complete, flawless.

This means that there are people who sacrifice their lives and give their souls to idol-worship, which is in a place where they have no meaning in life and see that their whole future is nothing but pain and agony.

This happens for various reasons. Some have come to that state by losing their property so they feel there is no point to continue living without property and think that this is the worst suffering in the world.

Alternatively, they are deep in debt and cannot repay and they cannot stand the shame from the debtors, which afflicts them terribly. They, too, think that this is the worst suffering in the world, and for this reason they have no desire to go on living. Hence, they commit suicide.

It follows that the offering of the sacrifice is not for the Creator but for themselves. This is called "making an offering to idol-worship."

Sometimes, a person is lost because of the above-mentioned causes and says that now he agrees to serve the Creator in complete devotion because he sees that corporeal life gives him no vitality but to retire from all the corporeal matters because he is bare and indigent, so he gives himself up to spirituality.

In that, too, although now he is making an offering to the Creator, there is still a flaw in this offering because the corporeal life he gives as an offering is flawed, so he is not deficient. If there were no flaw in the offering, he would not sacrifice the corporeal life but would take it for himself and not for the Creator.

A flawless offering means that it has no flaws, and yet he gives his soul to the Creator in order to give contentment to his Maker. Specifically that offering is called "My fire is a fragrance for the Lord," since he has no consideration of himself, but all his intention is only for the sake of the Creator.

# 570- General Attainment and Personal Attainment

There is a difference in seeing between general attainment and personal attainment.

"General attainment" means that one attains the matter in general. For example, when one sees a big city from afar and sees from afar that people are walking about in the city, and sees signs of houses, this is called "general seeing," meaning that all the details are included in the city.

This means that even though afterward he approaches the city and enters it, and sees each detail separately, such as the beauty of the city, the shape of the houses, the gardens, the towers, and the wealth of the city, that there are many factories and stores filled with abundance and all kinds of merchandise that exist in the world, many banks, and the mentality of the people, good people and bad people, educated and ignorant, the beauty of people, if they are great or small and so forth, but nevertheless, this does not add anything to the general, meaning that from afar he saw a city, and so he does now.

When he is asked, "Where were you?" he replies, "I was in the city," meaning both from afar and from nearby; it is all the same city.

The benefit of the details is that now he has impressions from what he saw inside the city, which he did not have before. Although when he was outside the city, he knew that there were many details, he still did not have impressions. When he was in the city, he could enjoy all the details that he could not enjoy from the city in general.

It follows that personal attainment is the main pleasure and delight, as it brings him vitality when he comes to know the details. This is not so with the general.

This applies in every single state, whether good or bad, since when he sees a situation that is bad in person, he is impressed by the bad feeling and can correct it, for the bad feeling brings him to reveal hidden forces, which he uses and finds profound tactics to be saved from the bad.

It is the same with a good situation. That is, in general, he knows that he has abundance, yet he does not have the feeling of impression of how much he can enjoy, since he lacks the details about all those things. For this reason, he cannot give praise and gratitude to the Creator as much as he should.

Since man's greatness depends primarily on one's attainments, and one does not attain except when he gives praise and gratitude to the extent of the attainment that he has been given, therefore, he must try each time to delve into the details so he can be impressed by the details and be able to give the proper praise and gratitude, and then he will go ever upward.

## 571- He Is One and His Name, One

We should discern between He and His name: "He" refers to the Creator. "His name" pertains to the created beings, for "His name" pertains specifically to the other one. With respect to Himself, there is no question of "His name." But when another speaks in the name of Reuben, by the word "Reuben," is he referring to Reuben himself, meaning that his name points to him.

It therefore follows that when we say that He is called "desire to bestow," His name is called when He is revealed to the other one. This means that the other one attains the good by Him filling him with abundance, and he has no lack so he can say that there is another guidance in this place, but rather that everything is good and does good.

According to the above, we should interpret the words of *Pirkei de Rabbi Eliezer*, "Before the world was created there was He is one and His name, One." "One" refers to one intention: to do good to His creations. The created being is the place of lack. If that place is filled with abundance, we see that His name is called "The Good Who Does Good," meaning that His desire to do good is revealed in this place.

It follows that the desire, when to do good is only in Him, His goodness is still not revealed to the created beings. And when the creatures, too, attain His goodness and have no place of lack, it is considered that they attain His name, which is "to do good."

But while there is still room for a lack, they feel about this place that His desire to do good is still not revealed. It follows that he still cannot say that He wants to do good, as it is with the Creator (since the lower ones are unfit to receive His goodness).

Hence, there is a difference between Him, whose desire is to do good, and the created beings, who have still not been rewarded with seeing His goodness to the extent that it is in the Creator, meaning the full measure with which He wants to delight them. Therefore, He and His name are not one.

This is the meaning of "Before the world was created," meaning before the concealment and hiding were made, which is the *Tzimtzum* [restriction], when the upper light filled the whole of reality and did not leave any aspect of pleasure unrevealed in that place called *Malchut de Ein Sof* [*Malchut* of infinity].

But after the *Tzimtzum*, when the light returned and did not shine in the quality of *Malchut*, leaving a place where the above-mentioned benefit was not revealed, meaning to the extent that she was revealed in the world of *Ein Sof*, it was impossible to say "One," who is to do good, since in this place there is a difference between "He," whose desire is to do good, and "His name," the place where the benefit should be, while the benefit is still not disclosed as the Emanator would like.

At the end of correction, it will be "He is one and His name, One," since then the creatures will be worthy of receiving all the abundance that He had contemplated in their favor. Naturally, it will be one, meaning one quality—only to do good. But before the correction, there is still room where it is not one, but rather in this place there is a lack.

# 572- Two Labors

"The arrow maker is slain by his own arrows" (sometimes the craftsman makes an arrow which kills the craftsman himself)

(*Pesachim* 28a), concerning the Passover leaven, which is by burning. We should interpret that the order of one's work in Torah and *Mitzvot* [commandments] when he wants to work for the sake of the Creator is that one must fight and defeat the evil inclination.

That is, it is human nature to toil when there is self-benefit. But when he sees that no self-benefit will emerge from this work, he cannot work. Instead, he complains and asks, "What is this work for you?" meaning what will you gain from exerting?

When a person overcomes it and says that he wants to work against nature and bestow upon the Creator, the evil inclination comes with a different argument, asking the question of wicked Pharaoh, "Who is the Lord that I should obey His voice?" It is possible to work for the sake of others only where I know that the other receives the labor.

However, when he has two labors, 1) He must overcome and go against nature, and work not for his own benefit but for the benefit of others, for the sake of the Creator. 2) He must believe that the Creator receives his labor.

These two questions are the main ones in the argument of the wicked one. The rest of the questions that come to a person are merely offspring of the two above questions.

It is possible to overcome these questions only by the power of faith, which is above reason. One must reply to the wicked one that from the perspective of the intellect, it makes sense to ask what he is asking. But above the intellect, in faith, when he believes in the words of the sages, this is the only way that is for the sake of the Creator.

That is, when one gives all his energy and efforts for the sake of the Creator, this is his only purpose, and the world was created for this purpose, as our sages said, "The whole world was created only for this" (*Berachot* 6b), meaning for the fear of heaven.

Hence, when he answers the wicked that he is going above reason, which is against the intellect, the intellect can no longer ask any questions because all the questions are within reason, whereas above the intellect there is no place for questions.

Hence, when the wicked one asks the questions, he is told that now is the time when I can do my work in faith. In other words, by the very fact that you are asking a question and I reply to you that I am going with faith, and I am not giving you an intellectual answer, this is a sign for you to know that my work is with faith above reason.

It follows that now you have caused me to make a *Mitzva* [commandment] in that only now does it become revealed to all that the path of the Creator is only faith.

By this we can interpret what our sages said, "The arrow maker is slain by his own arrows," meaning that the craftsman makes an arrow that kills the craftsman himself. This means that the same arrow with which he wants to kill the man, meaning the question that the wicked one asks, with this he is slain, meaning with the question itself, he kills the wicked one, meaning he replies to the wicked one with the question itself and kills him.

Thus, through the question he asks, he takes upon himself the commandment of faith above reason and thereby kills the wicked one, who does not want to give him a chance to perform *Mitzvot*.

# 573- They Shall Fear You

"And all the peoples of the earth shall see that the name of the Lord is called upon you and they shall fear you" (*Minchot* 35b). The great Rabbi Elazar says, "These are the head *Tefillin* [phylacteries]."

In the *Tosfot* there, he interprets in the treatise, that he wrote on them the majority of the Name, *Shin* and *Dalet*, and it seems that the *Dalet* and *Yod* in the straps are not complete letters and are not regarded as part of the name *Shadai*.

The *Tosfot* says the reason is that the head *Tefillin* is more visible than that of the hand, for "shall see" pertains to it, but the hand *Tefillin* should be covered, for it is said about them, "a token on your hand, for you as a token and not for others as a token." The *Shin* of the *Tefillin* is a law given to Moses at Sinai. It is written in the [book] *Shimusha Raba*, in *Tefillin* there are three heads in the *Shin* of the right [side], and four heads on the left.

We should ask:

1) Why is the head [*Tefillin*] exposed and that of the hand should be concealed?

2) Why are there three heads on the right, and four heads on the left?

3) We do not see that uneducated people fear the head *Tefillin*.

It is written in *Berachot* (p 6): "Rabbi Helbo said, 'Rav Huna said, 'Anyone who has fear of heaven, his words are heard, as was said, 'In the end, after all is heard, fear God and keep His commandments, for this is the whole of man.'"

Accordingly, we should ask, 1) Why until now, when we had so many righteous who had fear of heaven, why did they not reform the whole of Israel? 2) What is the meaning of the words, "In the end," so that one who fears heaven, his words are heard?

We should say in the work that the verse refers to the individual himself.

# 574- If You Come

"And all the peoples of the earth shall see that the name of the Lord is called upon you and they shall fear you" (Deuteronomy 28:10). "Shall see ... The great Rabbi Eliezer says, 'These are the head *Tefillin* [phylacteries],'" and the *Tosfot* interpreted that since there is the majority of the name *Shadai* in them, *Shin* in the boxes and *Dalet* in the straps (*Berachot* 4, 6a), meaning that "And saw that the name of the Lord" refers to the head *Tefillin*, where the majority of the name *Shadai* is visible.

The *Tosfot* asks a question (*Shabbat* [Sabbath] 28), as was said there, from what is permitted in your mouth and does not elicit straps. Also, in the *Megillah* (26), it calls the straps mere instruments of *Kedusha* [holiness], implying that the *Dalet* in the straps is not regarded as an integral part of the head *Tefillin*.

Thus, what is the meaning of the verse, "And saw," which pertains to the head *Tefillin*? He also gives a reason, that it is at the height of the head and is visible, for "and saw" pertains to it, while the hand *Tefillin* are covered, as it is written, "for you," as a token on your hand and not for others.

We should ask why the hand *Tefillin* should be covered and that of the head should not. From Baal HaSulam—the head *Tefillin* is regarded as Torah, and the hand *Tefillin* is regarded as faith.

# 575- The Purity of the Work

"Come and see, He replied, 'He was a bastard, for Tziv'on came unto his mother and begot a bastard.' And he came in this way because of the spirit of impurity that clung to him" (*The Zohar*, *VaYishlach*, Item 264).

It is known that when he comes and asks "Who" or "What," and wants to reply to this question, he "replied," from the words "You shall not reply unto your neighbor [a false testimony]," meaning that he testifies that he has found *Eymim* [horrors]. *Eymim* is from the word *Yomam* [daytime], which is lights and pleasures in servitude.

It follows that he testifies that his work is in the will to receive, called *Lo Lishma* [not for Her sake], since all his work is because he receives great pleasures, and if he did not have pleasures, he would not work at all.

However, we must know that all created beings were created only for His glory. It follows that the evil inclination, too, is the messenger of the Creator. Hence, by coming to him with its questions, it sorts out the source and foundation of his work. And since the work is a result of the desire, the thought and the desire are called "father," and the work is called "offspring."

Thus, he came to ask about his father, meaning who is causing him the work. This is the meaning of "Who found the waters... for Tziv'on his father," meaning that he testifies that the cause of the work is the *Lo Lishma* called Tziv'on, meaning *Tzviut* [hypocrisy] and not truth, called *Lishma* [for Her sake].

*The Zohar* asks how he had the ability to continue in the work thus far if his intention was founded on falsehood. However, there was a mixture here, meaning "Tziv'on came unto his mother."

"Mother" is called "the point in the heart," which yearns for the work of the Creator. It is an organ of the *Shechina* [Divinity], called "mother of the children." However, Tziv'on came unto her, namely the *Lo Lishma*, called for the sake of the will to receive, which is the body, and Tziv'on makes him think that it is worthwhile to work in order to be delighted with spiritual pleasures in which it is possible to receive more pleasure than in corporeal pleasures.

There is a mixture of one kind with that which is not its kind here. For this reason, the offshoot of this is a bastard, since the point in the heart should unite with the desire to bestow and not with the will to receive. It follows that the causes of the work, called "father and mother," are one kind with that which is not its kind. For this reason, he begets a bastard.

"Replied" was born from Tziv'on, his father. It follows that with his questions, he caused him to beget an offshoot, called "replied," meaning his testimony. This means that specifically the question causes him to beget a bastard.

The rule is that a bastard does not give birth, for offspring means the work. Hence, he can no longer continue the work because now it has been revealed to him that all his work is *Lo Lishma*, whereas before, he thought that he was working *Lishma*.

It follows that this revelation did him much good, for now he can aim his eyes and heart on correcting his state so as to be rewarded with coming to the real *Dvekut* [adhesion], and his only thought will be to bestow contentment upon the Creator.

This is the meaning of *The Zohar* continuing there, "And yet, every person who walks by the ways of the Creator and fears Him does not fear them." "The ways of the Creator" is called above reason, whether in mind or in heart. "Does not fear them" means he is not afraid of the questions of "Who" and "What."

This is the meaning of what is written in *The Zohar*, "Rabbi Yitzhak said, 'Likewise, all those desolate mountains are their dwelling places. And it is written about all those who engage in Torah, 'The Lord shall keep you from all evil.''" *Harim* [Mountains] are things that stand in the middle of the way and do not let one keep going in order to reach the goal. These are *Hirhurim* [thoughts], foreign thoughts that delay man's work.

This is the meaning of "Ascended up the mountain," meaning that they went into those mountains "and they were ruined" meaning lost all their attainment. This is why it said, "desolate mountains are their dwelling places," meaning that it brings them nothing but ruin. This is not so for those who walk on the path of the Creator. These ascend on the mountain of the Creator, as it is written, "Who will ascend the mountain of the Lord ... He who has clean hands and a pure heart," meaning mind and heart that are both in bestowal and faith above reason.

# 576- A Shabbat Dish

"The Caesar said to Rabbi Yehoshua Ben Hanania, 'Why is the Shabbat [Sabbath] dish so fragrant?' He said to him, 'We have a dish called 'Shabbat.'' He said to him, 'Let us have some of it.' He replied, 'Anyone who observes the Shabbat, it is good for him. But to one who does not observe the Shabbat, it is not good for him'" (*Shabbat* 119a). The MAHARSHA interpreted that the Caesar thought that there is a type of vegetable called "Shabbat."

We should ask how the Caesar knew that it was fragrant? He must have tasted it. Thus, what does "Let us have some of it" mean? Some interpret that it means "Give it to us," meaning that he himself would cook the dish, for only when Israel cooks, the foreigner can also taste and feel the taste, that it is fragrant.

But when the foreigner himself cooks, since he does not observe the Shabbat, he cannot feel the taste, that it is fragrant. This is the meaning of what Rabbi Yehoshua Ben Hanania replied to him, "Anyone who observes the Shabbat, it is good for him," etc.

The meaning in ethics is that it is known that within a person himself there is a Jew and there is a foreigner, meaning the Caesar, who is called "an old and foolish king," and there is the good inclination. The difference between Shabbat and the weekdays is that there is a time of work and a time of receiving reward. Shabbat is regarded as awakening from above, which means that there is no time of work on Shabbat, for Shabbat is a similitude of the next world, which means it is a time of reception of reward.

For this reason, it is forbidden to work on Shabbat, as it is a time of wholeness, and it is forbidden to cause any deficiency on Shabbat, and when he does work, it indicates that something is missing.

On weekdays, which is the time of work, it means labor in the war against the inclination, since man should work against nature, since human nature is to receive pleasure for himself, for man is unable to make a single move unless it yields pleasure for himself. For this reason, when he wants to work for the sake of the Creator, it is a great effort.

To the extent that he accustomed himself to work for the sake of the Creator, when Shabbat comes he tastes a taste on Shabbat. At that time, the body, too, enjoys the Shabbat, meaning that the foreigner, called Caesar, the old king, also enjoys. This is the meaning of what our sages said, "He who toils on the eve of Shabbat shall eat on Shabbat" (*Avoda Zarah* 3a), for Shabbat is the time of reception of the pleasure.

To the extent that he has *Kelim* [vessels] of "for the sake of the Creator," the Shabbat dresses in those *Kelim* and also spreads to the body, meaning to the gentile, too, as our sages said, "When the Lord favors man's ways, his enemies, too, make peace with him," referring to the evil inclination (*Jerusalem Talmud, Trumot*, Chapter 8). For this reason, the body, too, enjoys observing the Shabbat, since it feels a good taste on Shabbat.

This is the meaning of Caesar's question about the fragrant Shabbat dish, meaning that in everything he does on Shabbat, he feels a fragrant taste. This is why he said, "Let us have some of it," meaning that he himself wants to cook the dish and wants to have its fragrance for himself. That is, he wants to engage in Torah and *Mitzvot* [commandments] not for the sake of the Creator, yet taste the taste of Shabbat while working.

But why is it not fragrant when he works with the aim to delight himself? To this he replied, "We have a dish called 'Shabbat.'" That is, Shabbat is light that shines in the manner of the conclusion of heaven and earth, which is a similitude of the next world. This is why at that time, we taste pleasure on Shabbat. At that time, the body says, "Let us have it," meaning "I will cook for myself; I want to feel this flavor while I am performing the *Mitzvot* with the aim to delight myself, and then I will always perform good deeds and *Mitzvot*."

The whole difficulty about observing *Mitzvot* is that I want to enjoy the work I am doing, yet I do not feel any flavor. Hence, let me enjoy my work, and by this I will always let you engage in Torah and *Mitzvot*. Then he replied to him that to those who observe Shabbat, doing the *Mitzvot* helps them feel the taste. In other words, when can one feel the taste of Shabbat? Only when he observes Shabbat, for only on Shabbat is he careful not to awaken any lack, and wants only to praise the Creator, but his aim is not the pleasure.

During the weekdays, he works on his intention being for the sake of the Creator, and by this, when Shabbat comes, he has *Kelim* that are ready to receive the abundance, meaning he has desires that he wants to bestow contentment upon the King, and the abundance of Shabbat is poured into these desires.

Conversely, if he does not observe Shabbat, namely his intention is not to praise the King, but rather his aim is only to receive the pleasure, it follows that he is not observing the Shabbat so as not to desecrate it with the desires of the body, called "will to receive pleasure," so he has no *Kelim* in which the Shabbat can spread.

It follows from all the above that only when one's intention is for the sake of the Creator, he feels a flavor that is fragrant in Torah and *Mitzvot*, as it is written, "When the Lord favors man's ways, his enemies, too, make peace with him." But if his intention is only to please himself, he cannot taste the taste of Shabbat. For this reason, he does not feel any flavor in Torah and *Mitzvot*, for only the labor during the six workdays qualifies him to be worthy of receiving the light of Shabbat.

# 577- Concerning the Goal
8 *Adar, Tav-Shin-Lamed-Zayin*, February 26, 1977

The purpose of man's work is to achieve the intention to bestow, for there is nothing to correct in the external action, since the *Kli* [vessel] that was created by the Creator will not undergo any change. Rather, all the changes should be in the intention, meaning that since the purpose of creation is to do good to His creations, He created a *Kli* for this purpose, called "desire and yearning to receive pleasure."

However, in order not to have the bread of shame, but only through equivalence of form, a correction was made called *Tzimtzum* [restriction], so as not to receive unless it is in order to bestow. In other words, in the same *Kli* he had before, namely the will to receive, but with a different aim, meaning not to receive because he wants to satisfy his deficiency, but because of the *Mitzvot* [commandments] of the Creator, since He wants to do good to His creations. But for himself, he is willing to relinquish the pleasures.

It therefore follows that all the work is only on the aim to come to a person yearning to bestow. This is called "inner work," which is something concealed, not apparent on the outside. It is man's intention in the act that he performs.

However, in order to achieve the intention called "inner work," we first need external work, which is actions, something visible, meaning that his work is apparent. Conversely, the intention is internal and concealed.

Therefore, the work in Torah and *Mitzvot* enables us to achieve the intention through these actions. This is why our sages said, "The Creator said, 'I have created the evil inclination; I have created the Torah as a spice.'" In other words, the Torah and *Mitzvot* spice up the evil inclination so it becomes tasty, for the evil inclination is called the "will to receive."

For itself, it is tasteless, for the *Tzimtzum* is on it and it remains in the vacant space. But through the Torah and *Mitzvot*, he achieves the intention to bestow. Then, with this *Kli*, called "will to receive," he receives all the delight and pleasure.

It therefore follows that the external actions are means by which he achieves the goal, which is the aim to bestow. Hence, we should know when we engage in externality that it is only a qualification to reach the internality, which is the goal.

Then, when he has the real intention, the actions themselves are regarded as internality, meaning that inner light dresses in the external acts of Torah and *Mitzvot*. That is, with respect to root and branch, the upper abundance dresses during the performing of Torah and *Mitzvot*, as explained in the *Sulam* [Ladder commentary on *The Zohar*] in the introduction to *The Zohar*.

# 578- Half a Shekel – 2

Adar, Tav-Shin-Lamed-Zayin, February-March 1977

Concerning the matter of half a Shekel, that it should be explicitly half and not a quarter or a whole Shekel, according to what is explained in *The Zohar*, Shekel means Mishkal [weight], something we must weigh.

Accordingly, we should discern that Shekel means that a person must weigh his actions, to make a choice, meaning that he cannot complain that he is poor in knowledge and qualities, meaning that he was born without talents or virtues, so it is very hard for him to walk on the straight path, while his friends, who were born rich, meaning with great talents and inherent virtues, it is easier for them to sentence themselves to the side of merit.

The verse tells us about this, "The rich shall not give more." That is, wealth does not add to him, giving him better suitability and strength to sentence to the side of merit. "And the poor shall not give less," meaning his poverty does not deny him from making efforts to sentence to the side of merit.

Rather, concerning sentencing, everyone is equal. In other words, the Shekel—when a person weighs his actions, thoughts, and desires—is always only half, since as our sages said, "Anyone who is greater than his friend, his inclination is greater than him" (*Sukkah* 52).

In order to have choice, there must be an equal weight because when the two pans of the scale are equal, it can be said that he can choose. Conversely, if there is more and less, it is impossible to speak of deciding. This is as our sages said, "One should always see oneself as half guilty and half innocent" (*Kidushin* 40), for only then can we speak of deciding.

This is the meaning of "explicitly a half Shekel." It comes to teach us that one always has only half, since when he has a little bit of good, he has a little bit of bad. And when he has a lot of good, opposite that he has a lot of bad. This is the meaning of "God has made them one opposite the other."

## 579- I Will Remove the Stony Heart

Purim, 14 *Adar, Tav-Shin-Lamed-Zayin*, March 4, 1977

The stony heart means that a person wants to understand if it is worthwhile for him to engage not in order to receive reward. A person cannot understand this because it is against our nature, for we were born with a will to receive for ourselves. Hence, a person must work in faith above reason, meaning even though he does not understand how it is possible to achieve this degree, but it is rather a gift of the Creator.

This is called "Unless the Creator helps him, he cannot overcome it." This is called "I will remove the stony heart." That is, only the Creator can give him that power so the body will agree to work not in order to receive reward. But from man's perspective, he must only begin. That is, if a person yearns to achieve this degree and performs acts of Torah and *Mitzvot* [commandments], and prayer so as to achieve this, the Creator helps him.

But before this, if there is no awakening from below, one does not receive help from above for this. This is called "man's work," meaning what man should do, since prayer pertains to whether there is a prayer from below, which is called "raising MAN," meaning that a person raises the lack that he has and asks the Creator to satisfy his lack.

Hence, if he has a lack that he cannot work not in order to receive reward, the Creator gives him the *Mayin Duchrin* [MAD], which is the filling of the lack, namely the Creator gives him that strength. However, if a person does not ask for this, meaning about not being able to work not in order to receive reward, then we cannot speak of filling a lack.

In order for one to feel that this is called "a lack," there must be special education about this. Otherwise, we do not feel that this is called "a lack." A person feels only the lack of diminution of light, meaning that he has no pleasure in Torah and prayer the way he understands it should be. But the lack of a *Kli* [vessel], and that this is the real lack, not everyone is given this feeling.

This is why the world is educated only on a lack of light, and not on a lack of a *Kli*, since for the light to shine in him, he has a *Kli* because the will to receive feels only the absence of pleasure, as this pertains to the vessels of reception. But the absence of a *Kli* is the opposite of the vessels of reception. Hence, a person does not feel this naturally. This is why it is impossible to educate the general public on this lack, but they are rather educated on the lack of light.

For this reason, this lack requires special education, and not everyone can be educated in this manner. Rather, only people who have the quality of truth can be educated.

# 580- A Good Neighbor and a Bad Neighbor

A person has an evil inclination and a good inclination. Normally, there is a bad neighbor, meaning the evil inclination. But when a person achieves the degree of "with all your heart, with both your inclinations," meaning that he can love the Creator also with the evil inclination, he has a good neighbor.

When he can be a servant of the Creator only with the good inclination, he is called "mighty," as in "Who is mighty? He who conquers his inclination." But the "mighty among the mighty" is when he can make his enemy his friend, meaning that he will love the Creator with the evil inclination, as well, and then he has a good neighbor.

However, first, he himself must be good, and then it can be said that the good person has a neighbor who is either bad or good. For this reason, first, one must exert that the good inclination will have control, and then there can be the second prayer, that his neighbor, the evil inclination, will be good, as well.

## 581- The Act Is What Decides

25 Heshvan, Tav-Shin-Lamed-Vav, October 25, 1975

It is written in The Zohar, VaYera, Why at the oaks of Mamre and not elsewhere? It replies that it is because he advised him about his circumcision, since when the Creator told Abraham to circumcise himself, Abraham consulted his friends. Aner told him, "You are more than ninety; you will torment yourself." Mamre told him, "Remember the day when the Chaldeans threw you in the furnace of fire, and that hunger that the world had undergone ... and those kings whom your men chased and whom you struck, and how He saved you from them all ... Arise, do as your Master commands."

We should understand the question people ask, How can the Creator tell Abraham to circumcise himself and he goes to ask for advice whether he should obey the Creator; can this be?

We should also ask, Why is his advice more than the advice that Aner gave him? After all, both advised him. Also, according to what is explained (in Midrash Rabbah 42), Aner and Eshkol advised him not to circumcise himself, and Mamre advised him to circumcise himself, so why did he accept Mamre's advice, since he was one against two?

We can interpret that the Creator telling him to circumcise himself pertains to his body, so it will observe the commandment of the Creator. Since man has a good inclination and an evil inclination, he must see that the body agrees to do the Mitzva [commandment].

This is considered that he went to ask his friends, meaning the good inclination and the evil inclination. Thus, when one says, "It is all mine," and the other says, "It is all mine," how can one decide, meaning that each one makes him think that he is right. Thus, he needed an advice as to how to defeat the evil inclination because both made him understand that from their perspective, that they were speaking to the point.

We can understand this according to what is explained, "One should always see oneself as half guilty and half innocent; if he performs one *Mitzva*, etc., if he performs one transgression," etc. (*Kidushin* 40). Thus, if it is half and half, who can decide?

The answer is "Do!" That is, he cannot decide unless by acting, and not with the intellect. In other words, whatever he does, it later becomes revealed to the intellect whether or not it is a good deed. This is the meaning of Mamre giving him an advice about the circumcision, when he said, "Arise, do as your Master commands," meaning act, and then you will understand that the good inclination is right, and not the evil inclination. It follows that the advice pertains to the doing.

# 582- One Whose Wife Provides for Him

"Woe unto one whose wife provides for him." Provision means what a person enjoys; this is one's provision. We see that there are people in the world who have abundance and lack nothing, yet do not have joy in life and are regarded as poor, meaning they have no provision. In other words, they have nothing from which to receive pleasure.

Man consists of two forces: One is that which he receives, and what he gives to the other, regarded as the force of reception and the force of bestowal. The force of bestowal in him is called "male," meaning one who receives all his provision, namely his pleasure, from giving to others. There is also the contrary, when all his pleasure is from what he receives for himself. This is called "female," meaning a woman.

This is the meaning of "Woe unto one whose wife provides for him," when all the delight and pleasure are from receiving. This is called "Woe unto him," since he is in the place of *Tzimtzum* [restriction]. Conversely, if his delight and pleasure, meaning his provision, is from engaging for the benefit of others, he is close to the goal that one should achieve—to bestow contentment upon his Maker.

## 583- Righteous and Wicked

13 *Heshvan, Tav-Shin-Lamed-Vav*, October 18, 1975

"Even if the whole world tells you that you are righteous, be wicked in your own eyes."

There are two discernments in servants of the Creator:

1) One is regarded as "righteous." For example, one who has a fixed time when he rises before dawn, and when he wakes up from his sleep, he promptly gets up to work, for the body, too, understands that man must engage in Torah and *Mitzvot* [commandments] and it cannot be otherwise. He understands that one who was born in a good environment takes after the environment and has no foreign thoughts, God forbid, for how can it be otherwise?

That person is regarded as "righteous" because the things he does are in order to observe the *Mitzvot* of the Creator, to bring contentment to the Creator, and he does not feel any lack in himself. Rather, he always adds.

2) There are people, who, when they must rise before dawn at the usual time, the body disagrees and brings them foreign thoughts, asking "What is this work for? What did you gain yesterday when you got up before dawn? You learned and prayed, but who gained from this? What will it add to you that you've acquired more knowledge in the Torah or that you prayed? You could behave like most people: They get up on time, learn on time, and pray on time. Why do you need to rise early and exert more than most people?"

It follows that then he is in a state of "wicked" because when the intention, "What is this work for," arises, no excuse helps unless he can overcome with the quality of above reason.

In other words, he should tell the body, "You are right, meaning all your complaints are true and I cannot justify them. But now I want to observe the Torah and *Mitzvot* above reason, as in doing that precedes hearing, since only in action can he work, but not in the intention, since from the perspective of the intention, meaning the goal, the body cannot understand.

It follows that then he is in a state of "Be wicked in your own eyes." Eyes imply *Hochma* [wisdom], meaning that the thought and the intellect, which is called "purpose," the act, he knows what for. Therefore, when he does not know, meaning from the perspective of reason, he is wicked. Thus, he can work only above reason, called "doing only."

He tells his body, "Always do, and then you will be rewarded with hearing," for as long as he has not taken upon himself to engage above reason, he cannot understand the view of Torah. Hence, here is man's primary work—in above reason.

# 584- The Face of the Lord Is in Evildoers

After Shabbat, Noah, Tav-Shin-Lamed-Vav, October 11, 1975

"The face of the Lord is in evildoers, to cut off the memory of them from the earth. They cried out, and the Lord hears, and saved them from all their troubles."

We could ask, But the face of the Creator belongs to the righteous, and not to evildoers, as it is written, "By the light of Your face, you have given us ... mercy, and life, and peace." Only the *Achoraim* [posterior] is regarded as judgment, when He executes judgment on the wicked.

We should say that this means that those who want to walk on the path of the Creator, on the path of truth, see that they are always doing evil. They cry out to the Creator to save them from that state of evil, and everything that they could do but could not be freed from the evil, as explained about the exodus from Egypt, "And the children of Israel sighed from the work, and their cry went up to God," and He delivered them from Egypt.

Likewise, we should interpret here that the Creator shone His face to them, and then the concealment that they had departed from them. By "The face of the Lord is in evildoers," the face of the Creator cancels even the memory of the bad. This is the meaning of "cut off the memory of them from the earth." *Eretz* [earth/land] comes from the word *Ratzon* [desire]. Even a memory of the bad desire did not awaken in them because "They cried out, and the Lord hears, and saved them from all their troubles."

# 585- The Kingship and the Governance to The One Who Lives Forever

Man consists of two forces: a good inclination and an evil inclination, and each wants to rule over the other. The governance was given to man so he could control the evil within him, but in fact, the bad controls the good. At that time, the evil is told that the kingship and the governance belong to the One Who Lives Forever.

In other words, in order to be able to adhere to the One Who Lives Forever, meaning that the power and the governance that were given, were given only so he would control the evil in him, by this man can adhere to the One Who Lives Forever.

Then, if his evil controls his good, the person wants to control other people, too, for the reason that Baal HaSulam said, that a pleasure that one receives inside his own body, he should scrutinize whether it is for the sake of the good inclination or for the sake of the evil inclination. But if a person delights his friend, it is all for the sake of the good inclination. That is, that which a person delights outside his own body already belongs to the good inclination.

For this reason, if the good inclination governs in a person, he enjoys bestowing to other people. If the bad controls the good within him, that person wants to control other people, too, since with regard to that person, other people are regarded as the good inclination. Hence, as he governs the good in him, he wants to govern over others, since they are regarded as the good inclination.

## 586- Which Is the Straight Path

*1 Av, Tav-Shin-Lamed-Dalet, July 20, 1974*

"Rabbi says, 'Which is the straight path that one should choose? Anyone that glorifies its Maker and glorifies Him by man'" (*Avot*, Chapter 2).

The thing is that there is the matter of the correction of creation and there is the purpose of creation. The purpose of creation is to do good to His creations, and the correction of creation is equivalence of form. That is, as the Creator bestows upon His creatures, the creatures should come to a degree of bestowing upon the Creator.

It therefore follows that the correction of creation is called "glorifies Him by man," which is glory for man when he has corrected himself, when he achieves equivalence of form, regarded as bestowing in order to bestow, meaning when he has come to obtain the *Hesed* [grace/mercy].

The purpose of creation is when a person has achieved a degree where he can receive the pleasures of doing good to His creations, called "receiving in order to bestow." This is called "glorifies its Maker."

In other words, the beauty of the Creator is apparent when He reveals to the created beings the delight and pleasure that He wants to impart upon them, called *Hochma* [wisdom] that comes to expand in *Kelim* [vessels] of reception of pleasure. This is why this path is regarded as comprising two things together—*Hochma* and *Hassadim*.

## 587- The Upper One Scrutinizes for the Purpose of the Lower One

The upper one scrutinizes the GE for the purpose of the lower one (because "a prisoner does not free himself"). The upper one makes a *Masach* [screen] on the MAN of the lower one, meaning the rejecting force, until it is in the form of receiving in order to bestow, and only then is the light gripped in the MAN.

That is, MAN is a desire to receive. This is expressed through prayer, where prayer is regarded as raising MAN, and the answering of the prayer is called MAD, *Ohr Yashar* [direct light], upper abundance, bestowal. This prayer called MAN requires conditions, meaning that there will be the correction of a *Masach* in the prayer, namely that his intention will be for the sake of the Creator, called *Lishma* [for Her sake].

One must receive the power to work *Lishma* from the upper one, since the lower one is powerless to begin the work, but only in the form of *Lo Lishma* [not for Her sake], called "will to receive," for only the *Lo Lishma* gives the first moving force of the lower one, for when a person does not find sufficient flavor in corporeal pleasures, he begins to search for spiritual pleasures.

It follows that the root of the work of the lower one is the will to receive, and the prayer, called MAN, rises up, and then the upper one corrects this MAN and places on it the power of the *Masach*, which is a desire to delay the abundance before the lower one knows about himself that his aim is to bestow.

That is, the upper one bestows upon the lower one good taste and pleasure in the desire to bestow, by which the lower one feels

His exaltedness. At that time, he begins to understand that it is worthwhile to annul before Him and cancel his existence before Him. Then, he feels that all that there is in reality is only because such is His will, that the Creator wants the lower one to exist, but for himself, he wants to annul his existence. It follows that then, all the vitality he feels is regarded as *Lishma* and not for himself.

When he feels this, it is considered that he already has the correction of the MAN, and then he is also fit to receive the MAD, as well, for there is no contradiction between them anymore, since the lower one, too, wants the benefit of the upper one and not his own benefit.

It is considered that when the upper one gives the lower one *Mochin*, he also gives him the clothing of the *Mochin*, meaning that he gives the lower one the abundance, as well as the power of the *Masach*, which is the desire to bestow. This is the meaning of "from *Lo Lishma*, we come to *Lishma*."

# 588- *Malchut* of the Upper One Becomes *Keter* to the Lower One

It is explained in several places that *Malchut* of the upper one becomes *Keter* to the lower one. We should ask, Since *Malchut* is called "vessels of reception," what the lower one receives and which is considered the "I" that we attain, and *Keter* is called *Ein Sof* [infinity], and even *Keter* of *Assiya* is called *Ein Sof*, so how can it be said that *Malchut*, which is called a *Kli* [vessel], will be called *Ein Sof*?

According to what is explained there, *Keter* being called *Ein Sof* refers to the Giver, since in the Giver, there are no names or differences of which we can speak. All that we speak of is what is revealed from *Ein Sof*, and any change in the revelations depends on the ability of the attaining lower one.

Therefore, he says that the Giver of the world of *Assiya* is also called *Ein Sof*, since *Ein Sof* is called the "thought of creation," referring to His desire to do good to His creations.

For this reason, anything that is bestowed upon the lower ones is according to the power of the attaining. But among the attaining there are changes. For this reason, each time, the Giver is given a different name according to how the lower one attains Him. He names the Giver after his attainment.

With corporeal names, we call Him "Healer of the sick," "Freer of the imprisoned," "Who makes the blind see," etc. Likewise, in spiritual bestowal, when we receive *Assiya* from the Giver, He is called by the name *Assiya*.

When we say that *Malchut* of the upper one becomes *Keter* to the lower one, it is in the sense that *Malchut* of the upper one causes the lower one to receive from the upper one.

This means, as is said, that the *Reshimot* that remain from the upper one cause the lower one to want to attain. In other words, *Malchut* of the upper one causes the lower one a need for the lower one to need to receive abundance from *Ein Sof*. Likewise, the connection between upper and lower also refers to the medium there is between the need that the upper one lacks and the need that the lower one lacks.

However, to the Giver, when the lower one causes the quality of *Ein Sof* to be born, but *Malchut* of the upper one causes the lower one to have a need to receive from the upper one, at that time, the quality of *Ein Sof* is born in the lower one, meaning that at that time the lower one extends the quality of *Ein Sof*, meaning a giver.

It is as *The Zohar* interprets in *BeHukotai*, "'And do them,' do not pronounce it *Otam* [them] but rather *Attem* [you]," as though you have made them. He interprets in the *Sulam* [Ladder commentary on *The Zohar*] that by the lower ones needing the Creator to fill them, the lower one attains the Giver by receiving abundance from the upper one. But if the receiver does not receive anything from the Giver, how does he know that there is a Giver? This is called "By Your actions, we know You."

## 589- God Did Not Guide Them

*Shevat, Tav-Shin-Lamed-Zayin*, January-February 1977

"God did not guide them through the land of the Philistines even though it was near ... lest the people might reconsider when they see war and return to Egypt."

Concerning "near" and "far": "Near" means close to the mind, and "far" means far from the mind. The mind asserts that it would be better if the way to come to the land of Israel, meaning to come into the work of the Creator, the Creator had to make each one who begins the work of the Creator have the scrutiny of "bitter and sweet," as is explained in the introduction to the book, *Panim Masbirot*.

After the sin of the tree of knowledge, the scrutiny was done in "good and bad," meaning that something could be sweet yet bad for him, or vice-versa, that he would taste a bitter taste, yet it would be for his best.

Hence, according to man's perspective, there should have been a sweet taste to Torah and *Mitzvot* [commandments], and in corporeal things there should not have been so much pleasure. Then, since man yearns for pleasure by his own nature, which extends from the purpose of creation, when the pleasure is revealed, each one would reject corporeality and would give all his energy to Torah and *Mitzvot*.

But the pleasures are revealed in corporeality, and there is concealment in Torah and *Mitzvot*. For example, when a person wears a *Tzitzit* [prayer shawl], he does not feel any flavor in this. But when he wears a new outfit, he does feel a flavor. Hence, it is difficult to observe the Torah and *Mitzvot*. This is called "a faraway road." Conversely, if the pleasure of Torah and *Mitzvot* were revealed, it would be called "a nearby road."

"God did not guide them ... when they see war, and return to Egypt," for then, when they see war, they will say, "Everything I do in Torah and Mitzvot is in order to have pleasure, so why go to war in order to get more pleasure? I settle for the corporeal pleasure."

However, when He guides them through the faraway road, meaning that the scrutiny of Torah and Mitzvot is in the manner of good and bad, meaning that the whole purpose of the work is only to bestow and not to receive, although it is a faraway road, for this work is far from the mind, if he wants to walk on the path of bestowal, he has nowhere to return, since one who begins the work knows that only in this way can he reach the goal.

But in truth, we must say that if the Torah and Mitzvot were revealed, what work would be there? It is clear that it should be for the sake of the Creator, and since it is difficult to aim for the sake of the Creator, he will say that he returns to corporeality, for at least there he can receive pleasure, even if small. But in spirituality, if he cannot aim, he is given nothing.

But when he begins the work in order to bestow, he promptly accustoms himself on the path of bestowal. Thus, the wars are not new to him, but he immediately begins to fight against himself. Thus, this is more successful and he will not return to corporeality, meaning to Egypt.

# 590- Those Who Walk to the Land of Israel

29 *Tevet, Tav-Shin-Yod-Het*, January 21, 1958

"Stretch out your hand and touch his self and his flesh ... but keep his soul" (Job 2).

In other words, He gave him control over all his possessions, but not over the soul, for the soul means faith, as in "A soul without knowledge is also not good." That is, He permitted him to touch him in everything but not in his faith.

The *Sitra Achra* [other side] can touch anything that a person acquires. The *Sitra Achra* can slander and say that his intention is not for the sake of the Creator. However, the *Sitra Achra* cannot have any touch on faith because the whole basis of faith is above reason. Naturally, the *Sitra Achra* cannot touch there because all the connection to the *Sitra Achra* is only where there is reason; there he has room to grip.

However, in a place that is above reason, he has no mouth. For this reason, "He who adds knowledge [*Daat* (reason)] adds pain," since there is room there for trials and torments.

Accordingly, do not think of saying "Why should I get into matters of reason?" He says about this the commentary: "A soul without knowledge is also not good." Rather, we must engage in possessions, too, since "the wisdom of the poor is wretched" and wealth, too, is required, as it is written, "Longevity of days to her right, wealth and honor to her left." "Longevity of days" is precisely in the quality of the soul, called "faith," since there the *Sitra Achra* has no reach.

This is called "right" [side], where there is no fear. But on the left side, called "Isaac's fear," meaning wealth and honor, the *Sitra Achra* can slander and say that it is not for the sake of the Creator but that he is receiving this for his own sake.

Yet, nonetheless, both are needed, as it is written, "If you are right, what will you give him?" However, the Creator makes us receive from Him all the good that has been prepared for our sake, meaning that we must reveal all the *NRNHY*, discerned as "wealth and honor."

"Rabbi Shimon said, 'Job's is not a trial from the Creator, as are the trials of the rest of the righteous,' since it is not written, 'And God tried Job,' ... Abraham sacrificed his only son to the Creator with his own hand, whereas Job gave nothing and passed nothing unto the Creator ... since it was evident to him that he would not be able to properly endure it. Instead, he was given to the hands of the slanderer" (*The Zohar*, Bo, Items 29-30).

We should ask what is the difference whether the trial comes from the Creator or from the slanderer, since he gave a reason that he was not tested by the Creator because he would not be able to endure the test.

We should interpret this according to the *Tzimtzum* [restriction] and *Masach* [screen]: If it comes from the Creator, although the Creator illuminates for him the abundance openly, he still sees that there is a higher desire to remove himself from all the abundance and work only in a manner of covered *Hassadim* [mercies]. At that time, he promptly chooses for himself the path of covered *Hassadim*.

It follows that he withstood the test, meaning he did everything out of free choice. That is, he had the choice to keep the abundance because the test came from the Creator, meaning he stood at the degree of the revelation of the abundance, which is called "the hand of the Creator." Then, when he withstood the test, meaning he did everything by choice and not by force, this is considered that the trial came from the Creator.

But if a person is unfit to withstand the test, meaning by choice, he is given to the slanderer, meaning from a *Masach* that is controlled by force. That is, the disclosure of the abundance is taken away from him, and this is called "in the hands of the slanderer," meaning that the test is during the departure—whether he complains about His attributes or not.

It follows that here the choice was not about giving back the abundance, since this was taken away from him against his will. He was not given choice here. Rather, he was given all the choice after the departure of the abundance.

It therefore follows that the trial by the hand of the Creator is considered that the test comes when he has the abundance, and the test by the hand of the slanderer means that the test comes after the departure of the abundance.

It was said about it in *The Zohar*, "And you shall love ... even if He takes your *NRN*." This is as David said, "I awaken the dawn [also means "black" in Hebrew], and the dawn does not awaken me," since he invokes the departure, and the departure does not awaken him to the trial, to complain about His attributes.

It is written (*The Zohar*, Bo, Item 30): "Moreover, it was done by the Creator's sentence, for having inflicted Israel with hard labor in Egypt" (as it is written in Item 15), since Job was among Pharaoh's counselors, and when Pharaoh wanted to kill Israel, Job told him, "Take their money and rule over their bodies with hard work."

## 591- Renewed Work

"Rather, he will take a virgin of his own people." He asks, Why should it be only a virgin, without a flaw? He replies, "A woman is a cup of blessing. If its taste has been flawed, meaning that it implies *Malchut*, called 'a cup of blessing' ... and the offering priest should be unblemished" (*The Zohar*, Emor, Item 38).

We should ask what this implies to us in the work. The ARI says about *Malchut* that she returns to her virginity each day. That is, the root of *Malchut* is a dot, and all nine *Sefirot* in her are regarded as an addition. Hence, each day she is built anew, meaning that each day begins a new work to build the *Malchut* up to her state of *Gadlut* [greatness/adulthood].

However, each day is a new discernment that we raise from *BYA* to *Atzilut* and take them out from the place where they fell into the *Klipa* [shell/peel], and raise them to *Kedusha* [holiness].

In the work, it becomes clear that each day, one should take upon oneself the burden of the kingdom of heaven anew, and not use what he had from yesterday, meaning to say that he divorced her and takes back that same kingdom of heaven, or that she has become a widow, meaning that the person died in the spiritual sense, as in "The wicked in their lives are called 'dead,'" or that he desecrated her.

Rather, each day, one should accept the kingdom of heaven as something new. He does not use the kingdom of heaven he had yesterday. Rather, now he takes a new discernment, meaning that he still did not blemish this *Malchut* because she is a new discernment.

All the teachings that he learns today concerning the work of the Creator should be with new interpretations, not those of yesterday, since he has already flawed yesterday's teachings. Rather, it must be a virgin.

# 592- The Names of *Malchut*

"Widow" means that the person died in the middle, meaning that he died in spirituality, as in "The wicked in their lives are called 'dead.'"

"Divorced" means that he ejected her—the kingdom of heaven—from his home.

"Desecrated" means he desecrated her where he should have sanctified her with a treatment of respect. He desecrated her honor and went to engage in secular matters.

"Prostitute" means that it nourishes and sustains a person. That is, only if *Malchut* gives him nourishment will he take it upon himself. Otherwise, he does not want it.

"Virgin" is like "virgin soil."

# 593- One Should Not Appease One's Neighbor When He Is Angry

One should not appease one's neighbor when he is angry because once he becomes angry, he is erring and cannot understand anything without erring.

"The Lord will lift up His face to you [favor you]." Another verse says, "Who will not lift up the face [be biased]." Here, it is when we do His will, and here it is when we do not do His will (*Midrash Rabbah, Nasso*, 11:7). This is perplexing: Why is bias required when we do His will?

We should interpret "doing His will." It is known that the Creator's will is to bestow. When the lower ones perform acts of bestowal, it is considered that they are doing His will, and then there is the matter of equivalence of form. At that time, the Creator can give them the lifting of the face, called "revelation of His face." That is, the *Tzimtzum* [restriction] and concealment that were on them are lifted.

But when they do not do His will, meaning when they do not exert in the matter of wanting to bestow, which is the Creator's will, there is no equivalence of form here, and then there must be concealment and hiding. This is called "Who will not lift up the face," but the *Achoraim* [posterior], which does not shine for them.

Also, we should interpret concerning help from the Creator, to whom He helps—to those who do the Creator's will. We should interpret that "doing" means like exerting, meaning that his work is that he exerts to have the desire of the Creator, meaning he tries to obtain the desire to bestow. At that time, the Creator lifts up His face to him, to help him achieve the desire to bestow. This is called "He who comes to purify is aided."

But when their work is not to do the Creator's will, when all their work is only in the will to receive, it is said, "Who will not lift up the face," meaning he does not receive help from above that the will to receive will not control them. Rather, as it is written, "He who comes to defile, it is opened for him," and not "is aided." This is called "who will not lift up the face," meaning that He does not help them.

# 594- The Commandment of Repentance

*The Zohar* (*Nasso*, Item 28): The *Mitzva* [commandment] and anyone who repents, it is as though he returned the letter *Hey*, which is *Malchut*, to the letter *Vav*, etc. *Teshuva* [repentance] has the letters of *Tashuv Hey* [the *Hey* will return] to the *Vav*, since when a person sins, he causes the *Hey* to depart from the *Vav*, and this is why the Temple was ruined.

A king whose decrees are harder than Pharaoh's, and they will repent against their will, "unto the Lord your God," to complete the *Hey*.

Repentance, which is *Malchut*, is called "life," without work and without labor.

Interpretation: The work and labor is to go against nature, meaning for the sake of the Creator. By this one comes to equivalence of form, and the abundance is poured out without effort because the labor was not in order to receive reward. It follows that afterward, he receives life through the equivalence of form, which is called "without work." "The image of the Lord does he behold," as a reward for "And Moses hid his face from looking."

## 595- The Measure of the Greatness of the Creator

It is written in Psalms, "As Your name is God, so is Your glory." That is, to the extent that one assumes the greatness of the Creator, to that extent he can praise Him. Hence, if one wants to thank and praise the Creator, he should first assume the greatness of the Creator, and then he will be able to praise Him.

## 596- Nothing New Under the Sun

"There is nothing new under the sun," but only above the sun. "Sun" means "day" and "reason," as our sages said, "If the matter is as clear to you as day," and as it is written, "The murderer arises at day." It follows that below reason, when one wants his reason to yield renewal in the work, it is written about it, "There is nothing new." But above it, which is above the sun, there is renewal, meaning that above reason, a person can receive renewal in the work.

## 597- A Generation Goes and a Generation Comes and the Earth Forever Stands

"The earth forever stands." Earth means "dust," regarded as "still," motionless. This is called "faith above reason," when there is no rhyme or reason. To the body, this tastes like dust.

But when a person takes upon himself this work, he has no descent. Rather, he always remains standing, as it is written, "The earth forever stands," meaning she has no falling.

"A generation goes and a generation comes" means ups and downs. "The earth" means the still. "Forever stands" means that in the earth there is no falling because there is nothing lower than the earth.

## 598- What It Means that Shabbat Is Called "Guest" in the Work

We must prepare food and drink to honor the arrival of the guest, called "Queen Shabbat [Sabbath]."

Question: 1) Does the guest, Shabbat, eat and drink? Also, we must change our clothes in honor of the guest. In corporeality, when an important guest arrives, we prepare good food and drinks in honor of the guest, and we should also wear nice clothes in his honor.

2) We can understand having to prepare food and drinks to honor the guest, but why do we need to wear nicer clothes to honor the guest? We should say that we show the guest that we are very happy that the guest arrived, and this is why we wear respectable attire, showing that we are honoring the guest. For example, when a person is alone at home, he might wear slippers and not wear a frock, since garments means respectable attire. That is, the clothes a person wears are in order to respect others.

Hence, one who does not have nice clothes is ashamed to go into a party because he is embarrassed that everyone will know that he is poor. Hence, he puts on nice clothes. The wisdom of the meager is wretched, as it is written, "The wisdom of the poor is wretched." Hence, even if a person is wise, he is despised and a person cannot tolerate contempt. For this reason, Shabbat, which is an important guest, requires handsome and appropriate garments.

For this reason, we should say that Shabbat being called "a guest" means that the Shabbat dresses in a person, and this is called "an additional soul" that a person receives on Shabbat. This is why it is regarded that we eat.

## 599- Arise, O God

"Arise, O God, and judge the earth, for You possess all the nations." That is, there are wicked judges in one's heart who take a bribe. Therefore, if the Creator is the judge, everything will be fine.

## 600- From the Depth I Called You, Lord – 1

At the bottom of Sheol, it is written, "From the depth I called You, Lord," meaning "I called You from the depth of trouble." Hence, a person should think before the prayer how big is the lack in him, so the Creator will help him on a big deficiency.

It follows that one should pay attention in order to feel one's lack. This is called "a prayer from the bottom of the heart" from the perspective of the receiver. However, there is also the matter of minding the Giver. That is, one should have great faith that the Creator will help him.

In other words, we see that in corporeality, a real prayer is when a person comes to ask a favor from someone, such as money. There are two conditions here: 1) The giver should have the thing he wants from him. If he wants money, he should first know that that person is rich. 2) He must have a kind heart.

If one of the terms is missing, there is no room for prayer, as in "Israel are holy; he has and does not want, he wants and does not have."

We should interpret with regard to the Creator that when Israel ask of the Creator, they are holy from the perspective of the act of prayer. Although there are those who believe that the Creator has what they are asking, such as provision and health, and He can give, but He is not merciful. Others believe that He is merciful but cannot give. That, too, is considered holy.

However, a real prayer is when one believes that the Creator has what he wants, and He is also merciful, as it is written that the Creator is called "Father of mercy, and His mercy is on all His works."

But in corporeal matters we should only believe that He gives, but we do not have to believe regarding the deficiency, since in corporeality, a person feels his lack.

"Israel are holy," etc.: The Creator has but He does not want to give because a person is undeserving due to his actions. He wants to give him but the Creator does not have what he wants. That is, he wants Him to give him in the vessels of reception but He does not want to give into vessels of reception.

# 601- Prayer and Request

A prayer is what our sages have arranged for us. This is in general. A request is a personal matter, what each one asks, what he feels he needs.

Hence, a prayer should be with the mouth, or else there is no grip to the prayer, since there are words in the words of the prayer that a person has no idea why they are needed. Hence, the grip on the prayer is when a person says the words that are written.

Conversely, a request that a person asks, when he feels what he is lacking, he need not utter it verbally. Rather, it is enough that he feels in the heart what he is missing. In other words, what a person feels he needs is called "a request," when the heart wants that someone who has the ability to give him what he wants will give to him.

Since a religious person wants the Creator to satisfy his wish, and the Creator knows the thought of each and every one, what his heart demands, it is therefore enough if a person feels his deficiency—this is a prayer to the Creator for the deficiencies in his heart. Conversely, the words of the prayer were established in the hearts of our sages, what they had in their hearts.

## 602- One Should Not Be Ashamed of the Mockers

*Ezov* [moss] comes from the word *Azuv* [forsaken], when one feels that he is forsaken of good deeds. "One should not be ashamed of the mockers" means that when a person wants to do something good, Torah, or prayer, or good deeds, charity, almsgiving, and there are thoughts or desires in his heart that mock him and tell him, "Why do you need to do those things? What will it give you that you want to exert?" It is written about it, "One should not be ashamed of the mockers."

## 603- There Is *Shechina* in the Wall

13 Av, Tav-Shin-Chaf-Gimel, August 3, 1963

"Rabbi Yosi started, 'Hezekiah turned his face to the wall and prayed to the Lord' ... it is as it is written, 'Those who honor Me I shall honor, and those who despise Me shall be despised.' One who looks at the *Shechina* [Divinity] while praying, how can one look at the *Shechina*? Rather, it is to know that the *Shechina* is indeed standing before him during his prayer, so he must not open his eyes, as it is written, 'Hezekiah turned his face to the wall.' For this reason, nothing must part between a man and the wall" (*The Zohar, VaEtchanan*).

We should ask, 1) Why the association between "Hezekiah turned" and "I entreated"? 2) What is the answer to the question, "How can one look at the *Shechina*?" when he says "it is to know that the *Shechina* is indeed standing before him"? 3) What does it mean that the *Shechina* is there, namely in the wall? Is the *Shechina* specifically in the wall? After all, "The whole earth is full of His glory." Also, what does it mean that there should be no partition? If there is a partition, is this enough to separate from the *Shechina*?

## 604- Why He Waited until the War Against Amalek

Question: Why did he wait until the war against Amalek? The answer is that he saw that when they fall from faith, they have to work by themselves. This is the meaning of "awakening from below." If they are adhered to Moses, who is regarded as the Torah, through the Torah they can be rewarded with faith. Therefore, he had to go to Moses in order to learn from him the ways of faith.

Moses is called "the faithful shepherd," the shepherd of faith, since Moses is called "Torah," as it is written, "Remember the Torah [law] of My servant Moses." Hence, when they are adhered to Moses, they take strength for faith. This is why he had to go to Moses, so as to receive from him the strength.

## 605- And Jethro Heard

"And Jethro heard." *The Zohar* asks, Did Jethro hear and all the nations did not hear? After all, it is written, "The nations will hear, be angry." However, Jethro heard and was broken, and all the nations heard and were not broken. Therefore, their hearing is not hearing.

We should ask why Jethro broke when he heard the tearing of the Red Sea and the war against Amalek. He saw two things here: 1) On the part of the Creator, the Creator said to Moses, "The Lord will fight for you and you will be silent." Concerning the war against Amalek, it is written, "And Moses said to Joshua, 'Choose us people and go fight against Amalek.'" Concerning Moses, it is written, "His hands were hands of faith until the sun set."

We should say that when he went out from Egypt, they believed in the Creator. At that time, because of the faith, they did not need an awakening from below. Rather, the Creator told them that they must only continue to have faith, and the Creator will fight for you. The power of faith is to deliver him from all the troubles.

This is so because faith is actually an awakening from below, as our sages said, "Everything is in the hands of heaven but the fear of heaven." Conversely, the war against Amalek, which is "how he met you along the way," bringing heresy to the people of Israel, as they interpreted, "And attacked the stragglers at your rear," cutting the words and throwing them upward, casting words upward and saying, "The commandments You commanded Your people Israel, how has this helped them?" This is how the [book] *Siftey Hachamim* interprets it. For this reason, the matter depends on faith, which is the meaning of fear of heaven, and this is in the hands of man. This is why they had to fight.

# 606- *Those of Little Faith*

Having little faith means that he does not want only to bestow. "He who makes his voice heard during his prayer is of those of little faith."

We should ask, When one prays to the Creator, he certainly believes in the Creator, so what is the difference? If he makes his voice heard, is he no longer regarded as believing in the Creator, but if he prays in a whisper, he is regarded as believing in the Creator? What is the difference, since whether in a whisper or out loud, one must believe that the Creator hears the prayer? This implies that if he prays, he must have faith, so what is the connection of one to the other?

We should say, as is explained in the *Sulam* [Ladder commentary on *The Zohar*], that prayer in a whisper that we learn from Hannah, as it is written, "And her voice was not heard," he interprets that the voice of *Malchut*, called "will to receive," is not heard. Rather, the prayer is for the quality of the desire to bestow, meaning for the Creator to send him from above the power of purity called "desire to bestow."

It follows that one who sounds his voice, meaning the voice of the will to receive, although he believes in the Creator and asks the Creator to help him, he is of those of little faith, since the heart of the faith when a person believes in the Creator should be for the Creator to send us the spirit of purity, called "desire to bestow," and then the delight and pleasure that is in the purpose of creation can clothe in the desire to bestow.

# 607- Remember that You Were a Slave

"Remember that you were a slave in the land of Egypt." Here it implies to us that when a person is in a state of ascent, he should learn what he had at the time of descent, since during the descent, there is no one to speak with, since then a person is devoid of consciousness in the spiritual life and is concerned only with filling his body with pleasures, and it does not matter to him from which place the pleasures come to him, but only "Give!"

However, during the ascent, a person can learn and gain from the state of descent. This is the meaning of "Remember."

# 608- Not because You Were Many

"Not because you were many," since when the people of Israel ascend, they are more than everyone. When they descend, they are below everyone.

In the work of the quality of *Yashar-El* [Israel/lit. "straight to the Creator"], during the ascent, one feels that they are standing at a degree above the general public. When they descend, they see that they are worse than the general public.

Assorted Notes

## 609- God Is More Terrible than Your Sanctifiers

"The God of Israel is more terrible than your sanctifiers; He gave strength and power to the people; blessed is God" (Psalms 68:36).

We should interpret "God is terrible." How can one accept the fear of God? It is through "Your sanctifiers." That is, by sanctifying himself in what is permitted to him, when he wants everything to be for the sake of the Creator, by this he can be rewarded with the fear of God.

"The God of Israel"–at that time, a person receives the name "Israel," which means *Yashar-El* [straight to the Creator], when he wants to do everything for the sake of the Creator, meaning in order to bestow, which is the quality of *Hesed* [mercy/grace], called *El* [God]. At that time, a person enters the quality of *Yashar-El*.

Then "He gives strength and power to the people," for then He can extend to man power and might by which one receives the name of His people, Israel, as it is written, "to the people," and then one can bless God for bringing him closer.

Thus, the order is, 1) In order for one to obtain fear, he must sanctify himself. 2) Through the fear he receives from above, it gives a person strength and power, and then one is called by the name of His people, "Israel." 3) Afterward, "Blessed is God," a person thanks the Creator.

## 610- Buying a Woman

"Send forth. Rabbi Yehosha says, 'What were they like? Like a king who brought to his son a fair-looking woman of good upbringing and wealthy, etc. He saw her, etc., I give her only to your son,'" etc. (*Midrash Rabbah*, 16:7).

When a person begins the work, the Creator promises him that He will give him a fair woman, etc., meaning a soul, called a "woman." But the person says, "I want to see her." That is, since the *Kli* [vessel] of the soul is called "faith above reason," and the person wants her to be within reason, it means he does not want to believe that she is worth taking.

In other words, a person cannot believe that the purpose of creation, to do good to His creations, is found in Torah and *Mitzvot* [commandments], and in order to receive it we must pay, meaning give her something, where through the reception of the matrimony money, she agrees to be his wife and serve him. But if he does not give her something for which she agrees to take him, she is not dedicated [wedded] to him.

In the literal, we should ask how it is possible that because he gives a penny to a woman, she agrees to be his wife, and without a penny she does not agree. Is it worth taking him as a husband for a penny? How does the penny help in this matter, which makes it the deciding factor?

To buy a wife, one must pay with his life, as our sages said, "The Torah exists only in one who puts himself to death over it."

# 611- Capital and Fruits

"'There is an evil which I have seen under the sun, and it is heavy upon men.' This evil is the force of the evil in the heart that wishes to dominate the worldly matters and does not watch over the matters of that world" (*The Zohar*, BeHaalotcha, Item 140).

The Creator gives him wealth so that through it, he will be rewarded with the next world, for wealth is called "There is none who is poor except in knowledge." It follows that the Creator gave him knowledge, which is Torah and good deeds, so that through it, he will be rewarded with the next world. The next world means *Bina*, meaning vessels of bestowal, and he uses the Torah and *Mitzvot* [commandments] in order to be rewarded with this world, called *Malchut*, which is the will to receive.

There is the capital and there are fruits [yields]. The capital is for the next world, and the fruits are to eat in this world.

# 612- Concerning This World and the Next World – 2

A person eats its fruits in this world, meaning the Torah, the 613 *Mitzvot* [commandments], which are counsels, are called "fruits," meaning the light in it reforms him.

When a person sees that the Torah and *Mitzvot* have reformed him, this is regarded as seeing the fruits of his work in Torah and *Mitzvot*. What is the capital? It is the next world, meaning the next state, which should come when the 613 *Mitzvot* are as deposits. At that time, the Torah is discerned as the names of the Creator. The next state is discerned as "the next world."

It follows that "Those things whose fruits a person eats in this world," meaning that they are as 613 counsels. This is called "the light of the Torah that reforms him," and the capital is mainly for this.

# 613- When a Woman Inseminates

"Come and see, when the Creator is with the assembly of Israel, and she evokes first, *Malchut* is filled from the right side, which is *Hassadim*, male. When the Creator evokes first, everything is in the form of female, as when a woman inseminates" (*The Zohar, Tazria,* Item 60).

In the work, a "woman" means the whole of Israel, and the Creator is called "man." If the awakening comes from above, "she delivers a female child," called "receiving and not bestowing for herself." If the person awakens first, then "she delivers a male child," regarded as a giver, meaning he can extend to himself.

This is when a person overcomes his desire and sees that he cannot overcome and asks for help. Then "she delivers a male child." But when he waits to have an awakening from above, this is called "she delivers a female child."

## 614- Bitter Herb

If he swallows the bitter herb, he did not do his duty. Rather, one must chew, meaning we must feel the bitterness.

## 615- The Reward for the Work

When one works because the Creator needs his work, the Creator should pay the salary and the reward. But if a person works for himself, to correct, how can he ask for a reward?

## 616- The Governance of *Malchut*

*Parsa* is called *Malchut*, which stands in *Bina* of the *Guf*. Below *Malchut* means below the governance of receiving in order to receive. That is, he comes with thoughts of reception and cannot break loose. Hence, there must be a shattering.

Above *Malchut* means above the governance of *Malchut*, when we can break loose from thoughts of reception.

## 617- Peace at Home

The home is the heart, and it is not whole with the Creator, as it is written, "I will hear what He will say ... He shall speak peace unto His people." Instead, there is separation of hearts between the Giver and the receiver. To have peace, meaning equivalence of form, this is all our work...

## 618- Awakening – 2

Male is called *Hassadim* [mercies], meaning that the lower one receives from above the desire to bestow, which is called "male." That is, the lower one awakens and wants to approach the Creator but cannot. It follows that "When a woman inseminates," meaning the person, who is extended from *Malchut*, "she delivers a male child."

Man means the Creator. When the awakening comes from above, "she delivers a female child," meaning that this is called "female light." "She receives and does not bestow" means that when he is given an awakening, he receives, and when the giving stops, he stands and waits to be given an awakening. At that time, "she delivers a female child," meaning that only light that receives and does not bestow can emerge from this work.

## 619- King of the Nations

*Shevat, Tav-Shin-Chaf-Dalet, February 1964*

The *Zohar* (*Mishpatim*, Items 33-34) asks about the verse, "Who will not fear You, King of the nations"? "Is the Creator the king of the nations? He is the king of Israel! ...And should you say that He is called 'King of the nations,' it is a praise for them that the Creator rules over them, and not as they say, that they were given to His servants and appointees. Moreover, the end of the verse writes, 'For among all the wise men of the nations and in all their kingdoms, there is none like You.' All this is praise to the rest of the nations."

It explains, "If you say that it says about the Creator, 'King of the nations,' it is not so. Rather, 'Who among the kings of the nations will not fear You, for among all the wise men of the nations and in all their kingdoms, there is none like You.' 'There is none like You' is the word that spreads among them in their wisdom and they all admit it."

We should ask about this since reality does not show this, and I wish there were the spreading of the word "none like You" among the Jews!

In ethics, we should say that there are two states in the work of the Creator: a state prior to repentance, and a state after the repentance.

It is written in *The Zohar* (*Mishpatim*, Item 76): "Come and see, anyone who is rewarded with thirteen years or more is considered a son of the Assembly of Israel. And anyone who is twenty years of age or more and is rewarded with it is considered a son of the Creator, as in 'You are sons of the Lord your God.'"

We should understand the difference between being a son of the Assembly of Israel, which is regarded as *Malchut*, and being a son of the Creator. It is explained that the hand *Tefillin* [phylacteries] is called "faith," and the head *Tefillin* is called "Torah." A prayer is called "work in the heart," and faith is acquired through work, since it is considered *Malchut*, who is called "poor and meager."

When a person must take upon himself the burden of faith, the body kicks back. Hence, it is a lot of work to be able to overcome it. Also, Torah is called "a gift," as our sages said, "from Matannah [Hebrew: gift] to Nachliel." We should say that the difference between faith and Torah is that faith is called *Tzedakah* [charity/righteousness] and Torah, a gift. The difference between charity and a gift is that charity is a necessity, and a gift is an accessory.

For example, if someone gives a poor person a sack of flour that costs twenty pounds, we will say that he received a sack of flour as charity. But if someone sends the poor a watch that costs twenty pounds, we will say that he received the watch as a gift.

Faith is necessity, for without fear of heaven there is nothing. But Torah is like an accessory. Hence, faith, which is the first state, is called "a son of the Assembly of Israel," which is faith. The second state, regarded as Torah, is called "a son of the Creator."

A person's thoughts and desires before he repents are called "gentiles." When he repents, it is considered that he is king over these nations. This is the meaning of what he says, "Who among the kings of the nations will not fear You?" since if he has no fear of heaven, he is not called "king of the nations," "for among all the wise men of the nations and in all their kingdoms, there is none like You," for everyone says that there is none like You.

We should say that even after he becomes a king, he says that all his wisdom and in all their kingdoms, and every time he had control over his nations, it all came to him from "there is none like You," meaning that only the Creator helps him, as our sages said, "Were it not for the help of the Creator, he would not overcome it," etc.

# 620- *Concerning a Blessing*

Av, Tav-Shin-Chaf-Bet, August 1962, Tiberias

"'And it came to pass because you hear these sentences ... and you shall eat and be satisfied, and you shall bless the Lord your God, etc.,' This *Mitzva* [commandment] to bless the Creator for everything one eats and drinks and enjoys in this world, and if he does not bless, he is called 'a thief from the Creator,' as it is written, 'who robs his father and his mother' ... because the blessings that a person blesses the Creator come to extend life from the source of life to the name of the Creator" (*The Zohar*).

We should ask, 1) Why is a person called a thief when he does not bless the Creator? 2) To understand the reason that *The Zohar* gives, "because the blessings that a person blesses the Creator come to extend life from the source of life to the name of the Creator," what is the connection between extending abundance and man's blessing?

The thing is that the purpose of creation is to do good to His creations. For this purpose, the lower ones were created with a desire to receive the benefit, and through this disparity of form they became separated from the root. When there is separation, the lower one cannot receive. Hence, we must correct the separation, meaning to be able to receive the upper benefit.

Therefore, when a person blesses the Creator, he bestows upon the Creator. Therefore, even the pleasures he receives, his intention is not to receive, unless in order to be able to bless on it. This is called "equivalence of form." This is why the abundance comes for His name, etc.

A "name" indicates *Malchut*, regarded as "the whole of Israel" or the Assembly of Israel, which is everything. For this reason, what a person does in private, surfaces and sentences the entire collective, as our sages said, "One should always see oneself as half guilty and half innocent. If he performs one *Mitzva*, happy is he, for he has sentenced himself and the entire world to the side of merit" (*Kidushin* 40). The reason is that every individual influences the whole collective through his actions.

Therefore, if an individual works for the sake of the Creator, namely that in everything that he enjoys he needs a blessing so he can bless the Creator, it means that his aim is to bestow. At that time, the abundance extends from the Creator to the Assembly of Israel, meaning to the *Shechina* [Divinity], which is the unification of the Creator and the *Shechina*.

Assorted Notes

# 621- A Minor *Mitzva* [Commandment]

It is written in *Midrash Tanchuma*: "'And it came to pass,' as the writing said, 'Why should I fear in days of adversity, when the iniquity of my foes surrounds me' (*Hulin* 49), blessed be the name of the Creator, who gave Torah to Israel, in which there are 613 *Mitzvot* [commandments], and there are minor ones and there are major ones among them."

Because there are minor *Mitzvot* among them, which people do not notice and throw under their heels, meaning that they are of little importance, David feared the judgment day and said, "Master of the world, I do not fear the major *Mitzvot* in the Torah, for they are major. What I fear are the minor *Mitzvot*, lest I transgressed with one of them, if I did or did not do because it was minor. And You said, 'Be vigil with a minor *Mitzva* as with a major *Mitzva*.' For this reason, he said, 'Why should I fear in days of adversity, when the iniquity of my foes surrounds me?'"

We should ask what is the minor *Mitzva* that he says people throw under their heels. Our sages said (*Avodah Zarah* 2b), "In the future, the nations of the world will come and say, 'If You had forced the mountain on us like a cask as You did to Israel, would we not have received it?' etc. Promptly, the Creator tells them, 'The first ones will hear, as was said, 'And the first ones will hear.' The seven *Mitzvot* that you received, where did you observe them?'"

It is mentioned above that they did not observe them, as Rabbi Yosef teaches, "He stood and surveyed the earth; He looked and startled the nations." What did he see? He saw the seven *Mitzvot* [commandments] that the sons of Noah took upon themselves and did not observe. Since they did not observe them, He permitted it for them. They said to Him, "Master of the world, give us in advance and we will do them." The Creator said to them, "Fools, he who toiled on the eve of Shabbat [Sabbath] will eat on Shabbat. He who did not toil on the eve of Shabbat, from where will he eat on Shabbat?"

"Yet, I do have one minor *Mitzva*, whose name is *Sukkah*; go and do it. And Rabbi Yehosha Ben Levi said, 'Why is it written, 'I command you this day, today to do them and not tomorrow to do them'? Today, to do them and not to take reward. However, the Creator does not complain against His creations.'"

Why did He tell him, "a minor *Mitzva*"? It is because lack of money in it, and lack of money means precisely for the sake of the Creator. This means that in the action there is no difference between working for the sake of the Creator or for one's own sake. The matter of *Sukkah* refers to the thatch, which is a shade. The shade must be more than the sun.

"Major" means action. In this regard, he was certain that he observed all 613 *Mitzvot*. But about "for the sake of the Creator," he had to scrutinize.

# 622- Overcoming

*Heshvan, Tav-Shin-Chaf-Dalet, October-November 1963*

Concerning Abraham asking for advice about the circumcision, it is explained in *Siftey Hachamim* that it is to receive a greater reward for the *Mitzva* [commandment], and he thought that perhaps they would object to him.

We should interpret that Abraham saw that since he had a *Mitzva* that he could do only once in his life, meaning that he could make an effort on this *Mitzva* only once, he thought of an idea to ask his friends. Should they resist, he will have great labor to overcome them, and "According to the effort, so is the reward." For this reason, he put himself into the test in order to receive reward.

We see from this that he so wanted to do the Creator's will that it was worthwhile for him to put himself to a test only because he understood that doing the Creator's will should be with a power of overcoming.

For this reason, although we do not need to put ourselves to tests, it is rather a daily thing that the world and the environment object to the work of the Creator and that we must overcome them and not consider what they say, and understand that this is to our benefit, that it is in order for us to receive a reward for this.

When some resistance to the work appears, we must be happy, since only now will it be possible to gain a great reward, just as when one is happy when he sees that he will make a great profit. He does not look at the effort, but only at the reward. As it is written, we must overcome in Torah and *Mitzvot* [commandments].

When we have disturbances, we will have joy from being given an opportunity to gain a great reward.

Likewise, with charity, we should overcome more than the environment obligates. Instead, each one should give more than he is able, and then it is regarded as overcoming.

## 623- *Purify Our Hearts*

Tevet, Tav-Shin-Chaf-Dalet, December 1963

"Purify the filth of my deeds lest my agitators say, 'Where is the God who made me?'"

We should ask, What is the connection between the Creator purifying man's actions and "lest my agitators say"?

The thing is that what the agitators say is because they do not see that the Creator's guidance is good and does good, but that it is rather in concealment. Why is it concealed? It is because before one achieves the state of bestowal, when his intention is for the sake of the Creator, there must be a concealment. Only after a person purifies his actions does the Creator behave with him with open Providence.

For this reason, we pray to the Creator to purify our actions, as in "A pure heart, create for me, O God." And why does one pray that the Creator will purify his actions? It is not because he wants to be rewarded with open Providence, but in order to shut the mouths of the agitators.

# 624- *Ushpizin* [Sukkot Guests]

Baal HaSulam interpreted the matter of *Ushpizin*, that it is a matter that is introduced in *The Zohar*, a way by which to pass, for the light of *Hochma* cannot shine in it consistently.

This is the meaning of "luck," that "Sons, life, and nourishment depend on luck," as written in *The Study of the Ten Sefirot* (Part 13). This comes from the words, "Water will pour out from his buckets." Pouring means that it is only dripping, meaning it illuminates intermittently, whereas a stream means illuminating ceaselessly.

For this reason, the guests love that he will have a spacious place. But when they come and the place is narrow, they cannot enter. This means that the light of *Hochma* cannot shine unless by clothing of *Hassadim*, and *Hassadim* is called "wide," as explained in *The Study of the Ten Sefirot*. The light of *Hochma* is called *Ushpizin*; therefore, if he has no *Hassadim*, it cannot clothe.

# 625- The *Mitzva* of *Sukkah*

In the *Yotzer* [prayer] of the Monday morning prayer, the poet says there: "Let the *Mitzva* [commandment] of *Sukkah* not be light in your eyes, for it is equal to all the *Mitzvot* [commandments] of His laws."

We should ask why a *Sukkah* is equal to all the *Mitzvot*. Baal HaSulam explained that *Sukkah* means faith, a "shadow of faith." Naturally, we understand that faith is equal to all the *Mitzvot*. That is, to the extent of the faith, so he observes the *Mitzvot*.

Likewise, we can understand what is written there: "For no harm will come to all who observe it." That is, one who has faith cannot be harmed by anything. "In the future, He will curse all who despise it," since they have no faith. Therefore, they did not observe the Torah and *Mitzvot* for the sake of the Creator but rather *Lo Lishma* [not for Her sake], so from whom can they demand reward if they engaged not for the sake of the Creator?

As I interpreted concerning a minor *Mitzva*, in which there is no lack of money, it means that aiming for the sake of the Creator does not require special funds or a special time.

# 626- Anything that the Merciful One Does, He Does for the Best

Sukkot, *Tishrey, Tav-Shin-Chaf-Dalet*, October 1963

*Avid* [Aramaic: do] comes from the word *Avud* [Hebrew: lost], for the *Ayin* and *Aleph* are interchangeable. In other words, when a person comes to a state where he is truly lost, when he does not see how he can exist in the world or that he has anything to hold on to, and he has exhausted all the tactics and ideas, and sees that after all the labor and exertions, everything is lost, he must brace himself and say, "Everything that the Merciful one does is for the best."

In other words, the Creator brought upon him all those states of being lost, and they are for the best. That is, through them he has come to a state where he is at the lowest degree, and by this he will be able to rise up, as it is written, "The Lord is high and the low will see," for there is no greater lowliness than when one feels completely lost.

This is the meaning of "Everything that the Merciful one does, He does for the best." Afterward, when he begins to work once more and correct his actions, and makes repentance from love, he says, "This, too, is for the best," meaning the states when he was lost, and there is no greater transgression than a person coming to a state of being lost.

When he repents from love, he sees that this, too, is for the best, that from the bad itself, the good was done. It follows that there is a difference between "Everything that the Merciful one does" and "this, too, is for the best."

# 627- Law and Judgment – 1

"If there is no advocate opposite the prosecutor, tell Jacob the words of law and judgment."

We should ask about the meaning of "words of law and judgment" that we ask of him.

We should say that when a person wants to take upon himself to draw near the Creator, he promptly feels his own inferiority and lowliness, that he is constantly engaged in nonsense like the rest of the world, so why does he suddenly want the Creator to bring him closer more than his contemporaries? This seems like insolence on his part.

This is the meaning of "If there is no advocate opposite the prosecutor," when the litigator begins to mention his sins and crimes, and the person cannot justify them, we ask, "Tell Jacob," meaning the point in the heart, which is regarded as *Akev* [heel], regarded as a *Mitzva* [commandment] that one tramples with one's feet, "the words of the law," for it is a law from Him that no outcast shall be outcast from Him. Thus, even the least of the least will draw near to the Creator. Why should it be so? It is a law. Then, it is by judgment that he should accelerate the time soon in our days, Amen, and we will be able to draw near right away during the prayer.

ASSORTED NOTES

## 628- The Qualities of "Idol-Worshippers" and "Israel"

Ten Penitential Days, *Tishrey*, *Tav-Shin-Chaf-Dalet*, September 1963

"Rabbi Yochanan said, 'An idol-worshipper who engages in Torah must die, as was said, 'He commanded the Torah to us; we are permitted, and not they'" (Sanhedrin 59a).

"Anyone who engages in Torah before an uneducated person, it is as though he had intercourse with his betrothed woman in front of him, as was said, 'Moses commanded the Torah to us as inheritance; do not pronounce it 'inheritance' but 'engaged' [similar sound in Hebrew]'" (*Pesachim* 49b).

We should understand the meaning of an idol-worshipper learning Torah having to die. It means that if a person does not repent, he is regarded as an idol-worshipper. Then, when he learns Torah, and the Torah is called "life," as it is written, "For it is your life and the length of your days," he can obtain this only when he is Israel, meaning when he is a servant of the Creator.

But when a person serves himself, which is regarded as work that is foreign to us [idol-worship], at that time, he cannot enjoy the life in the Torah, since he is still doing idol-worship. It follows that he has incurred death on himself, which is called that he must die.

In other words, although he is learning, and according to the learning of Torah he should have been given life, meaning that he would be rewarded with life from the Torah, since he is doing idol-worship, he must die and not live, meaning that he does not feel the taste of life in the Torah.

This explains "An idol-worshipper who engages in Torah is as a High Priest." That is, he knows that he is still idol-worshipping and regrets it. Then it was said that he will certainly repent and will be rewarded with being Israel, since the light in it reforms him. But when a person learns Torah and does not know he is an idol-worshipper, meaning he does not feel that he is idol-worshipping, he incurs death on himself.

## 629- One Who Despises a Wise Disciple

"Anyone who despises a wise disciple, there is no cure to his illness" (*Shabbat* [Sabbath] 119b). This means that only one who has an illness cannot receive the cure. But one who does not have an illness has nothing to fear.

We should say that "his illness" means that every person who has still not repented is an afflicted person, and the healing for his affliction means that he will repent. Since every person consists of "uneducated people" and the quality of "wise disciple," called the "point in the heart," if he despises the wise disciple within him, he will never be able to repent and will remain in his lowly state, and there is no greater affliction than this.

Rather, only when he respects the wise disciple within him, meaning he is concerned with benefitting him, and each day he searches how he can benefit him, what nourishes the wise disciple, meaning Torah and prayer, then he can hope that there will be healing to his affliction, meaning that he will repent.

I heard that Baal HaSulam said that one who despises a wise disciple, meaning his teacher, if he cannot respect his teacher properly, he cannot be cured because to the extent of the greatness of his teacher that the student assumes in his heart, to that extent his teacher can benefit him and bring him closer under the wings of the *Shechina* [Divinity].

# 630- And There Was Evening and There Was Morning

Why was it not said, "And there was evening and there was morning, the seventh day"? It is known that absence precedes presence, for there is no light without a *Kli* [vessel]. Hence, first there must be evening, and both together are one day, for if one does not feel a lack, he has no need to draw the filling.

This is precisely during the six workdays, when there is an awakening from below. At that time, there must be darkness first, for otherwise he will not draw the filling. This is why it is written concerning the six workdays, "And there was evening and there was morning."

But on Shabbat [Sabbath], which is an awakening from above, he does not need to first feel the state of evening in order to draw the filling, since Shabbat is regarded as extending from above without the assistance of the lower one. This is why it was said "the seventh day," since on Shabbat, the light and the *Kli* come from above.

# 631- Kedusha [Holiness] and Tahara [Purity]

"The Torah is called *Kedusha* [holiness], for it is written, 'for I the Lord am holy.' This is the Torah, which is the upper, holy name. Hence, one who engages in it is purified and then sanctified, as it is written, 'You will be holy.' It does not write, 'were holy,' but certainly, 'will be holy'" (*The Zohar*, Kedoshim, Item 13).

This means that the Torah purifies. The question is what is a Torah that purifies, by which they will certainly achieve *Kedusha*. He says that the Torah is the upper, holy name. This means that although when we look at the Torah, we see that the Torah speaks of corporeal matters, we must nonetheless believe that it is all holy names. Hence, by their merit, we purify ourselves and are rewarded with *Kedusha*.

However, we should understand what is *Kedusha* and what is *Tahara* [purity]. In the literal sense, it is just as if you have a purified *Kli* [vessel] in corporeality; you can put food in it, but if it is dirty, you cannot put anything inside.

Accordingly, we should say that *Tahara* pertains to the *Kli*, and the filling to the light. Since dirt pertains to the *Kli*, called "will to receive," which is called a "dirty *Kli*," we cannot fill it because anything that we will place in it will be soiled. That is, the will to receive is called *Av* [thick] and crass, and dirty, and the purification of the *Kli* means that we have corrected it to work in order to bestow. At that time, the *Kedusha* will come by itself, as it is known that no change happens from the perspective of the Emanator; He wants to give, but due to the disparity of form, the *Kli* is considered dirty and cannot be filled.

Hence, when he is purified, it is thanks to the Torah—which are the names of the upper, holy name—he is rewarded with the purification of the *Kelim* and subsequently with *Kedusha*. *Kedusha* means that he has been rewarded with attaining the holy names according to the merit of his *Tahara*.

# 632- I Will Always Yearn

"I will always yearn and I will add to all Your glory" (Psalms 71:14).

We should interpret that when one feels that he has closeness to *Kedusha* [holiness], and it must be that the Creator drew him near, he must praise the Creator for pulling him out of his lowliness and admitting him into a state of feeling the *Kedusha*. But one should not settle for this, although he should value his state, and as much as he can depict it as very important, meaning that as much as he may be able to appreciate its importance, this quality is still higher than his attainment.

Yet, he says, "I will always yearn," meaning there are higher degrees than I can depict.

But how is this possible? After all, as much as he may depict this as important, how can something be more important than what can be depicted? About this, "I will always yearn," meaning that I will be able to depict a more important reality than I can depict now. Naturally, "I will add to all Your glory."

It follows that although now, for the present, I am praising You, by always yearning that I will be able to attain more understanding of Your importance, I will be able to add more glories.

# 633- Revealing a Portion and Covering Two Portions – 2

"Revealing a portion and covering two portions." That is, at first, everything was covered, and he came and revealed a portion and then covered two portions. Therefore, we should ask if it would not be better had he not revealed at all. The place that he revealed, had he revealed a portion and covered a portion, it would have been the same as before he revealed the portion. But if he revealed a portion and covered two portions then now it is more concealed than before.

We should say that previously, when it was concealed, it was not known that it is concealed. That is, there is a big intimation here, since if he covered the portion he had revealed, it would be as concealed as before he revealed. So what did he gain by revealing? Also, if he did not cover what he revealed, the matter would be revealed to all, and the revelation is not beneficial to everyone.

Hence, if he revealed a portion and covered two portions, it means that there is a cover here that they did not feel before. That is, if it were as before he revealed, it would not be known that there is a cover here, since when one feels that there is a cover here, there is something to grip, as this cover will invoke a person who is looking for ways to reveal.

This is similar to a person having to believe that the Creator hid Himself from the lower ones. But not everyone believes in the Creator, to say that He hid Himself. It follows that one who believes in concealment, believes in the Creator.

# 634- Fear of Heaven

Yom Kippur [Day of Atonement] 10 Tishrey, Tav-Shin-Chaf-Hey, September 16, 1964

"Antiganos Man of Socho complained to Shimon the Righteous ... but rather be as slaves serving the rav [great one/teacher] not in order to receive reward, and the fear of heaven will be upon you" (Pirkei Avot, Chapter 1).

We should ask about the connection between "And the fear of heaven will be," etc., and "not in order to receive reward."

If a person works not in order to receive reward, the question is, Who obligates him to work? By nature, it is the reward that obligates one to work. If one has no intention to receive reward then who obligates him? When a servant serves the rav, it is because he has no choice, for the master governs him. But here, in the work of the Creator, it is a matter that is given to choice.

The answer to this is "and the fear of heaven will be upon you." That is, the reason that obligates the work will be only the fear of heaven. The matter of choice pertains to the fear of heaven, as in "Everything is in the hands of heaven but the fear of heaven." This was given to man to choose for himself his own fear of heaven, and each one has his own measure.

## 635- This World and the Next World – 1

"One hour of repentance and good deeds in this world is better than all of the life of the next world, and one hour of contentment in the next world is better than all the life in this world." We should ask about this, since it is known that usually the reward is more important than the work, since man observes "By the sweat of your brow," and his reward is "you shall eat bread." That is, if a person enjoys his work, but at the same time his salary is far greater than his work, how did they say that one hour of repentance and good deeds in this world is better than all the life of the next world?

In other words, by exerting in repentance and good deeds in this world, one is rewarded with the next world. It therefore follows that one should calculate, and if he wants to see how much his reward in the next world is worth, he can assume that the whole of the life in the next world is worth one hour in repentance and good deeds.

But who would want to work in Torah and *Mitzvot* [commandments] when he knows what taste he feels in Torah and *Mitzvot*? It therefore follows that the next world is even worse!

But according to the *Sulam* commentary [on *The Zohar*], the "next world" means lights of *Hassadim*, regarded as *Bina*, and "this world" is called *Malchut*, which is lights of *Hochma*.

He tells us that if a person has been rewarded with the next world, which is the quality of bestowal, he should know that it is worthwhile to work in repentance and good deeds of the quality of this world, which is the quality of *Hochma*, since this is regarded as reception in order to bestow, and this is the purpose of creation.

Hence, one should not position oneself in the state of bestowing in order to bestow, which is the quality of light of *Hassadim*, the quality of *Bina* or "the next world." Rather, one should continue one's work and achieve the quality of "this world," regarded as *Malchut*.

# 636- The Need for Flavors of Torah

Questions:

1) Concerning the NRNHY in the world of *Assiya*, he explains these are the NRNHY of *Assiya*. We should explain the NRNHY of *Yetzira* and *Beria*.

2) If we must observe the *Mitzvot* [commandments] in the literal way, as our sages said, "Why do we blow? The Merciful One said to blow." Thus, what does it mean that we are seeking books that explain the meaning of the *Mitzvot*?

Answers:

1) Baal HaSulam said that we must learn the intention of the *Mitzvot* of the ARI. It is good for one to know that there is something in each and every *Mitzva* [sing. of *Mitzvot*], and to ask the Creator to open our eyes and reveal to us the flavors of Torah and the flavors of the *Mitzvot*. However, for ourselves, we should be willing to serve the Creator in the simplest way.

This is regarded as "Let wisdom be given to the wise," since a person needs a *Kli* [vessel]. That is, there must be an evident force to absorb the wisdom within him, and all the information he learns are only in order to increase the *Kli*, meaning that he will have a need for it and it is permitted.

However, when he begins to accustom himself in the literal way, he no longer believes that there are terrible secrets in it, that it is worthwhile for him to draw near the King, so the King will grant him attainment.

He does not need attainment because if he knows the reasons, he will work harder. It follows that he needs assistance, but because "He who does not know the commandment of the upper one, how will he serve Him?" It means that then he will know what and how to serve the Creator.

If he does not have the knowledge, he will still be happy that he nonetheless has the privilege of being given the means to serve the King as a simple servant without any understanding. It follows that he wants to obtain the flavors of Torah only in order to know how to serve Him.

All the reasons that they said what He is, and we learn from books that say not to use it, it is in order to have a desire and yearning for the Creator to reveal the secrets of Torah. But if one already understands the reasons, he has no need for the Creator to bestow upon him.

The most important is the *Kli*, meaning the yearning for the matter. It follows that by learning the reasons and the concepts, he increases the need to understand and to attain, but the attainment should come from the Creator, and if he does not learn, he will not have the need. This is the meaning of "Let wisdom be given to the wise."

# 637- *Four States in the Work*

Beauty: This pertains specifically to the seeing of the eyes, which is the quality of *Hochma* [wisdom].

Wealth: This means "left" [side], as it is written, "and wealth to her left."

Attributing: This means ZA, which is not regarded as an entity but is attributed to "right" and "left."

Ugly, etc., as long as you crown me with gold: According to the RASHI interpretation, after the marriage, meaning *Malchut*, where reception is forbidden, there is concealment on this place. Hence, it is an ugly thing, for we do not see any merit there, for anything that is there does not belong to her authority and we can receive it only in the quality of faith.

This is called "for the sake of the Creator," since we do not see any merit there that will make it worthwhile to bond with her. But after the acceptance of faith, we must extend all the degrees to her.

## 638- Man's Inclination

London, 1 Av, Tav-Shin-Chaf-Hey, July 30, 1965

"Man's inclination overcomes him every day, and unless the Creator helps him, he cannot overcome it." We should ask about this: It is known that everything is in the hands of heaven but the fear of heaven, so why did they say, "unless," etc.?

The thing is that faith is called above reason, meaning above nature, since everything that is within reason is called "within nature and reason," for that which a person understands, he can do, unless he is lazy. But above reason, he cannot do this. Therefore, anything that is above nature is regarded as a miracle.

All the miracles are attributed to the Creator, meaning regarded as an awakening from above and not as an awakening from below, since the lower one cannot do something that is above nature. But in order for a miracle to be done to him, a person should pray that a miracle be done to him.

Hence, the work from the perspective of the lower one, meaning that he will make a choice, was said only about the prayer, and then the Creator hears the prayer. Therefore, one is given one's wishes, and the rule is that a prayer pertains specifically to a deficiency.

For this reason, a person must create within him a need and a deficiency for faith, for only when one sees and feels that he is lacking faith, and to the extent that he needs it, since he sees that for himself he cannot receive the above-mentioned, then he makes a true prayer that the Creator will help him, and then the Creator makes a miracle for him and gives him the light of faith.

However, one must be careful not to enjoy this light, as our sages said, "One does not enjoy the work of miracles." This means that acceptance of faith should be only for the purpose of bestowal and not for the purpose of reception, for then there is room for the spirit of *Kedusha* [holiness] to be on him.

If he wants the above-mentioned light in order to have pleasure, since he feels that the corporeal pleasures are not eternal, so he wants an eternal pleasure, and this is why he asks for faith—he immediately loses the light of *Kedusha*.

Instead, one must ask because the *Shechina* [Divinity] is in exile, meaning that he wants to sanctify the name of heaven in him, and not to have foreign thoughts, since he cannot tolerate the slander that the body says about *Kedusha*, as it is written, "All day long, my enemies curse me." At that time, the Creator makes a miracle for him and gives him faith above reason, and he is rewarded with permanent faith.

# 639- This Is the Making of the Menorah [Temple Lamp] – 2

Zurich, 20 Sivan, Tav-Shin-Chaf-Hey, June 20, 1965

"This is the making of the *Menorah* [Temple Lamp], hammered work of gold; from its base to its flowers it was hammered work; according to the pattern which the Lord had shown Moses, so he made the *Menorah*."

We should understand the matter of hammered work in ethics. RASHI interpreted, "It was one talent [piece] of gold. He would strike with a hammer and cut with an axe to fashion its pieces appropriately, and it was not done piece by piece by connecting."

In other words, it was one whole, and many parts were made of it. Here lies the main difference between the way of Judaism, which maintains that the foundation should be faith, while that of the nations of the world is by knowing. That is, they think that by researching Him they will attain Him. Hence, they walk on the path of detail-by-detail, meaning intellectual understandings that they learn about Him.

Each time, they think that they understand Him better. That is, they take organ by organ and turn them into a *Menorah*, meaning that by learning more about Him each time, they will finally have the quality of a *Menorah*.

But the way of Judaism is the opposite. The way is that they take the talent of gold, called "will to receive," from the word *Ze-Hav* [give this/lit. gold], and strike with a hammer, meaning they go with the qualities of mind and heart, and this is called "hammered work," since they go by the way of faith. At that time, he has many questions, since the matter of faith begins specifically where the intellect does not agree. Naturally, it is hard for him to accept the faith above reason.

The verse also adds, "from its base to its flowers." "Its base" means while he is still at the time of concealment, from the words "As a thigh is concealed." "To its flowers" means that he begins to blossom and wants to take the blossoming as a foundation for his work. This, too, is forbidden. Rather, it must be hammered work from beginning to end, "according to the pattern which the Lord had shown." This is the meaning of the work of the *Menorah* in which Moses was perplexed.

The order is that in order to obtain *Hochma* [wisdom], we follow an order of degrees, meaning from a small mind to a bigger mind until we are rewarded with the real mind. Also, he gives an opposite order, meaning that the basis is faith above reason.

Precisely by this, we are rewarded with the knowledge of *Kedusha* [holiness], meaning that we begin by accepting the work as "hammered work," and there is no cutting of limbs in the work of the *Menorah*, meaning not any work, but only faith.

Precisely through the beatings, called "striking with a hammer," we come to obtain details, for there is a difference between one *Mitzva* [commandment] and the next.

It follows that if in the beginning it was one talent of gold without any discernments, afterward it became many details that have one connection. Conversely, the way of the nations of the world is the opposite, as it is written (in the "Introduction of *The Zohar*, 161) that a philosopher asked Rabbi Shimon, etc.

# 640- A Blessing and a Curse

Manchester, Av, *Tav-Shin-Chaf-Bet*, August 1962

"I see... the blessing that you will hear the commandment of the Lord your God that I command you this day. And the curse, if you do not hear the commandment of the Lord your God, and you stray from the path that I command you today, to follow other gods whom you do not know."

The interpreters ask:

1) Why does he say in the blessing, "that you will hear," and in the curse he said, "if you do not hear"? Why does he not say "If you hear" also in the blessing?

2) Why does he separate in the curse between the "the commandment of the Lord your God, and you stray from the path that I the Lord command you today," and in the blessing, immediately following "the Lord your God" comes "that I command you today"?

We should say in the manner of intimation, concerning the verse, "the blessing," that he interprets the blessing, that you will hear the commandment of the Lord your God, which I command you today. Concerning the curse, he interprets the curse, if you do not hear the commandment of the Lord your God. He interprets what will happen—that you will "stray from the path that I command you today," and all that you will have is to "follow other gods whom you do not know."

We should ask the following:

1) Why did he say "that" in regard to the blessing, and "if you hear" in regard to the curse? Why does he not say "if you hear" concerning the blessing, too? It seems to imply that it is a condition: If you hear, you will receive a blessing.

2) Why, with the curse does he separate between "your gods" and says that you will "stray from the path that I command you today"? Also, why does he not say in the blessing, too, "and you will walk on the path that I command you today," but rather said, "that you will hear... your gods, which I command you today"?

3) What is the meaning of the words "that you will hear"? What if you do not hear? Is this a matter of hearing? Why does He not say, "If you walk or do in My laws"? What does the word, "hearing" mean?

The thing is that at the time of the reception of the Torah, Israel said, "We will do and we will hear." Hence, all that it talks about here is doing, and the Creator interprets the reward called "hearing."

Hence, He made the blessing so you would hear, and the curse, when do you know that you have a curse? When you do not hear. Then you will know that your work is inappropriate. This is why they said, "you shall stray," etc., "to walk," which is "doing." But if the doing is fine, there should be hearing.

# 641- Inheritance of the Land

28 Av, Tav-Shin-Chaf-Bet, August 28, 1962

"Justice, justice you shall pursue, that you may live and inherit the land that the Lord your God is giving you."

We should ask how inheritance of the land is connected to justice, and why we cannot inherit the land without justice. If someone does not walk in justice, can he not inherit his father's lots?

We should understand that the inheritance of the land that the Creator promised our forefathers does not pertain to the corporeal land, since we see that to the nations of the world, the Creator gave bigger lands than our land. Also, King David already said about corporeal matters, "Behold, these wicked and those who are tranquil in the world gained riches" (Psalms 73).

Rather, inheritance of the land pertains to spirituality, as I heard from Baal HaSulam regarding the verse, "How will I know that I will inherit it." The Creator replied to him, "Know for certain that your descendants will be strangers," and he replied that through the exile they will have suitable *Kelim* [vessels] and will have a need to receive the higher land.

This is the meaning of "Justice, justice you shall pursue," meaning that you will calculate justly if the corporeal matters are on the path of Torah, and also concerning spiritual matters, meaning Torah and prayer, if they are on the side of purity.

If a person calculates justly, he sees "who will be just before You in judgment," meaning that for his part, man is still unable to work in purity. Hence, the person will need the Creator to give him the inheritance of the land, meaning the higher land, called "instilling of the *Shechina* [Divinity] and the secrets of Torah."

It is called "inheritance" because the person did not labor for it, since man's labor is not enough to be able to acquire the spiritual things. This is why it is called "inheritance of the fathers": That which the Creator gave to the forefathers, He gave the same thing to him as an inheritance. This is called "the light of faith," and afterward we are rewarded with the reception of the Torah.

This is called "a gift," as our sages said, "It is not an inheritance to you." Rather, each one is given a different measure in attainment of the Torah.

However, concerning faith, it is the same discernment, divided by each and every tribe, meaning that every tribe has a part in the matter of the land, and the matter of faith comes by inheritance.

Conversely, the Torah is called "a gift," regarded as each veteran disciple being destined to renew his part in the Torah. However, inheritance requires qualification, meaning a need, and the need for the inheritance is through "Justice, justice you shall pursue."

"Justice, justice you shall pursue." One to pursue Torah and *Mitzvot* [commandments], called "justice," and this is regarded as *Lo Lishma* [not for Her sake].

The second justice is after he already engages in Torah and *Mitzvot*. He must pursue the second justice, which is the quality of *Lishma* [for Her sake], since the beginning is in *Lo Lishma*. This is called "justice" with respect to corporeality, when all the corporeal things are as a lie compared to the Torah and *Mitzvot*, even in *Lo Lishma*, called "the first justice."

## 642- *Justice, Justice You Shall Pursue*

6 *Elul*, Tav-Shin-Chaf-Dalet, August 14, 1964

"Justice, justice you shall pursue, that you may live and inherit the land that the Lord your God is giving you."

The interpreters ask about the duplication, "Justice, justice." Also, we should ask about "that you may live." If a person does not pursue justice, can he not live? Also, concerning "and inherit," when the people of Israel were in their land, how was it relevant to say "and inherit," in future form?

It is known that "from *Lo Lishma* [not for Her sake] we come to *Lishma* [for Her sake]." We should ask why one does not begin one's work immediately in *Lishma*.

First, we should explain the matter of *Lishma* and *Lo Lishma*. The simple meaning of *Lishma* is for the sake of the Creator, when all that he thinks and wants is to benefit the Creator, called "to bestow upon the Creator." It is known that man is born with the evil inclination, as it is written, "for the inclination in man's heart is evil from his youth."

## 643- Supporters of the Torah

"If any man of you brings an offering to the Lord." The matter of the offerings implies to us that one must bring oneself closer to the Creator, that *Korban* [offering/sacrifice] comes from the word *Hitkarvut* [drawing near], as it is written, "And to cleave unto Him," which means "Cleave unto His attributes, as He is merciful, so you are merciful." But when a person works all day only for his own good, by this he draws far from the Creator, and one who is far from another cannot receive anything from him.

Hence, when one observes, "so you are merciful," this is called *Dvekut* [adhesion], and at that time he unites with the Creator. For this reason, when a person makes an offering, meaning gives the Creator a part of his possessions, from his self-benefit and pleasure, by this he draws near to the Creator.

This is the meaning of "If any man of you brings an offering," meaning that one must give a part of you to the Creator, where by observing "so you are merciful," he draws near to the Creator. This was at the time when the Temple stood.

But now, because of our iniquities, the Temple is ruined and the everlasting fire has been cancelled, and we have no priest in his work, or a Levite on his stand, or Israel in his position, and you said, "that we may present the fruit of our lips." Our sages said, "This is the law of the offering," as though he offered an offering of sin, etc.

But he did not give everyone a chance to learn Torah. This was given to us by the participation of Issachar and Zebulun, who made one engagement out of the two of them. Therefore, when they support the learners of the Torah, it is as though they themselves are learning Torah. Hence, by this we will be rewarded with nearing the

Creator, and by this we will be rewarded with "It is a tree of life to those who hold it, and those who support it are happy," and we will be rewarded with complete redemption soon in our days, Amen.

# 644- Passing the Dead before the Bride

Our sages said, "Passing the dead before the bride, and both before the king of Israel" (*Ketubot* 17a).

We should ask about this in ethics. This phrase shows us the order of the work of the Creator:

1) First, we must remove the bad that is within man's heart. This is as in "The wicked in their lives are called 'dead.'" Therefore, the bad is regarded as dead.

2) Then we go to the bride. The bride is called *Shechina* [Divinity], as it is written, "Go my beloved, toward the bride." This pertains to faith, since before we remove the bad, we cannot be rewarded with faith, which is called "bride."

3) "Both before the king of Israel." This is the Torah, for the Torah is called "king," and faith is called "kingdom of heaven" or "fear of heaven," which means accepting the burden of the kingdom of heaven, for only after we are rewarded with receiving the *Malchut* [kingdom] can we be rewarded with the Torah.

Also, we should interpret in another way, according to the order of the preparation for the work of the Creator. At that time, the order is 1) Torah, called "king of Israel," 2) bride, called "faith," and 3) we go and bury the dead.

In the order of preparation, when we begin the work of the Creator, we must begin with the Torah, meaning to learn Torah. When we begin, we must begin in *Lo Lishma* [not for Her sake], and from *Lo Lishma* we come to *Lishma* [for Her sake], since the light in it reforms him. Afterward, when he learns Torah with the aim that the Torah will reform him, he is rewarded with faith, since faith is regarded as good, and its opposite is bad.

Subsequently, once he has been rewarded with faith, he can extract the dead from within him, for then he can bury the dead within him, as our sages said (*Shabbat* [Sabbath] 105b), "Which is a foreign God that is in a man's body? It is the evil inclination," and then he observes "And you shall root out the evil from within you," as our sages said concerning King David, that he killed it through fasting.

Afterward begins a new order, for once he has rooted out the evil, he is rewarded with fear of heaven, since the first discernment is called "faith" in the sense of "fear of sin," and the second quality of faith is called "fear of heaven."

Afterward, we are rewarded with the Torah, called "king of Israel," and the faith of the fear of heaven is called the "assembly of Israel." It was said about this, "Learning Torah is equal to all of them," since it is impossible to be rewarded with the Torah before we are rewarded with admitting a bride and extracting the dead.

# 645- By Your Actions, We Know You

Av, Tav-Shin-Yod-Zayin, August 1957, Boston

It is known that the purpose of the creation of the worlds is to do good to His creations. It is also known that we speak only of what extends from Him, but in Him, Himself, there is no thought or perception. Accordingly, we should understand why we say that the thought of creation is to do good to His creations, since we do not attain His thoughts, as it is written, "My thoughts are not your thoughts."

However, we should say as in the known rule, "By Your actions, we know You." It was interpreted that through the actions, we know His thoughts. Since the righteous of the world were rewarded with all the delight and pleasure, by this act they concluded that such was His intention: It is to do good to His creations.

It therefore follows that everything we say is only from the place where there is a connection between the Creator and the created beings, where the act is already apparent in the created beings, as in the verse, "You have made them all with wisdom." That is, we are speaking only from the perspective of actions, as it is written in the *Poem of Unification*, "By Your actions, we know You." However, we have no utterance or a word to speak of the Creator without His created beings, as was said, "There is no thought or perception of Him whatsoever."

Accordingly, why should we not ask why we say that Creation does not add anything to Him, so why did He create it if it does not add anything, since this question is asking whether the Creator had a need for Creation before He created it? It follows that we want to speak of Him prior to creation, meaning before there was a connection between the Creator and the created beings, and we said above that prior to this connection, "there is no thought or perception whatsoever."

However, we see that this was His intention. The proof of this is that He gives us abundance when we are ready to receive the King's gift, and there will not be any flaw in the gift, meaning when the bread of shame is not felt in the gift, namely when man's intention is only for the sake of the Creator.

At that time, when one receives from the Giver, it is also with the above-mentioned aim, meaning that he wants to receive the King's gift because he feels that this is His will, and not for the sake of self-benefit, and then he is rewarded with receiving all the delight and pleasure.

And to add clarification, it is as it is written, "The whole earth is full of His glory," as it is written in *The Zohar*, "There is no place vacant of Him." Yet, we do not feel it for our lack of tools of sensation.

We can see that with a radio receiver, which receives all the signals in the world, the receiver does not create the sounds. Rather, the sound exists in the world, but before we had the receiving device, we did not detect the sounds although they did exist in reality.

Likewise, we can understand that "There is no place vacant of Him," but we need a receiving device. That receiving device is called *Dvekut* [adhesion] and "equivalence of form," which is a desire to bestow. When we have this machine, we will immediately feel that there is no place vacant of Him, but rather "The whole earth is full of His glory."

# 646- The Generations of Jacob Joseph

23 *Kislev, Tav-Shin-Lamed-Het*, December 3, 1977

"Observe and sanctify it from its beginning through its end." It was interpreted in *The Zohar*, What is Shabbat [Sabbath]? The name of the Creator.

Accordingly, what does it mean that we should observe the sanctification of the holy name? I would understand it differently—that we must sanctify ourselves, as it is written, "You will be holy."

The thing is that *Kedusha* [holiness] means something important, and secular means something unimportant. It is our nature to appreciate that which concerns our body, meaning we value anything that concerns self-love. When a person does things that he does not see what they will yield to self-love, but that he must aim everything for the sake of the Creator, then his work is unimportant in his eyes.

This is the meaning of having to sanctify the name of the Creator, meaning that the work will be important to us when we must work for the sake of the Creator—called the name of the Creator. This work will be the main thing for us, and our engagement in the work of the body is only so we can serve the Creator with the body.

Yet, how do we achieve this? The body is full of questions and it always asks, "What will you gain from working for the sake of the Creator?"

RASHI writes as follows about the verse, "These are the generations of Jacob Joseph": "Another thing: 'And Jacob sat. The camels of that linen merchant came in loaded with linen. That coal merchant wondered where all that linen would be placed. A clever man replied to him, 'One spark from your blower burns it all.'"

We should ask what is clever about this if he asked where it would be placed. If he is clever, he should have given him ideas how to fit it in, while he told him to burn all the linen. Thus, this reply is inappropriate.

Yet, we need to understand how RASHI concludes: "Jacob saw all the champions that are written above, he wondered and said, 'Who can conquer all of them?' What is written below? 'These are the generations of Jacob Joseph,' and it is written, 'Then the house of Jacob will be a fire and the house of Joseph a flame, and the house of Esau will be as stubble, a spark setting off from Joseph that consumes and burns them all.'" What does "The house of Jacob will be a fire" mean? It is enough to write "And the house of Joseph a flame."

But the allegory is this: Where will they place all this linen? That is, when the linen enters the store of the coal merchant, he will have no place to work because the linen will be a burden on him, and he will no longer be able to throw out the linen. This is why the clever man told him, "Before the camels with the linen come into your place, set off one spark and it will promptly burn it all," and then they will not be able to do harm although they are many.

But if they have already entered, you cannot overcome them and throw out the linen because all this burden will be on you, and you will have no choice. This is why the clever man said, "One spark will burn it all."

The lesson is that when he saw all the champions, Jacob wondered how he could conquer them. They explained that one spark will emerge from Joseph, since Joseph is the quality of "righteous," called "a giver." When he takes to himself the quality of bestowal, he has a way to prevent them from entering because they will be burned immediately by the intention to bestow.

But if he lets them in, he will not be able to overcome them, as with the linen. When they enter, when the heavy burden falls on him, he cannot throw them out.

This is the meaning of "the house of Joseph a flame," for a flame is not something permanent, but a bursting flame in ups and downs. Therefore, whenever the questions of Esau arrive, he immediately increases and inflames by the power of the desire to bestow, and does not let those champions into his heart. Then, from all the many flames, a constant fire will be made, which is the quality of Jacob.

That is, by flaming time after time in ascents and descents, he is rewarded with a permanent fire.

# 647- A Prayer Requires a Deficiency

13 Tishrey, Tav-Shin-Lamed-Het, September 25, 1977

"Rabbi Shimon says... and when you pray, do not make your prayer permanent, but mercy and pleading before the Creator" (*Pirkei Avot*, Chapter 2, 18). Concerning the Torah, our sages said, "Set times for the Torah."

We should say that regularity means that although one has no desire or need, he must still learn Torah because the Torah itself brings him *Kedusha* [holiness], even though he feels no need to learn.

This is the meaning of "Great is the learning that yields action," meaning that he will be among men of action, since one who has a need for something acts in order to obtain it. Therefore, the learning will bring him the need. This is why it was said "regularity in the Torah."

However, a prayer means that he is lacking something and he is praying to be given what he is lacking. But if he has no lack, how can he ask when he has nothing to pray that he would be given?

For this reason, Rabbi Shimon said, "Do not make your prayer regular," since this is not regarded as a prayer. Rather, what is a prayer? "Mercy and pleading before the Creator," meaning that he is lacking something and asks the Creator to give it to him. By this we can understand what our sages said, "One does not pray unless in great seriousness."

## 648- The Joy of the Giver

If one receives joy from serving the King, it means that he enjoys the King's pleasure, but his joy from serving the King does not merit a name.

For example, say, after he takes his suitcase, he feels a wonderful pleasure about it. Yet, if he knows that there is another person who, if he takes his suitcase, the King will be more pleased, if he relinquishes the pleasure because his whole aim is to delight the King.

## 649- Preparation for the Light

In order to reach the light, we must first make preparations, so the light will help as in "the light in it reforms him."

## 650- Criticism on Bestowal

The will to receive is self-love. The desire to bestow is love of others. The question is, Why would one want to love others? If it is because self-love, called "will to receive," knows it will be better for it to be a giver, and therefore rejects the will to receive and takes upon itself the desire to bestow, this should be called "bestowing in order to receive."

Thus, when one chooses love of others and revokes self-love, the question is why he does this, who causes him to take upon himself love of others? If you say that the reason is shame, then one who is ashamed, it is still self-love.

## 651- Day and Night

"Day" means that one is happy even without taking any action. He feels that he is in a good mood like the sun that shines without my actions.

"Night" means I cannot be happy unless through corrections. For example, if we want to have light at night, we must light up a candle or an electrical lamp.

## 652- If Any Man of You Brings an Offering

*Iyar*, May

"If any man of you brings an offering ... from the beast." The matter of offering is specifically from the beast, as in "he pretends to be as a beast and not as humans." This is so because all the *Korbanot* [offerings/sacrifices], meaning the *Hitkarvut* [nearing] the Creator, are from the beast. Conversely, one who wants to offer from the quality of man commits a transgression, as one who gives his son to Molech, which is an offering to idol-worship.

Israelis offer only from the beast, and not from man (and he also said "And I will remove the stony heart from within you." Even [stone] comes from the word *Avin* [I will understand], meaning that he wants knowledge. As long as this works in his organs, he is deficient. Rather, it must be from the quality of a beast).

Man should not pray for any spreading of knowledge into himself. Rather, he must work in the current state, even if it is the smallest *Katnut* [smallness/infancy] in reality.

He only needs to see that it is permanent, without having anything that might disqualify the slaughter (a puncture in the gullet, even the slightest, and much less a delay, disqualifies the slaughtering. Slaughtering means that in a wise disciple, signs of slaughter are seen by themselves). One should pray for the expansion of the knowledge only for the sake of the collective.

# 653- Concerning Threshing

Iyar, May

"Indeed, your threshing will last for you until grape gathering, and grape gathering will last until sowing time."

The matter of "threshing" means things that a person tramples with his feet, meaning he extracts the abundance from under his feet. By this he comes to a state of narrow. Since it becomes narrow to him, he feels that this is bad. Then, once he has obtained these discernments, he is guaranteed to walk on the good path. But before one attains this, he walks in circles ("if there is no reason that distinguishes where from," but when he obtains these discernments in his mind, he can then distinguish).

## 654- Who Despises the Day of Smallness

"Who despises the day of smallness?" This means that one should be happy about work in *Katnut* [smallness/infancy] more than about work in *Gadlut* [greatness/adulthood] because the bigger the light, the more there is fear that the external ones will blemish it. Hence, it is covered so as to be seen, but only in the form of *Katnut*. Conversely, a smaller light can be revealed because there is less concern.

One should believe that there is more contentment from servitude in the time of *Katnut* than in the time of *Gadlut*, for the above reason.

## 655- Shoots Like an Arrow

Any sperm that does not shoot like an arrow does not beget. This means that as long as one does not feel that it is so bad that it is like the shooting of an arrow, that any discernment of bad shoots like an arrow in his bones, and he feels that he will die from these arrows, then he begets and builds the structure of *Kedusha* [holiness]. This is the meaning of the entrance to Rebecca and threshing her, meaning that the entrance to the sty and the shed and the threshing in it, from saying that a person threshes with his feet, extracting the abundance to the external ones, which is the will to receive for oneself.

## 656- For the Iniquity of the Amorite Is Not Complete

"For the iniquity of the Amorite is not complete." It is known that there is a limit to man's *Kelim* [vessels], to how much he can receive, meaning to feel and attain. Hence, if a person reaches his maximum, he no longer feels any feeling. It is like the heat in a fire, where if the heat of the fire is at its peak, it has no sensation to it.

# 657- What Is Reality and What Is Imagination

Spirituality is called "that which will never be cancelled," and the will to receive is called "corporeality," since it will be cancelled and will eventually be inverted to work in order to bestow.

Reality means that anyone who comes there, to that place, sees the same form as the other. Conversely, in something imaginary, everyone imagines it differently.

When we refer to the seventy faces of the Torah, it means that they are seventy degrees. In each degree, the Torah is interpreted according to that degree. However, a world is a reality, meaning anyone who comes to any of the seventy degrees attains the same form as all the other attainers who came there.

From this extends what our sages say, meaning interpret the verses of the Torah and say that this is what Abraham would say to Isaac. The question arises, How did they know this? Because those who reached the degree where Abraham stood, they see and know what Abraham knew and saw. For this reason, they know what Abraham would say.

It is likewise with all the sayings of our sages that interpret the verses of the Torah, since they, too, attained the degree.

## 658- This World and the Next World – 2

There is a discernment of the next world, called "faith," and there is the discernment of this world, called "attainment." It is written about the next world, "Will be satisfied and will be delighted," meaning there is no end to the satiation. This is so because all that is received through faith is unbounded.

Conversely, what is received through attainment is limited because anything that comes into the *Kelim* [vessels] of the lower one, the lower one limits it. This is why there is a boundary to this world.

## 659- What Are Torah and Work?

With regard to the Creator, we can speak of Torah, since work pertains specifically to the created beings.

Work applies only to the created beings. Hence, when we speak of work, it means that we learn what one should do. In that state, a person should say, "If I am not for me, who is for me?"

Afterward, we should extend the quality of Torah on this work, regarded as what the Creator does. That is, we must extend the discernment of private Providence and we must not say, "My strength and the might of my hand has gotten me these riches." This is the meaning of the Torah being called "the names of the Creator," meaning that the Creator does everything.

Man's work is included in the Torah of the Creator, meaning that man attributes all his work to the Creator. This is the meaning of what is written, that the Torah is called "the names of the Creator."

In everything, we should discern between Torah and work, for when one engages in Torah, one must always have before him the reward he hopes to obtain from learning Torah: 1) Work. "The light in the Torah reforms him," and from this he will have strength to work, so that everything he does will be in order to bestow. 2) Torah, to be rewarded with the holy names, since "One who does not know the commandment of the upper one, how will he serve Him?"

# 660- How Did They Sin?

In the event at Mt. Sinai, they became free from the angel of death, and only by the sin of the calf did they return to their filth. The question is, How could they sin? Indeed, we should also understand how *Adam HaRishon*, prior to the sin, when he was at such a high degree, could still sin.

# 661- Branch and Root

An instantaneous reward is that a person should value the fact that he is observing the *Mitzvot* [commandments] that the Creator commanded and the Torah [law] that the Creator gave. The whole reward is that he is obeying the Creator and is rewarded with speaking with the Creator. Another reward, such as receiving for himself, which is called "self-benefit," is not regarded as work for the sake of the Creator.

The connection between spirituality and the corporeal body is called "branch and root." It is impossible to attain this before one is rewarded with Torah *Lishma* [for Her sake]. Prior to this, everything is a lie since before we attain the roots, it is impossible to connect them with the branches.

Instead, we must believe that all that there is in this world extends from Him, He sustains everything, and without Him, there is no force that will sustain this corporeal world. He even sustains the *Klipot* [shells/peels], as it is written, "And His kingship rules over all," "And You sustain them all," even the *Klipot*.

## 662- Four Discernments in the Desire

There are four discernments in the desire:

1. Receiving in order to receive;

2. Bestowing, observing *Mitzvot* [commandments] in order to receive the next world as a reward;

3. Bestowing in order to bestow;

4. Wanting to receive pleasure in order to bestow because he wants the Creator to receive pleasure from him.

A corporeal will to receive means that he wants corporeal things. A spiritual will to receive means that he believes in the next world and in attaining the internality of the Torah, and wants everything out of self-love, meaning that through this, the will to receive, which wants to enjoy, will have what to enjoy.

## 663- If He Is Rewarded, His Work Is Done by Others

"If he is rewarded, his work is done by others." But if he is not rewarded, his work is done by himself.

We should understand the importance of being rewarded, that his work comes through others. If so, then this is regarded as the bread of shame, so what is the benefit?

We should interpret that "others" means *Achoraim* [posterior]. There are *Kelim de Panim* [anterior vessels], which are called "vessels of bestowal," and *Kelim de Achoraim* [posterior vessels], called "vessels of reception." For this reason, before one becomes complete, while he has not achieved the degree of "rewarded," his work, the holy work, is done by the *Kelim de Panim*, which are vessels of bestowal, and he can work with them in the holy work.

But once he is rewarded, his work, the holy work, is done by others, meaning that he can also use the *Kelim de Achoraim*, which are vessels of reception, for the sake of the Creator.

# 664- Feeling the Sin Increases the Light

"Had Israel not sinned, there would be only the book of Torah in them." This means that by feeling that they were sinners, they "cried out to the Lord" to save them, and any help is through the light of Torah.

It follows that every sin that they felt and for which they asked for help always adds the light of Torah from above. This means that the illumination increased for them by feeling that they had sins within them. Instead, one who does not feel a sin, does not need the help of the Creator and naturally does not have proliferation in the Torah, as he does not need the Torah to help him.

# 665- Counsels against the Inclination

If a person sees that his inclination overcomes him, he should read the *Shema* reading [Hear, O Israel...]. If this does not help him, etc., he should remember the day of death; this will certainly help him.

We should ask why he is not told to remember the day of death right away. Why should we wait and use other counsels, and only when we see that there is no other way do we tell him to remember the dying day?

We should say that first he is told to take advice from fear of the Creator, which is on vessels of bestowal. If this does not help him and he has no choice, he should take advice from the fear of the body.

## 666- He Who Comes to Purify Is Aided – 2

"He who comes to purify is aided," but He who comes to defile, it is opened for him and he does not receive assistance. What does that come to tell us?

To defile, a person runs and wants to defile himself with vessels of reception. However, it is closed and locked because he has no connection to spirituality. But when one who has begun to work in spirituality comes to defile, it is opened for him and he runs without assistance from above. And why is it opened for him? So he will have room for choice.

Then, when he makes a choice and then comes to purify and sees that he is incapable on his own, although he wants to, then he is aided.

## 667- A Descent and Ascent in the Work

A descent in spirituality means that spirituality has descended in its value. An ascent in spirituality means that the value of spirituality has increased, meaning it has become more important.

Torah and work. "Work" means the work of the *Kelim* [vessels], meaning the qualities in mind and heart. "Torah" is the filling with abundance that comes after the correction of the qualities, or the abundance that comes for the purpose of the correction of the qualities.

## 668- In a Place Where Repentants Stand

"In a place where repentants [people who repented] stand, complete righteous cannot stand."

"Complete righteous" means "right line," when one learns Torah *Lishma* [for Her sake], called "bestowing in order to bestow." "Repentants" means receiving in order to bestow. The act is called reception, meaning moving away, but through the intention, he returns the act to its root. This is called repentance, when he returns to his root. This is *Teshuva* [repentance], when [the letter] *Hey* returns to [the letter] *Vav*.

## 669- The Good Inclination and the Evil Inclination

"For [He will command] His angels" (Genesis 32). That is, the evil inclination and the good inclination both guard a person so he will achieve the goal.

## 670- You Shall Give Him His Wages On His Day

Normally, we work during the day and not at night. The reward from the side of judgment is "You shall give him his wages on his day before the sun sets" (Deuteronomy 24:15).

This implies that when one feels that he is working with himself, this is already called "day," meaning that he is already being called from above and he is told, "See how far you are from spirituality."

When he completes the work, he receives the real reward, after which he is rewarded with faith.

# 671- Sorting Food and Waste

On Shabbat [Sabbath], we sort the food from the waste, meaning good things that are found in the body. On weekdays, we sort the waste from the food. We do not look at good deeds that exist in the body and for which we should thank the Creator for the deeds that the Creator awarded us with doing. Rather, we look at the waste that is in the body, and at that time we do not look at the good. Hence, there is room for prayer.

A wise disciple is in a state of Shabbat on weekdays, too. In other words, when he engages in Torah, he should look at the food from within the waste and thank the Creator for rewarding him with engaging in Torah.

# 672- The Creator Craves the Prayer of the Righteous

The Creator craves the prayer of the righteous. What did He do? He caused them harm so they would pray to remove the harm from them and turn it into good (*The Zohar, VaYishlach*, Item 45).

# 673- The Death of a Righteous

Rabbi Elazar says, "Anyone who engages in Torah *Lishma* [for Her sake], his death is not by the evil inclination, which is the angel of death... For this reason, righteous who engage in Torah, their body is not impure after their death" (*The Zohar, VaYishlach*, Item 47).

We can interpret that their descents, called "death," are not due to the angel of death, who is impure, but because the Creator craves the prayer of the righteous. For this reason, the Creator gives them descents so that through them they will rise to a higher degree. This is called that they are not impure.

## 674- To Admonish Another

"'[One] who does not know how to be careful.' It did not say "to warn," but "to be careful" (*The Zohar, VaYeshev*). A person wants to admonish others, for everyone wants others to work with vessels of bestowal, for if all the friends work in bestowal, they will bestow upon him everything he needs. However, to admonish himself, that he will be a bestower, in that case his will to receive would lose. But when the *Kelim* [vessels] of others work in bestowal, his will to receive gains. Therefore, each one wants the other to be pure.

## 675- The Quality of Joseph

"Jacob sat." RASHI interpreted, "Jacob sought to sit in peace; Joseph's anger jumped on him. Righteous seek to sit in peace. The Creator says, 'Is it not enough for the righteous what awaits them in the next world, but they also seek to sit in peace in this world?'"

We should ask, since our sages said many times, "Happy are you in this world and happy are you in the next world," so why does the Creator say, "Is it not enough for the righteous what awaits them in the next world?" etc.

We should say that "this world" is called *Malchut*, which is a vessel of reception. The "next world" is called *Bina*, which is a vessel of bestowal. Thus, it is not enough that they engage in vessels of bestowal in order to bestow, they also want to be rewarded with reception in order to bestow. This is called "Joseph's anger jumped on him," who is the middle line, the *Sefirot NHY*, called *NHY* of the *Kelim* and *GAR* of the lights. He was angry because he has still not been rewarded with the revealed *NHY*, called *Yesod*, which is the quality of Joseph.

## 676- *Being Privileged*

The privilege that one has to serve the King is expressed when he wants to work in order to bestow. These thoughts are considered that the Creator brings him near and lets him serve Him.

But when he cannot aim in order to bestow and has other intentions, and not to bestow upon the Creator, he is serving others. And who are the others? At that time, one can look at one's intentions.

## 677- *Why Matza Is Called "Bread of Poverty"*

Let us explain the matter of *Hametz* [leaven] and *Matza* [unleavened bread], why *Matza* is called "bread of poverty," and why the *Omer* is made of barley, which is food for beasts, and the two loaves of bread, from wheat, which is food for man.

To understand the verse, "On Passover, he is judged on the crops, and on the *Atzeret* [eighth of the assembly], on the fruits of the tree." According to the RASHI interpretation of Rabbi Yehuda, according to him, the tree from which *Adam HaRishon* ate was wheat (*Rosh Hashanah* 16).

Concerning circumcision and removing: The circumcision is the removal of the foreskin, and the removal is the division between *Mitzva* [commandment] and Torah. "A candle is a *Mitzva*, and the Torah is light."

The removal of the will to receive is called "Turn away from evil." Through *Mitzvot* [commandments] and good deeds and assistance from the Creator, we are rewarded with removal of the foreskin. Afterward, we are rewarded with the Torah, called "man is the tree of the field." Also, a beast is called *BON*, *Malchut*, as in "His wealth will be only for the Creator."

# 678- Male and Female

Rabbi Yitzhak said, "Rabbi Ami said, 'A male comes to the world, his loaf comes with him,'" *Ze-Kar* [*Zachar* (male)], and it is written, "And he prepared a great feast for them." *Nekevah* [female], *Nekiya Ba* [comes clean], until she said, "I did not give her my food," and it is written, "Name me your wages, and I will give it" (*Niddah*, 31b).

Interpretation: Sustenance depends on the man, but the woman asks from her father or from her husband. She is clean, meaning she has nothing. Until she marries, the work of her hands belongs to her father. Once she is married, the work of her hands belongs to her husband. This is why the giving force is called "male," and the receiving force is called "female."

# 679- Signs of the Son of David

"The Son of David [Messiah] does not come until all pennies have run out from the pocket" (Sanhedrin 97a). A "pocket" means the *Kelim* [vessels] where man's energy is placed, meaning that he has done all that he could, and then he will be rewarded with redemption.

The son of David does not come until they give up on redemption, as was said, "And none is stopped and abandoned," as though there is no supporter or helper to Israel.

Rabbi Hanina said, "The son of David does not come until a fish is sought after for a sick man, but it will not be found" (Sanhedrin 98a). *Dag* [fish] comes from *De'agah* [concern/worry] (as it is written, "And the fish that was in the Nile died").

# 680- Annulment—the Baal Shem Tov Way

The way to annul the body used to be through abstention. But there is another way, which is annulment before the rav [great one, teacher]. This is the meaning of "Make for yourself a rav." "Making" is clarified by force, without any intellect.

As abstention revokes the body only through action and not through the mind. Likewise, annulment before the rav is by force and not through intellect. That is, even in a place where one does not understand the view of one's rav, he annuls himself and the Torah and the work, and comes to the rav so he will guide him.

There is guidance in the manner of the general public, called *Ohr Makif* [surrounding light], which is light that shines only from outside, and is without words, but only by coming to the rav and sitting in front of him, sitting at his table during the meal or during the service. Yet, there is another way, which is internal, and this is specifically through "mouth-to-mouth."

## 681- When a Woman Inseminates – 2

The book *Kedushat Levi* (*Tazria*): In the work there is sowing, conception, and birth. "Sowing" means an awakening that awakens people's hearts to the work of the Creator. "Conception" means one who wants to perform the *Mitzva* [commandment]. "Birth" is when a person performs the *Mitzva*.

"When a woman inseminates" means that the receivers will be givers. "She delivers a male child" means *Gadlut* [greatness/adulthood]. "When a man inseminates" means the Creator, called "Giver," "male," which is only an awakening from above. "She delivers a female child" is *Katnut* [smallness/infancy].

This is the meaning of "A female, her face is turned upward" toward the giver. This is the meaning of "His force waned like a female," and he only waits for an awakening from above. "When a woman inseminates, she delivers a male child," meaning as one who always has the strength to overcome. This is the meaning of "And you have grown strong and have become a man."

## 682- Exit and Entry in the Work

*Tzeva'ot* [hosts/armies] is a connection of two things: *Tze* [exit/leave] and *Ba'ot* [coming], which is exit from the work and coming to the work. Through the two of them, the holy name is made, using the word "armies," since the war is only through two things. In this way we should interpret what King David said, "Go out and stretch out your hands in the battalion..."

## 683- A Wise Sees the Future

Concerning the pleasures of this world, the authors of ethics said, "Its beginning is sweet and its end, bitter." This is as it is written, "Who is wise? He who sees the future," meaning that its end is bitter and he has the strength to retire from them. Also, "One does not sin unless a spirit of folly has entered him." Therefore, he does not see what will become of his end.

## 684- The Quality of Moses

Why was Moses called specifically "Moses"? It is because he was given Pharaoh's daughter. We should say that it is after the saving, for I *Mashitihu* [pulled him] from the water.

In the work, a person drowns in the evil water called "What" and "Who," and by this you were saved from the evil water. This name is very important because the beginning of the entrance into *Kedusha* [holiness] ...

## 685- The Creator Complements the Desire

The main thing required of man is the desire, to have a desire and yearning to work in order to bestow. Although he cannot control himself, since man cannot go against nature, but when man wants, the Creator complements his desire.

## 686- The Most Important Is the Right

Elisha asked the Shunammite, "What do you have in the house?" and she replied, "Nothing but a jar of oil." He replied to her that it was good, "Go and borrow vessels."

That is, precisely where there is oil, which is the quality of "right," there is room for *Kelim* [vessels], meaning to find in oneself deficiencies. But when a person lacks oil, when he is in the quality of "right," it is forbidden to awaken the left, meaning the scrutiny, if his work is in truth.

## 687- Make for Yourself an Ark

Aba Hanan said in the name of Rabbi Eliezer, "One verse says, 'Make for yourself an ark.' Another verse says, 'Make an ark' [in plural form]. How come? Here, when Israel do the Creator's will, according to the RASHI interpretation, the work is named after them. Here, when they do not do the Creator's will, it is named after Moses" (*Yoma* 3b).

We need to understand what is the actual reality, Moses or Israel. We should say that the ark is the place where the Torah is placed. "Time" means the *Kli* [vessel], which is the desire for the Torah. The Creator gives the Torah, and the desire belongs to the created beings.

It is written, "When Israel do not do the Creator's will," and their whole intention is to do their own will, the ark is named after Moses, meaning that their desire to receive the Torah is not their own, but Moses'.

In other words, the Torah, which is the quality of Moses, obligates them to do its will. But for themselves, they have no desire. Yet, since the Torah obligated them to receive the Torah, they receive the Torah. This is why it is Moses' will.

But when they do the Creator's will, meaning that their only aim is to bestow, it is considered that they themselves are making their desire to receive the Torah. This is (like) a youth who has the Torah of his own volition, or he needs the overseer to give him the desire to learn Torah.

Rabbi Yochanan wondered: It is written, "Make for yourself an ark," and it is written, "Make" [in plural form]. Hence, a wise disciple, whose townspeople command him to do his work, RASHI interpreted that in the beginning he charged the work to Moses, and afterward charged it to the public (*Yoma* 72b).

In ethics, we should say that "ark" means the desire to receive the Torah. First, the verse obligated Moses to be a servant of the Creator only with the good inclination, and then with the evil inclination. That is, his townspeople, namely the organs and desires in the body, surrender and do the work of the good inclination. This is the meaning of "with both your inclinations."

# 688- *Raise a Contribution for Me – 2*

Shevat-Adar, February-March

"Raise a contribution for Me," meaning *Tarum* [raise] *Hey* [the letter], which is *Malchut*. This is the meaning of *Teshuva* [repentance], of which *The Zohar* said *Tashuv Hey* [the *Hey* will return] to the *Vav*, namely the unification of the Creator and the *Shechina* [Divinity].

In other words, the whole of Israel is regarded as the assembly of Israel, which is about reception. We must make a unification with the Creator, who is regarded as the Giver.

"Raise a contribution for Me." From where? "From every man whose heart is willing, you shall take My contribution." The question is, From whom can we take the contribution, meaning that he is able to lift himself up to the Creator? He replies about this, "from every man whose heart is willing."

The *Zohar* said that it is he who is a man, meaning a man of war, the war against the evil inclination. In other words, every person who wants to enter the war, as it is written, "One should always vex the good inclination over the evil inclination" (*Berachot*), meaning wage war against it.

"Man's inclination ... unless the Creator helps him, he cannot overcome it." Hence, if the Creator must help, then any person can be awarded ... and from the perspective of the Creator, there is no difference between a great help and a small help.

# 689- *The Matter of Father and Son*

"A son makes the father worthy, but the father does not make the son worthy." King Hezekiah was righteous. Although his father, Ahaz, was a complete wicked, he has the next world thanks to his son, Hezekiah. But Menashe [Manasseh], son of Hezekiah, does not have a part in the next world although his father Hezekiah was righteous (Sanhedrin 104).

It is known from holy books that the sons come to correct what the parents did not complete. Hence, when Abraham completed the quality of *Hesed* [mercy/grace], Isaac was born in order to complete the two other lines. When Isaac completed only the line of *Gevura*, Jacob came and completed the quality of *Tifferet*, which is the middle line. Likewise, all the generations complete what the earlier generations did not.

This has continued since the sin of the tree of knowledge, for after the soul of *Adam HaRishon* divided into 600,000 souls, all the generations after him must complete the soul of *Adam HaRishon* that he corrupted.

From this extends that "A son makes the father worthy," meaning the next generation corrects the former generation, but the former generation does not correct the next generation, for if the earlier generation corrected everything, there would not need to be a next generation. This is the meaning of reincarnation, that one who did not complete the correction must reincarnate in order to complete what he did not correct in the previous incarnation.

Hence, although Hezekiah was righteous, had he completed what he had to, he would not have had to have sons, since the sons, who come after him, come to correct what their father did not correct.

Therefore, Hezekiah corrected what his father did not correct, and this is why Ahaz has the next world. But Menashe had to correct what Hezekiah did not correct. And since he was wicked, he did not correct what he had to, and Menashe remained without correction. This is why he does not have the next world.

"The righteousness of the righteous will not be remembered on the day of his wickedness." In ethics, father and son are regarded as cause and consequence, meaning the former act and the following act. The following act is called "a son." Hence, one who did bad deeds, it is considered that his father was wicked. When afterward, he does good deeds, it is because he repented.

Therefore, repentance corrects the previous actions, according to the value of the repentance he has made: If it is repentance from fear—the sins become for him as mistakes, and if it is repentance from love, the sins become for him as merits.

It follows that his actions after he has repented are called "sons" with respect to the previous actions. Thus, the son, meaning deeds that come after bad deeds, are corrected by the son's repentance.

However, one who first does good deeds is called "father," and bad deeds he did he does afterward, which are called "son," so the father does not correct the son. That is, the good deeds he did before cannot cleanse the bad deeds that follow them, since "The righteousness of the righteous will not be remembered on the day of his wickedness." But if it is to the contrary, if the son does good deeds, he can correct the bad deeds.

# 690- This World and the Future

Adar, Tav-Shin-Chaf-Bet, March 1962

In this world, a man builds a building and then ruins it.

In other words, anything that one does, any construction, and a construction means it is something sustainable, such as when a person does some corporeal lust, the lust is not regarded as a construction because it is only temporary. When the lust passes away, nothing is left of it, such as eating and drinking, and so forth. But when one learns or prays, this exists after the action, too.

This is called a "construction." However, that construction is not for one's own sake, but rather another dwells in it. In other words, he builds the building for another. Like a contractor builds houses for other people, one who engages in Torah and *Mitzvot* [commandments] for others, it is called *Lo Lishma* [not for Her sake]. It follows that it is not for himself.

But in the future, he will not build so that another will dwell. That is, when a person engages in Torah and *Mitzvot Lishma* [for Her sake]—meaning that now he engages in Torah and *Mitzvot* in order to achieve *Lishma*, and he will be rewarded with the quality of *Lishma* afterward, which is called "in the future"—there the building, meaning the Torah and *Mitzvot*, will not be built so that another will dwell in it. Rather, he himself will dwell in it because the engagement in Torah and *Mitzvot* is for his own purpose.

We should also say that when one works for the purpose of this world, meaning in order to receive, he cannot enjoy it because there is a *Tzimtzum* [restriction] on reception. It follows that "another will dwell in it." That is, through the exertion he is making, it is so that, as it is written, "If he is rewarded, he takes his part and the part of his friend in the Garden of Eden." That is, one who is rewarded with entering the Garden of Eden takes the labor that others labored in Torah and *Mitzvot*.

This is considered that they are raising the Torah and *Mitzvot* of the general public, as in "A thousand enter a room, and one comes out to teaching." But in the future, one who exerts to achieve *Lishma*, meaning the aim to bestow, will be rewarded with receiving the reward for the labor he had made. It follows that he himself will dwell in it.

# 691- The Torah Was Given in Secret

"Let it be given to the upper ones and let them not be given to Moses." The Torah should be given when one is ascended. "And let them not be given to Moses," as Moses is called "the faithful shepherd," and the hands of Moses are regarded as "faith." At that time, Satan slanders and says that the Torah cannot be received when one is unworthy of it. So the advice is that Moses has the ability to receive, meaning in the quality of faith, for then he is above reason, and there, there are no questions, since all the questions are only within reason.

Hence, when one wants to receive the Torah in public, he understands that he has a need for the Torah for a reason that is *Lo Lishma* [not for Her sake]. But in a manner of concealment, there is no issue of *Lo Lishma*. Then, when he receives the Torah, it is only with the aim that the Torah will bring him the quality of faith. Hence, it must be in secret, and only during the *Katnut* [smallness/infancy]. But during the *Gadlut* [greatness/adulthood], the Torah is called "healing" and "the potion of life."

This is the meaning of "another thing," which is called *Tohu*, meaning "the earth hangs on nothing." This is why Rav Hanin interpreted that it exhausts a person's strength, for then he sees that he is devoid of faith. It follows that all mean the same thing.

# 692- The Torah Is Called *Tushiya* – 1

Sanhedrin 26b: "Rabbi Hanin said, 'Why is her name *Tushiya*? It is because she *Mateshet* [wanes/exhausts] a person's strength.' Another interpretation: *Tushiya*, since she was given in secret because of Satan." RASHI interpreted that he slanders and says, "Let it be given to the upper ones and let the tablets not be given to Moses." "Another interpretation: *Tushiya*, matters of *Tohu* [formlessness], on which the world is based."

RASHI interpreted, "Matters of *Tohu*, speech, and aimless reading, and any speaking without real substance, like that *Tohu*. And yet, the world is based on them. The acronym is *Tav-Yod-Vav*, *Tohu*, *Shiyha*—based."

Ulla said, "A thought helps even words of Torah, as was said, 'revokes the thoughts of the cunning, and they will not make it *Tushiya*.'" RASHI interpreted—helps, causes them to forget what they learned. "Revokes the thoughts of the cunning": He gives them nourishment and cancels the thoughts in their hearts that did not let them perform *Tushiya*.

Another interpretation: A thought that a person calculates—I will get this and that—helps to arrest the matter, so his thought does not come true, even for words of Torah, like one who says, "Until this and that day, I will learn this and that many treatises in the Talmud." "Revokes the thoughts of the wicked," meaning his thoughts do not succeed even for *Tushiya*.

*Tosfot*: RIBA interpreted: Man's concern for his nourishment causes him to forget all his other thoughts, even thoughts of words of Torah. Some interpret "helps" as "lying and will not succeed." That is, if a person contemplates becoming rich, as well as words of Torah, he will not succeed, but only when he works *Lishma* [for Her sake].

The MAHARSHA: We should also say about words of Torah, that what works most is the thought in the heart, and it is not enough to learn it in the mind. Rather, it must be chewed in the mouth, as well, as was said, "By twisting the lips, it is an act." This is as it is written, "revokes the thoughts of the cunning." He who learns Torah only in thought, revokes, and it is forgotten from him. "And they will not make it [*Tushiya*]," so the Torah does not become an act, unless by speech.

Raba said, "If one engages *Lishma*, it does not help, as was said, 'Many are thoughts in a man's heart, but the counsel of the Lord shall be established.' A counsel in which there is the counsel of the Creator, this will be established."

# 693- The Torah Is Called *Tushiya* – 2

Our sages said, "Rabbi Hanin said, 'Why is her name *Tushiya*? It is because she *Mateshet* [wanes/exhausts] a person's strength.' Another interpretation: '*Tushiya*, since she was given in secret because of Satan.'" RASHI interpreted that he slanders and says, "Let it be given to the upper ones and let the tablets not be given to Moses." "Another interpretation: *Tushiya*, matters of *Tohu* [formlessness], on which the world is based." RASHI interpreted "Matters of *Tohu*, speech, and aimless reading, and any speaking without real substance, like this *Tohu*. And yet, the world is based on them. The acronym is *Tav-Yod-Vav, Tohu, Shiyha*—based" (Sanhedrin 26b).

We should ask:

1) Here he says that it exhausts a man's strength. However, our sages said, "His head aches, let him engage in Torah; his whole body aches, let him engage in Torah, as was said, 'a healing to all his flesh'" (*Irovin* 54a). So how did they say the opposite here?

2) What is the slandering of Satan, who argues that they should be given only to the upper ones and not to Moses? What flaw did he find, to the point that he had sufficient argument, and in order for him not to be able to slander, it was necessary to give the Torah secretly?

Also, if Satan is right, why indeed was the Torah given to Moses? Is there bias above? Certainly, one of them is right, and if he has some complaints, he should be given a real answer and not to give it secretly so he does not see, for this implies that there is no answer to his arguments.

3) What does it mean that the world is based on words of *Tohu*, and as RASHI interpreted, any speaking is insubstantial like that *Tohu*, so why was there a need to establish the world specifically on *Tohu*?

We should interpret this in ethics. Satan's slandering is that since the Torah is something precious and very important, we must give the Torah to the upper ones, meaning someone who is at a high degree, who has a big mind and all the manners of his work are only within reason, and not to Moses, since Moses' hands are regarded as faith, which is against reason.

But it is to the contrary: One who wants to go within reason will never attain the Torah within reason.

Just as there is a general Satan, so there is Satan in every individual. The Satan within claims that he wants to observe the Torah only in the way of the upper ones, meaning to be able to understand the ways of the Creator through the intellect, meaning within reason, and not walk in the ways of Torah, above reason, which is called "in the hands of Moses." Hence, as long as one does not grasp the guidance of the Creator in the mind, he does not want to observe the Torah.

To this comes the answer that the Torah will be received only through the hands of Moses, and this is the intimation, *Tushiya*, indicating that the Torah can be received only in secrecy, which is in concealment. That is, it is concealed from the mind, and the mind does not attain it, but specifically above reason. Conversely, "in public" indicates that it is revealed to all, meaning it is revealed to the intellect that they can attain within reason.

By this we reject the argument of Satan, who claims that the Torah should be given within reason, called "the quality of the upper ones," for it is about this that the intimation comes, that the Torah is called *Tushiya*, that it was given secretly and not publicly.

The matter of "Walk in concealment with the Lord" means that it should not be revealed within reason, but rather specifically with the quality of faith is there an ability to receive the Torah. This answers Satan's complaint, and not the literal meaning that "secret" means that Satan does not see.

If Satan is an angel, how can it be said that he does not know that the Torah is given, so we can say that it was given secretly? Rather, "secretly" means not publicly, meaning that it is not revealed within reason.

Indeed, why must we receive the Torah above reason? Why should the Creator mind giving the Torah within reason?

The thing is that according to the rule that Baal HaSulam gave, we should know that every action must be in the quality of bestowal, whether in mind or in heart. Hence, it must be above reason, for then there is room to receive the Torah in order to bestow.

Only then is there the matter of work in reward and punishment, which is the matter of choice. Otherwise, there would be no room for choice. The reason for the choice is also the above-mentioned intention that by this, one can come to the degree of receiving in order to bestow.

Also, to understand what was said, "Another interpretation: *Tushiya*, matters of *Tohu* [formlessness], on which the world is based," another interpretation does not dispute Rabbi Hanin. Rather, it interprets more, that the world, namely everything we should do in the world, which is Torah and *Mitzvot* [commandments], is based on *Tohu*, meaning on faith above reason, for there is no basis on the path of truth except in the quality of faith.

This is called "words of *Tohu*," since man does not understand, so he is always in a state of *Tohu*. Specifically in this way is there existence to the world, meaning that specifically by this the world will achieve its completion.

# 694- Great Is a Transgression that Is *Lishma*

"Rabbi Nachman Bar Yitzhak said, 'A transgression *Lishma* [for Her sake] is greater than a *Mitzva* [commandment] *Lo Lishma* [not for Her sake],' and this is what Rabbi Yehuda said, 'Rav said, 'One should always engage in Torah and *Mitzvot* [commandments], even *Lo Lishma*, since from *Lo Lishma* he will come to *Lishma*.' Rather, say, 'as a *Mitzva* that is *Lo Lishma*,' as it is written, 'Blessed than women is Ya'el, the wife of Heber the Kenite, more blessed than women in the tent.' Who are the women in the land? Sarah, Rebecca, Rachel, and Leah'" (*Nazir* 23b).

In the literal meaning, some interpret that the forefathers acted out of envy. It follows that they had multiplication *Lo Lishma*. Others interpret that because a woman is relieved from multiplication, it is called *Lo Lishma*. Also, we should understand the question about "From *Lo Lishma*, one comes to *Lishma*," etc.

But in ethics, we should ask what it means that a transgression that is *Lo Lishma* is preferable, or the explanation of the Gemara that it is as a *Mitzva* that is *Lo Lishma*, meaning that they are of equal weight. Why does it matter to the Tana which is greater than which? After all, it is written, "Be careful with a minor *Mitzva* as with a major one, for you do not know the reward for the *Mitzvot*." Thus, what does it come to teach us?

There is a rule: "If you come across a *Mitzva*, do not miss it." Thus, if he comes across a *Mitzva* in *Lo Lishma*, he must do it even if we say that the transgression of *Lo Lishma* is greater, since it is forbidden to breach the *Mitzvot*. Also, if he comes across a transgression *Lishma*, he must also do it first.

In ethics, we should understand that here the question is which way a man will walk when he performs a *Mitzva Lo Lishma*. Should he be happy that he has performed a *Mitzva*, or should he be sorry that he now transgressed by not aiming *Lishma*, meaning that his transgression is that he did not act in *Lishma*.

There are two things to discern here concerning the *Mitzva* that is *Lo Lishma*: 1) He performed a *Mitzva* in practice. 2) He performed a transgression in thought, since before he did the *Mitzva*, it was still not revealed to him that he is engaging *Lo Lishma*. Rather, by doing the *Mitzva*, the transgression was revealed in the matter of *Lishma*—that he cannot aim *Lishma*.

Hence, the question is what should one do? Should he be happy about the *Mitzva* that he did or sad about the transgression in *Lishma*? At that time, Rabbi Nachman Bar Yitzhak said, "A transgression that is *Lishma* is great," meaning it is more important that he will know that he is committing a transgression in *Lishma*. The importance is that he will afflict himself and pray to the Creator, which will cause him to come to be able to aim *Lishma*.

The Gemara asks about this: "And this is what Rabbi Yehuda said, 'Rav said, 'One should always engage ... since from *Lo Lishma* he will come to *Lishma*.''" This means that the *Mitzva* that he does *Lo Lishma* will bring him to *Lishma* by way of "a *Mitzva* induces a *Mitzva*." The Gemara answers, "but rather say, 'as a *Mitzva* that is *Lo Lishma*,'" and RASHI interpreted that the two are the same, and the RA'ASH interprets that both enter.

In general, we should ask why there is a link from "From *Lo Lishma*, one comes to *Lishma*," to a transgression *Lishma*, since there he will come to perform a *Mitzva Lishma*, and with a transgression *Lishma*, he has already acted *Lishma* in doing the transgression, and there is nothing to add to it. Conversely, in *Lo Lishma* he has more to add, meaning to achieve *Lishma*.

With Ya'el, the act was a transgression and the thought was for the sake of the Creator. We should ask, If she intended for the sake of the Creator, why is it called "a transgression," for by this she did a lot of good to the people of Israel?

We should say that the act was only a preparation for a *Mitzva* and not an actual *Mitzva*, since her aim was to tire him in order to kill him, so you could say that preparation for a *Mitzva* is not a *Mitzva*, since the killing was a *Mitzva* and tiring him was only a preparation.

This implies that where the act itself is the end of the act of *Lishma*, this can be like a *Mitzva Lishma*. For example, had he died because of his exhaustion, the thought *Lishma* would have been carried out with doing the act. But here we should discern between a preparation for a *Mitzva* and the actual *Mitzva*, since tiring him was only a preparation.

According to what Rabbi Nachman Bar Yitzhak said, "A transgression *Lishma* is greater," etc., he would interpret the verse, "Blessed than women," meaning more than women. According to the explanation, "but rather say, 'as a *Mitzva* that is *Lo Lishma*,'" we interpret "blessed than women" as "like the women," and not "more than women."

We should learn from the story with Ya'el, for there the transgression was in the act, and a *Mitzva* in the thought. But sometimes the *Mitzva* is in the act and the transgression is in the thought, and this is called *Lo Lishma*. But the Gemara says that they are of equal weight.

We should discern in the work of *Lo Lishma* that there is a *Mitzva* in action, meaning to be happy about performing the *Mitzva*, and say that a *Mitzva* induces a *Mitzva*, and there is regretting about the transgression in regard to *Lishma*, that he did not aim for the sake of the Creator. By this we should understand, "Even if the whole world tells you that you are righteous," that it is in terms of the action. But in terms of the thought, meaning the intention, if it is still not for the sake of the Creator, he is regarded as wicked in that sense.

This is the meaning of "in your eyes." That is, in regard to the thought, the world should not know. Rather, the aim is given to man himself, and others cannot know what is in his mind. Hence, "Be wicked in your eyes." If the aim is not for the sake of the Creator, it follows that in the place of making the *Mitzva*, the transgression in *Lishma* immediately awakens.

Assorted Notes

# 695- And They Shall Take to You Pure Olive Oil

"And they shall take to you pure olive oil." Rabbi Shmuel Bar Nachmani said, "To you and not to me; it is not its light that I need" (*Minchot* 86b).

"Outside the veil of testimony in the tent of meeting," a testimony to all the people of the world that the *Shechina* [Divinity] dwells in Israel. If you say, "It is its light that I need, all forty years that Israel walked in the desert, they walked only by His light. Rather, it is a testimony to all the people of the world that the *Shechina* dwells in Israel." What is its testimony? Raba said, "It is a western candle, which places in it oil such as the measure of the others, and from it he would light, and in it he would conclude" (*Shabbat* [Sabbath] 22).

We should ask:

1) What fool could say that the Creator needs Israel to illuminate for the Creator? Does the Creator need corporeal light?

2) Why does he need to bring evidence from the desert that Israel walked by the light of the pillar of fire? Without the evidence, what would I say?

The goal is to do good. The receivers, who take the benefit, it means that they receive the light of the Creator, which is extended through the work of the lower ones. This is called "light from the side of Israel," meaning the forces of the people of Israel. When there is no preparation on the part of the lower ones, the Creator does not impart them with the upper abundance.

However, He cannot be limited and to say that without this, He cannot bestow upon them. He brings evidence from the desert, that the Creator illuminated for them without an awakening, and for this reason, they ate bread from the sky, meaning without work, and only when they came to the land, they were given the wholeness called "bread from the earth."

Hence, even when Israel made the *Menorah* [Temple lamp] in the Temple, they were given the testimony so they would know that the *Shechina* dwells in Israel even without an awakening from below, since the Creator does not need the light of Israel, meaning their preparation, for "If you are right, what will you give him?" Rather, it is only for man's benefit so as not to have the bread of shame.

This is why the testimony came from the "western candle," which illuminated in a miraculous way, for a miracle means above nature, since the Creator created the world with a nature that they will be able to receive pleasure only according to their work.

Hence, when giving half a *Log* [ancient liquid measure] of oil, the labor is that of half a *Log*, and the sages assumed that it would be enough to burn from dusk until morning. The fact that the "western candle" burned more than the measure of the labor indicated that it was burning miraculously, not according to the labor. From this we see that the Creator can impart abundance even without the work of the lower ones.

## 696- Your Strength to the Torah

A strong person is one who has a strong desire, and not one who has strong limbs, as in "Who is mighty? He who conquers his inclination," as is done with the powers of strong limbs.

For example, when one wants to go somewhere, but there are people who interfere with his walking on the path he wants to go, and each one pulls him to the place he wants, if he is drawn, he does not have the strength to subdue them, and then he is pulled away from the place where he wants to go to the place that the strongest one among them wants, since he subdues all the others because he is more powerful.

It is likewise with emotional strength. Man consists of many desires, and each of the desires wants to subdue the other desires and draw the body to go to its side. Here, too, the strongest among the desires prevails. And if there is a person whose desires are all equal, and none is more powerful than the others, he can be in a state of complete rest because he has no desire that overcomes the others, so they all stand and pull the body, and the body stands in the middle and does not move an inch, not here and not there, for all are pulling equally strong.

Then he naturally stays put without any movement. Even if he has great strength, they are all equally mighty forces, so no one can submit the other. Only when one desire is strong, that force can act, and the rest of the desires annul before it.

It therefore follows that if a person wants to succeed in the Torah, he must see that the desire to engage in Torah is stronger than the rest of the desires in him, and then they will surrender to it because the strong has the power to subdue the weak. Hence, the strong desire subdues the desire for idleness, for honor, and the rest of the lusts.

# 697- And You Shall Honor It, Not Doing Your Ways

"And you shall honor it, not doing your ways." "Honor it," so your Shabbat [Sabbath] attire will not be as your everyday attire, "and even as Rabbi Yochanan called his garments 'My honorers,'" and RASHI interpreted "My honorers," since they honor he who wears them (*Shabbat* 113a).

In ethics, clothing is regarded as a *Kli* [vessel] that dresses the light. That is, the place of the clothing of pleasure is called "clothing," by which one obtains pleasure, since pleasure is a spiritual light that cannot be obtained without clothing. Sometimes the pleasure is clothed in corporeal attire, and sometimes the pleasure is clothed in spiritual attire, meaning in Torah and *Mitzvot* [commandments].

Hence, on Shabbat, because of the glory of Shabbat, meaning to be rewarded with the light of Shabbat, we must prepare attire by which the light of Shabbat can be worn.

## 698- Two Kinds of Internality

1) Internality is called "desire of internality," namely the mind and the heart, which are the thought and the desire.

2) That which is clothed in the thought, meaning what one thinks or wants. This is regarded as the light that is clothed in vessels of thought and desire.

## 699- The End of Correction

The end of correction means that the *Kelim* [vessels] receive in order to bestow. When the light fills the *Kelim*, the *Kli* [vessel] is annulled before the light and does not merit a name. Hence, *Hitpashtut Bet* [second expansion] is light of *Hochma* in a *Kli* of *Keter*, meaning that the *Kli* is bigger than the light.

When the *Kelim* are corrected with the aim to bestow, they will receive all the abundance that was in the thought of creation, and the *Kli* will not be cancelled, since the cancellation extends from the oppositeness of form, and what is written in *Akudim*, that the *Kli* was cancelled although it was through a *Masach* [screen], which is the meaning of "in order to bestow."

## 700- Covering and Revealing

"When Israel do the Creator's will, their work is done by others." "Work" means the work on qualities (*Berachot* 35b). When one does the Creator's will, he sees no place that he should correct. But then the Creator makes for him the wings, which are a cover, and then he has a place where he needs to work in order to reveal the place and reveal the lack. In other words, the Creator does this work for him, revealing to him the lack.

## 701- Confidence

Confidence depends on faith. One who believes that his friend is very wealthy and generous is confident that he will give him what he asks. If he hesitates, meaning he is uncertain that he will satisfy his need, it is a sign that his faith is incomplete. Thus, the confidence testifies to the measure of faith.

## 702- From the Depths I Have Called You, Lord – 2

"From the depths I have called You, Lord." Therefore, one should pray from the lowest place. When one prays that the Creator will satisfy his needs, he must try to see how he is deep in the earth, that he is immersed in earthliness, and for this he must pray.

But when people pray for luxuries, meaning that they are actually fine but they would like some more, but do not know or see that they are at the bottom of Sheol [underworld], which is called the deepest that can be. And this is "for You hear the prayer of every mouth," whether a person is decent or not.

# 703- Miketz [After]

Rabbi Shimon said, "Until that event happened to Joseph, he was not called 'righteous.' Once he kept that covenant, he was called 'righteous' ... And what happened in the pit before, they moved away from it, and it is written, 'and they hurriedly brought him out of the pit,' he was removed from it and was crowned in a well of living water."

He interprets in the *Sulam* [Ladder commentary on *The Zohar*] that this should not be perplexing because through this act, he was rewarded with being called a "righteous." Thus, why did they place him in the prisoners' dungeon? He replies that he was initially in the pit because through it he ascended to kingship. It is written, "and they hurriedly brought him out of the pit," meaning he moved away from it, from the *Klipa* [shell/peel], and was crowned with a well of living water, which is the *Shechina* [Divinity] (*The Zohar*, *Miketz*, Item 35).

We should ask why it was necessary to first be in prison, which is called *Klipa* [shell/peel], in order to ascend to *Kedusha* [holiness]. As soon as he was called "righteous," by that deed, he should have entered the *Kedusha*. And yet, we see that Joseph was in the pit twice—1) by his brothers, as it is written, "And they threw him in the pit," 2) by the chief cook, as it is written, "and they hurriedly brought him out of the pit."

We should say that a pit means prison, that it is a person being under the control of the evil inclination, when one is incarcerated by it and cannot emerge from its authority.

By observing the *Mitzva* [commandment] of honoring the father, Joseph saw through the illumination of the *Mitzva* that he was in prison, since during the darkness it is impossible to see the truth. But that was only through his brothers, who are Israelis. That is, he saw that he was walking in the path of the Creator, but the reason that makes him work is the environment, that he is in an Israeli environment.

It follows that he was incarcerated by the environment, meaning had to engage in Torah and work because of the environment. When a person is rewarded with greater light, he sees the truth, that he is not in the prison of Israel, but he is truly in the hands of the *Klipa*.

The fact that he was called "righteous" because of the deed, at that time he saw that it was Potiphar who placed him in prison and saw that it was a real *Klipa*. At that time, there is room for prayer that the Creator will deliver him from prison.

The more one sees that he needs the Creator's help not for luxuries but for necessities, the more genuine is the prayer. Therefore, it is accepted above and the Creator delivers a person from imprisonment and is rewarded with being among the recipients of the face of the *Shechina*.

This is the meaning of the words of *The Zohar*, "And what happened in the pit before was removed in a well of living water," as it is written in the *Sulam*, "and they hurriedly brought him out of the pit," meaning he moved away from this *Klipa* and was crowned in a well of living water, which is the *Shechina*.

# 704- Why Was the Torah Given to Israel

"Why was the Torah given to Israel? Because they are fierce." RASHI interpreted, because Israel are fierce, they were given the Torah, which wanes the strength and subdues their hearts (*Masechet Beitza* 25).

We should understand the following:

1) This implies that the Torah was not given to the nations of the world because they are not fierce, and therefore have no need for the Torah.

2) After the Torah, they will no longer be on the same degree as the nations of the world.

We should say that "foreigner" means working for oneself, and "Israel" means that one is serving the Creator. When one wants to be Israel, he sees that he is fierce in both attributes and views, which are fiercely against the *Kedusha* [holiness]. This is why they were given the Torah.

But one who works for his own benefit is regarded as a foreigner. At that time, his attributes are not against the *Kedusha* and are not fierce, so they have no need for the Torah, which wanes their strength, meaning the power of lusts. "Subdues their hearts" means that all the desires surrender before the *Kedusha* because the light of the Torah reforms him, and then he feels the greatness of the Creator and receives the strength to subdue his qualities.

But when one works for oneself, he cannot see that he has bad attributes and views because for one's own sake, the body gives strength to work and does not show him any lack in the work.

# 705- *Impudence*

"Impudence, even toward the heaven, it is enjoyable" (Sanhedrin 105a).

Commentary: When one feels that what he is praying, for the Creator to grant him his wishes, is impudence on his part, since he is not worthy of the Creator's help, it is enjoyable (beneficial), and his prayer is answered. But when he feels that he deserves something, he is not given what he asks, for there is no person who is so virtuous that we can say that for his actions, he deserves the Creator's help.

## 706- By the Sweat of Your Brow

"And God said, 'Let the earth put forth grass... fruit trees bearing fruit after their kind.'" RASHI interpreted "fruit tree, that the taste of the tree will be as that of the fruit. But she [the earth] did not do so. Rather, 'And the earth put forth... fruit bearing tree,' and not a 'fruit tree.' For this reason, when Adam was cursed for his iniquity, she, too, was mentioned for hers."

"And to Adam He said ... 'Cursed is the ground because of you; in sadness you will eat of it all the days of your life; thorns and thistles will it grow for you, and you will eat the grass of the field.'" "Rabbi Yehoshua Ben Levi said, 'When the Creator said to Adam, 'Thorns and thistles will it grow for you,' his eyes teared. He said to Him: 'Master of the world, will I and my donkey eat off the same manger?' When He told him 'By the sweat of your brow you will eat bread,' his mind was eased'" (*Pesachim* 118a).

1) How can it be that the earth would transgress against the will of the Creator? Can it choose?

2) Why was she not punished for her iniquity right away, but He waited with the curse until after the sin of the tree of knowledge?

3) Why did he say that he and his donkey will eat from the same manger? Is it appropriate to say to the Creator that he wants better food? After all, our sages said, "Therefore, man was created after the creation of all the animals so that if he wants to boast, he will be told, 'The mosquito came before you.'" We should ask what this comes to teach us in day-to-day life.

The tree that bears fruit: We see that a thought yields an action, and the action should be like the thought, since the act that a person does is fine, and there is nothing to add to it. Even if he is the righteous of the generation, he will still not place *Tefillin* on his right hand. However, in the thought there is a difference between people.

It is the Creator's wish that the taste of the tree will be as that of the fruit, that the thought will be as complete as the act. Man is the tree of the field. Hence, he gave a hint in the land to know how man should behave. For this reason, the earth showed that the thought will not be as the act, meaning that it will be *Lo Lishma* [not for Her sake].

For this reason, afterward, *Adam HaRishon* came and sinned, meaning *Lo Lishma*, and was punished for this. That punishment should also be in the earth, so the man will see that the punishment was insinuated. Hence, precisely after the sin, when Adam was cursed, the earth was punished. Therefore, the earth does not have a choice, but such was the will of the Creator, that she would symbolize the shape of the man, and that she would symbolize the punishment.

Nachmanides writes that everything is in the form of unification; hence, the curse is also for correction.

Also, the matter of "thorn and thistle" means that he is not worthy of enjoying, that the taste of *Mitzvot* [commandments] *Lo Lishma* [not for Her sake] is as that of thorns and thistles, but all the flavor will be in corporeality, like the donkey.

"By the sweat of your brow you will eat bread," meaning through repentance.

# 707- A Treasure of Fear of Heaven

All the Creator has in His treasury is a treasure of fear of heaven, as was said, "The fear of God is His treasure."

We should ask, But there is no fear in Him, so how can it be said that He has such a treasure?

A treasure means something outside of a person, meaning there is the person and he has a treasure; these are two things. Also, we should say here as in, "The Torah and Israel and the Creator are one." But fear of heaven means something outside of him, meaning two things. This means that the Creator has a treasure of fear of heaven.

## 708- The Prayer of the Righteous

"The Creator craves the prayer of the righteous." A prayer is specifically where there is a lack, since one who prays discovers that he has a lack. The lack is the *Kli* [vessel] that can hold the abundance within it, so as not to lose what he is given, since according to the importance that one feels from the matter, to that extent he tries to keep the present.

This is the meaning of "Who is a fool? He who loses what he is given" because he does not value the gift. It is written, "Better a wise and poor child than an old and foolish king who no longer knows how to be careful." Hence, the prayer and the yearning fashion the importance for him. For this reason, the Creator craves the prayer of the righteous.

## 709- Education

There are two aspects to education: 1) the practice, 2) the intention.

For example, when the father educates his son and tells him that it is forbidden to steal, the child hears about a practice. Afterward, the child asks about the intention in the matter, meaning why it is forbidden to steal, since he likes his friend's object and he wants to have it, but his father prevents him from stealing. At that time, the child asks, "Tell me, why is it forbidden to steal?"

If the child's mind is still not sufficiently developed, his father tells him that there is the police, and they catch thieves and put them in jail. So the child asks, "What is jail?"

Then he is told that there he cannot speak to whomever he wants, eat what he wants, or play where he wants, but he is limited in every way, and it is very painful. Therefore, although he will enjoy it if he steals the object, the pleasure is not worth it compared to the suffering he will feel when he is placed in jail...

# 710- Three Generations, Three Lines

Someone who he, his son, and his son's son achieved the Torah, the Torah never ceases from them, as was said, "will not depart from your mouth," etc.

We should ask about it, since we see that there are three generations of achievers of the Torah, yet the fourth generation no longer achieves the Torah. By intimation, we should interpret that three generations means three lines, since one who has been rewarded with the middle line is guaranteed that the Torah will not depart from him, since all the cessations he had had were in order to come to the middle line.

# 711- There Has Never Risen a Prophet Like Moses

There has never risen a prophet like Moses, but a sage did rise (end of *Yalkut HaReuveni*).

We should ask about this, since the whole Torah is named after Moses. We can say that Moses comprises all the discernments, as it is written in several places that Moses is the quality of *Netzah*, and also the quality of *Daat*. However, we always consider his own degree and not what he contains. That is, even if he has all the qualities, still, whichever quality he uses, the Torah (says) about this that with respect to prophecy, he was the greatest.

Also, there is the quality of Moses, which is the quality of the "faithful shepherd," meaning the quality of faith, which is *Hassadim* [mercies]. I heard from Baal HaSulam about the verse, "And Moses approached the mist and they did not approach," meaning that Moses could even endure* the mist, as it is written, "And Moses approached the mist" and attained the name of God because he excelled in that quality.

This is why Moses is called "the faithful shepherd" and "illuminating mirror," meaning that he always illuminated. It was said about this, "He is trusted in all My house." This is the quality of Moses.

However, in Moses there were also the quality of Solomon and the quality of Joseph, as it is written, "And Moses took Joseph's bones." This is what it means that they were all said to Moses in Sinai. This is also what it means that Moses is tantamount to 600,000, meaning that he included all of them. But when we regard the merit of Moses, it is his unique degree called "the quality of Moses."

Also, concerning what our sages said concerning fear in regard to Moses, "a small matter," since the essence of Moses is a higher quality, but he certainly contained all the qualities. And concerning what is written in *The Zohar*, that the quality of *Hochma* [wisdom] was higher than Moses, it means that they walked in a quality that is higher than Moses' because Moses had no personal interest in going there.

*There, and to attain His Godliness. But they will not approach, meaning where there was a mist, they had no access to Godliness.

# 712- *Desire and Intellect*

Desire and intellect: The desire is the essence, the ruler, and it has many servants at its disposal, such as a counselor called "intellect," and slaves that execute, called "hands and legs," and eyes and ears and nose, etc.

Although the intellect is smart and the desire is not smart, the desire is still the ruler. This is like a rich man who has several businesses around the world. In each business, he has great executives, skillful overseers, and adept lawyers at the disposal of the managers.

He died, leaving the inheritance to his son, who is still a child and does not know about negotiations, and for anything he wants to know or do, he must consult with the overseers and the lawyers at his service. Nevertheless, that child is the real owner and not the managers and overseers. So is the desire with respect to the mind.

# 713- One Who Walks along the Way

"Rabbi Yehoshua Ben Levi said, 'One who walks along the way without company should engage in Torah, as was said, 'For they are a graceful accompaniment'" (*Iruvin* 54). We should understand what it means that we need company when we set out on the road. To interpret this in ethics, "the road" means "the path of the Creator," and "company" means *Dvekut* [adhesion], as it is written, "Now this time my husband will accompany."

It tells us that one who walks on the path of the Creator and does not have *Dvekut*, the advice is that he should engage in Torah, since the reason he has no *Dvekut* is that he still has evil in his heart. When he engages in Torah, the light in it reforms him, and then he will be rewarded with *Dvekut*.

# 714- Torah of *Hesed* [Mercy/Grace]

"Rabbi Elazar said, 'Why is it written, 'She opened her mouth with wisdom and the Torah [law] of mercy was on her tongue'? Is there Torah of mercy and Torah that is not of mercy? Torah *Lishma* [for Her sake] is Torah of mercy. *Lo Lishma* [not for Her sake] is Torah that is not of mercy. It is said, 'Torah to teach is Torah of mercy; not to teach is Torah that is not of mercy'" (*Sukkah* 49b).

*Hesed* means bestowal for the sake of the Creator. "To teach" means to teach the body, as in "I have created the evil inclination; I have created the Torah as a spice."

# 715- Concerning Preparation for a Fast

Sorrow and joy, fear and love are all offshoots, consequences of various reasons, yet they are not the source.

Hence, when we want to expand and increase the result, meaning the sorrow and the joy, the sorrow itself, or the joy or the love cannot expand them. Rather, it is the reasons that must be expanded, and then the outcome of the cause will expand, as well.

This is similar to a person who has many numbers but he does not add them all together into one sum. For example, he has five ones but he does not add them up, making it five.

If I want to expand and increase the sum total, it is impossible. Instead, I must add details, and then I get the bigger sum, since the sum is a result of the details. Hence, if one adds in the reason, there is an addition in the sum total.

Likewise, one who wants to expand the love and the fear and the sorrow and the joy, meaning regards the thing he had and which was taken away from him, to the extent of the importance of the matter that he had, so grows the sorrow that he does not have it. Hence, when he wants to increase the sorrow, he should increase the preciousness and importance of the thing he lost.

# 716- Concerning Pride

"Anyone who is proud, says the Creator, 'He and I cannot dwell in the same abode.'"

A place of lack is specifically if there are walls to the place of lack, and then that lack is regarded as a *Kli* [vessel]. A lack that has no walls is not regarded as a *Kli*, as the space of the world is not going to be filled. Rather, according to the size of the walls, the part of the lack of the world enters there.

Through the walls in which there is the lack, it will be filled. Thus, although a person does not taste a flavor in Torah and *Mitzvot* [commandments], it is drawn through his engagement in Torah and *Mitzvot*. Thus, to the extent of the lack that is there, it is going to be filled.

But when a person engages in Torah and *Mitzvot*, and the Torah and *Mitzvot* bring him to wholeness, he covers the lack that the Torah and *Mitzvot* should bring him. Moreover, he regards himself as a complete person. It follows that he has no place that can be filled. It was said about this, "Anyone who is proud, says the Creator, 'He and I cannot dwell in the same abode,'" since he is not making a place.

This is the meaning of "From *Lo Lishma* [not for Her sake] we come to *Lishma* [for Her sake]." But while one is in *Lo Lishma* and regards himself as a whole person, there is no place where *Lishma* can help him because he has no lack.

# 717- Voice and Speech

"Voice" means the feeling that one is in the quality of "animate," but without any clothing in the intellect.

"Speech" means that the feeling dresses in the intellect. This is called "speaking."

Naturally, these things that are called "innovations in the Torah," meaning with respect to the Torah that brings him toward the Creator, each time new things are renewed in him with respect to nearing the Creator.

## 718- Anyone Who Mourns Jerusalem

Shabbat Hazon [the Sabbath preceding the 9th of Av] is a preparation for Shabbat Nachamu [the 1st Sabbath after the 9th of Av], as it is written, "Anyone who mourns Jerusalem is rewarded with seeing the consolation of Jerusalem." "Anyone who aches with the public is rewarded with seeing the consolation of the public."

"Mourning" means that he is looking at himself to see how much the Temple has been ruined, meaning that anything of *Kedusha* [holiness] was ruined and cannot be built. That is, in everything where one sees self-benefit, he is willing to build. But where he sees that there will not be self-benefit, but only for the sake of *Kedusha*, he has no power to make any movement for the sake of building the *Kedusha*.

## 719- And Judah Approached Him – 2

"And Judah approached him and said, 'My lord, may your servant please speak a word in my lord's ears, and do not be angry,'" etc. RASHI interpreted, "You learn from this that he spoke to him harshly."

We should ask what this means for Judah, since in the beginning he said, "We are my lord's slaves, both we and the one in whose possession the cup has been found." He replied to them, "The man in whose possession the cup has been found, he shall be my slave; but as for you, go up in peace." But why does he deserve to be spoken harshly to if he was lenient in judging them? That is, he said, "We are all slaves, including Benjamin," and he said that he settles for the least, that only Benjamin is enough for him.

Joseph's question, 1) Why did you steal the cup? Certainly not for money, since you brought me back the money that is in your pouches...

# 720- He Who Adds Knowledge, Adds Pain

We see that when a person is in *Katnut* [smallness/infancy], before he grows up, he draws vitality and pleasure from every single thing. Anything he encounters excites him and elicits from him good, when he loves the object and yearns to play with it, or bad, when he is afraid of the object and steers clear from it.

He grows through those two and expands and ascends higher and higher until within a short time—some seventeen or twenty years—he grows up and becomes a tall tree of about 1.60-1.80 meters [5'4" - 6'].

Then, once he has grown up, when he has obtained the quality of *Daat* [knowledge] and can measure each and every thing, whether he should receive it or move away from it, and even when it is worthwhile to receive it and he already wants it, he must still move away from it due to external causes, where as a child he did not have any external enslavement and he did what his heart desired.

Naturally, it is hard for him to find life and pleasure, for not everything can he bring closer. On the contrary, he must push away most things, since reason makes him think that those things do not become his personality. Thus, he becomes deficient of bread, and when he grows up, the tree can no longer spread to the length and to the width, but he is happy just to be able to endure and not lose what he already had.

When he was little, he wanted and desired everything, meaning that he could derive vitality and pleasure from anything. This is why we see that children always want new things, and before he obtains anything, he plays all kinds of tricks—whether asking or shouting—only to be given that object. But as soon as he gets the object, he throws it and wants new things.

But when he grows up, he criticizes every passion whether it is worth toiling for or should he give it up.

In truth, it is not worth toiling for anything corporeal. Hence, when he begins to think about them, he promptly has no *Kli* [vessel] for work; therefore, he does not continue with them. Thus, from where will he take vitality so he can grow?

Just as a tree needs new foods every day and without it, it dries up and dies, so man must receive corporeal nourishment in order to satisfy his corporeality. And also, he must satisfy his spirituality.

It therefore follows that the more his reason grows, the more he needs spirituality. And then, "he adds pain," since it is hard for him to always obtain such precious foods like spiritual nourishment.

And even when some intellectual thing comes to him, and he thinks that he is playing with this thing, as soon as he begins to examine with his mind, he does not always succeed in absorbing in the mind everything he saw and heard because he already has the power of criticism.

And the more his criticism grows, the more he is tormented because he becomes enslaved to his intellect, meaning he cannot receive anything before his intellect permits him, for without its consent he is forbidden to do anything. It follows that the more the intellect grows, the more the criticism grows. Thus, he who adds knowledge, adds pain.

At that time, it is hard for him to obtain nourishment because man has a mutual agreement with the mind that he is forbidden to do anything without its consent, and when one breaches this agreement, the reason promptly puts an end to its partnership with the man and departs.

Perhaps this is what our sages implied by the words, "There is none who is richer than a pig, and there is none who is poorer than a dog." That is, in *Katnut*, he always repeats his actions because he has no criticism. That is, even if he already decided that he must not do such things, he still repeats what he forbade. He is always rich, meaning that inferior food can always be found for sale in the market.

This is not so with a dog. When a person has a dog, meaning he pays attention to everything, as our sages said, "The righteous, their hearts are given to them," meaning that they have a heart, as it is written, "And every wise-hearted," etc., for then he cannot derive pleasure and abundance from anything, but rather everything must be calculated in advance, and then he decides.

It is possible that this is what was implied by "Bread is not for the wise," meaning that they are poor because they cannot derive pleasure from anything, for they have limitation on everything, since they must be criticized.

# 721- The *Segula* of Torah and *Mitzvot*

There is a *Segula* [power/cure] in Torah and *Mitzvot* [commandments] that if he learns with this intention, although his heart disagrees with it, and all that he does with this intention is against his will and heart, yet through compulsory work, he is rewarded with inverting his desire from self-love to love of others.

We should understand what is written, that it is harder to attain the concept of bestowal upon others as this is against nature. Nevertheless, through the power of Torah and *Mitzvot* in order to bestow, we can be rewarded with inverting our nature into aiming to bestow.

There is a question: When one is immersed in the nature of self-love, how can he engage in Torah and *Mitzvot* in order to bestow, since he has no desire or ability whatsoever to do anything unless it is for his own sake? Thus, how can one be educated into engaging in Torah and *Mitzvot* in order to bestow?

We should say that although man's nature is only self-love, and that which is against it is hard for him to do, to the point that all his organs go against him, but there is the matter of coercion, meaning that when he engages in Torah and *Mitzvot*, he learns against his will, meaning that he wants it to be only for the sake of the Creator, and then he learns and thinks only about things that speak of the matter of bestowal.

And although the body disagrees, through the labor in which he exerts himself, forcing his body to work with this intention, although his heart's desire disagrees with this intention, the light in it reforms him.

## 722- Action and Thought

There is a difference between action and thought. A person does not control the thought, meaning he cannot chase away a thought if the thought is in his mind. But with an action, he can do or not do the action, since on action, there is the matter of coercion, that he can overcome the act.

Hence, when one does a good deed, the Creator gives him a good intention and thought to be on the act, if he wants it. This means that he yearns for a good thought but cannot overcome the thought and the intention.

This is the meaning of "I will bless you in everything you do," when the Creator sends a blessing on the act, for blessing pertains to a place where one's hand does not reach. There, a blessing is pertinent, and this was said about the intention.

## 723- Tzimtzum

Tzimtzum Aleph [first restriction] is called "private Providence," and Tzimtzum Bet [second restriction] is Providence of reward and punishment. Through raising MAN, the light of AB from before Tzimtzum Bet illuminates.

As for *Malchut*, it is a rule that we do not speak of any *Sefira* but only of *Malchut*, since there is no light without a *Kli* [vessel]. That is, we do not speak of light without a *Kli* because all that is spoken of is what the *Kli* attains, for we cannot speak of that which we do not attain.

## 724- Balak Saw

"And Balak Ben Tzipor saw," etc. We should understand why "Moab feared," since it is written, "Do not harass Moab."

The Hatam Sofer explains, as Maimonides wrote in eight chapters, that the Creator strengthened the heart of Egypt and the heart of Sihon in order to avenge the transgressions they had committed, not that that were done now, for this, since the Creator is the one who strengthened and hardened their hearts against their own good, so how would they be punished for it?

Balak knew that Israel would not go against him, since they were warned, "Do not harass Moab." However, he feared that the Creator would strengthen his heart until he begins to afflict them with wicked afflictions, and then they would have permission to go against him. This is why he said that he saw and understood what Israel did to Sihon, meaning that his heart was made strong, and also that they took over Egypt, meaning also, as said above, "And he feared from the people."

## 725- Man's Soul Will Teach Him

8 Elul, Tav-Shin-Zayin, August 24, 1947

"Man's soul will teach him." The whole Torah is learned primarily for the purpose of the soul, meaning for those who have been rewarded with a soul. And yet, they must yearn and search words of Torah or other sages in order to learn from them new things that the predecessors invented in their innovations in their teachings.

This will make it easy for them to climb up the rungs because they will be carried by them.

However, there is a discernment in the Torah that must not be revealed, since each soul must make its own scrutiny and not that another will scrutinize the degree. Hence, before they make the scrutiny themselves, they must not reveal the words of Torah. For this reason, the sages tend to hide many things.

Besides, there is great benefit to the souls when they can receive from the innovations in the Torah of predecessors. This is why it is written, "Man's soul will teach him" how and what to receive and be assisted by innovations in the Torah.

## 726- Going on the Road

"Going on the road" means that first he was at home and was used to Torah and Mitzvot [commandments], and there, it was a habit for him. But now when he goes on the road, he diminishes what he had from when he went by habit. Then he is promised that he need not be afraid, but on the contrary, he will even have more.

## 727- The Most Important Is the Environment

"And choose life." The most important is the environment. Man is always in an environment and necessarily follows them. Hence, if one is immersed in thoughts of Abaye and Raba, he is necessarily influenced by them. But if, for a brief moment, he places his thoughts on a different matter during the study, meaning thinks about something related to corporeal matters, he is necessarily immediately placed in a corporeal environment. This means that he begins to yearn for desires that the environment obligates him.

Also, concerning Abaye and Raba, if he regards them merely as great scholars, he will only be able to yearn for erudition. But if he regards them as sages with attainment, he will yearn for attainments.

## 728- Faith – 2

"Rabbi Tarfon says, 'The day is short and the work is plentiful; the workers are lazy and the reward is ample, and the landlord presses'" (*Avot*, Chapter 2, *Mishnah* 15). That is, when one believes that there is a landlord, that there is no capital without a leader, and when he fully recognizes that there is a landlord, he feels the pressure. It is as though a person is in a sealed house where there is no air, he feels the pressure and does all that he can, to the point of giving his life, in order to get air, since he says, "If I get no air I'll die anyhow."

Likewise, if one believes that there is a landlord to the world, he feels the pressure to obtain the air of *Kedusha* [holiness], since otherwise he sees that he is dead, and he does all that he can to obtain air of *Kedusha*. It therefore follows that only the landlord presses. That is, when he believes that there is a landlord, it makes him feel the pressure and the need for air of *Kedusha*.

At that time, he sees that the day is short, the work is plentiful, and the workers are lazy. He also sees that the reward is ample, meaning that it is a wonderful pleasure to adhere to Him, more than all the pleasures of this world. He feels that not only is the pleasure so intense, but that it is impossible to live without it.

This is also the meaning of "If you learned plenty of Torah, you are given ample reward, and you can trust your landlord to pay you for your work. Know that the righteous are given their reward in the future."

## 729- This World Is Sanctified by Man

According to the literal meaning, all the matters of this world are bodily matters, and man's deficiencies, to be dust from the earth. One who wants to be pious cannot, unless he abstains from the pleasures as much as he can and does not enjoy except that which he must for his survival, and then he will be pious, turning away from evil, and with that act he will remain good because it is only the necessity in order to live.

According to the way of Kabbalah, the acts themselves return to being good and high corrections. And since he prepared the high desire, the matters of this world that a person uses for one's own need and pleasure become sanctified.

## 730- Nicer than Gold

Words of Torah: 1) They are holy. 2) They are sublime. 3) They are sweet, as it is written, "Nicer than gold and from much fine gold, and sweeter than honey" (*The Zohar*, Part 3, 149 [in Hebrew]).

We need to understand these three phrases. *The Zohar* advises that we should learn in order for it to bring *Kedusha* [holiness] to a person. This is the meaning of "The words of the Torah are holy." The *Kedusha* that a person wants is in order to achieve *Dvekut* [adhesion], meaning to bestow, called "an ascent," as Baal HaSulam said, that an ascent means *Hizdakchut* [cleansing]. This is the meaning of the words, "They are sublime."

At that time, we taste the sweetness of the Torah in it. This is why it is written, "They are sweet." Otherwise, when we learn Torah, it is utterly tasteless, and as one comes, so one leaves, and he does not know what is required of him, and does not know what is written in it. He does not agree with "You shall not commit adultery," meaning the quality of the heart and the quality of slander. It is written in it, "You shall not commit murder"; he does not agree. Thus, which ... he will have when I learn.

Rather, "We will do and we will hear," and this is the meaning of overcoming.

# 731- Charity for the Poor

Portion BaHar, Iyar, Tav-Shin-Yod-Het, May 1958, Sunderland, UK

Portion, *BaHar* [In the Mount (Leviticus 25:1-Leviticus 26:2)]: "If a countryman of yours becomes poor and his means with regard to you falter, then you are to sustain him." RASHI interprets, do not let him decline and fall, and it will be difficult to raise him. Rather, strengthen him from the time when his hand weakens. What is this like? Like a load on the donkey. While it is on the donkey, one grabs it and helps it stand. If it falls to the ground, five will not raise it to its feet.

It is written in *Midrash Rabbah*, "Happy is he who makes the poor wise; in the day of affliction, the Lord will save him." There are five interpretations here: 1) Aba Bar Yirmiah said in the name of Rabbi Meir: "It is the one who crowns the good inclination over the evil inclination." 2) Isi said, "It is one who gives a penny to a poor." 3) Rabbi Yochanan said, "One who buries a 'dead *Mitzva* [commandment].'" 4) Our great sages say: "It is one who runs away from the kingship." 5) Rav Huna said, "It is one who visits the sick."

We should understand the following:

1) Why is everyone straying from the literal? It is written "poor," and they interpret the words as "crowning the good inclination over the evil inclination" and "burying the 'dead *Mitzva*,'" and "running away from kingship," and "visiting the sick."

2) What is the connection to "If a countryman of yours becomes poor"?

First, we must know whom the verse calls "poor."

There is a verse in Ecclesiastes (9): "There was a small city with few men in it, and a great king came to it, surrounded it ... and found in it a poor and wise man. But the wisdom of the poor man is despised and his words are not heeded." RASHI, in the name of *Midrash Agadah*: "A small city is the body. 'Few men' are man's organs. 'A great king' is the evil inclination, whose organs all feel it."

It follows that the meager and the poor and indigent is called "the good inclination." Since his words are not heeded, the verse, "Happy is he who makes the poor wise; in the day of affliction, the Lord will save him," is said in this regard.

It is also said there in the *Midrash*, "More than the landlord does for the poor, the poor does for the landlord, for so said Rut to Naomi, 'The name of the man with whom I did today is Boaz.' It is not written 'he did,' but rather 'I did.' She said to her, 'I did many good deeds with him today for the penny he had given me.'"

Now we can understand the above *Midrash* [treatise]: Since a poor man is called "the good inclination," for this reason, Aba Bar Yirmiah said in the name of Rabbi Meir, "It is the one who crowns the good inclination over the evil inclination," and Isi comes to interpret how and with what we can crown the good inclination over the evil inclination.

He said, "It is by giving a penny to a poor," through the power of charity, as our sages said, "Charity saves from death."

Rabbi Yochanan came and interpreted that through it, he will be rewarded with burying a "dead *Mitzva*" [someone who died but no one sees to his proper burial], meaning the evil inclination, for "The wicked in their lives are called 'dead,'" and we are commanded to bury the evil inclination.

Our great sages interpret this further: By this he saves himself from the kingship, meaning from the great king called "evil inclination."

Rav Huna interprets further, that by this he can come to visit the sick, since the soul is regarded as sick, as it is written, "for I am lovesick" (Song of Songs 2). In other words, the good inclination has love for the Creator to the point of sickness, except the evil inclination does not let one feel it. Yet, everyone is rewarded by giving a penny to the poor, since the merit of charity is so great.

## 732- Before the Face of the Menorah

Sivan, Tav-Shin-Yod-Het, June 1958

"Before the face of the *Menorah* [Temple lamp], the seven candles will illuminate." RASHI interpreted that it is so it will not be said that He needs its light.

The Gemara asks (*Shabbat* [Sabbath] 22b), "Does He need light? After all, all forty years that Israel walked in the desert, they walked only by the light of the *Shechina* [Divinity]. Rather, it is a testimony to the people of the world that the *Shechina* dwells in Israel. What is a testimony? Rav said, 'It is a western candle, which places in it oil such as the measure of the others, and from it he would light, and in it he would conclude.'"

The *Tosfot* there: "Why did it take forty years? Forever does the whole world walk by the light of the Creator."

We should ask, What fool is there in the world who would think such a folly? After all, we believe that it is one of the thirteen tenets, that the Creator is not a body, so how can it be said that He needs its light, to the point that we must bring evidence to this, "After all, all forty years ... they walked only by His light"?

Also, the question of the *Tosfot*, that the whole world follows the light of the Creator, and without this evidence, how will anyone think that the Creator needs corporeal light?

The thing is that the purpose of creation is to do good to His creations. In order not to have the bread of shame, we must perform the acts of *Mitzvot* [commandments] so it will be in order to bestow. The *Menorah* implies the light of the Creator that is revealed to the lower ones, and we, through an awakening from below, awaken the awakening from above, as it is written in *The Zohar*.

This is the meaning of "so it will not be said that He needs its light," meaning that the Creator cannot give us abundance without any good deeds, as it is written, "If you are right, what will you give him?" Rather, all the work of the *Mitzvot* is to cleanse Israel through them. Hence, the making of the *Menorah* comes to imply our work, meaning so that we will qualify ourselves so our intention is to bestow.

This is what the Gemara says, "Does He need its light?" implying that the Creator cannot give us abundance. But when Israel walked in the desert forty years and ate manna, which is called "bread from the sky," it was only an awakening from above. Nevertheless, they had abundance, since they were called "a generation of knowledge," a title that no other generation has.

The *Tosfot* asked, "The whole world follows the light of the Creator." That is, in the world in general, both Jews and the nations of the world are nourished without any awakening, indicating that the Creator does not need the performance of *Mitzvot*. Rather, it is only for us, meaning to qualify ourselves so our intention is only to bestow. At that time, there will be wholeness in the reception of the benefit of the Creator.

This is as was said, it is testimony to the people of the world that the *Shechina* dwells in Israel, meaning that the Creator truly is the operator, as it is written, that He alone does and will do all the deeds, even without our work. And Rav interprets, "What is a testimony? It is a western candle, which places in it oil such as the measure of the others, and from it he would light, and in it he would conclude."

In other words, if the Creator's benefit depends specifically on our actions, meaning to the extent of our work, then the western candle should not have illuminated more than the measure of oil that is placed in it, meaning to the extent of our work. This shows that the Creator can give not according to the measure of our actions, but that He is almighty, and all our actions are only in order to obtain completeness in the King's gifts.

The matter of the "western candle" is the meaning of *Shechina* in the west, which is the matter of faith, which is evening and not day. This is considered that the *Shechina* is regarded as poor, and this is the meaning of charity to the poor. This is the meaning of "Give tithing [a tenth of your income] so you will get rich," meaning that in that sense, there is no need for man's work, for He can complement his profits, since usually, according to one's work, so is one's reward. But in the case of charity, there is a testimony that here the Creator helps without an awakening from below.

# 733- In Its Time, I Will Hasten It

"Rabbi Alexandrai said, 'Rabbi Yehoshua Ben Levi Rami said, 'It is written, 'In its time,' and it is written, 'I will hasten it,' 'I the Lord will hasten it in its time.' If they are rewarded, I will hasten it. If they are not rewarded, in its time'"" (Sanhedrin 98).

In other words, the whole world must achieve the complete benefit and receive the purpose of creation, which is to do good to His creations, and the whole world must feel the good in the manner of "happy are you in this world."

Rabbi Eliezer says, "If Israel repent, they are redeemed. If not, they are not redeemed." Rabbi Yehoshua said to him, "If they do not repent, are they not redeemed? But the Creator places over them a king whose decrees are as harsh as Haman's, Israel repent, and He reforms them" (Sanhedrin 97b).

We should interpret the meaning of "a king whose decrees are as harsh as Haman's." This means that everything that the evil inclination sentences them to do, they will feel in these actions a flavor that is as harsh and as bitter as Haman. Then, since man cannot live without pleasure, everyone will pursue the Torah and *Mitzvot* [commandments] and will feel there the real pleasure.

This is the meaning of "And Israel repent," since they will not feel any flavor of pleasure in corporeal matters. It follows that the flavor that is as harsh as Haman, which they will feel in corporeal things, will compel them to reform.

# 734- *The Western Candle*

Why does the western candle indicate that the *Shechina* [Divinity] dwells in Israel? *Erev* [evening] means darkness, the opposite of day, for "day" implies seeing, when we see what we are doing. Conversely, evening is called "darkness," which means that we do not see what we are doing.

Faith means to believe in the Creator and observe Torah and *Mitzvot* [commandments], when we do not see what we are doing because in corporeal things, when a person does something, he immediately sees the benefit. But with Torah and *Mitzvot*, he exerts but does not see.

# 735- On the Day When the Tabernacle Was Established

"'On the day when the Tabernacle was established,' Abaye said that there is no building of the Temple at night, as was said, 'On the day when the Tabernacle was established.' It is established in the day, and it is not established in the night" (*Shavuot* [Feast of Weeks] 15b).

We should ask, If the building of the Temple is so vital to the people of Israel, why would it not be built at night, as well? It is written in *Midrash Rabbah* about the verse, "If a countryman of yours becomes poor and his means with regard to you falter, then you are to sustain him." This is as it is written, "Happy is he who makes the poor wise; in the day of affliction, the Lord will save him." There are five literal interpretations to the meaning of "poor."

We find that the verse interprets "poor" in Ecclesiastes (9), "There was a small city with few men in it, and a great king came and surrounded it ... and found in it a poor and wise man. But the wisdom of the poor man is despised and his words are not heeded." RASHI, in the name of *Midrash Agadah*, and there in the *Midrash*, "More than the landlord does for the poor, the poor does for the landlord, for so said Rut to Naomi, 'The name of the man with whom I did today is Boaz.' It is not written 'he did,' but rather 'I did.' She said to her, 'I did many good deeds with him today for the penny he had given me.'"

It follows from all the above that through the *Mitzva* [commandment] of charity, we are rewarded with the governance of the good inclination over the evil inclination, and the Torah is eternity, for man must build the Temple, and the building is through bricks and mortar, and each and every brick must be connected with silt, as this is what holds the bricks.

When a person performs a *Mitzva* and yearns to perform another *Mitzva*, by this the first *Mitzva* connects to the second, and a strong building is made. But when a person does and regrets, he thereby separates the first brick from the second.

The meaning of "day" is that we see what we are doing, and "night" means that it is dark and we do not see what we are doing. When a person believes and works with joy, it is considered "day," and then the *Mitzvot* [commandments] connect and become a building where there is the *Shechina* [Divinity]. But at night, when he is not joyful because he does not see what he is doing, this cannot yield a building.

There are two discernments about the matter of "night": 1) We do not see. 2) He is not in high spirits but is as depressed as one who cannot make a living the way he wants to, and then the world grows dark on him.

At that time, through faith, he is rewarded with joy.

# 736- *The Diminution of the Moon*

*Tammuz*, July

"One goat for a sin offering to the Lord." The Creator said, "Bring atonement for Me, for diminishing the moon."

We should ask the following:

1) How can it be said that He seemingly sinned by the diminution, that the Creator did?

2) If this is ostensibly a sin, why did He do it?

3) How does the offering of the beginning of the month atone for the sin?

4) In the "Sanctification of the Moon" [a prayer at the beginning of each month], we say, "May the blemish of the moon be filled." Why does He care if the moon remains with its blemish? Does the moon have feelings and will feel deficient if it has a flaw?

5) There is a rule that one who sins brings atonement. So why should Israel bring atonement for Him?

Our sages said, "Israel count by the moon, and the nations of the world count by the sun."

The "sun" implies knowing, as our sages said (*Rish Pesachim*) about the verse, "The murderer arises at dawn," "If the matter is as clear as light to you," meaning clear knowledge is called "sun," but if you are doubtful about it, like the night, for the governance of the moon is at night, implying *Malchut*, which governs at night, as explained in the writings of the ARI. This means that where reason has doubts, this is where the quality of faith belongs.

Prior to the diminution, the kingdom of heaven was in *Gadlut* [greatness/adulthood]. That is, in a state of *Gadlut*, a person can feel a wonderful and infinite pleasure when he accepts the kingdom of heaven, and then it would be easy to walk in the ways of the Creator.

But after the diminution of the moon, there was the matter that when one accepts the burden of the kingdom of heaven, he feels a burden without pleasure. However, he receives the faith as a force, "as an ox to the burden and as a donkey to the load."

It follows that through the diminution, there is a place where man will come to sin, meaning not want to assume the burden of the kingdom of heaven. It brings to man the spirit of heresy, and the Creator made it so that there will not be the bread of shame, since precisely where the pleasure is not revealed, it is possible to work not in order to receive reward. It follows that the diminution is a correction that enables man to achieve *Lishma* [for Her sake], meaning not to please oneself but for the sake of the Creator.

It therefore follows that the diminution is the cause and the reason that man can achieve the eternal wholeness. But along with this correction, there is another cause, meaning it causes man to be able to sin because through the diminution of *Malchut*, the person veers off from the work of accepting the burden of the kingdom of heaven. This is seemingly the same as not placing an obstacle before a blind person, since a person might trip because of this diminution.

It turns out that it is as though he sinned and needs atonement. This atonement can come specifically through Israel. However, the matter of the offering is about bringing himself near the Creator, where nearness means equivalence of form. That is, when a person takes upon himself the burden of the kingdom of heaven not in order to receive reward, but in order to bestow, this is called "nearing," and this is the meaning of an offering to the Creator.

It follows that by taking upon himself the work in order to bestow, the person corrects the sin of the diminution of the moon, since the diminution of *Malchut* causes man to be able to come to work in order to bestow.

It follows that it becomes revealed that from the beginning, this was not a sin. On the contrary, it brought man to be able to achieve wholeness, since were it not for the diminution there would be no way for man to be able to work in bestowal. At that time, we see that there was no sin here, but on the contrary, a correction that yields wholeness.

It follows that precisely Israel can bring atonement. That is, with the offering, the sin passes. This is why we pray, "May the blemish of the moon be filled," meaning that *Malchut* will illuminate in wholeness, and this is done through the correction of our actions in work in order to bestow.

# 737- *A Eulogy*

Our sages said, "Anyone who cries over a *Kosher* [fitting/worthy] person, all his iniquities are pardoned." "Rabbi Shimon Ben Pazi said, 'Rabbi Yehoshua Ben Levi said in the name of Bar Kafra, 'Anyone who sheds tears over a *Kosher* person, the Creator counts them and places them in His treasury, as was said, 'You have counted my wanderings; put my tears in Your bottle.'"'" (*Shabbat* [Sabbath] 105b).

We should ask what is the praise that the Creator places in His treasury. The MAHARSHA interpreted about this, that none is more important to the Creator as one who has fear of heaven, since the Creator has nothing in His treasury but fear of heaven.

The verse says, "What does the Lord your God ask of you? Only fear." It follows that one who has fear of heaven no longer lacks anything, and you find that all his iniquities are forgiven.

Also, we find in *Berachot* (p 6b): "Rabbi Helbo said, 'Rav Huna said, 'Anyone who has fear of heaven, his words are heard.'"

We should ask about this, since we see several people with fear of heaven who are admonishing but there is no desire to heed their words. However, we should interpret that this pertains to the person himself, since before one has fear of heaven, man's organs do not want to obey him, as it is written, "The wisdom of the poor man is despised and his words are not heeded." But when he has fear of heaven, all the organs surrender before him, as it is written, "And all the peoples of the earth shall see that the name of the Lord is called upon you and they shall fear you," since man's organs are called "the peoples of the earth."

Hence, there is no dispute with what the other one said. Rather, they are all of one view, that one who sheds tears over a *Kosher* person is rewarded with fear of heaven. Yet, we should understand why this is so. Our sages said, "One hour of repentance and good deeds in this world is better than all the life of the next world," since when a person dies he becomes free from the *Mitzvot* [commandments].

It follows that if we share in the loss that the person lost, that now he cannot do good deeds, and this matter touches our soul to the point where we shed tears, this causes us to truly take upon ourselves the burden of the kingdom of heaven and to be rewarded with pardoning of iniquities.

By the deceased causing people to come to fear of heaven, it is a great correction for him, since now the deceased cannot do good deeds. But if, by his demise, he causes people to repent, it follows that the deceased has made a great correction called "good deeds." This is the meaning of "Anyone who makes the collective cleansed, sin does not come through him."

## 738- A Covenant of Salt

30 *Shevat, Tav-Shin-Yod-Tet*, February 8, 1959, Tiberias, at a meal celebrating the completion of part six

"On all your offerings you shall offer salt." This is the covenant of the salt, which is a covenant against the intellect, for when one takes good things from one's friend, they should make a covenant.

A covenant is needed precisely when each one has demands and complaints against the other, and they might come into anger and separation. At that time, the covenant they made obligates them to maintain the love and unity between them, for the rule is that whenever someone wishes to hurt the other, they have a cure—to remember the covenant that they had made between them.

This obligates them to maintain the love and peace. This is the meaning of "On all your offerings you shall offer salt," meaning that any nearing in the work of the Creator should be through a covenant of salt, as this is the whole foundation.

## 739- Two Types of Attire

External attire, which is on the body, is called "clothes of *Hassidim* [pious followers]." An external attire, which is the body, is worn over man's internality, which are thought and desire, regarded as "mind and heart."

The first quality is called "externality of externality," and the second is called "internality of externality," which is the joy and awakening that one does at the time of Torah and *Mitzvot* [commandments].

In general, "externality" is that which is revealed outward, meaning that which one's friend can see. In the externality, there is a grip to the external ones. Hence, it is forbidden for man to dress up more than his surroundings, since the power of honor and pride latch on to the garments and keep within man the power of honor and pride, and do not give man the strength to be able to climb up the path that leads to work for the sake of the Creator.

# 740- Three Gifts

"And the Lord your God will keep for you the covenant and the *Hesed* [mercy/grace/]." The Creator gave three good gifts to Israel: merciful ones, shy, and alms givers, as it is written, "will keep ... and the *Hesed* [also means alms giving]" (*Jerusalem Talmud*, Chapter 1, 45).

"Merciful ones" means being givers, as in "As He is merciful, so you are merciful."

Shy means that one feels shame when he receives in order to please himself. Otherwise, he will not have a need to work in order to bestow.

Almsgiving is also the quality of bestowal, for mercy pertains to charity, when one has mercy on the poor. This pertains specifically to a time when one does not feel the taste of Torah and *Mitzvot* [commandments], and then it is considered that all his actions are regarded as *Tzedakah* [righteousness/charity].

Almsgiving pertains to both poor and rich, meaning that even if one already has a taste in Torah and *Mitzvot*, now he must exert because afterward, he will repay him equally for his labor, except he must believe him that he will pay him back later.

It therefore follows that there are two kinds of work:

1) Charity, when one exerts in Torah and *Mitzvot* and does not want any reward other than his work.

2) When he feels that he is not giving charity, meaning he is certain that afterward, he will receive reward for the labor.

Here, the main lack is in time, meaning that if one receives immediately following the labor, it is regarded as selling and buying, the way one gives money and receives something in return. But when one must wait for the return, as in "To do them today and to receive the reward for them tomorrow," this is already regarded as a loan and as almsgiving.

Man should acquire for himself these three gifts, meaning to try to be liked by the Creator so He will give him the three above-mentioned gifts, since usually, when someone is liked, he is given gifts.

However, before one is rewarded with gifts, a person is inherently incapable of doing such deeds, and only through upbringing can one come to the above.

However, this is not wholeness, since what one receives through rearing is regarded as without intention, meaning he does not have a choice, namely that everything he does is compulsory, and what is compulsory is neither condemned nor praised, since one does not do out of one's own volition, but because of a desire that the environment induced within him. If he were in a different environment, he would do completely different things than what he does.

However, when we receive this gift from the Creator, this is called "wholeness," and then he does everything out of his own volition.

## 741- To Cleanse the People
### 1957-1958

There is a story that Turnus Rufus the Evil [an epithet given to Quintus Tineius Rufus, a provincial governor under the Roman Empire] asked Rabbi Akiva, "What deeds are good, those of the Creator or those of man?" He said to him, "Those of man." He replied, "But the sky and the earth, can man do the likes of them?" Rabbi Akiva replied, "Do not speak to me of something that is above people, that they do not control. Rather, speak of things that are found in people."

He said to him, "Why do you circumcise"? He replied, "I knew that you would ask me this. This is why I told you in advance that the works of man are better than the works of the Creator." Rabbi Akiva brought him stalks of wheat and cakes, and said to him, "These are the works of the Creator, and these are the works of man; are these not nicer than the stalks?"

Turnus Rufus said to him, "If He desires circumcision, why does the baby not emerge circumcised from its mother's womb?" Rabbi Akiva replied, "And why does its umbilical cord come out with it, and it is hanging by its belly and its mother cuts it? And what you are saying, why does it not emerge circumcised, it is because the Creator gave the *Mitzvot* [commandments] to Israel in order to purify them, as David said about it, 'Every word of God is pure'" (Psalms 18).

To clarify the argument between them, we should first present the reason for the creation of the worlds. It is explained that the purpose of creation is to do good to His creations. It is known that "There is no thought or perception in Him whatsoever," and all that is spoken of is "By Your actions, we know You," as it is written in the *Poem of Glory*, "They picture You not as You are, and they depict You by Your actions."

It therefore follows that what is written, that the reason for the creation of the worlds is to do good to His creations is because all those who said that this is the reason because they attained that this is so, this is regarded as "By Your actions, we know You." That is, they saw that the world is filled with abundant pleasures and there is no place for agony, so they determined and said that this is the reason.

They also attained that there is a discernment of reward and punishment. That is, sometimes the abundance stops, and sometimes it increases. So they also determined the reason that causes reward and punishment.

Where there is *Dvekut* [adhesion], meaning equivalence of qualities, the abundance increases more each time. Conversely, self-love— called "will to receive for oneself"—awakens, the fountain dries up, and the abundance stops. Then, they knew that we must go specifically with the quality of equivalence of qualities.

And why is this the Creator's will? They said that it is in order not to have the bread of shame, so there will be completeness in the benefit that the Creator gives. That is, when a person takes for himself, he is always limited, meaning that the delight and pleasure he received is enough for him.

But if he receives because of the Giver, since the Giver wants to give indefinitely, the lower one will not feel satisfied in the middle of his work and say that the spiritual possessions he has acquired are enough for him, and he does not need to extend anymore, since here the receiver is not taken into account. Rather, the only measurement to how much pleasure he will receive is the Giver.

Hence, in order to satisfy the desire of the Giver, he draws down more abundance each day, for otherwise he is regarded as cutting the plantations, unable to extend more fruits to the world.

And the reason he cannot is that there is no need for it. For this reason, in order to have completeness in the benefit, which is that His abundance will be drawn more each time and he will not be ashamed while drawing the abundance, but on the contrary, he will know that each time he continues to draw, he does his Maker's will, as it is written, "More than the calf wants to suckle, the cow wants to nurse," in order for one to achieve this degree, to have an intention to bestow, we were given the opposite work than what seems to us from the purpose of creation.

Because of the purpose of creation to do good to His creations, we were imprinted with a desire to receive for ourselves. When we want to work in a manner of bestowal, meaning not to receive, it is against the acts of the Creator, who wants us to receive the abundance, yet we reject all the pleasures.

This is what Turnus Rufus the Evil asked. That is, he asked the question of the wicked one who argued, "What is this work for you?" From the perspective of the Creator, the goal is to do good to His creations, meaning to use the will to receive, since the Creator's wish is for the lower ones to receive the delight and pleasure, as this is called "to do good to His creations."

But the created beings came and took action, and inverted the will to receive, wanting to work only with the desire to bestow. This is called "works of flesh and blood," since the works of the Creator is that the lower ones will receive, and you say that it is forbidden to receive for oneself.

This is why Rabbi Akiva replied to him that the works of flesh and blood is finer.

He asked, "But the sky and the earth, can man do the likes of them?" He meant that if the works of flesh and blood are better, then it is worthwhile to walk on a path that is opposite from the purpose of creation. So he asked, the sky and the earth, which are the upper worlds, the upper light, regarded as the filling that fills the *Kelim* [vessels], can man create the upper light, called abundance and pleasure?

Rabbi Akiva said to him, "Do not speak to me of something that is above people, that they do not control." In other words, the light and the pleasure precede creation. This is called "existence from existence," and we have no control, but only from creation onward, meaning from the will to receive, onward.

In other words, I can speak only from the perspective of the *Kelim* and not from that of the lights. From the perspective of the *Kelim*, our *Kelim* are finer than the *Kelim* that extend from the Creator, which are called "will to receive."

Then he asked Rabbi Akiva from the perspective of the *Kelim*, meaning "Why do you circumcise?" Circumcision is regarded as removal of the foreskin. Baal HaSulam explained that the foreskin means the will to receive. Although man was created to have a will to receive, he should still work to remove from him the will to receive and take instead a desire to bestow.

This is called "the works of flesh and blood," as it is written, "Everything is in the hands of heaven but the fear of heaven." Baal

HaSulam explained that from the Creator comes only the filling of the lack, meaning that the Creator gives abundance and pleasure called "to do good to His creations." But fear of heaven, called "correction," meaning not to receive so he will not be separated from the equivalence of form called *Dvekut*, this comes from the lower one.

It is explained that the light of the corrections, called "light of *Hassadim* [mercies]," comes only through an awakening of the lower one that wants to correct itself to also be a giver like the root.

Rabbi Akiva brought him stalks of wheat and cakes, by which we see that the work of people is finer. He showed him that the stalks of wheat are in the cakes, too, but now the stalks have been corrected by adding work on the part of the lower one, which is reception in order to bestow.

Then he asked, If He wants circumcision, why does the newborn not emerge circumcised from its mother's womb? That is, why is man not created with a desire to bestow to begin with, but must make great efforts in order to acquire the possession of bestowal?

Rabbi Akiva replied, "And why does its umbilical cord come out with it, and it is hanging by its belly and its mother cuts it?" In other words, even to acquire the desire to receive, the work of the lower ones is required, since before he emerged into the world, the fetus was its mother's thigh, eating what its mother eats, meaning he had no authority in and of himself, not even on the will to receive. Rather, he was denied of any choice and everything was as an upper force upon him.

When he emerges to the world and comes into his own, through cutting his connection with the mother, the blocked opens, and the opened becomes blocked, for only through corporeal food for thirteen years he acquires the will to receive in full.

Afterward comes the cutting of the foreskin, which is an act in order to acquire the desire to bestow. This is the meaning of the words, that the Creator gave the *Mitzvot* [commandments] only in order to cleanse them by them.

## 742- The Lord's Revenge Against Midian

"And the Lord spoke to Moses, saying 'Avenge the vengeance of the children of Israel on the Midianites' ... and Moses spoke to the people, saying ... to execute the Lord's vengeance on Midian." The famous question is why Moses changed the words of the Creator.

The thing is that the purpose of the Creator is to do good to His creations, meaning that Israel will receive the benefit. It follows that the vengeance against Midian is for the sake of Israel, for by this, Israel would receive the benefit.

But Moses, as the leader of Israel, instructs them the way of the work, that all the vengeance against Midian should be for the sake of the Creator, meaning to bestow upon the Creator and not for self-reception. Otherwise, they will become remote from the Creator and will not be rewarded with any wholeness. This is why Moses changed and told the people, "to execute the Lord's vengeance on Midian."

## 743- The Journeys of the Children of Israel

"These are the journeys of the children of Israel, who went out from the land of Egypt with their armies, by the hand of Moses and Aaron. And Moses wrote their places of exit to their journeys according to the word of the Lord, and these are their journeys according to their places of exit."

The interpreters ask why at one time, it is written "their places of exit," and at another time, "their journeys," before.

Exiting means exiting from the King's palace, when one feels a deficiency in that degree, and is therefore compelled to journey to another place where there is more wholeness. It follows that the exit is the cause of the journey, for were it not for this, he would not move from place to place. It follows that first he feels the lack, and then he makes the journey. This is why it is written, "their places of exit" before "their journeys."

Sometimes, a person does not feel any deficiency in the degree that he is in, and yet must make a journey. But afterward, during the journey, he recognizes that his previous state was deficient. This is why it is written, "These are their journeys according to their places of exit," meaning that the journey had to take place first, and then the feeling of deficiency.

This is perplexing: If he does not feel a deficiency, who forces him to make the journey? This is the meaning of "according to the word of the Lord," when a person himself cannot feel it. This is what it means that every person needs a teacher to guide him. A person must believe that everything that the teacher tells him is "according to the word of the Lord." Otherwise, the person will not agree to leave his place and take upon himself the jiggles of the road.

And the order of exits and journeys is precisely through Moses and Aaron, since Moses is called "the King's best man," and Aaron is the queen's best man. Aaron fixes the candles, meaning the correction of the qualities, so they are able and worthy of receiving the abundance. This is regarded as preparing the assembly of Israel. Moses is considered the drawing of the light of Torah, which is the meaning of being the King's best man, meaning extension of the abundance into the corrected *Kelim* [vessels].

# 744- Abraham's Gemstones

Our sages said, "There was a gemstone hanging from Abraham's neck, and any sick person who saw it was promptly healed."

We should interpret that "sick" means that his head aches. Each one thought that specifically through knowledge they could achieve wholeness, meaning that they could answer all the questions. But once they saw that on Abraham's neck was a place of vital breath, that he has *Margaliot* [gemstones], meaning a *Meragel* [spy], and with this quality he received the faith, this is why everyone could be healed.

## 745- *When the Creator Came*

It is written in *Midrash Rabbah* (*BaMidbar* 1): "Another thing: 'Why did they say, 'My people have descended; we will no longer come to You' (Jeremiah 2)? What is 'descended,' as it is said, 'for he oppresses the whole of the riverbank'' (1 Kings 5). He was told, 'You gave us a Temple but drove out Your *Shechina* [Divinity] from it, and what do you ask of us so we will no longer come to you?'

"He said to them, 'I wish I were in the desert now; where are all the miracles I did for you?' This is why he says, 'Who would give me a lodge in the desert, that I might leave my people,' where I was glorified, as was said, 'Let the desert and its cities raise their voices, courtyards where Kedar dwells, let the inhabitants of rocks sing aloud.'"

There is an allegory about a president who went into a country, and the countryfolk saw him and fled from him. He went into another one, and they fled from him. He went into a desolate city and was greeted and glorified. The president said, "This is the best city of all the country. Here I will build a handsome throne; here I will live."

Thus, when the Creator came to the sea, it fled from Him, as was said, "The sea saw and fled," and "the mountains danced as deer." He went into the desert of desolation, He was greeted and praised, as was said, "'Let the desert and its cities raise their voices, courtyards where Kedar dwells, let the inhabitants of rocks sing aloud.' This city is better for Me than all the countries; in it I will build a Temple and live in it." They began to rejoice that the Creator dwells in it, as was said, "The desert and aridity will rejoice."

## 746- Concerning the Fetus

When a newborn emerges into the world, he must acquire two forces: 1) the power of the will to receive, 2) the power of the desire to bestow.

For this purpose, the newborn was given two cuts:

1) The cutting of the connection from the infant's navel to the mother, by which the mouth opens and the navel closes.

When the mouth is closed, he still has no authority of his own. Rather, he eats what his mother eats, since eating means scrutinies, and through the scrutinies one buys vitality. There is vitality of *Kedusha* [holiness], and there is the opposite. This is called "the upper force." Hence, by cutting the connection with the mother, he acquires the will to receive. However, he does not acquire the will to receive at once, but over thirteen years.

2) The second cutting is done on the eighth day after his birth. Through this cutting, which is the removal of the foreskin, he acquires the desire to bestow. The time of acquiring this possession begins from thirteen years of age onward.

The difference between acquiring the will to receive and acquiring the desire to bestow is that the will to receive is regarded as an act of the Creator, from the perspective of the purpose of creation, namely to do good to His creations. Hence, a person must first acquire this possession, since this is the primary goal.

Acquiring the desire to bestow is called "the work of flesh and blood," since this is only corrections on the part of the lower ones, since the lower ones do not want the bread of shame, called separation from *Dvekut* [adhesion] with the Creator.

For this reason, a person must correct himself to have a *Kli* [vessel] ready to receive the purpose of creation, to do good to His creations. As long as one does not reach the benefit called "happy are you in this world," as it is written, "You will see your world in your life," it is a sign that he still has not qualified himself not to be separated when receiving the pleasure. Therefore, this is still not regarded as "happy are you in this world."

For this reason, the acquisition of the desire to bestow is called acts of flesh and blood, which is an act on the part of the lower one, as it is written, "Everything is in the hands of heaven but the fear of heaven." It is as Baal HaSulam interpreted, the Creator can only give, and the giving of the Creator adds only love.

But not receiving is man's work. This is as in "The Tannas, 'What is given from heaven is not taken back.'" That is, the Creator only gives and does not receive. Hence, the act of bestowal of the lower one is called "the work of flesh and blood." This is what Turnus Rufus the Evil asked, Which deeds were finer, those of the Creator or those of flesh and blood?

# 747- In the Heat of the Day

"In the heat of the day." Our sages said that the Creator took out the sun from her sheath so as not to trouble him with guests (*Baba Metzia* 86b).

In other words, after he was circumcised, he was rewarded with the revelation of the Creator to him, which is regarded as the Creator emerging from concealment to revelation. This is called "taking out the sun from her sheath." Naturally, he had no room for work on choice, which is called *Tircha* [labor], meaning that Terah [Abraham's father]—which is trouble and labor—begot Abraham.

# 748- To Renew the Reason

Any woman who does not have matrimony, not on it and not on others, the offspring is like her. And which one is it? The offspring of a handmaid and a foreigner. How do we know about a Canaanite handmaid? Rav Huna said, "Kara said, 'Sit here with the donkey,' with he who is like a donkey," meaning that matrimony does not apply. "Her offspring is like her," as Kara said, "The woman and her children will be to her master."

How do we know about a foreigner? Kara said, "You will not marry with them," meaning that matrimony does not apply. How do we know that her offspring is like her? Rabbi Yochanan said in the name of Rashbi, as Kara said, "For they will turn your sons away from following Me." Your son who comes from an Israelite is considered your son, and your son who comes from an idol-worshipper is not considered your son, but her son (*Kidushin* 68).

We should understand this in ethics:

Matrimony means a man who is rewarded with *Kedusha* [holiness].

An offspring is understandings that help the work.

An Israelite is the *Shechina* [Divinity].

A handmaid and a foreigner are the *Sitra Achra* [other side].

A Canaanite handmaid means a *Klipa* [shell/peel] of the quality of "donkey," which is the heart.

A foreigner means the *Klipa* of an ox, which is the mind.

"The offspring is like her" means that the Torah and work, which are the understandings and feelings that one obtains through Torah and work are like her. In other words, they have no other value, but what applies to them is what applies to the intention, meaning the obligator. That is, if the reason that obligates one to engage in Torah and work, the reason is called "mother," who delivers the obligation to his engagement in Torah and work.

By this we should understand "Your son who comes from an Israelite." That is, if the reason that obligates her to work is the *Shechina*, it is pertinent to say "your son," for the above reason that the consequence always follows the cause.

Also, we should say that this applies during the preparation, too. That is, even though he has still not been rewarded with entering the *Kedusha*, but he wants to enter the *Kedusha*, at that time the reason, namely the desire to be rewarded with *Kedusha*, the quality of Israelite, and the result, namely the Torah and work that he does in order to be rewarded with *Kedusha*, is named after her.

It is likewise to the contrary: If the reason that obligates is the quality of idol-worship and a Canaanite handmaid, although he is still not attached to these *Klipot* [shells/peels], the Torah and work are already named after the *Klipot*.

Hence, one must always renew the reason, so the result will be named after the reason.

# 749- The Commandment of the Upper One

"What is the burden of the kingdom of heaven? It is like that ox on which a burden is placed at first, in order to elicit from it benefit to the world ... If it does not take it on itself first, it cannot work" (*The Zohar*, *BaHar*, Item 3, in the *Sulam* [Ladder commentary on *The Zohar*]).

We should say that before one takes upon oneself the burden called "above reason," which is the whole foundation, it is impossible to elicit good from him. In other words, it is impossible to be rewarded with the flavors of Torah and the flavors of *Mitzvot* [commandments], since otherwise, everything goes toward reception for oneself. For this reason, he can come to separation.

But when the whole foundation is only as a burden, he needs the flavors of Torah and *Mitzvot* only because "He who does not know the commandment of the upper one, how will he serve Him?" It follows that he does not need support for his work, since his entire work is built only on the burden. Hence, only then can he elicit benefit to the world, meaning to be rewarded with all the concealed benefit.

## 750- How Terrible Is This Place

"How terrible is this place? This must be the house of God."

When a person wants to come under the authority of *Kedusha* [holiness], he must take upon himself fear, for if there is no fear, there is no wisdom. That is, if the wisdom cannot bring him to fear, it is not wisdom.

But the fear should bring him to wisdom, too, since "The ignorant has no fear of sin," for if a person truly received the quality of fear in his heart and soul, it is not inevitable that he will not be rewarded with wisdom. Rather, it must be that the fear, too, is not in the true manner. Hence, one must always examine the weight between the two, so they will cling to one another.

## 751- Anyone in Whom There Is Fear of Heaven – 2

"Anyone in whom there is fear of heaven." To achieve fear of heaven is as in "around him it was very stormy."

What is fear of heaven? It is faith, so he will not sin, meaning self-reception. Afterward, we are rewarded with *Dvekut* [adhesion], when we are rewarded with the revelation of the secrets of the Torah.

Afterward, there is the quality of fear, when he is cleansed from the perspective of heaven, but the desire of the upper one. This is as in, "All my life I have regretted. Why? Since such was the thought." This is a degree of fear of heaven, meaning the taste of heaven.

## 752- Before I Was Circumcised – 2

"And he ran toward them." In the *Midrash*: "Abraham said, 'Before I was circumcised, passersby would come to me. Now that I am circumcised, they do not come.' The Creator said to him, 'Before you were circumcised, uncircumcised would come to you. Now, I and My entourage are revealed to you,' as it is written, 'And he lifted up,' 'And he saw.'"

We should ask in the manner of ethics, since the matter of the circumcision is the cutting of the *Lo Lishma* [not for Her sake], and only his work after the circumcision was *Lishma* [for Her sake]. There is a rule that where there are always ascents and descents, a person is called "walking" and not "standing."

This is what he asked, why, before he was circumcised, he always had ascents and descents. This is the meaning of the word *Ovrim* [passersby], from the word *Averah* [transgression], which is a descent, and *Shavim* [returning] meaning returning in *Teshuva* [repentance], would come to me, and he was busy all day with ascents and descents.

But now that he has been circumcised, he could not always be in a state of passing and returning. If he had a descent, he was in that state for a long time until he could pick himself up, while it should have been to the contrary.

The Creator told him that before he was circumcised, uncircumcised would come to him. Even when he repented and began the Torah and work, it was in a state of *Lo Lishma* [not for Her sake], for this reason (this is not very important).

You had many causes to repent and return to Torah and work. But now in *Lishma* [for Her sake], which is the truth, there is resistance from the evil inclination. Hence, it is inconsistent.

We should also say that he asked, Why before he was circumcised, he was in a state of work and choice, which is the quality of passing and returning, and now that he has been circumcised, he does not have the work of passing and returning?

He replied to this, "Previously, uncircumcised would come to you," meaning thoughts and desires of the uncircumcised, so that you would make a choice. This is in order for you to be rewarded with *Lishma*, meaning the instilling of the *Shechina* [Divinity]. But now that you have achieved this and there is no longer a need for choice, meaning that the previous work caused you to now be rewarded with rest. Terah begot Abraham.

## 753- *Concerning the Evil Inclination*

It is written in the books that the evil inclination itself is satisfied when it is defeated. There is an allegory in *The Zohar* about a king's son, etc.

We should interpret that it is known that the evil inclination is called "will to receive," and on that will to receive there was a *Tzimtzum* [restriction], meaning it does not receive anything because it is not given. But when a person defeats the evil inclination, meaning works in order to bestow, he receives all the delight and pleasure. It follows that the evil inclination itself is happy that he did not yield to it.

This is the meaning of "Anyone who chases honor, honor flees from him." In other words, if he runs from reception of pleasure, the pleasure chases him and he receives the pleasure in full. But if he chases the pleasure, the pleasure runs from him because of the *Tzimtzum* that was on the quality of reception. This is why it was said about the righteous, "Their reward is twofold," whereas the wicked, "Their misfortune is twofold."

This is why it was said about the wicked, "Their days are short and rife with anger," for even when they obtain a state of day, it promptly leaves them. Hence, they are angry about that. Conversely, the righteous are rewarded with long days, meaning that the illumination with which they have been rewarded does not depart from them.

# 754- *The Complaint of the Angels*

We should interpret concerning the angels, who said, "Give Your glory on the heaven."

Ostensibly, we should ask, Is the Torah a corporeal matter? If it is given below, can it not be above, as well? After all, the Torah should be given to both people and angels.

We should say that the complaint of the angels was that the Torah should be given to people who are in the quality of angels. This is the meaning of "Give Your glory on the heaven," meaning on one whose desire is solely for the sake of the Creator. But when a person is on the earth, meaning his desire and yearning are for earthliness, how is he related to the Torah?

To this He replied to them, "Is there evil inclination in you?" This is as our sages said, "I have created the evil inclination; I have created the Torah as a spice." But when the people of Israel are in the quality of angels, they have no need for the Torah.

It therefore follows that the Torah is needed mainly in order to reform us. That is, the Torah and *Mitzvot* [commandments] are in order to reform us, and this is precisely when we do have evil. This is when we need the Torah and *Mitzvot*, meaning that the Torah and *Mitzvot* are regarded as a *Segula* [cure/power/merit].

Only afterward, when they have been rewarded with purification, are they regarded as Israel, and then the Torah is considered an essence.

At that time, "The Torah, the Creator, and Israel are one." That is, after the repentance, he is called "Israel" because then he receives the Torah, which is one with the Creator. At that time, the Torah is called "the names of the Creator," and naturally, the Torah and the Creator are one with Israel, for only then is it called "Israel," when the Torah and the Creator are one with the Israel.

## 755- To Enjoy in Order to Bestow

Why is it permitted to enjoy when a person receives the pleasure in order to bestow? After all, why does he bestow? It is because he has pleasure. Therefore, he already has pleasure from bestowal, for if he did not have pleasure, he would not be able to bestow.

Even if we say that he is forcing himself, the question is why he is forcing himself. After all, this is also for a pleasure. And even if we say that he will obtain the fear of punishment, he will still enjoy not being punished. If he forces, since he wants to be rewarded with wholeness, it is also a pleasure.

## 756- A Deficiency from the Light

A deficiency, meaning a deficiency from the light, except the light was shining. But after the *Tzimtzum* [restriction], through the will to receive, a deficiency from the light was created. And yet, there was a *Tzimtzum* as an adornment.

## 757- Toil

*The Zohar, VaYechi*: "He did not see iniquity in Jacob and did not see toil in Israel." Yet, there is the quality of toil in Jacob nonetheless, but in Israel, it is even gone. A place where there is no iniquity because one engages in Torah and *Mitzvot* [commandments] is called "toil." That is, they engage in Torah, which is regarded as reward and punishment. This is the quality of Jacob, *Katnut* [smallness/infancy].

However, in Israel there is not even toil, meaning they do not see or feel that they are exerting. Rather, everything is in private Providence. At that time, they are in degrees, that "He alone does and will do all the deeds." Naturally, no toil is seen in them.

## 758- The Measure of Overcoming

"Man's inclination overcomes him every day, and unless the Creator helps him, he cannot overcome it." That is, the help that one demands is that only the Creator will help him, and not another force, meaning that he will truly have faith in the Creator. To the extent that he obtains faith, to that extent he overcomes his inclination.

This is the meaning of "He who comes to purify is aided." *The Zohar* interprets, With what? With a holy soul, where through this force he defeats his inclination.

## 759- Man as a Whole

As a whole, man consists of two discernments: 1) his own existence, 2) the existence of reality.

The existence of reality is divided into three discernments:

1) Necessity, without which reality would cease to be. For this, it is enough to eat a small slice of dry bread and one cup of cold water a day, sleep for a few hours with one's clothes still on, and on a bench, not even in a house, but in a field or in some cave during the rains to keep from getting wet. His clothes, too, can be nothing but patches over patches.

2) Behaving as ordinary middle-class, but not wanting to resemble the rich, who have many rooms, elegant furniture, fine paraphernalia, and nice clothes, and not wanting to eat and drink everything the way the rich are accustomed to eating and drinking.

3) There is a craving and demand in his body to resemble the rich. Although he cannot obtain what he wants, his eyes and heart are dedicated to it, and he waits and labors to obtain that—to be admitted into the class of the rich.

4) This one exists in all of the three previous discernments: If he has earned enough for today, he does not worry about tomorrow. Rather, each day is regarded as his entire life span.

Usually, people are concerned with satisfying their needs only for seventy years. But past one hundred and twenty years, a man is not concerned with his provision. Also, sometimes a person thinks that each day should be in his eyes as new, meaning as a new creation.

It is like reincarnation—that yesterday's person has incarnated into today's person and he must correct everything he did the day before, both in good debts or in merits, meaning whether he did *Mitzvot* [good deeds] or transgressions.

For example, if he took something from his friend, he must return it. And if he lent something to his friend, he should receive it from him, since collecting a debt is a *Mitzva* [singular of *Mitzvot*], so he must collect from his friend.

And now we will speak of love for the Creator. First, one must know that love is bought by actions. By giving his friends gifts, each gift that he gives to his friend is like an arrow and a bullet that makes a hole in his friend's heart. Although his friend's heart is like a stone, still, each bullet makes a hole. And from many holes, a hollow is created, and the love of the giver of the gifts enters in this place.

The warmth of the love draws to him his friend's sparks of love, and then the two loves weave into a garment of love that covers both of them. This means that one love surrounds and envelops them, and then they two become one person because the clothing that covers them is a single garment. Hence, both are cancelled.

It is a rule that anything new is exciting and entertaining. Hence, after one receives the garment of love from another, he enjoys only the love of the other and forgets about self-love. At that time, each of them begins to receive pleasure only from caring for his friend, and they cannot worry about themselves because one can labor only where he can receive pleasure.

Since he is enjoying love of others and receives pleasure specifically from that, he will take no pleasure in caring for himself. If there is no pleasure, there is no concern and no place for labor.

This is why you sometimes find in nature that when the love of others is exceptionally strong, one might commit suicide. Also, with love for the Creator, sometimes a person is willing to give up the above-mentioned third discernment for the love of the Creator. Afterwards, he is willing to concede the second discernment and then the first discernment, meaning all three discernments in the existence of reality.

But how can he cancel his own existence? The question is, "If his existence is cancelled, who will receive the love?" But the Creator grants love with the power to divert a person from the right path. In other words, he stops being rational and wants to be cancelled out from reality by the power of the love, and his rational mind has no strength to detain him.

Therefore, if we ask, "How can one come to such a state?" there is one answer to that: "Taste and see that the Lord is good." This is why nature necessitates annulment, even though one does not understand it rationally.

Now we can understand the verse, "And you shall love ... with all your heart and with all your soul and with all your might." "Your might" means the existence of reality, "Your soul" means his own existence, and "Your heart" is already a high degree, meaning with both your inclinations—the good inclination, as well as the evil inclination.

# 760- *The Material of the Soul*

Concerning the soul, which is a part of God above, the kabbalists compared it to a stone that is carved from a mountain. The question is, How can it be said that it is the same material as the mountain, for it is from His essence?

We should interpret that they mean that it is discerned as existence from existence. This is why they made a comparison to a stone from a mountain. The difference is that it is a part of the matter, which He divided, to be called a "soul." This is the will to receive, meaning that this part is called "Creation," meaning existence from absence.

Conversely, the light in it is regarded as existence from existence, but of course this "existence," which is received in the soul, already has its own form and changes between each soul. All this is done by the will to receive, and all the changing is according to the will to receive according to the corrections of the desire to bestow. But the filling in the soul, meaning the light and vitality that the soul obtains, is called "existence from existence."

# 761- Two Discernments in the *Kelim*

There are two discernments in the *Kelim* [vessels]: the part that they receive and the part that they give.

For example, the *Kli* [vessel] of *Bina* is regarded as having a little bit of reception, but it is enough to correct itself and create equivalence of form, that it wants to bestow. Hence, from the part of reception that exists in *Bina*, we say that *Malchut* is included in *Bina*, but not in the quality of bestowal. But upon the ascent of *Malchut* to *Bina*, *Malchut* is also included in the quality of bestowal.

# 762- Degrees of *Aviut*

What is the difference between *Aviut* [thickness] *Shoresh* [root], called *Salik BeRe'uta* [lit. Ascended in desire. (from Aramaic): wanted], and *Aviut* of *Behina Aleph* [first discernment], called *Histaklut Dak* [lit. thin looking]? It is that in *Aviut Shoresh*, the light of *Nefesh* is clothed, and in *Histaklut Dak*, the light of *Ruach* is extended.

# 763- Inverse Relation between Lights and Vessels

An explanation to what is written in several places, that anyone who receives, receives first in the *Sefira Keter*, and only the quality of *Nefesh*. When he corrects the *Kli* [vessel] of *Hochma*, he is rewarded with *Ruach* in the *Kli* of *Keter* and the *Nefesh* descends to the *Kli* of *Hochma*, and so forth, likewise. This is so because it is easier to correct the finer *Kli*, and subsequently the thicker quality.

We can understand this through a depiction. The finer *Kelim* [vessels] are regarded as the time when a person wears a *Talit* [prayer shawl] and *Tefillin* [phylacteries], and reads the *Shema* reading. Clearly, at that time it is easier for him to correct himself. At such a time we can say that he will be rewarded with *Nefesh*.

Afterward, when he learns Torah, he also has the strength to correct himself. On the path of correction, it follows that then he obtains the quality of *Nefesh*, too, but evidently, one who is fine during the learning is certainly more excited during the *Shema* reading. It follows that at that time, the quality of *Ruach* shines for him.

One who can correct himself while eating and drinking, too, the *Nefesh* shines in him, as well. During the learning, a greater illumination shines for him, the quality of *Ruach*, and during the *Shema* reading he has the quality of *Neshama*. If his thought is in *Dvekut* [adhesion] while he is speaking to people, he obtains the quality of *Nefesh*. Certainly, when he engages in matters of *Mitzva* [commandment], greater illuminations shine for him, as in the above manner.

If he is in *Dvekut* when he engages in commerce or during his work, as well, he obtains the quality of *Nefesh*. However, for such a person, during the *Shema* reading, the quality of *Yechida* shines for him, meaning that the illumination of *Yechida* causes him the quality of *Nefesh* in simplest things. It follows that he always receives the greater illumination into the quality of *Keter*, which is the finest *Kli*, and the thicker *Kelim* he corrects, the more his illumination grows.

## 764- The View of Kedusha

Our sages said, "I the Lord," Rabbah said about it, why is it written, "All the kings of the earth will thank You, Lord, for we heard the sayings of Your mouth" (Psalms 138)? It did not say, "the saying of Your mouth," but "the sayings of Your mouth." When the Creator said, "I, and you shall not have," etc., idol-worshippers said, "He is demanding for His own glory." When He said, "Honor your father and your mother," they rethought and admitted the first commandments (*Kidushin* 31a).

We should ask what they saw in His saying "Honor," to the point that it was worthwhile to rethink. By intimation, "your father" and "your mother" are *Hochma* and *Bina*, as it is written in *The Zohar*. First, they thought that since the whole basis of Judaism is faith above reason, they said that He was demanding for His own glory, meaning that only the lower ones would serve Him above reason, and He would give them nothing in return.

Faith above reason is called "complete bestowal." When He said "Honor," it means that man should honor *Hochma* and *Bina*, which is the Torah, called *Hochma-Bina-Daat*.

*Daat* [knowledge] is the quality that connects the two, as in "And Adam knew his wife, Eve."

We see that there are two manners of *Segol* [a Hebrew punctuation mark]:

1) *Segol* of *Nekudot*, where the connecting line is below [∴]

2) *Segol* of the quality of *Taamim*, where the connected quality is above [∴]

The meaning is that *Daat* means *Dvekut* [adhesion] and connection, which is called "the giving force," since man must achieve a degree of bestowal called "equivalence of form," as in, "As He is merciful, so you are merciful." The beginning of the work should be in faith, which is called "I, and you shall not have," which is above the intellect.

This is called "learning Torah *Lishma* [for Her sake]." Afterward, one is rewarded with the secrets of Torah being revealed to him, which are called *Hochma*, *Bina*, and then he must renew the faith once more. That is, he should not say, "Now I have a basis of *Hochma* and I can serve the Creator because I already have support."

Therefore, we must renew the faith once more, so we work even now without any basis. This is "reason below," called *Hochma-Bina-Daat*, and this is called "*Daat* of *Kedusha*."

# 765- He Who Learns Torah in Poverty

"He who learns Torah in poverty will eventually observe it in wealth." Our sages said, "There is none who is poor except in knowledge" (*Nedarim* 41). That is, precisely by learning and seeing that he does not understand, where the more he learns, the lower he finds himself to be, without stopping the learning but rather exerting to understand the true meaning, in the end, the Creator will send him true understanding and knowledge, and this is called "wealth."

This is why it is written that he will eventually observe it, meaning that the Torah will exist in him plentifully, meaning with true understanding and a clear mind.

Also, in the literal, when a person learns out of poverty, meaning that he is pressed on eating, drinking, and sleeping, he will eventually observe it in wealth. Therefore, the sign is that if we see someone who observes the Torah in wealth, he must have observed it first in poverty, and by this he was now rewarded with observing it in wealth.

## 766- The Ability to Receive

The ability to first establish reception in order to bestow, for because he is blind, it means that he does not see his illumination descending. Rather, precisely when one is in ascent, it follows that he is near the light of *Hochma*, where he will not have the power to provoke the person to want to extend into the quality of reception.

## 767- You Shall Make Holy Garments

"You shall make holy garments for Aaron your brother, for glory and for beauty." "Let your clothes be white all the time, and let not oil be lacking on your head" (Ecclesiastes).

The commandment of garments of priesthood was said in proximity. It is interpreted that "oil" implies *Daat* [knowledge] of the mind, so it will be pure and clean. This is the meaning of "pure olive oil." "Holy garments" imply the body, which is the clothing of the soul, to be done properly for honor and for glory (*Sefat Emet*).

We should say that the "mind" is wise disciples who engage in Torah. They are the ones who draw the light of Torah, which shines to the body. The body is the supporters of Torah. This is the meaning of "She is a tree of life to those who possess her, and her supporters are happy." The "soul" is called "learners of Torah." The body is called "supporters of Torah." Together, they are one man, since there cannot be a soul without a body, meaning a head without a body.

## 768- The Suckling of the Klipot

Concerning the matter that a suckling for the Klipot [shells/peels] was made, which are regarded as "very thin light."

"Mixing" means that there is no distinction between one who serves Him and one who does not serve Him.

"A righteous falls before a wicked" means that until we are rewarded with the fiftieth gate, called "repentance," all the degrees fall into the Klipa [sing. of Klipot]. This is the meaning of "When the benefit and holiness increase, their lives increase," since when a person is on the lowest degree of Kedusha [holiness], such as in Behina Aleph, and the Sitra Achra [other side] makes him sin, she takes that degree.

For example, if one already has an order in the work and he can make efforts and has illumination in that quality, when the Sitra Achra makes him sin, she takes that degree. In other words, she fastens this quality to herself, and a person can no longer attach this action to Kedusha. Instead, he has no other choice but to take a higher degree.

For example, he should muster more strength and make greater efforts because the previous measure is already flawed in him. It follows that she holds it so he cannot perform any Mitzvot [commandments] or act in Kedusha in this manner, so he must accept a higher servitude, which the Sitra Achra does not know that he is working in this manner. When he feels that he is above, she chases him and holds that degree, as in the first.

Therefore, our only choice is to go to an even higher level until we come to forty-nine gates of Tuma'a [impurity]. And then, "He has swallowed up riches and he will vomit it up, and God will expel them from his belly." That is, he takes all the powers that fell into her authority and connects them to Kedusha.

## 769- Merging of the Body

Man's nature is according to the merging of the body, as it is written in *The Zohar* that there are four elements called "fire, wind, water, and dust." This has nothing to do with the evil inclination.

It is known that it is impossible to change nature. However, man can use nature for things that bring correction to the world, meaning to use each attribute for something that brings correction to the world and not destruction to the world, similar to corporeal things applied in the corporeal world.

For example, it is known that fire is harmful. If there is a fire somewhere, the fire consumes and burns bodies and property. And yet, if we use fire where it is needed, then fire gives light at night, warms the house in the winter, and cooks, and so forth.

We see that even the most harmful thing, if it is used in a manner of correction, makes the world benefit from the fire instead of running away from it.

This rule applies to everything. It is like the rain (*Rosh Hashanah* 17). If a drop is sentenced to be a fool, and He did not say whether righteous or wicked, how can one be righteous if he is a fool?

1) Why was he sentenced to be a fool? It comes from the merging of elements.

2) Why did not everyone have a good merging, so they would be able to advance? Answer: In order to show that the Creator is not limited, that He can help only the good ones who have good qualities. Rather, He helps everyone, as it is written, "The Good Who Does Good to the bad and to the good."

# 770- The Difference between the Soul and the Body

A "soul" is when one receives in order to bestow. A "body" means when he receives only for himself.

A "soul" means that he is receiving in order to bestow, namely the attaining individual, who is regarded as the quality of "body." By receiving the quality of a soul from the worlds of *Kedusha* [holiness], he can invert the reception to be in order to bestow. At that time, it can be said that he is receiving from the quality of the soul, since all the things that are said in the upper worlds, and the names, meaning when they have their final form.

# 771- Walking

It is known that as long as one is alive, he is regarded as "walking," where through his engagement in Torah and *Mitzvot* [commandments] he "walks" each day from degree to degree. After his death, he is called "standing," since "The dead are free," etc. But Jacob is called "walking" even after his death, since Israel's whole engagement in Torah and *Mitzvot* in every generation succeeds for them because he bequeathed them the qualities.

This is the meaning of the words, "Jacob did not die." From the side of *Tifferet*, Jacob's death is complete. The doubter did not understand, and thought that it meant that he actually died, and said to him, "I demand the literal text."

There are two kinds of wise disciples: 1) those who sit and learn for themselves, 2) those who are rewarded and make the public worthy and teach Torah to others.

The difference between them is that the second kind walk from degree to degree after their death, as well. This is why there is the custom to be appointed on the death anniversary, since on that day he is judged, and through his father's engagement in Torah and Mitzvot, which he left after him in this world, or that he strengthens a wise disciple, there is an ascent to the soul of the parents. This is the meaning of the duty of the son to cleanse the father, and this is the meaning of his duty to honor him upon his death.

## 772- Writing a Book of Torah

Raba said, "Although his forefathers left him a book of Torah, he is commanded to write his own, as was said, 'And you, write this song for yourselves.'"

We should ask about it, for if he has a book of Torah from his forefathers, why does he need to write his own? We should interpret this by intimation, as it is written, "Write them on the tablet of your heart." This is what it means that although his forefathers wrote on the tablets of his heart, namely educated him in the way of Torah, he is commanded to write his own, meaning by himself.

## 773- The Difference between Torah and Ethics

The difference between Torah and ethics: "Ethics" is called "the correction of creation," which is the qualification of the Kelim [vessels]. "Torah," in the sense of the names of the Creator, is the purpose of creation. "His names" means names of abundance, such as names of corporeal pleasures.

## 774- It Is Good to Thank the Creator

4 *Kislev, Tav-Shin-Chaf-Hey,* November 4, 1964

"A psalm, a song ... it is good to thank the Lord." We should ask why it is good to thank specifically on Shabbat [Sabbath]. On the six workdays, it is the place of work, and then the prayer is relevant. But on Shabbat, which is regarded as *Shvita* [resting/cessation], when he rests from the work of the inclination, the work is in the manner of "It is good to thank the Lord."

Hence, one who is a wise disciple and feels rest from the inclination in the middle of the week, it is also "good to thank." This is the meaning of "A wise disciple is regarded as Shabbat."

## 775- The Thoughts of a Gentile and Those of Israel

"Israel" is one who engages in *Mitzvot* [commandments]. A "gentile" means idol-worship, the bad in him.

Israel's bad thought is that he engages in Torah and *Mitzvot* not for the sake of the Creator. Israel's good thought is that his thought is to engage for the sake of the Creator.

A gentile's bad thought means that he sees that he does not want to engage in Torah and *Mitzvot* because he has no faith. A thought that is Israel means that his thought is for the sake of the Creator. Yet, in fact, he does not have the aim for this, for the heart does not agree to this, and he thinks that the act of love is called "the feeling in the heart."

# 776- Still of *Kedusha*

Rosh Hashanah, 2 *Tishrey*, *Tav-Shin-Yod-Tet*, September 16, 1958

There is still of *Kedusha* [holiness], and there is vegetative, etc. The "still" is considered all those things that one receives by upbringing. "Vegetative" means that which a person takes upon himself, things he did not acquire through his rearing.

The difference is that there is no criticism whatsoever on all the things that man takes upon himself by rearing. Moreover, there could be two opposites in the same carrier, since there is no criticism. But when one takes upon oneself things that he did not receive by education, on those there is criticism and he cannot receive two opposites in the same carrier.

The reason is that every new thing that he is going to do, the question is, "Why am I doing it? Who obligates me, and what benefit will I get out of it?" Also, "For whose benefit am I doing it?" Only the intellect that obligates him to work can he do it. Otherwise, he suffices for what he received through education.

But then, when he receives new things, he needs faith. And to the contrary, only then is faith pertinent, since he already has criticism, there are always contradictions, and he cannot receive anything if not through the power of faith.

This is not so in the manner of education, when he has no criticism. At that time, he does not have much need for faith, since he is used to doing all those things by habit.

# 777- A Prayer for the Exile of the *Shechina*

What is the meaning of the prayer, that we should pray for the exile of the *Shechina* [Divinity]?

The *Sitra Achra* [other side], which is the quality of knowing and receiving, controls the *Shechina*, which is regarded as bestowal and faith. The Creator created the world in order to do good to His creations, and the lower ones can receive the benefit only in vessels of bestowal, which are regarded as eternal *Kelim* [vessels]. The upper light, which is eternal, cannot clothe in transient *Kelim*.

The lower ones, which are placed under the rule of the *Sitra Achra*, want specifically reception and knowledge, causing separation to the upper unification. This is regarded as having a foreskin on *Malchut*, and this foreskin separates ZA from *Malchut*, regarded as the unification between the Creator and His *Shechina*.

It follows that there is the sorrow of the *Shechina* because she is unable to unite with the Creator because of this foreskin, for the lower ones are gripping her and are not leaving her so she can part from *Malchut*. Hence, we must pray to the Creator to send illumination from above so the lower ones will want to cancel the foreskin and remove it from the quality of *Malchut*. This applies to the individual and to the collective.

Perhaps this is why we need the creation of the lower ones, where he wrote in the preface to *Panim Masbirot*, that from the perspective of the worlds, there are two states: the state of the first nine, regarded as vessels of bestowal, and *Malchut*, which is regarded as a *Kli* [vessel] for reception, from whom the *Klipot* [shells/peels] nurse. In spirituality, one does not mix with the other.

For this reason, there is the discernment of time for man, where until age thirteen he is under the governance of the *Klipot*, and from age thirteen onward he begins to obtain the first nine. At that time, because he consists of *Malchut* of reception, he can correct her so it will be reception in order to bestow, and then the verse, "The darkness will shine as light" will come true. This means that *Malchut* is called "reception and knowing." At that time, he inverts his *Kelim*. Conversely, if he consisted only of the first nine, he would not be able to correct anything.

This is why we need the work of the lower ones. This is the meaning of the Creator craving the prayer of the righteous, meaning those who pray and want to be righteous, meaning ask the Creator to help them invert the quality of Malchut to the quality of the upper nine.

## 778- *Pleasure Cancels the Mind*

Pleasure cancels the mind and does not let it think about life's purpose, whether he derives pleasure from spirituality or from corporeality. For this reason, when one wants to see if he is walking on the path of truth, he should not think about the pleasure he is in now.

Likewise, suffering causes him to lose his intellect, so his only concern is to get rid of the suffering he is in now.

Only dissatisfaction from the state he is in brings him to think about his life's purpose, and the mind begins to contemplate why he is living in this world and what he should achieve.

## 779- *Bless the Fruit of Your Womb*

"Bless the fruit of your womb." Rabbi Natan says, "How do we know that a woman's fruit of the womb is not blessed unless from the fruit of a man's womb, as was said, 'Bless the fruit of your womb'? It did not say, 'the fruit of her womb' but 'the fruit of your womb' [in male form in Hebrew]" (*Berachot* 11b).

A woman is called the "will to receive." The will to receive is blessed only from the man's fruit of the womb, for a man is called the "desire to bestow." In other words, to the extent that one works to bestow, to that extent he can receive pleasure. This is called "receiving in order to bestow."

## 780- And You, Write

"And you, write about the Jews as you see fit ... for a decree which is written in the name of the king and sealed with the king's signet ring may not be revoked."

Baal HaSulam said that in the decree of the law it was written to destroy, to kill all the Jews. But it did not write who would be the killers and who would be the killed. Hence, we can interpret that the nations will kill all the Jews. We can interpret "to destroy and kill all," meaning all the nations. And who would be killing them? The Jews, "And you, write," about the word "Jews," "as you see fit."

We should understand that the Torah was given to everyone to interpret according to his will, and this is called "choice."

## 781- The Way of the Baal Shem Tov

19 *Kislev, Tav-Shin-Chaf-Gimel*, December 5, 1964

The way of the Baal Shem Tov is that he set up a *Heder* [room for learning Torah], meaning gave lessons on becoming rabbis, and anyone who graduated from the *Heder* received the title Rabbi.

Rabbi means "teacher," meaning that one who teaches one's friend Torah is called a "rav." Before the Baal Shem Tov, the custom was to give the title Rabbi only to those who learned with their disciples the revealed Torah. The way of the Baal Shem Tov is to call by the name Rabbi also those who learn with their students the hidden Torah, since he established a seminary for teaching the hidden Torah.

Prior to the Baal Shem Tov, there were no seminaries dedicated to learning the hidden, and all the seminaries that were at that time were only for learning the revealed Torah. Anyone who yearned to learn the hidden had difficulty finding a teacher for this purpose. For this reason, many forces were lost because they did not find a place dedicated to it.

But after the Baal Shem Tov established a special seminary for the hidden Torah, all the wise disciples whose heart yearned to learn the Creator and whose soul yearned for the hidden Torah knew where to turn. By this, the disciples learning the hidden Torah proliferated.

We should understand the difference between the revealed Torah and the hidden Torah. "Revealed" means that which is revealed to all. This was said about the practice.

The practice of Mitzvot [commandments], as well as the words of the Torah and the prayers are also regarded as part of the practice, as our sages said, "Twisting the lips is an act," meaning because it is revealed, so his friend can see if he is praying or learning. In order to know the orders of the work of the Mitzvot, meaning their measures and times, this is called "the revealed Torah," where the Torah teaches us how to practice the Mitzvot.

Concealed was said only about the thought and the intention in the matter, since one cannot know what his friend thinks during the practice of a Mitzva [commandment], whether it is for the sake of the Creator or to the contrary, only because of false piety. The learning of the thought and the intention is called "hidden" and "secret," as it is written, "The secret of the Lord is to those who fear Him." What is "The secret of the Lord is to those who fear Him"? It is that the Creator gives the gift of fear of heaven to a person, and this is considered that the secret of the Creator is to those who fear Him, meaning they have fear of Him, and this is a gift from the Creator. He gives this secret only to those He likes, meaning He gives him a thought that it should be for the sake of the Creator. This is called "the hidden Torah," which teaches how to be rewarded with the quality of thought.

## 782- How Great Is Your Name

18 Tammuz, Tav-Shin-Chaf-Hey, July 18, 1965, Antwerp

"How great is Your name ... on the heaven," for all those camps of angels thank and glorify this action, that was revealed on earth, and which was not revealed to them (*The Zohar*, Item 62 in the *Sulam* [Ladder commentary on *The Zohar*]).

In other words, a person must first achieve the degree of "angel," meaning that one should achieve the degree of "angel," where he can say songs and praises that the holy names are revealed to other people. But before he can praise its revelation to others, he becomes angry that the holy names are not revealed, except that he has still not been awarded the degree of "angel."

"Angel" means the quality of *Hesed* [grace/mercy]. Once they have been rewarded with the degree of "angel," they can be rewarded with the degree of "man of below," called "earth." The quality of "heaven" is regarded as the quality of "angels," and this is the meaning of "Give Your glory on the heaven," which he interprets that they are the angels that praise the fact that the holy names were revealed to those who are in the quality of "earth."

Afterward, the person himself is rewarded with the quality of "earth," called "reception in order to bestow," while heaven is called "bestowing in order to bestow," which is the quality of "angel."

## 783- A Ransom for His Soul

Adar Aleph, Tav-Shin-Chaf-Hey, February 1965

A ransom for his soul, half a *Shekel* [coin]. Why not a whole *Shekel*? What is the meaning of half, *Shekel*, rich, and poor?

Mentioned and done, for on that generation, Israel should have been obliterated, and the Gemara says it is because they bowed to idols or enjoyed the meal of that wicked one. From this we see that even if one is on the lowest degree, to the point where he should be obliterated, through fasting and crying out, one can still be rewarded with repentance from love, as in "observed and received," henceforth, willingly. It follows that one should never give up on mercy.

## 784- The Meaning of Shabbat

Shabbat [Sabbath] is called *Shin-Bat* (*The Zohar, VaYakhel*), where *Bat* [daughter/girl] means female, which is the quality of reception. When the upper pleasure is revealed and we receive it, this is called "female" and "daughter."

This is why *The Zohar* says that when the three fathers unite in the daughter, it is Shabbat. The three fathers are interpreted in the *Sulam* [Ladder commentary on *The Zohar*] as three lines by which the light of *Hochma*, called Shabbat, is revealed. This is why it is called *Shin-Bat*, and it is also called "the pupil of the eye," for the revelation of *Hochma* is called "eye," since vision is revealed in the eye.

There is hearing and there is seeing. To hear, one must believe that what the other is saying is true. But with seeing, there is no need to believe anyone because he sees for himself. Hence, when the light of pleasures appears on Shabbat, it is called "seeing" and the "pupil of the eye," meaning that which the eye sees, and the reception in the eye, is called "daughter."

## 785- Law and Judgment – 2

"If you walk in My laws and keep My judgments." It is asked why there is a repetition of words.

It is known that there is the quality of law and judgment, called the quality of faith and the quality of Torah. "If you walk in My laws" means that you will take upon yourselves the law, then "you will keep My judgments," from the words, "and his father kept the matter." This means that then you can hope to be rewarded with the quality of Torah, called "judgment."

## 786- The Lord Came from Sinai

"The Lord came from Sinai and shone on them from Seir." This means that from what the children of Seir said, that they do not want to receive, from this it shone for Israel and added to them much light and love. "Appeared from Mount Paran." From what the children of Paran said, that they do not want to receive, much love and illumination was properly added to Israel (*The Zohar, Hukat*).

We should ask why the love of Israel was contingent upon the children of Seir and the children of Paran not wanting. This implies that all the love that He has for the people of Israel is because the nations of the world do not want to connect to Him. It follows that this is not real love for the people of Israel. That is, if the nations of the world wanted to receive the Torah, He would love them as much as the people of Israel.

The explanation is that because the children of Seir and the children of Paran do not want, there is room for choice. By the quality of Israel choosing it, He loves the quality of Israel. But when they want, it is a sign that the person is still not working for the sake of the Creator, or he would not agree to receive Torah and *Mitzvot* [commandments].

Assorted Notes

# 787- *ABYA* in the Work

18 Elul, Tav-Shin-Chaf-Bet, August 30, 1961, London

There are four discernments concerning the work. The order is that "From *Lo Lishma* [not for Her sake] we come to *Lishma* [for Her sake]." There is also an order of internality and externality.

The internality and externality also divide into internality and externality, meaning that there are internality and externality in externality, and there are internality and externality in internality.

We should also know that externality is called *Levush* [clothing/garment] in which the internality dresses, in this externality.

The first *Levush*: A person must be wearing a Jewish attire so the body will know that there is a big difference between Israel and the nations, and will thereby understand and feel that internally, too, one must always be watchful and keep from his internality being similar to the internality of the nations of the world, meaning that he will not grow his hair, and will have a beard and *Pe'ahs* [orthodox side-locks], etc.

This is called the "externality in the externality," and it is called "doing," meaning it pertains to the world of action, where he must do the externality in practice and does not need any thought, for there is no need to think in order to do these things. All it takes is to walk in Jewish attire.

For example, the buttons should not be left over right, but right over left, and one should also leave the *Pe'ahs*, etc., all of which are regarded as actions, and not as thoughts or imagination.

The second *Levush* is called "internality in externality." This is regarded as *Yetzira* in the work, since this *Levush* is done by depiction. When a person depicts to himself some depictions during the Torah and work, and these depictions inspire him to tears, or inspire him to joy, this is called *Yetzira*.

This is already regarded as internality, since it must come through imagination and depiction, which are things that come from man's internality.

However, that, too, is regarded as externality, since what is revealed outside, meaning what another can see, is already regarded as externality, and in externality, there is a grip to the externals.

This means that the prime basis of Judaism is faith in the Creator, regarded as fear of heaven. In other words, the reason for the work should be the fear of heaven.

# 788- He Raises the Poor from the Dust – 1

"He raises the poor from the dust, lifts the indigent from the trash."

We should ask the following: 1) what is dust, 2) what is poor, 3) what is trash, 4) what is indigent.

"Dust" is as in, "A serpent, all its food is dust." That is, he tastes the taste of dust in Torah and work, due to lack of faith. At that time, one must strengthen oneself with confidence that "Even if a sharp sword is placed on his neck, he should not give up on mercy," which is the mind.

"Poor" means that he is deficient of faith.

"Trash" means heart, when one is immersed in worldly lusts.

"Indigent" is *Av-Yaven* [in Hebrew]. *Av* [father] means "desire," from the words, "and he did not *Ava* [want] to send them away." *Yaven* comes from *Tit HaYaven* [quicksand like material]. When one's desire falls there, it sinks deeper each time. This is one who has no desire, who does not really want to immerse himself so low, meaning he does not have the sharpness in the will to receive because he only acts without thinking. Conversely, one who thinks and wants acts sharply about executing the will to receive.

And yet, when a person is on the lowest degree in terms of the mind and heart, he must believe that the days of mercy and good will assist one to be rewarded with exceptional success, meaning with a quality that is not in him by way of cause and consequence in a gradual manner, but in the manner of skipping over degrees.

## 789- From the *Peh* and Above, It Is Not Considered a *Kli*

The *Kli* [vessel] is *Aviut* [thickness], which is the will to receive. On this there is the power of judgment that it is forbidden to receive with this intention. On that there is a correction called *Masach* [screen]. There is a rule that *Aviut* is present only from itself downward, and not above it. We should ask why the *Aviut* is apparent only in *Malchut* and not above it.

It is known that before the desire awakens, we cannot speak of any reality, since the reality we can speak of is only when the feeling in the lower one begins. Until then, it is considered that the upper one is working and the lower one does not feel the action of the upper one. But when the lower one comes to feel it, he knows that there is a reason that caused him to feel the matter.

This is similar to one who sends a gift to his friend, and the gift goes through several hands until it reaches its recipient. Nevertheless, the recipient does not know about these hands it went through before he received the gift.

But when he receives, he understands that until it came to him, the gift went through several messengers because he received the gift from abroad.

Naturally, he cannot take away or add anything to the past state. Rather, all we can do is from here on, which is regarded as from him and below, meaning that he can make changes from the time of the reception of the gift onward. This is considered that the judgment does not work from *Malchut* of the *Rosh* and above.

## 790- Be Careful with What Comes Out from Your Lips

"Be careful with what comes out from your lips." "Remember and keep were said in one utterance."

"Lips" means *Malchut*, which is the acceptance of the burden of the kingdom of heaven. This requires great care because acceptance of a burden does not pertain to remembering, for remembering is something that is done with the intellect, while keeping pertains to something that is done in practice, and one must keep oneself from failing in that practice, or he must keep himself so as to observe that practice, or it will be an obstacle to him.

This is the meaning of "what comes out from your lips." This means that things that the lips utter, meaning whose root comes from faith, need keeping. This pertains to faith, meaning things that faith asserts are regarded as "what comes out from your lips."

"Remembering" pertains to the quality of Torah, which means light. This is the meaning of "All that there is in keeping, there is also in remembering."

This means that to the extent that one is in a state of "keeping," meaning that he has a grip on keeping, which is called "faith," to that extent he can be rewarded with the light of Torah, called "remember." One who does not have a grip in the quality of keeping has no attainment in the quality of remembering.

## 791- Demand and Receive Reward

Concerning "Demand and receive reward." The thing is that there are things that one can achieve and attain so he must learn how to behave and obtain the required qualification in order to attain them, meaning things that come through an awakening from below.

There are things that one can obtain only in a manner of "Demand and receive reward." "Demanding" means that a person comes to a state where he is utterly unable to obtain them because he sees that he does not have the qualified *Kelim* [vessels] for this.

In that case, it makes sense that he has nothing to do about it because to him, this is regarded as "In order for you to rise to the firmament." This is regarded as "never happened" with regard to that person. And yet, there is room to demand, from the words, "Zion, no one requires her, meaning that a demand is required." It was said about this, "Demand and receive reward." That is, the demand itself is the reward.

The words "Demand and receive reward" mean that one must picture to himself before Whom he stands and asks. That is, he must be able to show that he needs only the demand and not the fulfillment. If his intention is the fulfillment, then the Torah is endless, so he has room to ask for the things that exist in creation.

# 792- A Stubborn and Rebellious Son

"There never was nor ever will be a stubborn and rebellious son. Rather, demand and receive reward" (Sanhedrin 71).

We should ask, since it is known that the Torah is called "the names of the Creator," meaning that all the practice of *Mitzvot* [commandments] pertain to the internality, so there are things that do not have a grip on the corporeal world. The Torah means the internality of the Torah, and there, all 613 *Mitzvot* apply.

Although in corporeality, a person cannot observe all of the 613, such as levirate marriage, still, because all the things in corporeality are generally applied by the general public, it is possible for the individual to observe all 613 *Mitzvot*. This is the meaning of "Demand and receive reward."

In ethics, we should say that it is known that man must observe the Torah, in return for which he will receive a reward, as it is written, "And it came to pass that if you surely listen ... and I will give grass in your field," etc., and as our sages said, "The Creator wanted to reward Israel; therefore, He gave them plentiful Torah and *Mitzvot*."

This means that through the Torah and *Mitzvot*, man will be corrected and will be able to receive pleasure, and the intention will be for the sake of the Creator and not for his own sake. It follows that the reward is that he is doing the Creator's will and receives pleasure.

There are also things that one cannot attain, that are too high for man to obtain, meaning that there has never been anyone who attained them nor will there ever be one who attains them. The Torah gave this only for the discernment of "Demand and receive reward," where "demand" is as in "Zion, no one requires her."

# 793- Write Them on the Tablet of Your Heart

Raba said, "Although his forefathers bequeathed him a book of Torah, it is a *Mitzva* [commandment] to write his own, as was said, 'And you, write this song for yourselves'" (Sanhedrin 21b).

Indeed, we should ask: If his forefathers bequeathed him a book of Torah, why should he write another book of Torah?

We should understand this in ethics. The verse says, "Write them on the tablet of your heart." But why must we write on the heart? We should understand the meaning of "heart" and "writing."

"Writing" is black over white. "Blackness" means labor, when one exerts, since labor is called "darkness" and white is called "light of day," as it is written in *Pesachim*, "By the light of day."

## 794- The Place of Attainment

In GAR there is no attainment, and all our attainment is in VAK.

We should interpret that GAR means mind, where it should be only by faith. We must believe that this was His will. VAK means "heart," meaning an impression in the heart, and here, it is apparent in one's quality of love and fear. This should be with clear attainment, meaning that the impression should be revealed in him, and not by faith.

However, to the extent that the impression is felt in the heart, so is the measure of one's attainment. Here it is a commandment to expand his feelings. Conversely, in the mind, his greatness depends on the extent to which he can work in the manner of above reason.

It follows that they are two opposite things. If his mind is above reason, and the impression he feels in the heart is in the mind, this is called *Gadlut* [greatness/adulthood]. That is, on one hand, it is above attainment, yet it is felt in the heart. The measure of *Gadlut* depends on this, on the measure of oppositeness between mind and heart, for then one must overcome above reason, and the heart is precisely within reason, meaning in the feeling.

Only one who has the quality of "Israel" can walk on this path, but a foreigner cannot work in two opposites. This requires great strengthening so as to be able to march forward on this path.

## 795- Hear, My Son, Your Father's Morals – 2

*Tammuz, July*

"Pinhas, son of Elazar," etc., "Rabbi Elazar started and said, 'Hear, my son, your father's morals' is the Creator. 'And do not forsake your mother's teaching,' this is the assembly of Israel." The assembly of Israel is the *Shechina* [Divinity], which is the whole of the soul of Israel, regarded as "faith." She is called "Torah," and we must include the quality of Torah in faith, and we must include morals in the Torah.

The matter of faith should be as clear as the Torah, which is understanding and intellect. That is, a person must establish faith in Him in his heart to the same extent as though he understood everything.

Torah is regarded as "morals," for "morals" means admonition, as *The Zohar* interprets that there are several admonitions and punishments in it, as it is written, "My son, do not reject the morals of the Lord or loathe His admonition."

The difference between Torah and faith is that Torah is called a "gift," as our sages said, "From Matannah [gift] to Nahliel," where precisely when one feels pleasure in Torah and *Mitzvot* [commandments], this is when it is called a "gift." But when one exerts, when the Torah and *Mitzvot* are a burden and a load on him, it is called "faith," which is a burden.

For this reason, he says that even when a person feels the sweet taste of the Torah, he should limit himself so it is for the sake of the Creator and not for his own benefit, as this is the morals and the admonition, and he is punished if he breaches these limitations.

# 796- *The Real State*

"And it came to pass on that day that he came home to do his work, and none of the people of the household were there in the house." "And it came to pass on that day," the day when the evil inclination governs in the world and descends in order to mislead people. When? In the day when a person comes to repent for his sins or to engage in Torah and to do the commandments of Torah. At that time, he comes down in order to mislead people.

It seems difficult to understand these words. How can it be said that precisely when a person comes to repent or when he engages in Torah, the evil inclination comes to control him and divert him from the straight path? Does the evil inclination have no control when a person does not engage in Torah and *Mitzvot* [commandments]?

We should say that if a person does not engage in repentance, he cannot see his true state.

## 797- *A Gift*

Raba Hezia to Rav Hamnuna about prolonging his prayer. He said, "We leave the everlasting life and engage in transient life." RASHI interpreted "everlasting life" as Torah, "transient life" is for health, peace, and nourishment" (*Shabbat* [Sabbath] 10a).

We should interpret that "transient life" is a *Mitzva* [commandment], which protects and saves when engaging in it. This is why it is called "transient life." "Everlasting life" means Torah, since it protects and saves even when one does not engage in it.

We should understand that the meaning of *Mitzva* [commandment], which is faith, is only a correction, which is a temporary means. Conversely, Torah is a gift, which is the goal, and not the means to achieve the goal. The means are only transient.

A *Mitzva* is called "work"; the reward is called the "fruits" obtained through the work, and fruits are regarded as Torah, which is the gift that one obtains through the work. The path of the work is called "faith," by which one obtains the quality of Torah, and the Torah itself is the gift that one obtains, which is the reward that one obtains after the completion of the work.

# 798- The Merit of the Little One

A lesson on 1 Av, Tav-Shin-Yod, July 27, 1949, Tel-Aviv

"Who satisfies you with good." That is, the Creator gives such abundance to a person that he becomes satiated by the measure of goodness of the Creator. At that time, a person becomes a witness to the quality of the Creator, that He is called "The Good Who Does Good." *Adyach* [you] comes from the word *Edut* [testimony]. It follows that the good itself is the testimony.

Should you ask why are not everyone receiving this good, but only a chosen few are worthy of receiving the abundance, the thing is that there is a difference between types of people: There is a type that receives in the will to receive, and a type of people who work in order to bestow. The difference between them is from one end to the other.

It is known that the whole *Kli* [vessel] to receive the abundance is praise and gratitude. The more one expands the *Kli* with this desire, the more one can taste the flavor of the abundance.

The abundance itself is like an ocean. There is one who draws with a thimble, and there is one who draws with a bucket, and so forth. It is all measured according to the *Kli*.

If we say that the praise and gratitude are the *Kli*, for according to the feeling, so is the gratitude, since if one prevails as soon as he feels the salvation of the Creator and gives praise and thanks, by this he sustains and extends the abundance more powerfully and more strongly. Through the gratitude, the Giver of the abundance is imprinted in all his organs, and the more he feels who is the Giver, the more his *Kli* to receive the abundance expands.

It follows that this matter pertains only to the giver, and not to the receiver, since in the receiver, the Creator becomes indebted, and there are no praise or gratitude toward one who is indebted, for so is nature, just as there is no gratitude in a son toward his father.

But if a person off the street does something good for another, he praises and glorifies him. To the extent of the remoteness, so is the measure of gratitude. The reason is that to the extent of the closeness, so he becomes indebted. One who is far from another becomes indebted to him because of *Hesed* [mercy/grace]. Naturally, the opposite occurs where the other one becomes indebted to praise and glorify him.

One who receives, the more he is given, the more the Creator becomes indebted to him in his eyes. It is like one who gives each day one penny to his son. After some time, the power of love for his son increased in the father, and he wanted to benefit him so he gave him five pennies. The little one, who sees that today he received from the father a greater gift, is impressed by this and wants to thank his father for it. But afterward, when his father wants to give him one penny, as usual, the son becomes furious with his father for the decrease in his reception.

It follows that yesterday's addition not only did not bring closeness to his son, but through increasing the good he grew far from him for in his eyes his father has become indebted, so the little one wants his father to add each day. If not, all his presents mean nothing to him. To the receiver, it is as our sages said, "One does not die with half one's wishes in one's hand," since one who has one hundred wants two hundred.

Conversely, in one who bestows, the Creator does not become indebted, so he can always praise and glorify. If He sometimes gives him a greater gift, he glorifies Him more, since he knows about himself that he is utterly unworthy of the Creator bestowing upon him, and all he wants from the good that he receives is that greater praise of the Creator will emerge from it.

By this we will understand what our sages said, that where those who repented stand, complete righteous cannot stand.

It is known that it is impossible to be a complete righteous without prior repentance, since "Man is born a wild ass." Rather, it is certain that he had repented. When he repented, and the Creator accepted his penance, he clearly felt his smallness. At that time, he had the most intense feeling of praising and glorifying the Creator, for he saw then that "He lifts the indigent from the trash."

But later, after a few days, he sees that he is a complete righteous. And so it truly is—that he is a complete righteous. It follows that he lacks the sensation of lowliness of the time of repentance, so his praise and gratitude have waned. Thus, now he is smaller than those who repent, meaning from before. Perhaps this is the meaning of the words, "He who is great is small, even if he is actually great."

This is the meaning of "The Lord is high and the low will see," meaning that there is a desire to connect to something small, since doing something small and making it similar to something great is a wonder. Even in corporeality, we see that small things that are similar to big things have more value. This is why there is a desire in the upper one to connect to little ones. For this reason, even when one becomes a great righteous, it does not mean that he has become great, but rather that the Creator has become great in the eyes of the righteous.

Therefore, when a person is proud, the Creator tells him, "If it were great ones that I needed, I have greater ones above."

# 799- *The Birth of the Moon*

The birth of the moon. Moses was perplexed.

The moon is called *Malchut*. It is called "the renewal of the moon" because we must accept the burden of the kingdom of heaven each day anew. Yesterday's acceptance is not enough, since each time, says the ARI, we must raise the sparks that fell to *BYA* and raise them to *Kedusha* [holiness]. It follows that when a person accepts a new burden each time, it is considered that each time, he takes a part of the separation and admits it into the unity of *Kedusha*.

This is the meaning of *Malchut* returning to being a dot each day, and in *The Zohar* a dot is called "a black dot in which there is no white." That is, it does not shine, since "white" means that it illuminates. This means that it must be renewed each time.

However, we must know that it is not the same quality as it was before. Rather, it is as it is written, there is no renewal of light that does not extend from *Ein Sof* [infinity].

This is called "*Ibur* [impregnation] of the month." *Ibur* comes from the words "anger and rage." That is, a person must overcome while the kingdom of heaven is as a dot in him, meaning that the kingdom of heaven does not illuminate for him so he will be in gladness, as it is written, "Serve the Lord with gladness," but it is rather in sadness in him.

This is the meaning of *Ibur*. This is similar to an impregnation in corporeality, that the impregnation begins, and then, if the proper conditions are given, an offspring will emerge.

It follows that when one begins the work and sees how far he is from the Creator, and it hurts him, this is regarded as being rewarded with *Katnut* [smallness/infancy], meaning that he feels his own *Katnut*. This is called "a lack of a *Kli* [vessel]," and to that extent he can later obtain the light, called *Gadlut* [greatness/adulthood], according to the measure of the *Kli*.

A dot is called "*Shechina* [Divinity] in the dust," and rising is called "the sanctification of the month." That is, that which was in a state of "dust," he admitted this discernment into *Kedusha*. This is called "raising the *Shechina* from the dust."

# 800- A Broken Heart – 2

"A broken and contrite heart, O God, You will not despise."

When the work is built on the basis of above reason, one always needs the mercy of the Creator, to hold him, since he has nothing else. This is precisely so when the heart, which is the will to receive, called "body," is broken and contrite, and cannot receive any support from the body, as in "One who loves the Creator, his body is broken so the soul will reign."

But when the heart, too, understands what he is doing, he no longer needs the mercy of the Creator and can already say, "My power and the might of my hand," meaning that his own wisdom helped him and he no longer needs His help. At that time, it can be said that he despises His help.

# 801- The *Klipa* of Ishmael

"You shall build the altar of the Lord your God of complete stones."

*Even* [stone] comes from the word *Havanah* [understanding], meaning that he wants to understand. At that time, he also has wholeness, meaning that he accepts everything with faith. Then, "You shall offer on it burnt offerings to the Lord your God."

*Ola* [burnt offering] means it is all for the High One [*Ola* also means ascending]. That is, although he is already complete in the quality of "heart," he still needs the quality of "mind," which is complete stones, since there is no wholeness in the mind, for tomorrow he might think differently. But in faith there is wholeness, for there, there is no change once he has the degree of faith.

However, faith, if he has a desire to understand, it is called the *Klipa* [shell/peel] of Ishmael.

## 802- If Any Man of You Brings an Offering – 2

"If any man of you brings an offering," specifically "man," and specifically "from you." "Man," "You are called 'man'" (*Yevamot* 60). "I have found one man out of a thousand. A thousand enter a room, and one comes out to teaching" (in the *Midrash*).

This means that in the whole of Israel, too, not everyone is called "man," but only one out of a thousand. "Man," "In the end, after all is heard, for this is the whole of man."

Fear of heaven. This means that there is fear of earthliness, as it is written, "There is no advantage to man over beast, since all is vanity." Fear of earthliness is called "the people of the earth," meaning that one is afraid that he might not provide for the needs of the body, and fear of heaven means that he is afraid he might not obtain the things that are the needs of heaven, meaning *Kedusha* [holiness], *Tahara* [purity], Torah and *Mitzvot* [commandments], and *Dvekut* [adhesion] with the Creator.

The matter of "fear" pertains specifically to something that man craves. To the extent of the intensity of the desire, so is the measure of the fear. That is, if one does not have a great yearning for something, he is not so afraid that he might not obtain it.

In order to achieve such a desire, which pertains to the quality of "man," one must begin with offerings, meaning to make an offering from the beast to the Creator. This is the meaning of "If any man of you brings an offering." That is, "from you," Israel, if someone wants to approach the Creator and be discerned as "man," "If any man of you brings an offering," the order is an offering from the beast to the Creator, etc.

In other words, all the needs that pertain to beastliness must be offered to the Creator, and by this one enters a kind of the quality of man, a kind that is related to fear of heaven.

# 803- The Order of Conveying the Wisdom

The learning for one who yearns for it, the most successful way is to look for a sage, a true kabbalist, and obey him with whatever he tells him until he is rewarded with understanding the wisdom with his own mind, meaning the first discernment. Afterward, he will be rewarded with its conveyance orally, and this is the second discernment, and then to understanding in writing, since then he will inherit all the wisdom and its instruments easily from his teacher, and he will have all the rest of his time to add expansion and development.

Indeed, there is a second way in reality, where because of all the yearning and great desire in a person, the fear of heaven will open up to him and he will attain by himself all the sources that are the first discernment. But afterward, one must toil and exert very much in order to find a wise teacher before whom he can bow and obey, and receive the wisdom as conveyance from mouth to mouth, which is in the second discernment, and afterward in the third discernment.

But because he was not supported by a kabbalist sage from the beginning, the attainments come to him with great effort and take a long time, and he is left with little time to expand in it.

Or, sometimes it happens that the mind comes completely after the time, as it is written, "And they will die without wisdom." These are ninety-nine percent out of a hundred, and we call them "entered but did not exit."

Yet, not everyone succeeds in the first way, since most of them, once they are rewarded with attainment, become arrogant and cannot bow or obey their teacher sufficiently, so the sage must hide from them the tenets of the wisdom.

All this applies to the conveyance of the wisdom. There are rigorous and strict conditions that stem from necessary causes, and therefore few succeed in being favored by their teacher until he finds them worthy of this thing.

## 804- Raises the Poor from the Dust – 2

"He raises the poor from the dust, lifts the indigent from the trash."

"Dust" means not having any movement of his own, but everyone messes with it. In other words, anyone who wants to, builds his house on it and it cannot protest. Therefore, both good things and also to the contrary.

Therefore, the meager, who is the poor one, meaning the point in the heart, when a person comes to such lowliness that he cannot protest against undesirable people from building their homes, since the person received an inheritance from his teachers not to let anything be built on this dust, except for the Temple.

One should pay attention in the days between *Kesseh* and *Assor* ["ten penitential days" (between the Jewish New Year and the Day of Atonement)]. *Kesseh* means that he has a *Kissui* [cover] over Providence, and *Assor* comes from the word *Isru Chag Baavotim* [chain the festival with shackles]. This means one's hands and legs are tied and he cannot protest against his indecent thoughts, so they do not build their home there.

This is the meaning of what our sages said, "Seek the Lord while He is found; call upon Him while He is near" (*Yevamot* 105). Why is He near specifically at that time? It is because "The Lord is high and the low will see," meaning the quality of the mind. "From the trash" means the heart, when one is placed in the trash, namely the lusts of this world. At that time, a person comes to full recognition that "Unless the Lord builds a home, its builders labor in it in vain." For this reason, precisely then we must not give up on being rewarded with building the Temple.

# 805- Concerning Joy

Joy is a testimony. If a person becomes stronger in the matter of faith, to believe that the Creator is good and does good, that there is none above Him, although in the situation he is in right now he has nothing to rejoice with, meaning to be happy about, and yet he reinforces himself and says that the Creator watches over him in a manner of good and doing good, if his faith is sincere, it stands to reason that he should be happy and delighted. And the measure of joy testifies to the level of sincerity in his faith.

By this we can interpret what is said about Rabbi Elimelech, who would say that when he passes away and is told to go to hell, he will say, "If this is what the Creator wants, I will jump in." That is, this is regarded as Providence of good and doing good. Thus, he is always happy.

# 806- Esau's Head Is Holy

When Jacob went to receive the blessings from Isaac, why did he not tell Isaac that he deserves the blessings because he had bought the seniority? According to what RASHI interprets on Esau's saying, "This one delayed me twice," meaning he took his seniority by deceit, and Isaac replied to him, "He, too, shall be blessed," meaning that Isaac took the selling of the seniority into account, meaning that because of it, Jacob deserved the blessings.

Thus, why did Jacob not (say) to Isaac that he deserves the blessings because now he is the senior?

To understand the above, we should first interpret what is written in the name of the ARI, that Esau's head is holy but his body is impure. Baal HaSulam explained that it is because each degree spreads to *Rosh* and *Guf* [head and body, respectively], where *Rosh* means when he is not receiving, and *Guf* means when the abundance is clothed in the *Kelim* [vessels].

The discernment of *Rosh* in the left line is always holy because *Rosh* means resistance to clothing. Only when it is received is it forbidden to accept the left line. This means that from the *Peh* and above, it is permitted to extend, but not from the *Peh* down.

This is why it is written, "And Isaac loved Esau for there was game in his mouth," meaning he showed Isaac that he was receiving all the good things only up to the *Peh*, but not below the *Peh*.

## 807- Fire Is Called "Judgments"

Fire is called "judgments," which are similar to fire. If we use them in the place of correction, it yields the existence of the whole of reality. But not in the place of correction, it causes the ruin of the world (*The Zohar, VaYakhel*, Item 259).

## 808- Wholeness and Deficiency – 2

In corporeality, there is no wholeness and there is always a deficiency. In spirituality, there is wholeness and there is no deficiency.

Man was created with a deficiency. That is, from the perspective of man's substance, called "creation," it is only that within which there is the will to receive, which is regarded as a deficiency. Since man feels that he is deficient, meaning he lacks vitality, since the desire to do good caused a deficiency in the lower one, meaning to always yearn to receive pleasure and vitality, but when he can receive pleasure only from corporeal clothing, there is no wholeness in it so we can say that from this he will always be able to extend vitality. Instead, as soon as his deficiency is satisfied, the flavor and vitality in the matter disappear from it.

According to the rule that the yearning gives the flavor to the pleasure, where there is no yearning for something, that something does not give all the pleasure in it, and the matter gives him pleasure only according to his deficiency. But where he has no deficiency, it is as though he has no *Kli* [vessel] in which to place that pleasure.

Hence, if man is filled with pleasure, then he has no yearning for it. Therefore, he no longer receives vitality and pleasure from this thing. But if he is not completely satisfied by the pleasure, then there is still a deficiency in him. This is considered that he still has a *Kli* to receive pleasure.

The deficiency that one feels about himself, that he has no pleasure, means that he has nothing from which to receive pleasure. This is like a person who is on one of the islands in the ocean where there is no food, and he must starve from hunger and thirst.

In spiritual pleasures there is wholeness, meaning that we do not feel that there is a need for higher wholeness because there cannot be any lack in spirituality. Hence, spirituality shines in a way that there is nothing to add to it.

## 809- Wholeness in Life

"One does not die with half one's desire in one's hand." "He who has one hundred wants two hundred."

The question is, What is it like in spirituality? Is there no wholeness in life there, too, and one always lives in deficiency?

One does not feel a lack for spirituality so as to say that he cannot live without it, since man's lack, which he feels in himself, is that he must receive pleasure. He is filled by corporeal things, which is nourishment that is abundant in the world, since this was prepared for us by the Creator so that by them we would be able to exist in the world.

In other words, since the desire to do good impels us to receive pleasure, we satisfy the desire for pleasure with corporeal pleasures.

This is akin to food that is not very expensive, meaning that we do not need to make great efforts in order to buy them.

Only when one has been filled with all the corporeal pleasures and has no deficiency that he did not satisfy, and no deficiency or yearning for corporeality is left in him, then he has no vitality or pleasure, for only the deficiency and yearning give flavor to something. At that time, he begins to feel that it is worthwhile to see if there is vitality and pleasure in spirituality.

Also, sometimes a cause from aside takes from him the deficiency and yearning for corporeality. It follows that then, too, he has nothing from which to receive pleasure. Therefore, he must approach spirituality, perhaps he will be able to draw some pleasure from there.

That cause sometimes comes through inheritance of qualities from the forefathers, who revoked these pleasures either through morals or because they tasted the light of Torah and saw that it was not worthwhile to turn to the deficiency and desire for these pleasures. Although now they do not feel the taste of Torah, by receiving a temporary illumination, they loathe corporeal pleasures and now have a need for spirituality.

# 810- He Who Fears Me

"Your heads, your tribes." Although I appointed for you heads, elders, and officers, you are all equal before Me, as was said, "Every man of Israel" (*Midrash Tanchuma*).

We should ask what is so remarkable about everyone being equal before the Creator, as none are transcendent from the perspective of the Creator.

We should interpret that in the way of reward and punishment, there is a difference, as He says, "Although I appointed for you," and "You are all equal," meaning in private Providence. This means that from the perspective of the Creator, namely what the Creator does, there is no difference from the perspective of the Creator between great and small, and He can bestow upon everyone.

We should also say in regard to choice, that the whole difference between "your heads" and "your tribes" is only with regard to the person, meaning in *Lo Lishma* [not for Her sake]. However, before Me, meaning in *Lishma* [for Her sake], there is no difference, as it is written in *Midrash Rabbah*: "Verily, anyone who fears Me and does words of Torah, all the wisdom and all of the Torah are in his heart."

# 811- *Returning to One's Origin*

"He and I cannot dwell in the same abode." Repentance means returning to one's origin, annulling before Him. When a person always thinks about increasing the glory of heaven, while he himself is annulled before Godliness, this is called "repentance," when he returns to his origin.

But when one is proud, meaning he does not want to annul before Him, it means that he does not want to be in the same abode with the Creator, since he wants specifically his own authority. This is called "two authorities," the authority of the Creator and his own authority. This is why "Anyone who is proud, it is as though he commits idol-worship" because of the two authorities.

It follows that when the Creator says, "He and I cannot dwell in the same abode," it is because the Creator says to the person that it is impossible if you do not want to annul before Me.

## 812- Turn Away from Evil and Do Good – 3

Man's work begins with "Do good," and then he can keep the "Turn away from evil," since by education he cannot perceive the bad as bad. Rather, man yearns to satisfy his wishes because he feels great pleasure is satisfying his passions.

When one is told that satisfying his desires is bad, he does not know why. Instead, he must believe above reason that this is bad and he must turn away from this path.

Also, when one comes to engage in doing good, such as to wear a *Tzitzit* [a Jewish fringed undergarment], he does not feel anything good about it because he feels no pleasure when wearing the *Tzitzit*, so he can say about it that it is good. Instead, he must believe above reason that it is good.

But later, when he walks in this way above reason, whether in good or in bad, he is given from above some taste of "Do good." To the extent that he feels good when doing the commandment to do, he begins to taste a bad taste in bad things. At that time, he has a good feeling in "Do good," and a bad feeling in "Turn away from evil." In that state, he has reward and punishment in this world.

But for those who work in order to receive reward, through faith in reward and punishment they observe the "Turn away from evil," even though they feel a passion for pleasure. Nevertheless, they turn away from the pleasures because they cannot tolerate punishments in the next world.

Also, when one observes "Do good," he can also observe the commandments to do although he does not feel any flavor in it, but he believes that he will be paid a reward for this, so he has the strength to observe.

But when he wants to engage not in order to receive reward, the question is, For whom does he observe the "Turn away from evil and do good"? Clearly, he must understand that this is the

King's commandment. Yet, the question is, Why does the King need it? After all, He is not deficient, lacking the Torah and *Mitzvot* [commandments] of the lower ones.

Evidently, this is for us, so we may correct ourselves. At that time, a person begins to scrutinize the benefit that he derives from this. For this reason, the first work is in faith above reason, and then he gets help from above, which is called an "illumination from above," until he obtains the NRNHY of his soul.

## 813- *The Desire to Bestow – 2*

Everyone asks: When we say that His desire is to do good to His creations, and when the created beings receive His abundance, it means that His desire is satisfied, meaning that He enjoys the fact that He is giving. Thus, since we have a rule that the Creator only gives and does not receive, how then do the two interpretations coincide?

We should understand, since we should ask the same question about the person himself.

How can man, whose quality is to receive, be able to invert the vessels of reception into vessels of bestowal? After all, even when he bestows, we must say that he enjoys bestowing or he would not bestow, for without reward, we cannot comprehend that we will do something, since one who has any intellect cannot do anything unless it yields him a reward.

The answer is: "Were it not for the help of the Creator, he would not overcome it." This is a miracle, above reason, and was given only as a gift from the Creator. Moreover, with respect to the Creator, we cannot understand that there is a reality of bestowal without reception, as this is above our minds, since our root is reception.

## 814- Times in the Work

It is explained that there are the discernments of *Rosh* [head] and *Guf* [body] in each and every degree. These are regarded as potential and actual.

The *Rosh* is regarded as Emanator and *Ein Sof* [infinity] with respect to the *Guf*, since the *Rosh* is regarded as "from below upward," meaning by resistance to *Hitlabshut* [clothing].

It is regarded as light without a *Kli* [vessel], for *Hitlabshut* in the *Kli* means revelation, since the light is revealed only in a *Kli*, which is regarded as a desire to receive, meaning that the receiver attains it. Where it has still not been attained, it is regarded as light without a *Kli*, and this is called *Ein Sof* and Emanator, since it is not attained.

For this reason, at the *Rosh* of the degree, which is one's engagement with the *Masach* [screen], meaning by overcoming the will to receive, which is only about detaining one's desire to receive although he has a great desire and yearning, when all his work is to overcome his desire, and the force that impels him to overcome is his desire for equivalence of form.

Only when he knows that it is worth his while to receive because this is the desire of the upper one and not because of his own desire, he receives some of the light, meaning that abundance and attainment are poured down to him to an extent that he is certain that all his intention is because of the desire of the upper one.

It therefore follows that in the order of the preparation, before they are rewarded with entering the King's palace, there is also this order. In other words, when a person comes to perform some *Mitzva* [commandment] and the will to receive does not want to do this, a person does what he can and overcomes his desire. By this he has done his work by deciding to the side of *Kedusha* [holiness], by acting against his will.

By overcoming, he will take upon himself "as an ox to the burden and as a donkey to the load," and a spirit from above will immediately rest on him to the extent that he overcame his desire, meaning according to the revealing of his forces.

The spirit from above that is on him is revealed to a person as pleasure and not as work, since after the work, there always comes a state of rest and joy.

It follows that this should be divided into two states: 1) a time of work, 2) a time of contentment.

Hence, we must say that "a servant of the Creator" is called so during the work and not during the time of contentment. Yet, a person always yearns for the state of contentment and not for the state of work.

This is regarded as "the view of the landlord is opposite from the view of Torah." The view of the landlord is that the best state is the time of contentment. During the work, they regard it as *Katnut* [smallness/infancy], since they have the scrutiny of good and bad. This is a sign that there is still bad in them.

Conversely, during the contentment, it is a sign that they are in a state of a world that is all good. In truth, the contentment is only a continuation of performing the *Mitzva* of choosing good and bad, called "work of scrutinies."

Yet, during the time of contentment, he is not in a state of work but in a state of rest, called "a state of standing" and not "a state of walking." This is precisely when he works in unifications, meaning when he unifies everything with the Creator, regarded as equivalence and bestowal.

Thus, that state is called "work," and the second state is called "rest." However, we also need the second state because a servant cannot work if he is not nourished. It follows that the rest is only in order to have strength for work, since the *Kedusha* he puts into his internality gives him strength to be able to overcome all the desires.

But when he does not work, meaning when it is not the time for profits, such as one who sits in his store all day and earns money, and in the evening returns home and enjoys his meal, it will never occur to him that this is a time when he is earning something. On the contrary, it is a time of spending and not a time of earning.

## 815- Bo [Come]

"Come unto Pharaoh, for I have hardened his heart and the heart of his servants, that I may set these signs of Mine within him."

The interpreters asked about the words, "I have hardened": Since the Creator gave him the hardening of the heart, meaning that the Creator denied him the choice, why is it his fault? They also asked about the words, "Come unto Pharaoh": It should have said, "Go unto Pharaoh," since "come" means "Let us go together," meaning that the Creator will go together with Moses.

To understand the above, we should begin with what is written, "Our sages said, 'One should always see oneself as half guilty, half innocent. If he performs one *Mitzva* [commandment], happy is he for he has sentenced himself to the side of merit'" (*Kidushin* 40b).

We should ask, 1) How can one say that he is half... while he knows about himself that he has more transgressions than *Mitzvot* [pl. of *Mitzva*]? 2) "If he performs one *Mitzva*," they said that he has sentenced himself to the side of merit. But they said, "always," meaning that even after he has sentenced himself to the side of merit, he should also see himself as half and half, so how can such a thing be said when he has already performed one *Mitzva*? 3) If he knows that he has more merits than iniquities, why must he say "half and half"?

Our sages said, "Anyone who is greater than his friend, his inclination is greater than him" (*Sukkah* 52a). We should ask why he deserves such a harsh punishment that if he is great, he is given more evil inclination than a small person is given.

The thing is that our sages come to teach us the way in the work of the Creator, to advise us how to emerge from the authority of the evil inclination. Therefore, they instructed us that one should not say that since he has few merits and many iniquities, he can no longer decide that from now on I will walk on the good path, since he sees that he is under the authority of evil because he has many faults and few merits, and he concludes that all this extends from his being born with bad qualities and he has no way to emerge from the governance of evil.

The choice that one is given, to decide to the side of merit, pertains specifically to one in whom the powers of good and bad are equal. At that time, it is possible to decide to the good. But for one whose bad is greater than the good, he can no longer decide.

Our sages said about this: "One should always see oneself as half guilty," as in "Anyone who is greater than his friend, his inclination is greater than him," since if someone becomes great and remains in the bad from before he became great, he will have much good and a little bit of bad, and in this way, it is impossible to make a choice, since just as there cannot be choice if the bad is more than the good, there cannot be choice if the good is more than the bad.

Therefore, one who is great, whose good is great, his evil must be increased from above, so he will have the exact same measure as the good. Then, when the two are equal, there can be choice.

It therefore follows that if a person sees that his good is very small, he should know that his bad is also very small. Although he knows that he has made many transgressions, he should still know that from above, the bad in him was diminished because the good in him was diminished, so he would be able to make a choice. As for the many bad deeds he did, there are corrections for this, through hell or through repentance from fear or from love.

But concerning doing, henceforth there are corrections that diminish the bad so it is not greater than the good, so he will be able to choose.

Thus, a person can always choose, since before he has performed one *Mitzva*, the authority of the bad is not greater than the authority of the good although he has many bad deeds. After he has performed one *Mitzva* and decided to the side of merit, his evil is increased, meaning the bad is empowered so as to govern to the same extent as the good. It follows that then, too, he is half and half.

By this we will understand the verse, "Come unto Pharaoh, for I have hardened his heart." Once Pharaoh has sentenced himself to the side of merit, saying, "The Lord is righteous," he was great. Therefore, he could no longer make a choice. For this reason, there was a need for the Creator to harden his heart, meaning increase his evil, since only in this way is there room for choice.

It follows that through the hardening of the heart, the ability to choose was not taken away from him. On the contrary, here he was given the possibility to make a choice.

## 816- Observed and Received

The children of Seir and the children of Paran did not receive the Torah. The advice of "We will do and we will hear" means that through doing they will come to hearing, meaning that the body will agree. The matter of coercion means that through the pleasure, they did not have any other choice and they could feel the pleasure by accepting the doing. But the nations of the world, who did not have this qualification of doing, could not feel the flavor of Torah and *Mitzvot* [commandments].

Concerning the great protest against the Torah, meaning that it was by coercion and swallowing, when one does not feel the pleasure, they have a choice to revert. But "observed and received" means by choice, namely that it is out of unconditional love.

## 817- The Meaning of "Poor"

The meaning of "poor." According to what Baal HaSulam explained, she is called so because everyone works for her, while she herself does not work, for work is forbidden in her and she is fed only by what others have (perhaps this is why it is forbidden to work on Shabbat [Sabbath]).

According to the above-said, we should interpret that the nourishment of anything is the reason, for anything that we understand in our reason that we should do, we do it and use it. But if a person sees that he is negligent in the use, he must add mind and intelligence into the matter, meaning to understand that he needs this matter. At that time, that knowledge sustains him, meaning he receives a new strength to engage in the matter because the mind obligates him.

It follows that the reason sustains this matter. This is why it is considered that we use this thing by a force that this matter itself mandates. It follows that this quality is called "rich," since "There is none who is poor except in knowledge."

This is not so if one uses something without knowledge, when reason does not obligate him to engage in it. As a result, each time when it needs to be revived, to be given nourishment, meaning knowledge and intelligence why it is worthwhile to use it, and it must not be given knowledge, this is why it is called "poor and meager," and all the nourishment that is received from other things should be given to her. That is, all the concepts that one receives from other things where knowledge is permitted should be extended to her.

In other words, we must say that all the nourishment he receives from other things is thanks to her. By using and entertaining with her, even when he has no knowledge about it, he is given knowledge elsewhere, as in "Give tithing so you will become rich."

By tithing [giving ten percent of one's earnings], which is doing without knowledge, and saying that this tithing is holy, thanks to this he has wealth elsewhere, meaning he receives knowledge, called "wealth," from things.

For this reason, he will have nine qualities, meaning that in these nine qualities he receives knowledge, and the tenth will be dedicated to the Creator. In other words, he is entirely for the Creator, and he has no attainment in it. This is why it is called "to the Lord." The quality that the landlord receives, called "will be for him," is what the owner can attain.

This is the meaning of "'Test Me please by this,' said the Lord of Hosts, 'if I do not open for you the windows of heaven and pour out for you an endless blessing.'" "This" means the above-mentioned wealth. If you accept this above reason, will not all the wealth in the world flow to you?

## 818- Happy Are They Who Keep Judgment

"Happy are they who keep judgment, who practice righteousness at all times."

*Tzedakah* [righteousness/charity] is as it is written, "And he believed in the Lord, and He regarded it for him as righteousness." "Faith" means "charity for the poor," and this work should be at all times, as one always needs to see that the basis of the work is revealed before him in the quality of "poor."

At the same time, one must be a keeper of judgment. "Judgment" means specifically with the intellect, since "judgment" means everything we understand. The thing is that we must extend the intellect of the Torah and the flavor of the *Mitzvot* [commandments], for by this we build the *Shechina* [Divinity].

Through the mind of the Torah and *Mitzvot* that we extend, everything must be based on a calculation that is above reason. Precisely by taking her quality above reason, one is rewarded with the knowledge of *Kedusha* [holiness] in Torah and *Mitzvot*.

It follows that the intellect obligates him to walk on the basis of above reason, and the minute he fails in the foundation, when he wants to receive based on reason, too, even the knowledge he had in Torah and *Mitzvot* promptly departs from him. This sets in his heart the faith in the quality of fear, meaning fear of sin, for as soon as reason awakens on the basis, he immediately falls from his state in Torah and *Mitzvot*.

It follows that through these obstacles, he already knows how to keep himself from a foreign thought.

There is also the fear of heaven, which Baal HaSulam interpreted that sometimes there are people who are standing at a degree where they no longer have anything to fear, yet they maintain the faith not for fear of punishment, for they already see that there is nowhere to fall, and they keep the faith because of fear of heaven. That is, they see that such is the will of the upper one.

It follows that by engaging in other things by way of intellect and knowledge, by this they build the *Shechina*, which is called "faith." That is, they see that it is worthwhile to keep the quality of faith, since all the profits are gained only when one sustains the foundation.

This is called "working in one place, gaining there the mind and the intellect, and giving her all the powers in a manner of *Tzedakah*." In other words, with the vitality and intelligence he has received from things that he engaged in, with these forces he must serve the commandment of faith.

This is called "raising the *Shechina* [Divinity] from the dust," when he sees the importance of faith, that precisely by going with this basis does he make all the gains. Naturally, this quality becomes important to him.

# 819- Borrowing Vessels

Why was Isaac afraid to say, "What iniquity is there in me that I blessed the little one before the older one and changed the order of relation?" Esau began to shout, "He delayed me twice!" His father told him: "What did he do to you?" He said, "He took my blessing." He said, "This is what I regretted and dreaded that I might have broken the letter of the law. Now, my blessing to the elder, 'he, too, shall be blessed'" (*Midrash Tanchuma*).

This means that this is why Isaac blessed Esau, because of the birthright. Therefore, we should understand why Jacob had to deceive his father that he was Esau. He could have told him that he deserves the blessings because of the birthright. Nachmanides interpreted the verse, "And Esau despised the birthright," that this is why he said to Isaac, "I am your elder son," telling him that he deserves to be blessed.

We should also understand the verse, "And Isaac loved Esau for there was game in his mouth." What is the precision, "in his mouth"? Baal HaSulam interpreted why Isaac wanted to bless Esau, since it is impossible to give anything spiritual to one who has no desire for the matter. Otherwise, the spiritual matter yields no blessing to a person, but on the contrary, a curse.

"Blessing" means that his situation will improve, he will grow and expand, and will be able to go higher and higher to the sought-after wholeness. But if a person is given something spiritual while he lacks the *Kelim* [vessels] to receive, meaning that he has no need, this matter brings him nothing but losses, the opposite of a blessing.

Jacob was a smooth man, as it is written, "and I am a smooth man," meaning without any deficiency. "And I will bring upon myself a curse and not a blessing. And his mother said to him ... but obey my voice." Conversely, Esau was hairy. *Se'arot* [hair] comes from the word *Se'arah* [storm], meaning deficiencies, for over deficiencies there can be a storm.

Hence, it is precisely Esau who had the *Kelim* to receive the blessings, unlike Jacob. Rebecca advised him, meaning he wore the best garments of Esau. As RASHI interpreted, he coveted them from Nimrod, meaning that those garments belonged to wicked Nimrod.

Esau took from him these *Kelim*, and she also dressed his smooth parts with leather from young goats. In other words, he wore Esau's desires and thus had a lack in which to receive the blessings.

By this we can explain and say that for this reason, when Esau came and said, "He delayed me twice," meaning that he also took from me the birthright, his mind was eased that he had blessed the little one. That is, before he knew that he was the elder, he thought that he had no place of deficiency, and therefore no connection to the blessings.

But once he learned through Esau, that he took the birthright from him, Isaac (saw) that Jacob himself tried to obtain *Kelim* so he would have a place in which to receive the blessings, since he tried to find by buying the birthright.

This is why Isaac said, "He, too, will be blessed," for now Jacob is suitable for the blessings. Prior to the correction of borrowing Esau's *Kelim*, buying the birthright in and of itself was not enough to receive the blessings. Hence, there was no point in telling him that he has the birthright from Esau, since this is only the beginning of the making of the *Kelim*.

By borrowing the *Kelim* of Esau, he had the suitable *Kelim*. This is similar to the borrowing of the *Kelim* of the Egyptians, as it is written, "And each woman shall borrow from her neighbor," for the people of Israel, too, needed to borrow a place of lack so they could receive the *Mochin* of great possessions, similar to borrowing the garments of Esau here.

We can understand the matter of borrowing *Kelim* through a depiction. It is a rule that it is impossible to provide any answers if he does not have the questions. Jacob did not have any questions, so it was considered that he took the questions from Esau in a manner of borrowing, meaning in order to extend the answers. Yet, he promptly returned and gave him back all the questions.

# 820- The Discernment of "In Everything"

*Heshvan, October-November, Manchester*

"And Abraham was old, advanced in age; and the Lord had blessed Abraham in everything. And Abraham said to his servant..."

There is a question: Why is there a proximity between the commandment not to take a wife "for my son from the daughters of the Canaanite," and "you will go to my country and to my kindred," meaning he should take a wife specifically from his family?

In *Midrash Rabbah* there are three views concerning the meaning of "in everything." Rabbi Yodan: "In everything" means female. Rabbi Nehemiah: He did not have a female whatsoever. Rabbi Levi: He reigned in his inclination.

A female means a lack, since he was created deficient like all creations, and the Creator gave him a blessing in this lack. This is the view of Rabbi Yodan.

According to Rabbi Nehemiah, he did not have a female whatsoever, meaning his blessing was that he never had any deficiency, and there is no blessing greater than if one's deficiencies are taken from him.

Rabbi Levi said that it is that he reigned in his inclination. That is, he did have a deficiency, and a deficiency is called the "evil inclination," but he had the power to control it so as not to receive anything for himself, but only for the sake of the Creator.

It follows that there are three discernments here: 1) He has no deficiency at all; the evil inclination has been taken away from him, and he bestows in order to bestow. He reigned in his inclination, meaning he does not receive at all. Also, that he had a female, meaning that he had a deficiency but he was using it only in a manner of blessing, by receiving in order to bestow, and then it is regarded as a blessing.

1) He does not receive.

2) He bestows in order to bestow.

3) He receives in order to bestow.

In other words, the three views are the order of the work to achieve the completeness of the goal, and each one thinks that he is the most important. One thinks that the most important is the beginning, which is not to be a receiver, and that this was the whole blessing, and the rest simply follows.

The next one thinks that the most important is to bestow in order to bestow. If he is blessed here, the rest follows by itself.

The third one thinks that the final goal is the most important because we must be rewarded with this blessing.

The verse says, "It is not good for the man to be alone; I will make for him a help made against him." In other words, his wife will be an aide in fighting against the opposition, which is the evil inclination.

Abraham had Sarah as an aide. For this reason, he wanted Isaac his son to also take for him an aide from his family. As Sarah was his brother's daughter, Rebecca was the daughter of his brother's son. By having this aide from the side of his wife, he will achieve the complete wholeness, just as Abraham achieved wholeness, meaning that he was rewarded with the quality of "everything," which is wholeness.

# 821- We Will Do and We Will Hear – 2

In the verse, "And the man Moses was very humble," the meaning of humbleness is lowliness, meaning that person annuls himself before the other, not necessarily in external annulment, but also internally. Externality means that which is revealed outside, which is regarded as "revealed," when it is visible to everyone that he does not consider himself as anything, but that he regards his friend as being at a higher degree than his own. This is shown by the things he does before his friend.

But there is also internality, called "hidden." These are the thought and the mind, which he must also annul before his friend. This is the meaning of "My soul shall be as dust to all." The question is, How can an intelligent and knowledgeable person say that his mind will be annulled before each and every one, while he knows and feels that he is a hundred times higher than his friend?

However, there is a discernment of "part," and there is a discernment of "all." The collective is higher than the individual, and one must annul before each and every part, in that he is part of the "all." In other words, the whole of Israel, although they do not have such great importance individually, with respect to the collective, each one is very important from the perspective of the whole collective.

One must annul his personal needs before the needs of the collective, and since man must annul his view and thought before the Creator, he must accustom himself in externality, called "doing." This is called "We will do." All those annulments will influence him so he can annul his mind and thought before the Creator.

It therefore follows that one who is more opinionated has more work annulling himself before the Creator. Conversely, one who is a fool has no opinion to annul because he has no opinion. It follows that the whole merit of knowledge is in having something to annul. Only for this should one aspire for knowledge. One who is not ready for this, it is better for him not to have knowledge.

This is called "his wisdom is more than his deeds," meaning he is more opinionated than he can annul, since annulment is called "doing" and not "hearing." "Hearing" means understanding, and "doing" is only power without knowledge. This is "We will do and we will hear," meaning that if he has the power of "doing" then he can receive "hearing" because his basis is faith and not knowledge.

# 822- A Handmaid Who Is Heir to Her Mistress

"A handmaid who is heir to her mistress."

Corporeality is called "handmaid," which should serve spirituality, called the mistress. There are people who engage in corporeality in order to have the strength to engage in Torah and *Mitzvot* [commandments], and there are people who engage in Torah and *Mitzvot* in order to have corporeality. It follows that the mistress, who is the Torah and *Mitzvot*, serves them in order to bring corporeality, who is called "the maid."

# 823- The Name *Shadai*

The matter of creation is as it is interpreted in *The Zohar*: The world was created with [the letter] *Bet* and not in the other letters, meaning that when He created the world with the *Bet*, His intention was that the *Bet* would govern in the world, that its power would work in the world. Also, Jacob's blessing was similar, that He gave power to Menashe and Ephraim that their quality would reign in the world, for through those two qualities the whole of Israel emerged from the general exile. It is likewise with every personal exile; he emerges individually from exile.

This is the meaning of "My name in the midst of him," meaning the name *Shadai*, which is *Yesod* of *Malchut*. Conversely, the quality of *Tav* is regarded as *Malchut* of *Malchut*, which has the quality of *NRN*, where even complete righteous are punished by it. For this reason, He did not create the world under the governance of the *Tav* (See, *The Zohar*, Part One, p 26 in the *Sulam* [Ladder commentary on *The Zohar*] in Hebrew). This is the meaning of "My name in the midst of him," that his name is as the name of his Rav [great sage/teacher], which is the name *Shadai*, meaning that He said to His world "*Dai* [enough], expand no further."

# 824- Internality and Externality

Humility means that in any manner, in action or in intellect, he annuls himself before the other, meaning that even his view he should annul before his friend.

There is "internality," and there is "externality." These are called "revealed" and "concealed," and "action" and "thought." Something that is revealed to all pertains to action, whereas a thought is not revealed; therefore, a thought is regarded as internal, meaning it is in man's internality. An act is called "externality," and within it there is an internal thought.

Therefore, when one must annul himself before his friend, it is not regarded as true annulment unless it is in two manners: in thought and in action.

It is not necessarily the action, but he should also annul his view and say that his friend's view is more important than his own. Otherwise, this is (not) regarded as "annulment." When he shows his friend an act of annulment, this is nothing but fawning, where on the outside he shows that his friend is more important, but deep inside he knows that his friend is not half as good as he is.

## 825- Choice

"Rabbi Yitzhak said, 'If there are serpents and scorpions in it [the pit], why is it written about Reuben, 'In order to save him from their hands, to return him to his father'? Did Reuben not fear for him, that those serpents and scorpions might harm him? ...But Reuben saw that while he was in his brothers' hands, the harm was certain, for he knew how much they hated him...' Because of this, in a place of snakes and scorpions, if he is righteous, the Creator will make a miracle for him. And sometimes the merit of one's fathers assists a person and he is saved from them. But once one is given to one's enemies, only a few can survive" (*The Zohar, VaYeshev*, Items 130-132).

We should understand why "once one is given to one's enemies" the Creator does not make a miracle for him. Concerning saving, we find two manners: 1) where harm is found, 2) where harm is not found.

Concerning animals, some harm out of appetite and not in order to anger. But certainly, we should discern among the harm-doers, that they do so because of their nature, meaning that it is natural for animals to harm people. That is, they have a general desire to prey on any living being.

Conversely, with an enemy, he has all the power and energy only for that person, for only him does the enemy want to harm. It follows that all the anger in him comes out on that person. This is why it is considered "where harm is found." Here, we do not rely on miracles.

Conversely, with snakes and scorpions, who do not have a special interest in that person, this is not regarded as "where harm is found," and there can be a miracle.

There is a difference whether man's energy is spent on many things, for then he spends some of the energy on some of the things, instead of all his energy being spent on one thing.

The second manner is animals that do not have free choice but do what nature obligates them to do. It follows that they are close to the Owner of nature; they walk and behave according to what the Creator imprinted in them. Since they are in the hands of the Creator, the Creator can do with them as He pleases, meaning to give them a nature not to prey now.

Conversely, man has free choice. The Creator has allowed man to feel that he is able to do and act independently of the Owner of nature. Hence, it cannot be said that the Creator places compassion in the enemy's heart, since man is the operator.

It follows that if the Creator makes a miracle for him, by this He takes from the enemy the choice. This is unlike animals, who have no choice, but act according to what the Creator has imprinted in them, meaning that the Creator is the operator. Therefore, now He can change their nature.

## 826- A Messenger to Circumcise

There is also the commandment that he must be circumcised, also by a messenger, meaning that the father should circumcise his son. Thus, the question is, Is this commandment to circumcise for the father or for himself? It is like Abraham, who circumcised himself, but Isaac did not circumcise himself, but Abraham circumcised him.

It follows that it is as though his father is also a messenger to circumcise his son. The commandment pertains to his father, who must circumcise his son, but the actual correction of the circumcision is on the son. In other words, if the son circumcises himself if he has no father, it is also on the circumcision because he could have done it through a messenger, meaning through a courthouse.

## 827- The Godliness Made the Concealment

We should ask about the words, "The whole earth is full of His glory." Also, it is written in *The Zohar*, "There is no place vacant from You." What does that mean? After all, there was the *Tzimtzum* [restriction], where the light does not shine, so there is a vacant place, as it is written that through the *Tzimtzum*, a vacant place was made.

However, we should interpret that all the restrictions that we speak of pertain only to the lower ones. From the perspective of the Creator, there is no place vacant of Him, but rather "The whole earth is full of His glory."

What does that come to teach us? Man should know that during the descent, when he thinks that there is no Godliness there that sustains the world, he is wrong. Rather, he should believe that even there, within the concealment, there is Godliness. That is, the Godliness made the concealment so he would have a need to reveal. If one does not believe it, he is escaping the campaign.

## 828- A Lot

"And He chose David His servant, and took him from the flock folds" (Psalms 78). *Michlaot* [folds] comes from the word *Maachal* [food]. *Tzon* [flock] means *Yetziot* [exits]. That is, He took David to be a king because his food consisted of many descents, called "exits."

"From behind the nursing ewes, He brought him to shepherd Jacob." From behind the ascents [sounds similar to "ewes" in Hebrew], meaning from states when he was after the ascents, meaning from the descents. "To shepherd Jacob," "shepherd" from the word "bad."

*Akev* [heel] means "end," and is discerned as *Malchut*, which is called "faith." That means that from what was after the ascents, meaning from the descents, from the states, he shepherds his faith. This is called "a faithful shepherd," when the nourishment that sustained the faith was from the work he did during the descent.

This is why it is written, "to shepherd Jacob," meaning to shepherd, so that his faith would grow, meaning that the descents expanded the "in Jacob," in faith. "His people," for then it is called "the people of the Creator," and then they were rewarded with inheritance, called a "lot."

## 829- The Basis of Learning the Revealed

This is already something that is acceptable by anyone in our generation, that learning the revealed is a must, as well as being proficient in Mishnah, and Gemara, *Rishonim* [First] and *Achronim* [Last], and that one should dedicate one's entire life to it and give his heart and soul, and starve his family, to the extent that our sages said, "as black as a raven," for the Torah exists only in one who becomes as cruel to his sons and daughters as a craw, and the Torah exists only in one who puts himself to death over it.

We should understand this racket. If you say, "to learn the rules and not fail in it," one should learn only the verdicts. As for the rest, it is enough if only one person in the city learns, so he will be a rabbi. Why is there an obligation to the point that they said, "For it is your life and the length of your days"? That is, does one who did not learn all six books of the Mishnah, not taste, "For it is your life"? But we see that each and every one says, "For they are our lives and the length of our days."

## 830- The Need for Gentiles

"Do not say in your heart... 'Because of my righteousness... to inherit the land,' but it is because of the wickedness of the nations that the Lord is dispossessing them. ... It is not for your righteousness or the integrity of your heart that you are going to inherit their land, but it is because of the wickedness of the nations that the Lord is driving them out before you, which the Lord swore to your fathers" (Deuteronomy 9:4-5).

We should ask: If the Creator is giving the land because of the wickedness of the nations and not because of the righteousness of Israel, does it mean that were it not for the wickedness of the nations, the Creator would not give the land to Israel? The answer is as Baal HaSulam said concerning "Know for certain," that they give the need for the inheritance of the land.

## 831- The Need for the Torah

After the future. Zebulun gives sustenance, meaning he receives sustenance in the manner of poverty, and in this manner he will learn Torah. It follows that the Torah gives *Malchut* the strength to sustain the poor, and the Torah will furnish the poor. Thus, power is called "sustenance." In other words, since he wants wars, he wants the Torah to give him the strength to work, and he works in order to have a need for the Torah.

## 832- Dead Fish

"Live *Dagim* [fish]" means he has *Daagot* [concerns] about work, but he is alive. That is, he has the power to work and find ways to mitigate his concerns. But dead fish means his concerns cause him death, meaning that all his powers to work have died and he has no vital spirit, having no strength to work and find solutions. This is called "dead fish."

In Egypt, when the *Klipa* [shell/peel] of Egypt was on the Jews, they ate live fish, but the quality of Egypt is called "dead fish," as it is written, "The fish that were in the Nile died," unlike the fish of the Jews, which are alive.

If the concerns are in order to achieve the aim to bestow, this is the concern of Israel, who is concerned over why he is not in the quality of Israel. This is unlike the concerns of the *Mitzrim* [Egyptians], for *Tzar* [narrow] means that he is under the rule of the *Tzar*, meaning the quality of mercy. This is the meaning of "The fish that were in the Nile died," meaning that these *Daagot* [concerns] yield death, the death of the powers, and he cannot do anything.

## 833- Turn Away from Evil and Do Good – 4

Man has two concepts: 1) When he sees that he is in a state of lowliness, and to worry and regret being in lowliness, or be worried over why he is not in a state of ascent.

Although they are seemingly the same thing, they are two things, according to the rule of Baal HaSulam, "Where one thinks, there he is." When one thinks that he is in lowliness, he is attached to lowliness. But when he thinks about how to ascend, he is attached to the discernment of ascension. This is called "do good." But from the bad, "turn away," since when one is attached to the bad, the bad controls the person. Therefore, "Do good."

## 834- "Grow!"

"You have not a blade of grass... that strikes it and tells it, 'Grow!'" In the work, this means that people are as the grass of the field. The angel that strikes is the suffering that the whole world suffers. In other words, the created beings want rest like the root, and the suffering is like a stick that tells (a person) "Go to work!" By this there will be development, and this is called "Grow!"

## 835- Gird Your Sword

15 *Tevet, Tav-Shin-Chaf-Gimel*, January 11, 1963

"'Put your hand under my thigh.' What is 'Your hand'? He started and said, 'Gird your sword upon your thigh, mighty one, Your glory and Your majesty.' And he says about this, 'Mercy and truth will greet you,' the face of the Creator is their share" (*The Zohar, VaYechi*, Item 30).

This means that when it is written, "Your hand," it refers to a sword, and a sword that has two edges, which are mercy and truth, *Hochma* and *Hesed*, see in the *Sulam* [Ladder commentary on *The Zohar*].

Our sages said, "He who reads the *Shema* reading by his bed, it is as though he holds a double-edge sword, as was said 'a double-edge sword in their hand.'"

Concerning the two edges, which are mercy and truth, it means that there is the good inclination, and there is the evil inclination. The beginning of man's work is with the good inclination, and afterward through the evil inclination, as our sages said, "And you shall love ... with all your heart, with both your inclinations."

Concerning *Hesed*, which is the quality of bestowal, it is a work of the good inclination. When one is rewarded with the quality of truth, meaning that the quality of the Creator's goodness is already revealed to him, that it is true, meaning the trueness of His aim, that it is to do good to His creations, then he has nothing against the work of the Creator, for then even his enemies make peace with him, as in, "When the Lord favors man's ways, even his enemies make peace with him," pertaining to the evil inclination.

This is the meaning of "Mercy and truth will greet you." This means that to be rewarded with the *Panim* [face/anterior] of the Creator, there must first be mercy and truth. When one is rewarded with the quality of truth, it is considered that then he is rewarded with the *Panim* of the Creator. Conversely, before one is rewarded with the quality of truth, it is considered that he only has the quality of *Achoraim* [back/posterior], regarded as concealment. At that time, he sees that only he is giving to the Creator, and this is discerned as *Hesed*.

In other words, he is doing mercy with the Creator, meaning that only he is giving. However, when one is rewarded with the quality of truth, he sees the opposite—that he is the receiver from the Creator, though it is in a corrected manner, meaning he is receiving in order to bestow.

This is the meaning of "One who reads the *Shema* reading by his bed," where *Mitta* [bed] is regarded as *Mata* [down/below], which is before a person moves into a state of lying down, which is sprawling of hands and legs, as in "I did not find my hands and legs at the seminary." This means that one has no attainment because at that time, he is in a state of concealment of the face, regarded as *Achoraim*.

## 836- Servant and Son

"Anyone who buys a servant, buys his master."

There is the discernment of "servant" and there is the discernment of "son." A servant means that a person says that he has no authority of his own. This is called "He who buys a servant, buys his master," meaning that he has no authority of his own, but his sole aim is to please his master. At that time, it is considered that he is working only with the good inclination.

A son means that he is rewarded with serving the Creator with the evil inclination, too, meaning that he is rewarded with receiving abundance from the Creator. At that time, he is rewarded with the Creator giving him as a father who is concerned only with satisfying his sons' will, as it is written, "As a father has mercy on sons." It follows that a son means that the person receives, but in order to bestow.

## 837- Adhere to His Attributes

Rains fall thanks to three things: thanks to the earth, thanks to mercy, and thanks to suffering (*Jerusalem Talmud, Taanit*).

We should ask what "thanks to the earth" means. Can the earth choose, that we can say that it has merits for following the path of the Creator?

We should understand this in ethics. "Earth" means the quality of *Malchut*, called "earth," which is the matter of faith. It is known that there is a discernment of "heaven" and a discernment of "earth," as it is written, "In the beginning, God created the heaven and the earth." "Heaven" means the quality of Torah, which is regarded as sublime and high, like the heaven, which is above.

The Torah belongs to the Creator, for He should give the Torah as a gift to a person. Conversely, faith is called "earth," since it belongs to man, who is in the earth, as our sages said, "Everything is in the hands of heaven but the fear of heaven." The matter of faith pertains to man, who should make the choice to take upon himself the burden of the kingdom of heaven during the concealment.

*Hesed* [grace/mercy] comes from the words, "Who is *Hassid*? He who says, 'Mine is yours,'" which means bestowal, as our sages said, "Adhere to His attributes, as He is merciful," etc. Otherwise, it is impossible to be rewarded with *Dvekut* [adhesion].

# 838- *The Trueness of Providence*

It is known that the purpose of creation is to do good to His creations. It is impossible to be rewarded with the goal before one corrects oneself with the quality of equivalence, called the quality of *Hesed*. Afterward, he will be rewarded with the goal, called "truth," and then the trueness of His Providence is apparent—that it is in the manner of good and doing good.

We see that the verse says, "What does the Lord your God ask of you? Only to fear Me." In other words, a person must be rewarded with fear of heaven. This is the only thing that one should try to merit, as it is written, "but fear." This is called "the quality of faith," where one must believe in the Creator, as our sages said, "The eye sees, the ear hears, and all Your deeds are written in the book."

A person can check if he believes in this, for he can take an example from the fear of flesh and blood. For example, when a person looks through the window into his neighbor's home, he will certainly not do anything unless it is good in the eyes of his friend, and he will certainly not do something inappropriate.

It follows that when a person is alone in the room, if he believes that "the eye sees," he cannot do anything that the Creator does not like, just as he will not do anything bad while his neighbor is looking at him.

For this reason, if one sees that he is doing things not according to the Creator's will, he must certainly say that he does not believe in "the eye sees." Otherwise, he would not be able to do these deeds.

Likewise, if his friend could look into his mind and would know what his friend thinks, he would certainly not think any bad thoughts because he would not want to be disgraced in the eyes of his friend.

Accordingly, if a person believes that the Creator knows the thoughts, how can one think thoughts that are not according to the Creator's will? Hence, he sees that he does not have real faith. For this reason, this is a true test to know whether he has faith.

When one sees that his faith is inappropriate, it is considered that he is lacking fear of heaven and needs the Creator to send him.

## 839- A Kosher Woman

Tiberias, 10 *Shevat, Tav-Shin-Chaf-Gimel*, February 4, 1963

"Who is a *Kosher* [fit/proper] woman? She who does her husband's will."

It is known that man is regarded as the quality of "woman," meaning a "female," who receives bestowal from her husband. The Creator bestows all the pleasures to His creatures. And when is one regarded as a *Kosher* woman? When she does her husband's will, meaning when he receives all the pleasures only with the aim to do "her husband's will," and not because of his own will.

## 840- Quick Nearing

One does not enter the work of the left, called "trouble," unless during an ascent. At that time, he enters the left, meaning while he is still not in a descent.

"Rabbi Elazar said, 'One should always precede trouble with prayer'" (Sanhedrin 44b). This means that even when one is in a state of ascent, he must ask the Creator to bring him closer with another, greater nearing, so he will advance in the work. If he feels no deficiency, he cannot advance. This is why he is given a descent from above, so he will have a lack. A descent is called "trouble," and then he prays.

Hence, there is an advice: Before the trouble comes to him, he already prays.

# 841- Coerced

"Will offer [also "bring closer"] him to His will." RASHI interpreted, "It teaches that he is coerced until he says, 'I want.'"

Baal HaSulam said about the words, "The Lord is your shade," that according to the acts of people, so happens above, at the root of one's soul. Hence, it follows that if one coerces himself below, he also causes coercion above, until the Creator says, "I want," and accepts your work.

# 842- The Work in General

The work in general is:

1) Fear: This is called "the first commandment." It is fear as in "great and ruling," which are two discernments: 1) He attains His greatness. At that time, by seeing the exaltedness of the Creator, fear is established in his heart because he attains the greatness of the Creator.

Then, the measure of the greatness determines the measure of the fear. On this, there is no work, since it is a natural thing for the little one to annul before the great one. Then, through the quality of "great"—when the measure of the fear is determined—comes the "ruler," for then he has true fear, a discernment of only the "ruler."

This means that even though he does not attain anything unless through faith above reason, on such a level is the true fear. However, the fear in the manner of "great" is required in order to know the measure of the fear.

2) Love: Likewise, there are two manners in love, as well—in the manner of the side of His goodness, and in the manner of the side of the harsh judgment. Love on the side of His goodness is only in order to determine the measure of love, meaning the measure of His greatness. Afterward, when he already knows the measure of love, he must receive this measure as unconditional love, as in "Even if He takes your soul." This is regarded as absolute love.

At that time, it is regarded that he is permanently adhered because nothing in the world can stop him because he does not need anything, for there is nothing more in the world than "taking your soul." Hence, one who is ready for devotion every moment is certain to go forward on the rungs of holiness.

## 843- *The Work Is the Reward*

"Great reward according to his work." We should ask, since even in corporeality, a person is rewarded according to the work. However, the work is the reward.

## 844- *Labor Is the Reward*

"According to the labor, so is the reward." In other words, afterward, he sees that the labor he gave was his reward. To the extent of the labor, so is the reward, since the labor is the reward, and the Creator gave him the desire to labor.

## 845- None as Holy as the Lord

"There is none who is as holy as the Lord." But is there one who is worse than the Creator but holy? "There is no rock like our God." Does that mean that there is another rock, which is a little worse than the Creator? Rather, there are holy ones and angels and souls, and all receive *Kedusha* [holiness] from the Creator. This is not so "because there is none besides You." Rather, You will give them *Kedusha* [holiness] (*The Zohar*, *Tazria*, Item 37).

We should ask what this tells us in the work. One must believe how all the overcoming in the work, and did he labor in order to be rewarded with the Holy one, as it is written, "You will be holy, for I am holy." At that time, one must know that all of man's work does not help him whatsoever. Rather, it is all from the Creator.

In other words, all the *Kedusha* [holiness] that one feels he has comes to him from the Creator. This is what it means that there is no *Kedusha*, meaning no *Kedusha* in the world that one can obtain by himself. Rather, everything comes from the Creator. This is why it is written, "There is none as holy as the Lord," and "There is no rock like our God."

It is known that *Kelim* [vessels] are called by the name *Elokim* [God], and lights are called by the name of *HaVaYaH*. It is written, "there is no rock," which is when one sees that he has vessels of bestowal. This is regarded that a new thing was created for him, which is called a "rock," meaning that in a place where he had vessels of reception, vessels of bestowal have been depicted in him. One should not think that he helped the Creator in any way and by this obtained vessels of bestowal. Rather, everything came from above.

Baal HaSulam said that prior to working, one must say, "If I am not for me, who is for me?" After the work, he should believe in private Providence, meaning that the Creator does everything. This is the meaning of what is written there: "The Creator draws a picture within a picture." We should interpret that within the form of the *Kelim*, which is reception, He draws there the form of bestowal.

## 846- Faith Is the Quality of *Malchut*

*The Book of Aluma*: One who does not believe is worse than an idol-worshipper, for he admits that there is a God, but he is wrong about who He is and is regarded as a beast in which there is nothing but eating and drinking.

Faith is the quality of *Malchut*. The faith of Israel is that they establish their faith in the Creator, which is the presence of Godliness in the lower ones. From within the *Shechina* [Divinity], they believe in Godliness.

This faith in Him did not come to us except through this *Sefira*.

## 847- Willows of the Brook

"Willows of the brook that grow by the stream, etc., Rabbi Zira said, 'Why is it called 'It is rooted by abundant water'; its name is a willow'?" (*Sukkah* 34, Ezekiel 17). This means that although they have neither taste nor smell, it is still as though there is abundant water here.

Water means "upper abundance." It is as though one feels in it a good taste and pleasantness, and derives from this joy, gladness, and merriment, from belonging to a people that is filled with delight, meaning that with their actions, they serve the King.

## 848- The Days of the Messiah

"Our sages said, 'Proselytes are not accepted in the days of the Messiah'" (*Yevamot* 24b).

The Messiah means the time of greatness of the clarity of the brain by which one cannot be rewarded with the eternity of the

Messiah. Rather, one converts oneself precisely during poverty. Then, when greatness comes, he is rewarded with eternity.

## 849- A Condition for Marrying a Woman

"One will not marry a woman he intends to divorce" (*Yevamot* 37b).

In other words, one should not accept the awakening if he intends to subsequently return to the vanities of time. Rather, he should move his mind away from this because he does not want to blemish the abundance.

## 850- A Proselyte Who Converted

"Rabbi Yosi says, 'A proselyte who converted is as a newly born child.' One is not punished for the past. Rather, why is one tormented? Because he is not proficient in the precisions of the *Mitzvot* [commandments] like Israel" (*Yevamot* 48).

In other words, once he has converted, he has ascents and descents, which are spiritual suffering, and this is because he is not proficient in the precisions of the *Mitzvot* of mind and heart, for only then is his eternity established in him, and he no longer leaves the King's palace.

## 851- A Desire for Levirate Marriage

"A certain heretic said to Raban Gamliel: 'You are a people with whom its God has performed levirate marriage,' as it is written, 'In their flock and in their cattle they shall go and seek the Lord, but they shall not find; He has slipped away from them'" (Hosea 5). He said to you, "You fool! Is it written 'released for them'? It is written 'released from them,' while a sister-in-law whom the brothers released, could there be any validity in her?

This means that if the brother-in-law releases the sister-in-law, since the sister-in-law does not want to perform levirate marriage, it means nothing. But if the brother-in-law does not want, he releases the sister-in-law from the brother-in-law. The Creator releases Himself from them, meaning He received the release from them. That is, when Israel does not want to perform levirate marriage, the Creator forces them.

## 852- Two Kinds of Scrutinies

Two kinds of scrutinies are found in the human species: bitter and sweet, and true and false.

Prior to the sin, *Adam HaRishon* was in the scrutiny of bitter and sweet.

"To serve it and to keep it" in the scrutiny of bitter and sweet. We, too, have similar *Mitzvot* [commandments]. The pleasure of Shabbat [Sabbath] and the pleasure of Good Day, and abstention from insects and reptiles that one's soul wants.

The serpent started with "Even though God said, 'You shall not eat from all the trees of the garden,'" meaning he started a conversation with her, since the woman was not commanded by the Creator. "And the woman said to the serpent, 'From the fruit of the trees of the garden we shall eat, and from the fruit of the tree that is in the midst of the garden, God said, 'You shall not eat of it or touch it lest you die.'""

The serpent asked: How did she know that the tree of knowledge was forbidden? Perhaps all the fruits of the garden were forbidden for you? The woman's replied, "You shall not touch lest you die."

1) How did she know about the touching?

2) Why the doubt, "lest you die"?

We should interpret that the answer "lest you die" pertains to the touching, for there is none as wise as the experienced. The serpent's reply, "You will not surely die, for God knows that on the day you eat of it your eyes will open and you will be as God, knowing good and evil." The serpent's argument was that it was foolish to think that God created something harmful in the world. Rather, all the bad comes only from the lower one, since only here the correction of bestowal is missing.

"On the day you eat of it," meaning with the aim to bestow, "You will be as God, knowing good and evil," meaning that just as it is sweet to the Creator, completely the same, so the good and bad will be to you, completely the same, if it is with the intention to bestow.

But the Creator did not inform you of this because He knows, meaning the Creator knows that if you pay attention and your eating is in *Kedusha* [holiness], your eyes will open to understand the grandeur of the matter by yourselves. "And the woman saw that the tree was good…"

# 853- *The Need to Recognize the Greatness of the Creator*

The need to recognize the greatness of the Creator is specifically in *Lishma* [for Her sake]. *Lo Lishma* [not for Her sake] means the gifts, so there is no need for recognition.

## 854- Takes His Part and the Part of His Friend

One asked Rabbi Meir after he went astray, "Why is it written, 'God has made one opposite the other'? He said to him, 'Everything that the Creator created, He created its opposite. He created mountains, He created hills; He created seas, He created rivers.'

"He said to him: 'Your teacher, Rabbi Akiva, did not say so. Rather, 'He created righteous, He created wicked; He created heaven, He created hell. Each and every one has two parts, one in heaven and one in hell. If he is acquitted, he is righteous and takes his part and the part of his friend in heaven. If he is convicted, he is wicked, and takes his part and the part of his friend in hell."

"Rav Mesharsheya said, 'Why is it written about the righteous, 'Therefore, in their land they shall inherit twofold' (Isaiah 61)? Concerning the wicked, it is written, 'And their destruction is twofold'"" (*Hagiga* 15a).

The MAHARSHA interprets, why does each one have two parts? It is because He created the Garden of Eden for the righteous, and He created hell for the wicked, each as he sees it.

Accordingly, we should ask: If so, then there is no free choice, since He created these as righteous and those as wicked, so they are compelled to remain on the same degree on which they were created. The MAHARSHA answers about this, that since man was given the choice to be righteous or wicked, since everything is in the hands of heaven but the fear of heaven, and the Creator does not deny the reward or punishment of any creation, for this reason, He created the Garden of Eden for all of them, perhaps all will be worthy.

But also, He created hell for all of them, perhaps all will be unworthy. It is as was said, "If he is rewarded, he takes his part and the part of his friend," as Rav Mesharsheya said above.

## 855- Wood and Stone

"She wept for her father and her mother for one month." Rabbi Eliezer: truly her father and mother. Rabbi Akiva—this is idol-worship, as was said, "They tell the tree, 'You are my father,' and to the stone, 'You gave birth to us'" (*Yevamot* 48b).

"Tree" means ideas. One who says that his own ideas helped him be able to walk on the path, it is as though he says, "My power and the might of my hand has gotten me these riches."

*Even* [stone] comes from the word *Havana* [understanding]. By understanding the words of the Creator, he has the strength to advance in the work. Otherwise, he will have no strength.

## 856- Man's Nature

We should understand that although man's nature is only in self-love, and that which is against it is hard for him to do, to the point that all the organs are against it, but there is the matter of coercion. In other words, the nature is that when he engages in Torah and *Mitzvot* [commandments], he learns against his will, meaning that he wants it to be only for the sake of the Creator.

At that time, he learns and thinks only about studies that speak of the matter of bestowal. Although the body disagrees, through labor he exerts himself and forces his body to engage with this intention, although his heart's desire disagrees with this intention.

Assorted Notes

# 857- The Need for a *Kli* without Light

Purim, *Adar Aleph, Tav-Shin-Lamed-Vav*, February 1976

Complete faith is faith that yields wholeness. It is as Maimonides said, "What is repentance? Until He who knows the mysteries will testify."

In the "Introduction to The Study of the Ten Sefirot," he interpreted that he means until the Creator opens his eyes and he is rewarded with nearing the Creator. This is regarded as the Creator testifying to him. It also follows that his intention is that wholeness means that the Creator brought him closer and admitted him into His hall, all of him says, "Holy."

Ten *Sefirot* were made in *Nekudim*, but the completion of their work was in *Atzilut*, since in *Akudim* there was only one *Kli* [vessel], meaning the *Sefira* of *Malchut*, which was dark because there was a *Tzimtzum* [restriction] on her quality and she remained in the dark.

It follows that according to the rule that only *Malchut* is the receiver, it turns out that *Malchut* obtains the first nine that emerged through the *Zivug de Hakaa* that *Malchut* did. This is regarded as one *Kli* and one dot, since only her quality remained in the dark after the *Tzimtzum*.

In *Nekudim*, where *Malchut* ascended to *Bina*, it means that *Malchut* uses only the vessels of bestowal in each and every *Sefira*. Thus, *Malchut* attains the GE in the first nine, and the *AHP* in each *Sefira* departed from the degree. It follows that it became dark in every *Sefira* because no light was extended to the vessels of reception.

Afterward, during the *Gadlut* [greatness/adulthood], when they did extend abundance into the vessels of reception, the *Kelim* [vessels] broke because they were small *Kelim*. That is, the *Masach* [screen] could not stop itself from receiving in order to receive.

In *Atzilut*, even after the *Gadlut* returned, the real *AHP* in each degree remained empty from the abundance because only *VAK de Hochma* illuminated. This is regarded that there was no *Zivug* on

*Malchut* herself, but only on *Malchut* that is sweetened in *Bina*. Thus, in each *Sefira*, an empty quality remained, and this is discerned as a *Kli*, meaning without light.

The reason we need a *Kli* without light is that only then is it apparent that there is still a lack that we must correct. Otherwise, we would think that we have achieved wholeness.

## 858- Moses Assembled

"And Moses assembled." RASHI interpreted, "They assembled by his word." What does that come to teach us? Otherwise, I would say that he would collect them with the hands.

The interpreters say that the tabernacle came to atone for the calf. The matter of the calf was that they said, "These are your gods, O Israel," meaning seeing. This is called "hands." Hence, when he assembled them, it was not with the hands, which is reception, but through speech, for "speech" is called "The heavens were made by the word of the Lord," and as it is written, "I have a good gift in My treasury, and its name is Shabbat [Sabbath]; go and let them know." Gift is a good thing, unlike charity.

## 859- You Shall Increase Their Inheritance

"Among these the land shall be divided. ...To the large you shall increase their inheritance, and to the small you shall diminish their inheritance; each shall be given their inheritance according to those who were numbered of them" (Numbers 26:53-54).

"To the large you shall increase their inheritance, and to the small you shall diminish." That is, "large" means "right," wholeness, greatness, concerning the greatness of the Creator and the wholeness of man. By having some grip on the work of the Creator, their inheritance will grow. There we need to increase their inheritance, meaning to give more time than the hours of his work.

"And to the small" means a lack, when one sees one's lowliness, meaning that he has no *Kelim* [vessels], no Torah, and no work. This is called "left," meaning a place of deficiency that requires corrections. "Diminish" means to allot little time for his work.

# 860- With What to Aid?

"He is aided." With what is he aided? It says, "with a holy soul." Thus, how are souls born? Precisely through deficiencies that receive assistance from above.

# 861- The Work of the Lines

"It was said, 'Since it is a time of good will, let us ask for mercy for the inclination to commit an offense.' They asked for mercy and it was given to them. He said to them, 'See, that if you kill it, the world will end.' They incarcerated it for three days and sought an egg that was born on that same day, but throughout the land of Israel, none was found. They said, 'How will we do it? If we kill it, the world will end! And if we ask for mercy for half, half is not given from above.' They poked out its eyes and let it go, since one does not tease one's kin" (*Yoma* 69b).

"The inclination to sin" is the inclination to receive pleasure, discerned as *Hochma*. "If we kill it, the world will end," meaning that the purpose of creation—to do good to His creations, to receive pleasure—will be revoked.

"And if we ask for mercy for half," meaning that it will spread downward only to half of the degree of *Hochma*. That is, why should we make the middle line? To cancel the left line, but there is fear that they will not extend the middle line. Hence, it is best if it spreads down only half of the left line, meaning only illumination of *Hochma*, as it will be later by the decision of the middle line.

"Half is not given from above." Only wholeness comes from above, since when spirituality is revealed below, it is always in wholeness.

"They poked out its eyes and let it go." That is, precisely through the middle line, for *Hochma* is called "eyes." RASHI interpreted that he was blinded by blue, as in "You put a boundary to the sea," meaning that he does not see below that it is expansion from above downward, and he feels only in his place. "One does not tease one's kin" means that he has it during the *Dvekut* [adhesion].

## 862- Will Give Wisdom to the Wise

"Will give wisdom to the wise." "One does not sin unless a spirit of folly has entered him." Hence, one who wants the Creator to help him achieve *Lishma* [for Her sake] is given a gift. However, it is difficult for a person to achieve *Lishma* without help from the Creator.

## 863- Korah's Complaint

A person should include the left in the right, and then the Creator dwells within him (*The Zohar*, Korah, Item 30). This means that one should not stay in the left and wait for his prayer to be answered. Rather, he should promptly shift to the right, above reason. Korah's complaint was within reason.

## 864- See Life

See life with the woman you love, for she is your part in life. One must include life from the tree of life, which is ZA, in this place, which is *Malchut*, who is called a "woman." One must also include the quality of day in the night, meaning ZA in *Malchut*, for "She is your part in life," since there is illumination of *Hochma* only in *Malchut* (*The Zohar*, Korah, Item 28).

"Everything that your hand can do, do." This means that one should include the left in the right. "That your hand finds" means left; "to do by your strength" is right.

"Brings down to Sheol [netherworld] and raises up." Baal HaSulam said that when one feels that he is in Sheol, it causes him to ascend. This means that one comes to a state where he says that it cannot be worse than this, so he gives a heartfelt prayer "and rises up," meaning then he ascends to *Kedusha* [holiness].

## 865- Wholeness Is One Hundred

*Teruma* [donation/contribution] is two out of a hundred (Korah, Item 48), meaning to unify Him twice daily, meaning two out of a hundred, which are two times the *Shema* reading, evening and morning. These are two times 49, minus two to complete to one hundred. At that time, *Bina* and *Malchut* complete to one hundred, for *Bina* is called *Ima* [mother] and is called *Me'ah* [one hundred, same letters as *Ima*].

## 866- Peace to the Far and to the Near

"'Peace, peace, to the far and to the near,' said the Lord, and I will heal him." Peace comes to those who are near the Creator, which is "the right pulls closer, and the left pushes farther." The peace of the Creator can be specifically through both, through far and near, meaning right and left, and then there can be peace.

## 867- The Governance of Peace

Man can toil and labor if no correction results from it. But for a small thing, which does not require much effort, if it is on the path of correction, there is no strength, since the corruptions come from the breaking of the vessels of the sin of the tree of knowledge.

Since this is still not corrected, corruptions still reign. This reign gives power, which is not so on the path of correction. This requires a different governance, called "peace."

## 868- The Reason that Obligates

Receive reward. If not, you will receive punishment. It follows that the reason that obligates him will be self-benefit. But how will it be otherwise, meaning because He is great and ruling? And why is it not considered for the sake of the Creator, in order to bestow?

## 869- Matrimony

Any woman who does not have matrimony, not on it and not on others, the offspring is like her. And which one is it? The offspring of a handmaid and a foreigner. How do we know about a Canaanite handmaid? Rav Huna said, "Kara said, 'Sit here with the donkey,' with he who is like a donkey," meaning that matrimony does not apply. "Her offspring is like her," as Kara said, "The woman and her children will be to her master."

How do we know about a foreigner? Kara said, "You will not marry with them," meaning that matrimony does not apply. How do we know that her offspring is like her? Rabbi Yochanan said in the name of Rabbi Shimon Bar Yochai, as Kara said, "For they will turn your sons away from following Me." Your son who comes from an Israelite is considered your son, and your son who comes from an idol-worshipper is not considered your son, but her son (*Kidushin* 68).

In the work, "matrimony" means a man who is rewarded with *Kedusha* [holiness]. An "offspring" is understandings that help the work. An "Israelite" is the *Shechina* [Divinity], a "handmaid" and a "foreigner" are the *Sitra Achra* [other side], called "the *Klipa* [shell/peel] of a donkey," meaning a "handmaid," and the *Klipa* of an ox is called a "foreigner."

## 870- *Adam HaRishon* Was a Heretic

"*Adam HaRishon* was a heretic." We should ask, Since if the Creator spoke to him, how can it be that he was a heretic, meaning a disbeliever? He denied the faith because he had knowledge and he could not work in the manner of faith.

## 871- A Scorpion and a Snake

"The pit is empty; there is no water in it," meaning there is no Torah in it. But there are snakes and scorpions in it, meaning that if (there is no) Torah in it, there are immediately snakes and scorpions in it.

*Akrab* [scorpion] is called *Kar-Av* [cold-thick] where the coldness comes to him because of *Aviut* [thickness]. It has no eyes, meaning the quality of *Hochma* [wisdom]. This means that it does not argue with the intellect, but simply with *Aviut*. A "snake" is regarded as the mind, which argues with the intellect, as it is written in the Jerusalem [Talmud], "And the snake was cunning" and argued with Eve. It started and said, "Although God said," etc. This is why everyone agrees that a scorpion determines, but not a snake.

## 872- Who Makes a Way through the Sea

*Nukva* is units, *ZA* is tens, *Ima* is hundreds, *Abba* is thousands, *Keter* is ten thousand, KLA.

Commentary: *Elef* [one thousand], *El-Af* [God-nose]. The nose is the *Kli* [vessel] of life, as it is written, "And He breathed into his nose the breath of life." This *Kli* was actually taken from MIKVEHON, but the *Ruach* that emerges from it emerges only from the side of *Ima*, and therefore can come into the nose once more, like death and resurrection. However, if the *Ruach* comes from MIKVEHON, what emerges from the nose is *Ruach* that leaves and does not return.

It is known that the *Aleph* ascended in KLA, and there is the ten thousand because she is included in all of them. When she was sorted from there and descended to OMETZ, it is in the manner of "I will teach you *Hochma* [wisdom]," as rising without standing there, for lack of adornment. Hence, she descends to *Bina*, as in

"I will teach you *Bina* [intelligence]" in adornment, which is *Me'ot* [hundreds], from the words *Min-At* [heretic-you (female form)], for there she borrows from the daughter, or from the word *Ot* [letter], since it emerged from his nose and became a stranger.

When she descends to ZA, it is in the manner of tenth, everyone, as in "A king chained to troughs." When she descends to *Malchut*, it is in units, for it is a very small number, the smallest there is.

*Aleph* is a view of MIKVEHON, *Bet* is a view of *Hochma*, *Gimel* is their merging with one another into one where they are indistinguishable. This is why the light is in *Aleph* of MIKVEHON. However, in *Lamed-Hey* and *Lamed-Shin*, the day and night work together until the second day, when the firmament was made. But from the words "to the stamper embroiders" because he wove two noses together will be doubled and divided between male water and female water, since from *Tabur* and above it were males and they do not have a nose, and from *Tabur* down "They have a nose and they smell." Until the third day, when all the water from *Tabur* down gathered into one place, and the dry land that is the sealing under OMETZ emerged outside of the *Rosh* and was seen outside. Thus, the dry land was for the living, and the water for the dead. By this, the two *Mi* [two *Mi* make the word "water"] and the *Tav* connected in the upper one, too, which is the *Tav* of *Mitta* [death], from *Yod* and *Tav*.

Afterward, the dry land, too, which is from *Tabur* and above, a sealing before the MIKVEHON, which now receives the form of below the *Tabur*, but in the manner of "standing."

Understand that the water gathered in the *Kli* of "nose" of the first day like a mother who lends her clothes to her daughter. The dry land, which is the *Kli* of *Ima* from the second day, emerged from the *Kli* of "nose" in the manner of "standing." There, the light of the first day was included; hence, she is fit for life, since the control is mainly in the form of the *Kli*. This is the reason for the twofold "it was good," meaning the dry land, since the two *Mi* in *Mayim* [water] returned to prepare life in itself. This is the meaning of TADSHE [will put forth grass], as an acronym, the image of his father.

"Herb yielding seed," etc., means that if he is entirely as a mantle of hair, his name is called "herb." Herbs grow on the dry land and cover it until the earth is not seen. It follows that the herb of the field is regarded as *Saar* [storm] of *MIKVEHON*. Yet, from the text, they grow and emerge from within the dry land, which is the sealing of *OMETZ*.

This is the meaning of "yielding seed after their kind," meaning that the herbs that grow first are not seeds at all. However, after plowing for some time, they become an actual seed, as in "They were as antenna of grasshoppers, and He plucked them out and replanted them and they grew," see *The Zohar, Beresheet*.

Similarly, "A fruit tree, a fruit bearing tree": Likewise, a fruit tree in the first place does not bear fruit until they are relocated.

"With seed in them after their kind": That is, it is known that its seed is in it to begin with, before the *MIKVEHON*, meaning in the place called "dry land." For this reason, the seed is "after its kind," meaning "kind" [type] of utterance, and in the upper *Peh*, and there is no grip there to the outer ones.

This explains the meaning of "dry land" and "water," that they are in collaboration but the water is present. The water, which is light, covers the abyss, which is the *Kli*, the light of *Behina Bet* and the *Kli* of *Behina Dalet*. The opposite of it is the dry land, for the dry land is the sweetening of *Behina Bet*. The herb, which is *Behina Dalet*, covers it and conceals it.

Thus, all that is apparent on the water is the quality of *Ima*. This is the meaning of "As waters cover for the sea," while *Behina Dalet* sinks like a stone and disappears. For this reason, anyone who drowns dies from the stormy wind of the abyss, and anyone who drinks or licks from the face of the water revives himself by the power of *Bina*, which is the "living God."

This explains the essence of the water, which is very dangerous to man's life, for anything that comes into it sinks and drowns in the abyss.

Even a ship that tries to sail across the sea, sometimes a stormy wind emerges from the abyss deep in the sea, from the quality of *MIKVEHON*, and then "the water will rise" by the power of *Behina Bet*, and "will descend to the abyss" by the power of *Behina Dalet*, "and their soul will delight in evil," where their seed is not blessed, for "all their wisdom will be swallowed" because the big chasm and the little chasm mix with one another and the *Hochma*, too, is blemished, meaning the quality of "living soul" in it, and their living soul delights in evil.

This is the meaning of "who makes a way through the sea and a path through the mighty waters," meaning that "He caused the storm to be still, so their waves were hushed." The thing is that the whole danger is from the stormy wind at the sea, from which all of the sea's inclinations come, as in man's heart. There is the *Nukva* of the abyss, as in "And His wonders in the deep," meaning in the depth.

Hence, "When He spoke, He raised a stormy wind," where when he emits he has, and from above, he does not have. This is the opposite of the manna in the desert, which he had from above and he did not bring it out (however, "when the sun grew hot, it would melt," since by the unbounded radiance, which is the bringing out of the sun from its sheath at high noon, at that time, it melts and disappears as in the sealing of *OMETZ*).

For this reason, "and it lifted its waves," as in the verse, "He uncovered himself inside his tent," since he attributed his corruption to the upper one. This is the meaning of "He raised a stormy wind," which is not as "breathed" or "blew" or "walked," since it is not back and forth, but forth without back. This is why it seems like one pillar from below upward that wants to destroy everything.

This is the meaning of "He caused the storm to be still," since that storm will swirl on the head of the wicked, who deny the word of the Creator. But when they recognize the storm by the force of the Creator on the water, at that moment, they promptly silenced and "their waves hushed," since they became very yielding. Hence, "They were glad because they were quiet." That is, although they had nothing to be glad about, since they already threw all their possessions off the ship and into the sea, they were happy about the silencing itself, since they saved their lives.

This is the meaning of "He caused the storm to be still," meaning that the storm itself becomes a source of silence. And from then, "He guided them to their desired haven," since they were rewarded with obtaining their wish. This explains the meaning of the danger of the fierce water at sea.

Two objects: 1) MAALAD, which is the looting of Egypt, which is adornment and the looting of the sea, which is rising. This is the meaning of "He seems to them as a young man," meaning discerned as the elders of the land, but as ZA itself, who rises through the power of his forefathers. This is the meaning of "a handmaid saw," etc., since this rising reached the world of Assiya, externality.

For this reason, it is called "the tearing of the Red Sea," for it is the lower water of MIKVEHON. This is the meaning of "The nations will hear and be angry," etc., what our sages said at the time of the reception of the Torah, that the nations did not want to receive, as it is written, "And shone to them from Seir, appeared from Mount Paran," one clung to murdering, one clung to adultery, and only the children of Israel said, "We will do and we will hear," since He appeared to them as a merciful old man, meaning that in all His inclinations there was mercy.

This is so because there is a need for the power of judgment, too, as was said, "One must learn a tiny bit of folly," etc., for then they could come to the promised land of Canaan to plow and to sow, "each man under his vineyard and each man under his fig." However, by this, it was revealed that there is a tiny light in the *Klipot* [shells/peels], too, which sustains them, and this is why Seir and Paran braced themselves and did not yield. This is what it means that He appeared to them as an old man.

Old man and young man: The meaning of the young man is explained, that his illuminations come to this world. Hence, "The nations will hear and be angry." The meaning of the old man is the inner ascension and scrutinizing them. For this reason, the nations do not yield at all, and only Israel yield and not the nations. Then the "Righteous in their land will inherit twofold," rising and adornment. Conversely, in Egypt, which is a land that is not theirs, they had only adornment, meaning food and drink, but no rising.

"What rumor did he hear and come?" the tearing of the Red Sea and the war against Amalek. The first two objects (which are "We will do and we will hear"), the looting of the sea and the tearing of the Red Sea were not enough for them because they came into the dryness inside the sea. After the pleasantness of the miracle, the *Klipa* [shell/peel] of the dryness reawakened as the Sinai desert and not as a mountain, for they became thirsty for water.

Also, "They came to Marah [Hebrew: bitter]," etc., since they tasted there the bitter taste of MIKVEHON, for water that covers a person put him to death, while drinking a little bit of it revives him.

You saw *Abba*: There they tried the Creator, "If there is the Lord among us or not." This is perplexing, for it is not written simply that the people were thirsty, and it is not written at all that they tried the Creator by this, for they almost died of thirst, which is the meaning of the dryness and fire of thirst. Moreover, this is what grows out of rising where there is no testing.

This is the sublime secret that is called "When he lowered his hands," which is the striking of the rock. For when he raised his hand, the power of Israel and their sanctity became clarified, as AVI. When he lowered his hand to MIKVEHON, the power of Israel weakened. However, because "the people complained about Moses," for they could not resist the power of ascension like Moses, as MA, but rather as rising, as in, Datan and Aviram are standing in pride.

It has also been explained that the rising was as in a young man at which time all the nations surrendered, where the thirst for water is a faithful *Hesed* [mercy/grace], for therefore, "and Moses lowered his hands" and struck the rock. In other words, that verse taught them "If there is the Lord among us or not," and "much mighty water, waves of the sea" promptly came out. However, they drank a little to quench the fire of thirst, then they were rewarded with life again, which is the adornment.

"And Amalek came." That is, by the striking of the rock, that *Klipa* that disappeared before, in the tearing of the Red Sea, returned and was reinforced. "And fought," etc.

This is the meaning of "And you are tired" from the dryness, which the fire of thirst burned. "And weary" by the striking of the rock. They searched again for the two precious objects, "Have you seen *Abba*?" A tidal wave rose on them from *MIKVEHON*, in the image of a dog, and it is called a "tail," like the Red Sea. And then, "They came to the Sinai desert," for there is "Mount Horev," and it became Mt. Sinai, where God appeared to him in Moses' voice, as a merciful old man.

Rephidim means *Rifion Yadaim* [limpness of hands], when Moses lowered his hands, like the striking of the rock. At the time of the war against Amalek, everyone saw that when Moses raised his hands "Israel prevailed." Hence, they had a true preparation to receive the Torah as an old man, which is the *Netilah* [washing] of the hands as in mountains. This is the meaning of "And they took a stone and put it under him," and he seemed to them like that stone that sank in the fierce water. However, it was under Moses, for he needed it very much.

Were it not for the stone, there would be thirst for water. However, underneath him because "Moses' hands were heavy," since they caused them thirst.

Aaron and Hur supported him. Aaron is *Abba*. Hur is Miriam's husband and the son of Caleb. This is the meaning of "My uncle stretched out his hand from the hole, for it is Hur [also "hole" in Hebrew] son of Caleb.

By this force, they journeyed from Rephidim and "came to the Sinai desert," and were rewarded with limitation by the dryness and the thirst. They were rewarded with the revelation of the Creator by "And it came to pass when he raised," and Aaron's support.

This is the meaning of "And they saw the God of Israel, and under his feet was as the making of the sapphire brick. Yet He did not stretch out His hand against the nobles of the sons of Israel."

This miracle and wonder was allotted them by the victory over Amalek, for the hand under Moses, and naturally, He did not stretch out His hand against *Atzilut*, as in "his neighbor's work."

This is the meaning of "What rumor did he hear," etc., for Jethro was the priest of wickedness and knew that Moses sent for his wife and her two sons, for he did not need them after the adornment and the rising, those two above-mentioned objects.

However, after the war against Amalek, he said, "If she does not come out because of me," as in stretching out a hand in the manner of a priest of wickedness, "come out because of your wife," as in "And they saw God, and they ate and drank," meaning as adornment and rising together. At that time, Moses came out toward his father-in-law, for he was his eyes in the desert, for he told you, "and you will see."

# 873- *Ibur* [Conception] – 2

*Ibur Aleph* [first conception] is done by the upper one, like a person who receives an awakening from above. *Ibur Bet* [second conception] means that the lower one must work by himself by the power of the awakening he had received. In other words, he must add, through the awakening he had received from the upper one, and work by his labor. Otherwise, he loses everything and returns to being a black dot, meaning that his spirituality is regarded as darkness that does not shine.

By this we can interpret, "His first wife is called upon him from above, 'The daughter of so and so to so and so,'" meaning as said above, *Ibur Aleph* comes and calls on him from above, which is an awakening from above. "His second wife is according to his actions," as said above, like the example of *Ibur Bet*, that it is by himself, meaning according to his actions.

## 874- Rest and Joy, Light to the Jews
*Sivan, Tav-Shin-Mem-Dalet, June 1984*

"Rest and joy, light to the Jews" (Shabbat [Sabbath] evening songs). This means that it was light only to the Jews. But to the nations of the world, rest and joy are regarded as darkness. Can this be? Who does not want rest and joy? Also, we need to understand what our sages said about the verse, "The dove came to him toward evening, and behold, in her mouth was a freshly picked olive leaf." They said, "In her mouth," as though speaking. She said, "I prefer my foods to be as bitter as an olive from the hand of the Creator than as sweet as honey from the hands of flesh and blood" (*Iruvin* 7).

We should also understand what our sages said, "Rabbi Yohanan and Rabbi Elazar both said, 'When one needs people, his face changes as chrome. It was said, 'as when vile things become high in the eyes of people''" (*Berachot* 6).

To understand all the above, we must know that we can speak of rest only after exertion. Since we are speaking of Jews, it means that we are speaking of things that pertain to Jews, which means matters pertaining to serving the Creator, which pertains to Jews. Therefore, we should speak of work that one needs to do the holy work, which is bestowing contentment upon the Creator. This is why we were given the six workdays to work with the body to emerge from self-love and bestow upon the Creator.

Since the body does not agree to this because this is against its nature, the labor begins, since labor is that with which the body disagrees. When one wants to go against its opinion and will, it is a great exertion, since the body uses all kinds of arguments to make him think that this is unjust, that he is demanding intolerable things.

This is as it is written in *The Zohar*, "'And they returned from touring the land.' 'They returned' means that they returned to the bad side, saying, 'What have we gotten thus far? We labored in the Torah, yet the house is empty, etc. Who will be rewarded with that world, and who will come into it? It would have been better had we not toiled so, etc., but who can be rewarded with it? etc., and we also saw the descendants of the giant there,' meaning that you need a body as strong and as mighty as a lion. They who have faith, what did they say? 'If the Creator wants us, He will give it to us'" (*The Zohar*, *Sulam* [Ladder commentary on *The Zohar*], *Shlach*, Item 63).

It follows that the spies did not lie, but they had to believe above reason that "if the Creator wants us," He can help us. This is as our sages said, "He who comes to purify is aided." This is what *The Zohar* says, that those who have faith said, "If the Creator wants us," etc., for then the Creator shows His glory, meaning we begin to feel the glory of the Creator because this is all we need, since to us the work of bestowal is regarded as *Shechina* [Divinity] in exile, for our body does not feel the importance of the King, and therefore does not value serving Him and working for Him and thinking about Him all day and how one can please Him.

But if one could feel the importance of the King, we see that it is in our nature that we have the strength to serve an important person and it does not tire us at all. On the contrary, we seek all day how and with what we can do some service for him, and we expect no reward for the work because the work itself is his reward.

For example, the leader of the generation comes to the airport, and all the townspeople come out to greet him. He brought with him a small suitcase, picked one of the townspeople and gave him the suitcase to bring it to his lodging place. Afterward, he wanted to pay him for his work, since he was his porter, and since he is a very important man, he wants to pay him as if it were a big suitcase, for then you need to pay a good sum of money, and he wants to pay for his porterage a considerable sum for his little effort.

Clearly, this man will not take any payment for his work because he is an important person, so any sum of money he might pay him will be meaningless compared to the pleasure he derives from being chosen by the sage to serve him, rather than another person from the town. It is human nature that this costs him no exertion. Rather, according to the sage's importance, so is the pleasure of serving him.

It follows that the work itself is the reward and he does not look for any payment. On the contrary, all the rewards one might receive in return for the work is completely inconsequential compared to the work itself with which he has been granted, and this is his reward.

Conversely, if he is serving a common person and there is no importance in serving him, it is not worthwhile for the body to work for the sake of others, much less for the sake of the Creator, since for the sake of the Creator also contains the matter of faith, which is not such a simple matter.

Hence, when Shabbat [Sabbath] comes, when the light of Shabbat shines in the manner of the name of the Creator, as it is written in *The Zohar*, that Shabbat is the revelation of His name, meaning that the importance of the Creator becomes revealed, then he gets rest from his labor of the body not wanting to work in order to bestow because he did not feel the importance of the Creator. But when one feels the light of Shabbat, the body agrees to work in order to bestow because it is of great importance to him that he has been rewarded with serving the Creator, and then he does not want any reward, since any reward he might be given is meaningless compared to the value of the servitude he did while serving the Creator.

It follows that by having rest, meaning that he was rewarded with feeling the importance of the Creator, which caused his body to agree to work only in order to bestow contentment upon the Creator, this is his joy. However, from where did it come to him to feel the importance of the Creator? This happens through the light of Shabbat. This is why he says, "rest and joy." It comes by the coming of "light to the Jews," for Shabbat shines only for the Jews, as was said, "rest and joy" come from the light of the Jews, whereas for idol-worshippers, the light of Shabbat does not come.

This is not so on weekdays. At that time, it is called "*Shechina* [Divinity] in exile," when the importance of the Creator does not illuminate, that it is worthwhile to serve Him. This is called "*Shechina* in the dust*.*" Just as dust is unimportant, so is serving Him. At that time, we have great labor if we want to work only in order to bestow, for the body argues that "Since you do not feel the importance of the Creator, work for yourself," meaning only for reward.

In other words, you must always have in your hand what you are working for and not relinquish any self-reception when you taste the taste of pleasure, for this determines how much we can enjoy what we are doing, and what we do not enjoy, why toil for it? Thus, the body argues, "Why should you labor and work and relinquish self-benefit and work for the sake of the Creator, meaning bring contentment to the Creator?"

By this we will understand what our sages said, that the dove said, "I prefer my foods to be as bitter as an olive from the hand of the Creator than as sweet as honey from the hand of flesh and blood." Ostensibly, this contradicts what our sages said, "When one needs people, his face changes as chrome. It was said, 'as when vile things become high in the eyes of people,'" etc. This means that if nourishment is placed in the hands of flesh and blood, meaning that one must receive his nourishment from people, it is not sweet. On the contrary, his face changes like chrome, etc.

Also, in the blessing for the food, we say that we are blessing the Creator so we ask and tell Him: "And please do not make us need, the Lord our God, not the gift of flesh and blood, and not their loan, but only Your full hand," etc. This means that if the foods are dependent on flesh and blood, they are not sweet. Rather, precisely when it is in the hands of the Creator, it means that they are sweet. But here the dove said the exact opposite, that from the hand of the

Creator they are as bitter as an olive, and from the hand of flesh and blood they are as sweet as honey. But we see the opposite of the reality that the dove said.

We should also understand what the dove said, that in the hands of the Creator, they are as bitter as an olive. Why should the foods be as bitter as an olive in the hands of the Creator? Since the dove said this, it means that there is such a reality, so why should it be so, meaning why did the Creator create such a reality?

To understand the above, we must first understand the meaning of "in the hands of the Creator," and what "from the hands of flesh and blood" means, and what is the meaning of "foods."

"Foods" are that which feed man. Through reception of foods, meaning that the foods with which man feeds himself come in several types of pleasure such as eating, drinking, sleeping, money, and honor. All those things give him satisfaction, and he says that for these foods that he obtained in order to sustain his body, he says that it is worthwhile to live in order to receive these nourishments that sustain him if he receives what he wants. When he calculates, after he has obtained all the things he craved, he says that it was worthwhile to be created and worthwhile to live.

Also, we [see] that often, although a person has many things and lacks nothing, and he has abundance, he still has nothing from which to sustain himself. We see that there are many very rich people in the world who nonetheless do not enjoy their lives and have nothing on which to sustain themselves.

The reason is as presented in the introduction to *The Zohar*, that any pleasure that one receives is precisely from things for which he yearns. To the extent of the yearning, so is his ability to enjoy, not more and not less. The measure of the pleasure from a meal is to the extent of the hunger, and there is no pleasure from drinking more than he is thirsty, as our sages said, "One who drinks water when he is thirsty says, 'Everything is done by His word' [the blessing for water]," for then, when he enjoys, he can give thanks for the pleasure. Also, there is pleasure from rest only according to the labor.

Therefore, the very rich, who do not lack anything so they have something to yearn for since they have abundance, because there is yearning only where there is a lack, and they do not even enjoy rest because they do not work, since they have many managers for all their businesses, and have plenty to eat and drink, as well as nice clothes and stately houses and so forth, because they are devoid of yearning, they are devoid of pleasure. Nothing can nourish them, and they are regarded as poor because they have no foods.

Now we will come to clarify the meaning of what the dove said, "I prefer my foods to be as bitter as an olive in the hands of the Creator, than as sweet as honey in the hands of flesh and blood."

The thing is that when one begins to work in order to provide foods for himself, there are two options about it: 1) The foods will be in the hands of the Creator, as our sages said, "Israel sustain their Father in heaven." In other words, he decided that all his foods, which man enjoys, are that he wants to bestow contentment upon the Creator, that he is in *Dvekut* [adhesion] with the Creator, called "equivalence of form," as in "As He is merciful, so you are merciful." It follows that his nourishment is that he wants his foods to be placed in the hands of the Creator, and when he feels that he is working entirely in order to bestow, this is called "in the hands of the Creator," and the hands of flesh and blood do not reach there. "Hand" means a vessel of reception. When all his work enters the *Kli* [vessel] of the Creator, and not in his own vessels of reception, called "self-love," it is considered that his nourishment is in the hands of the Creator.

Now we will explain why when his foods are in the hands of the Creator, they are as bitter as an olive. Since "by the hand of the Creator" means in order to bestow, and since it is against nature, for the nature we are born with is only to receive, when one wants to work against nature, his body resists this work.

Instead, the body wants its nourishments to be in the hands of man, for the hands of flesh and blood are called self-love, called "receiving in order to receive." This is the meaning of what the dove said, "as sweet as honey in the hands of flesh and blood," for where one sees that the work he is doing will yield nourishment, meaning pleasures, which feed his will to receive, this is called "in the hands of man," where the foods are as sweet as honey because they come into the hands of flesh and blood.

And while he wants only to turn the order of life completely upside down, meaning that if previously, all he wanted and thought about was delighting his will to receive, now he wants to relinquish all his pleasures if he sees that they come with the aim of self-benefit. Although he has not achieved this degree of a desire to bestow, but only thinks about it, the body already begins to betray him and does not want to give him strength to work. Then, when he begins to go against the body, he promptly begins to feel a bitter taste in his work.

The dove said that she agrees to it although she tastes a bitter taste, since this is the truth, meaning that this is the real way to achieve the goal for which this world was created, which is to do good to His creations, and one cannot achieve this degree before he is rewarded with equivalence of form called "in order to bestow contentment upon the Creator." Otherwise, the point of *Tzimtzum* [restriction] lies on him, which is the concealment of the face of the Creator.

This is why the dove said that she wants her nourishment, meaning her pleasure, to be that she can concentrate on how from all her work she will be rewarded with everything going to the hands of the Creator and not to self-reception, since this removes her from the goal for which she was created. Hence, during the work, when one tastes a bitter taste and it is impossible to work without overcoming in ascending and descending, that time continues until a person gets help from above, as our sages said, "He who comes to purify is aided." *The Zohar* asks, "How is he helped?" With a holy soul, meaning he is given the light of Torah called "the light in it reforms him." At that time, there is no longer work with his body because all the forces that resist the Creator annul before the upper light.

For this reason, when the light of Shabbat comes, when a person begins to feel his additional soul, all the forces that oppose the

Creator are revoked, so there is no more room for labor. It follows that he is at rest. This is called "rest and joy." Where does it come from? From "light to the Jews," when the light that belongs to the Jews shines on him, meaning that this light that comes from above makes a person Jewish.

Conversely, the nations of the world, which "All the good that they do, they do for themselves," meaning in order to receive, the light that comes to assist and by which they can achieve the aim to bestow, they do not want it whatsoever, since they regard it as death. Hence, when the light of Shabbat comes, it is rest and joy only to the Jews.

## 875- Three Lines
### Sivan, Tav-Shin-Mem-Dalet, June 1984

"Which is a dispute for the sake of the Creator ... and one that is not for the sake of the Creator is the dispute of Korah and his congregation." There is a question: Why does it not say "Moses, and Korah and his congregation," as it is written about Hillel and Shammai?

To understand the above, we must know the meaning of "for the sake of the Creator." *The Zohar* interprets that "for the sake of the Creator" means *Zeir Anpin*. It is interpreted in the *Sulam* [Ladder commentary on *The Zohar*] that the dispute between Shammai and Hillel is the matter of the right line and the left line. Since the right line is incomplete by itself, since it does not contain *Hochma*, and the left line is also incomplete although it contains [*Hochma*], it still lacks *Hassadim*, which is the clothing on *Hochma*. Without this clothing, he is in the dark.

It follows that through the dispute, where each shows the other that there is no wholeness in it, and shows him the lack in the line of the other, it causes the two lines to merge with one another, meaning that both come into the middle line, called *Zeir Anpin*, which is the middle line in the *Partzufim* [pl. of *Partzuf*]. *Zeir Anpin* is called "for the sake of the Creator." This shows that if there weren't a dispute, each would remain in his line. Hence, the dispute was in order to achieve "for the sake of the Creator."

Conversely, Korah and his congregation went by the left line and wanted to remain in the left line. That is, they wanted to stay in *Hochma* without *Hassadim*. They wanted the goal, which is to do good to His creations, without the clothing of *Hassadim*. This is the meaning of what our sages said, "Korah was clever." That is, they wanted to remain on the left line, which is *Hochma* without *Hassadim*. It follows that the dispute of Korah and his congregation was not for the sake of the Creator, meaning in order to get to the middle line, called "for the sake of the Creator," which is *Hassadim*.

Conversely, Moses certainly included the middle line, since Moses is called *Daat*, which is the middle line, as it is written in *The Zohar*, that Jacob is regarded as *Tifferet*, and Moses is regarded as *Daat*. Hence, Moses' quality was for the sake of the Creator, which is why they did not say, "The dispute between Moses and Korah" is called "not for the sake of the Creator," since the quality of Moses is certainly regarded for the sake of the Creator.

The matter of the right line and left line applies even during the work of preparation, meaning even before one is rewarded with entering the King's palace, since in order to enter the King's palace, one must be rewarded with the quality of *Lishma* [for Her sake], as it is written in *Masechet Avot* (Chapter Six): "Rabbi Meir says, 'Anyone who engages in Torah *Lishma* is rewarded with many things... and the secrets of Torah are revealed to him," and then it is considered that he enters the King's palace.

There, in the secrets of Torah, begins the matter of right line, called *Hesed*, and left line, called *Gevura*. This is as it is written in *Elijah Started*: "*Hesed* is the right arm; *Gevura* is the left arm." Only in the secrets of Torah are all these matters explained truthfully. But before one is rewarded with emerging from self-love and doing everything in order to bestow, called *Lishma*, although he learns all these matters as they are, they are only names without any clarification, meaning that he has no attainment in those things that he is learning, since he has no knowledge about the material of the upper roots, called "the holy names," or *Sefirot* and *Partzufim* [pl. of *Partzuf*].

We can learn the upper matters, called "the wisdom of Kabbalah," only by way of *Segula* [remedy/power], since they can bring a person desire and yearning to adhere to the Creator because of the *Kedusha* [holiness] of the matters that speak of the holy names. Conversely, in the revealed Torah, he must believe that the whole Torah is the names of the Creator. It follows that these matters are more capable (as explained in the essay, "The Giving of the Torah").

When a person learns the upper matters in order for it to bring him closer to *Kedusha*, it causes a nearing of the lights. This means that this learning will cause him to thereby be rewarded with aiming all his actions in order to bestow. This is called "work in the manner of preparation," where he prepares himself to be worthy of entering the King's palace and to adhere to Him.

Here, too, in the work in the manner of [preparation], we learn the correction of lines, which extend by way of branch and root. "Right" is called *Hesed* [mercy/grace] and is regarded as covered *Hassadim*, which is the quality of "above reason," and is discerned as "for he desires mercy," when he does not need anything and he is happy with his lot, with what he has, and says that he suffices for whatever he was given from above as a gift—to have a grip on Torah and *Mitzvot* [commandments].

Although he sees that he observes Torah and *Mitzvot* only because of his upbringing, that he was brought up this way and that upbringing does not count if he was reared when he was little or when he was educated when he was older, it does not matter. Rather, any beginning of work starts with education. But this is still not regarded as "right line," since there is right only when he has two lines. Then he is told that the first is called "right," and the second is called "left."

But afterward, when he scrutinizes and begins to work in his own right, and wants to know his purpose in life, when he yearns for something, he reflects on whether through this yearning, he will achieve some goal, and mainly, what is the purpose of creation. He sees that it is written everywhere that it is to do good to His creations, and he sees that he still does not feel any delight and pleasure, so he asks himself why he is not feeling the delight and pleasure of the purpose of creation. Yet, in relation to this, he sees a reason, that first one must achieve equivalence of form, and only then can we come to feel delight and pleasure.

In order to achieve bestowal, called equivalence of form, his work is done by scrutiny and examinations whether he is truly walking on the path of love of others. Otherwise, it is impossible to achieve *Dvekut* [adhesion] with the Creator, called "Adhere to His attributes; as He is merciful, so you are merciful."

If he sees that he is still in self-love and has not moved one bit from his lowly state, he sometimes falls into despair. Sometimes, not only does he not progress, he even feels that he has regressed. At such a time it is hard for him to observe Torah and *Mitzvot* with joy. Instead, he is sad all the time, and sometimes the world grows dark on him because the sadness brings him many thoughts and desires that truly contradict the goal he wants to achieve. That state is called "left line," for something that requires correction is called "left."

When one comes to the left line and sees his state, that he is completely empty, he must shift to the right line, for when he has the "left," it is possible to speak of the "right," and "right" means wholeness. Before one has "left," it is regarded as merely a line because there cannot be "left" if there is no "right." Hence, the first line, regarded as wholeness, now returns to this line, since here is the basis from which we build the whole building called "above reason," since now he has a mind that sees his true state—that he has no grip on spirituality.

In other words, from the perspective of the intellect, he is in complete darkness, and now comes the time to go above reason and say "They have eyes but they will not see; they have ears but they will not hear." However, he is delighted that he has been rewarded with observing the *Mitzvot* of the Creator, who commanded us through Moses. Although he does not feel any flavor or understanding about it, above reason, he still believes that it is a great privilege that he can observe the commandments of the Creator in a simple manner, while others do not even have this. He believes that everything comes from above, and others were given only the enjoyment from nonsense that is suitable for beasts and animals, while he was given a thought and desire to see that their whole lives are nonsense and vanity.

Therefore, he regards this present as a great fortune and he is always elated because of this importance. It is as important to him as though he was awarded the highest degrees. At that time, it is called "right line," "wholeness," since precisely by being happy, one has *Dvekut* with the Creator, as our sages said, "The *Shechina* is present only out of joy." Since now he is in a state of wholeness, he has a reason for gladness.

Hence, even during the preparation, there is a place where he can receive illumination from above. Although this illumination cannot be permanent in him, even some connection with spirituality is a great profit because one cannot evaluate even the slightest contact with spirituality.

This right line is called "truth" because wholeness is built on the basis of truth. That is, he does not say that he has great possessions in Torah and *Mitzvot*, meaning feeling, attainment, and understanding. Rather, he says that whatever he has, whatever he is given from above, even if he feels that he is in a worse state than what he received by education, he still regards it above reason as having great importance to him that he has been rewarded with having some contact with spirituality.

When he works on this, on settling for little and being happy with this share, and he wants to honor Torah and *Mitzvot* as if he felt the flavor as true knowing and feeling, when the body, too, agrees to this work, which is called "even his enemies make peace with him," but when he must work above reason, the body resists this work, this is called "true work." In other words, he sees his true state, yet overcomes it as though he had knowledge. This is called "right line."

All this is because he wants to glorify the Torah above reason. Although it seems as though he builds it on a structure of reason, when he says that many people have no connection to Torah and Mitzvot, so it makes sense that he already has something to be happy about because he has a possession that others do not have, this is true, but to say that this is something important and worth being happy about, he must have the quality of above reason. This is called "a joy of Mitzva [commandment]," meaning it is built on a basis of faith, and then he can sing and dance, and it is all true because it is above reason.

The left line, which extends from the root of Gevura, and Gevura means Hitgabrut [overcoming], since a person calculates how close he is to Kedusha, meaning how much energy he can put into love of others, to perform acts of bestowal without any return, for the sake of the friends, he can measure this by the amount to which he is willing to make concessions for the sake of the friends without wanting any return for this. Then, if he sees his true state—that he is still unfit for any concession—there is no other choice but prayer. This is considered that the left line brings him room for prayer.

It follows from the above that the right line brings him a place where he can praise and glorify for being given wholeness, and then there is no room for prayer because then he has no place of lack. Also, there is no room for Banim [sons], which are called Havana [understanding] in Torah and Mitzvot, since then he has no questions for which he needs answers, and then he has no multiplication in Torah.

Conversely, the left line, which is Gevura, when one must overcome, because we see that we must overcome but we haven't the strength for this, then there is room for prayer, and there is also room for sons there because through the forces that come from above, which he extends through his prayer, it brings him multiplication in Torah.

However, we must know that these two lines must be equal, meaning used equally. At that time, it can be said that the third writing comes and decides between them, namely the middle line. The decision is that it integrates the two into one.

If one is greater than the other, they cannot be included in one another because the greater one does not want to be included in the other because it feels that its quality is more beneficial. Therefore, we must try to make them equal.

What is the benefit? When he has two lines, he must also see that they are equal so he will obtain the middle line. We must know that the middle line is called "the abundance that comes from above," which is revealed on the two lines.

We can interpret this according to what our sages said, "There are three partners in man: his father, his mother, and the Creator. His father gives the whiteness, his mother gives the red, and the Creator gives the soul." "Whiteness" means "white," as it is written, "Though your sins be as scarlet, they shall be as white as snow." This means that then he always walks in a state of "white," and this is called "right line," when he sees no deficiency in his situation. Rather, he is always happy with his share. Even though he feels that he has no possession in his work, he is still happy.

We can understand this according to a story that is told, that once a princess became ill and no cure was found to her illness until a wise man came and said that he could heal her, but only through a *Segula* [power/remedy]: If she wore a white garment of a person who is happy with his share, she would be healed by this. What did the king do? He sent messengers to the wealthiest people in the nation, who asked them if they were happy with their shares. Then, each one let them know what they lacked. Afterward, he sent out to ask the middle class, perhaps there was one among them who was happy with his share, but he did not find one, until they had given up.

But finally, a man came and told the king that far away from here there is a forest, and he heard that in that the keeper of the forest is always happy with his share. Naturally, the king sent high ranking officials to the keeper. When the officials came to the keeper, he asked them, "I see that you are distinguished people; why have you come to me?" They told him about the whole matter of the king's daughter. "This is why we came to you, and we would like to know if it is true what they say, that you are happy with your share." Then, he told them, "Indeed, no doubt, I feel that there is nothing that I need in life and I enjoy everything." "In that case," they said, "Give us one of your shirts for the king's daughter." Then he replied to them, "Believe me, if I had a shirt, I would give it to the princess, but I have none."

From this story we can see that if someone wants to be happy with his share, it must be unconditional. This is called "wholeness," when you do not need anything in order to be able to say that because of this you can be happy with your share. This is called "right line," when he does not need a thing, for if he needs something, anything at all, he can no longer be in wholeness.

"His mother gives the red," as it is written, "Though your sins be as scarlet," where there is a line of redness, for because he criticizes the good deeds he is doing, he sees that he cannot go forward. On the contrary, he is regressing. This is called "a line of redness," when the body makes him think that it is impossible to walk when the line is red. At that time, his only hope is to increase his praying.

This is as it is introduced in *Yalkut* (in the *Hagadah of Pe'ilim*): "Israel said to the Creator, 'When will You redeem us?' The Creator replied, 'When you go down to the lowest level, then I will redeem you.'"

It is precisely when one comes to a red line, when he feels that he is at the lowest degree, then comes redemption, since then the Creator gives the soul, and then the upper light shines on him, when he obtains help from above. It is as our sages said, "He who comes to purify is aided," and *The Zohar* asks, "With what is he aided?" and it replies, "With a holy soul," for then there is the third partner, the Creator, who gives the soul, and this is called the "middle line."

Assorted Notes

## 876- The Creator Created the Evil Inclination, He Created for It the Torah as a Spice

*Sivan, Tav-Shin-Mem-Dalet, June 1984*

"The Creator created the evil inclination, He created for it the Torah as a spice" (*Baba Batra* 16).

We should understand what is the evil inclination and what is the spice. And there is more we should understand: When we cook a dish, the main thing is the dish, and the spices only give flavor to the dish. Thus, how can it be said that the main thing is the evil inclination, and the Torah is only a spice? Also, when it says that the Torah is a spice, it means that the Torah and *Mitzvot* [commandments] are only a means, as our sages said, "The *Mitzvot* were given only in order to cleanse Israel with them" (*Beresheet Rabbah*, Portion 44). Does this mean that after the cleansing, we do not need to observe Torah and *Mitzvot*?

So what is the meaning of the evil inclination? It is known that the purpose of creation is to do good to His creations. For this reason, He created in the creatures desire and yearning to receive delight and pleasure. In order for the created beings to have wholeness while receiving the pleasure, meaning that they will not feel any shame while receiving the pleasure, there was a correction called "in order to bestow," which means that they will not want anything for themselves, but only to bestow upon the Creator. Then they will not feel any shame because they will not be receiving anything for their own sake, but only for the sake of the Creator and not for themselves.

However, we must know what we can give to the Creator that He will enjoy. Hence, the Creator notified us through Moses that He is giving us 613 *Mitzvot*, and we must observe these *Mitzvot* in order to bestow upon Him contentment. At that time, He will be able to give us abundance, since the *Kelim* [vessels] of the lower one are called will to receive only for himself, which is called "bad" because he does all the ruining, stealing, and murdering. This is what does bad to others.

Yet, we must know that the will to receive also harms itself, for besides causing harm in corporeality, it also spoils our entire spiritual state, since we cannot achieve the goal, which is to do good to His creations. We are meant to receive delight and pleasure, but it obstructs us because the will to receive is opposite from the desire to bestow, for the Creator is the Giver and we want only to receive, and without equivalence of form, we have no *Dvekut* [adhesion].

Therefore, we should be happy that He alerted us through Moses that if we observe the Torah and *Mitzvot*, we will receive the correction called "equivalence of form." Had He not alerted us what He wants us to give Him, we would not know what to give Him. But now that He informed us that we should observe the 613 *Mitzvot*, we know what to give Him.

This is similar to a vegetarian, who enjoys only fruits and vegetables, and so forth, but he invited an important person over and wants to prepare a meal for him. He is used to preparing only meals that vegetarians eat, so it is a great effort for him to find out what the important person is used to eating. If the guest were to give him a plan for his meal, what he likes, he would be very happy that he knows what to prepare for his meal.

Likewise, we should be happy that He informed us through Moses what He enjoys. Therefore, we do not have much labor finding how we can delight Him, which is through the 613 *Mitzvot* that He has given us to observe. When we aim, during the performance of Torah and *Mitzvot*, that we want to please Him, we achieve equivalence of form, called "adhere to His attributes," and by this we are rewarded with *Dvekut* [adhesion] with the Creator.

But His wanting us to bestow upon Him, is it because He lacks something so we can delight Him? It has already been explained in several places that it is for the purpose of a correction for our sake, so the delight and pleasure He wants to give us will not be mixed with shame. But why did He choose specifically these 613 *Mitzvot*?

It is said that He knew that specifically these *Mitzvot* will help us achieve the degree of bestowal and emerge from the governance of self-love, as this is a new quality that is not inherent in us. This is the meaning of the words of our sages, "I have created the evil inclination; I have created the Torah as a spice."

However, we must understand that according to what we say, that the Torah and *Mitzvot* are only a means to correct the evil, called will to receive, what does observing the 613 *Mitzvot* give us once we have corrected our will to receive to work in order to bestow? To understand this, we must delve into what is written in the "Introduction of The Book of Zohar" ("General Explanation for All Fourteen Commandments and How They Divide into the Seven Days of Creation," Item 1): "The *Mitzvot* in the Torah are called *Pekudin* [Aramaic: deposits], as well as *Eitin* [Aramaic: counsels]. The difference between them is that in all things there are *Panim* [anterior/face] and *Achor* [posterior/back]. The preparation for something is called *Achor*, and the attainment of the matter is called *Panim*.

"Similarly, in Torah and *Mitzvot* there are 'We shall do' and 'We shall hear,' as our sages said, 'doers of His word, to hear the voice of His word. In the beginning, they hear, and in the end, they do' (*Shabbat* [Sabbath] 88). When they observe Torah and *Mitzvot* as 'doers of His word,' prior to being rewarded with hearing, the *Mitzvot* are called '613 *Eitin*' and are regarded as *Achor*. When rewarded with 'hearing the voice of His word,' the 613 *Mitzvot* become *Pekudin*, from the word *Pikadon* [Hebrew: deposit]. This is so because there are 613 *Mitzvot*, and in each *Mitzva* [sing. of *Mitzvot*] a light of a unique degree is deposited, which corresponds to a unique organ in the 613 organs and tendons of the soul. It follows that while performing the *Mitzva*, one extends to the corresponding organ in his soul and body, the degree of light that belongs to that organ and tendon. This is considered the *Panim* of the *Mitzvot*, and in that quality of the *Panim* of the *Mitzvot*, at that time they are called *Pekudin*."

From all the above, it follows that the 613 *Mitzvot* give us two things:

1) During the preparation, when a person is still enslaved to his evil, meaning to the will to receive, and has no power to do anything for the sake of others, at that time a person is separated from the Creator because of the disparity of form. Then, the 613 *Mitzvot* give us the power to be able to emerge from their control. This is called "I have created the evil inclination; I have created the Torah as a spice," and then the 613 *Mitzvot* are regarded as a means.

2) Once a person has achieved *Lishma* [for Her sake], which is equivalence of form, he is rewarded with the revelation of the secrets of Torah, as said above. "Rabbi Meir says, 'He who learns Torah *Lishma* ... and the secrets of Torah are revealed to him'" (*Avot*, Chapter 6). At that time, the 613 *Mitzvot* become 613 organs of the soul, where each *Mitzva* is a special place for a special light. As in corporeality, we see that in everything corporeal that a person takes from corporeal pleasures, there is a different flavor. In bread there is one taste, and in meat there is another taste, and in fish there is also another taste, although all are regarded as foods for the body. Nevertheless, there is a different flavor in everything. In spirituality, it is much more so, that in each *Mitzva* there is a different flavor, and then the 613 *Mitzvot* are called an essence and not a means.

At that time, the whole Torah is the names of the Creator, as he says in the "Introduction to The Study of the Ten Sefirot" (Items 135, 140): "However, when one is rewarded with the revelation of the face ... it is said about him, 'Your Teacher will no longer hide Himself, and your eyes will see your Teacher'" (Isaiah 30:20), since from then on, the dresses of the Torah no longer hide and conceal the teacher, and He is revealed to him forever, for the Torah and the Creator are one.

According to the above, we will understand what we asked, why our sages said, "I have created the evil inclination; I have created the Torah as a spice." It implies that the evil inclination is what is important. It is similar to making soup. The main thing is the soup, and the spice only adds flavor to the soup. God forbid that we should say about the Torah that it is only a spice. Rather, as said above, the Torah gives us two things: One is called *Kelim* [vessels], and the other is called "lights."

*Kelim* means that we are fit to receive the upper abundance. *Kelim* of *Kedusha* [holiness] consist of two discernments:

1) This is the main thing, the yearning for something. To the extent of the yearning for that thing, so we taste pleasure in that thing. The yearning, great or small, is measured according to the suffering he has for the matter. That is, if he does not receive the thing he yearns for, he will feel intense suffering. This is called "great yearning." Conversely, if he does not suffer very much when he does not receive that thing, it is regarded as small yearning. To that extent, the measure of pleasure that he feels is measured while receiving the pleasure.

However, this does not complete the *Kli* to be fit to receive upper abundance, since while receiving the pleasure, he feels unpleasantness upon receiving the pleasure, which is the matter of the bread of shame.

It follows that although he will receive the pleasure, he will feel that the taste is flawed, like a soup with a missing spice. At that time, the Torah of the first kind comes and corrects the desire to work in order to bestow, and then the *Kli* can receive the pleasure without feeling any lack in it.

This is what we said about the matter of "I have created the evil inclination; I have created the Torah as a spice." In other words, the light in the Torah has the power to correct the will to receive in us to work in order to bestow, and then the *Kli* [vessel] is able to receive and there will be no flaw in that reception. This is considered that the 613 *Mitzvot* that came to give us the correction of the *Kelim*, meaning that by observing Torah and *Mitzvot*, it will invert our vessels of reception to work in order to bestow, and then we will be able to receive the abundance for the sake of the Creator.

The second discernment is that the Torah and *Mitzvot* came to give us lights, and then *The Zohar* calls the 613 *Mitzvot*, 613 *Pekudin*. That is, in each *Mitzva* [commandment], a special light is deposited, meaning that when he performs the *Mitzva*, in doing so, he extends a special light that belongs to that *Mitzva*. This is regarded that the 613 *Mitzvot* give us lights.

By this we will understand what we asked concerning the Torah and *Mitzvot*, that it implies that it is only a means and not the essence. This is so only during the correction of the *Kelim*, for then the *Kli* to receive the pleasure is only the will to receive. However, in order to have wholeness while receiving the pleasure, in order to have taste in it, the Torah and *Mitzvot* must give us the taste, like the spice in the soup.

But later, once the *Kelim* have been corrected and he comes to the second state, which is the lights, the 613 *Mitzvot* are regarded as the essence, and then they are regarded as "the names of the Creator." At that time, the order is that the light comes and dresses in the *Kelim*. This is considered that he receives delight and pleasure, and at the same time, he is in *Dvekut* [adhesion].

## 877- Three Prayers

Balak, *Tav-Shin-Mem-Dalet*, July 1984

It is written in the Shabbat [Sabbath] evening songs (in "Anyone Who Sanctifies"): "The Lord, God of Israel, the love of the innocent [also "whole" or "naïve"]; the Lord, God of Israel, everlasting salvation."

We should understand the importance of innocence [also "wholeness" or "naivety"]. On the face of it, it seems as though one who has less of an intellect can be more innocent, and one who has more intellect and more ability to criticize cannot be naïve. It follows that the quality of naivety was given to those with little knowledge.

But Baal HaSulam interpreted that first, one sees only *Mumim* [flaws], and then he makes of it *Tamim* [naïve/innocent/whole]. The explanation is that when one sees only flaws in the world, in individuals and in the collective, this is called *Mumim*, and it is called "left line." Afterward, he accepts everything above reason, and this is called *Tamim*.

It follows that one who has more knowledge has more flaws, as it is written, "He who adds knowledge adds pain," and he should accept all this above reason. It follows that his innocence is built on greater knowledge. Thus, his innocence is greater than one whose innocence is built on smaller knowledge.

It says, "The Lord, God of Israel, the love of the innocent; the Lord, God of Israel, everlasting salvation." This means that in order for a person to have the strength to overcome once he sees a world full of flaws, he cannot help himself and needs salvation from above to be able to go into innocence above reason. This is the "Lord, God of Israel, everlasting salvation," meaning to bring all the flaws into the above reason, which is called *Tamim* [innocent/whole]. This is the meaning of *Ol-Mim* [*Olamim* (everlasting) split in two]. *Ol* [burden] comes from the word *Ayil* [Aramaic: entering], meaning to insert a *Mum* [flaw] in the *Tamim*.

By this we will understand the words of *The Zohar* (Balak, Items 187-188). It is written there that a prayer for the poor precedes the rest of the prayers. This is the meaning of "A prayer for the poor when he envelops." "Envelops," from the words, "And the enveloped, for Laban," which means delayed. That is, it delays all other prayers in the world. He asks, Why does the prayer for the poor delay all the prayers? It is because the poor is brokenhearted and the poor always quarrels with the Creator, and the Creator listens and hears his words, see there in the *Sulam* [Ladder commentary on *The Zohar*].

We should understand why the Creator hears the prayer of the poor before all other prayers. He says that the reason is that the Creator is near to the brokenhearted. We should understand the importance of the brokenhearted to whom the Creator is close. In *The Zohar*, *Malchut* is called "poor, for she has nothing of her own except that which her husband brings her." This matter is explained in several places in the *Sulam*, that there are two states in *Malchut*. Once it is explained according to the first state, that she is called "poor" because she has no *Hassadim* [mercies], and elsewhere, he calls there, in the *Sulam*, the second state of *Malchut*, that she is called "poor" because she must receive from *Zeir Anpin*, her husband.

We should interpret that the kingdom of heaven—when one wants to take upon himself that all his actions will be for the sake of the Creator, not in order to receive reward—at that time *Malchut* is called "poor" because she has nothing to give to the person working for her. Normally, when someone works for someone, he receives a reward for his work. But when a person works for the Creator, not in order to receive reward for his labor, it follows that he is working for a poor one, meaning it is like working for a poor person who has nothing with which to pay him.

According to the above, we should interpret a prayer for the poor: A person prays to the Creator that his prayer will be for the poor. That is, he prays that everything he does will be for the sake of the Creator, meaning he wants to work in order not to receive reward. This work means that he wants to work *Lishma* [for Her sake]. That is, even though he has not achieved it, he still wants to. This is the first discernment in the work of the Creator. Before one achieves the state of *Lishma*, he works not for the sake of the Creator, but for his own sake.

By this we will understand why the prayer for the poor is accepted before all the prayers, to the point that *The Zohar* says that it delays all the prayers, that it precedes the prayer for David and the prayer for Moses. We should ask why it should delay the rest of the prayers. Is it impossible to answer everyone at the same time, but they must be answered one at a time?

We can understand this if we learn all these three prayers in one person. Normally, we should discern three prayers: 1) A prayer for Moses, who is the quality of the Torah. 2) A prayer for David, who is *Malchut* [kingship]. That is, he has been rewarded with the quality *Malchut* but he prays that the kingdom of heaven with which he has been rewarded will not depart from him. 3) A prayer for the poor, when he wants to begin to emerge from self-love and come into the work in order to bestow and not receive any reward, but only for the Creator. Then the body begins to resist this work because it is against his nature. At that time, he comes to a state where he sees that he is bare and destitute. That is, he has no support from which to receive fuel for the work. In other words, when he thought that he should engage in the work *Lishma*, he was fine. He had Torah and prayer and good deeds, and he had possessions to enjoy. He looked at people with whom he came in contact and felt that he was far above them.

But now that he has begun to walk on the path that leads to *Lishma*, he feels that he is more deprived than all his contemporaries, since they have vitality. He feels them just as he had felt himself before he began to change his way. At that time, he feels that the world has grown dark on him, as it is written, "Ever since I came to Pharaoh to speak in Your name, he has done harm to this people, and You did not save Your people at all. And the Lord said to Moses, 'Now you will see what I will do to Pharaoh, for with a mighty hand he will send them, and with a mighty hand he will drive them out of his land'" (Exodus 5:23).

We should interpret that before Moses came to the people of Israel as a messenger of the Creator, that He wanted to lead them out of Egypt, the people of Israel engaged in work of the Creator but were enslaved to Pharaoh king of Egypt. Pharaoh king of Egypt is the will to receive that is found in the created beings, which cannot do anything if not for its own benefit. This is the ruler in all created beings and it afflicts all those who want to emerge from its dominion, meaning to work for the sake of others.

Moses came to the people of Israel and told them that the Creator wants to deliver them from under the governance of Pharaoh, to lead each and every one of the people of Israel from under Pharaoh's control, which is found within each and every one.

Accordingly, each one understands that Moses' mission is that we must begin the work *Lishma* [for Her sake], so it makes sense that now, if we begin to walk on the path of truth, meaning for the sake of the Creator, where each one has the aim to bestow while doing the work of the Creator, now each one will begin to work harder and with great enthusiasm, and the passion will be so intense that it will be difficult for him to retire for a minute to think about corporeal needs, too, which are utterly necessary, since now he is working only for the sake of the Creator. And although he has not begun this work, to feel that he is working for the sake of the Creator, since he wants to walk on the path of truth, the body will certainly agree to make more concessions for him than it did while he was not working on the path of truth, meaning *Lishma*.

But the reality is opposite. Precisely when we want to walk on the way of *Lishma*, the body begins to resist. At that time, it begins with all its arguments, meaning the argument of Pharaoh king of Egypt, which is the argument, "Who is the Lord that I should obey His voice?" and the argument of the wicked, who says, "What is this work for you?" At that time, the work becomes heavy, and each time he needs more reinforcement.

We should interpret this matter in the above-mentioned verse, "Ever since I came to Pharaoh to speak in Your name, he has done harm to this people." That is, when Moses came to speak "in Your name," meaning that they should work for the sake of the Creator, "He has done harm to this people," they become worse. In other words, before Moses came to say that we must work only for the sake of the Creator, everyone served the Creator and considered themselves righteous. They had the strength to work and the fuel to know why they were working was clear to them. But after Moses came as an emissary of the Creator, that we must work for the sake of the Creator, they have become worse. Thus, accordingly, they would be better off not getting into the work of *Lishma*.

To this came the answer, "And the Lord said to Moses, 'Now you will see what I will do to Pharaoh, for with a mighty hand he will send them.'" The answer was not that they did not tell the truth, but what I want from them is to feel the truth, that they are so far from the truth, meaning from working for the sake of the Creator.

Then, when they have this kind of demand, that they cannot work *Lishma*, then you will see how I give you the strength to work for the sake of the Creator. I do not demand that you will be able to walk on the path of truth. All I need is for you to have a *Kli* [vessel] to receive the abundance. Hence, when you begin to work in order to bestow, you will see that you are incapable of this work, and then I will give you what is called "with a mighty hand he will send them," as it is written, "And I also heard the groaning of the children of Israel, that the Egyptians enslave them, and I remembered My covenant, etc., and I will deliver you from under the afflictions of Egypt" (Exodus 6). It follows that once they have a *Kli* to receive, I will give them the power required for it.

Now we will explain what we began, concerning the prayer of the poor—why this prayer delays all other prayers. Since we are speaking of one person in whom all these states unfold, it follows that the prayer of David cannot be accepted, as it is when he has already been rewarded with the kingdom of heaven, but he prays that the kingdom of heaven will not cease from him. One can pray for this after he already has the kingdom of heaven, but anyone who is still far from the kingdom of heaven, who is still under the rule of Pharaoh king of Egypt, how can he be given so that this matter will not cease in him while he still has nothing?

Hence, first the prayer of the poor is accepted, meaning that first he must be rewarded with the kingdom of heaven, called "poor and meager." This is the first discernment—that a person must enter in the work. Afterward comes the next degree, which is a prayer for David, meaning that his kingdom of heaven will not cease. Then comes the third degree, which is a prayer for Moses, which is the Torah.

## 878- *Their Leg Was a Straight Leg*

Tammuz, Tav-Shin-Mem-Dalet, July 1984

It is written in *The Zohar*, Pinhas (Item 317 in the *Sulam* [Ladder commentary on *The Zohar*]): "'And their leg was a straight leg,' for the legs of the harm-doers are crooked. And their leg, meaning the legs of the holy animals, it was said about them, 'and their leg was a straight leg,' on the part of *Haya*, which is Israel. Israel comprises three animals, of which it was said, 'the patriarchs, they are the *Merkava* [chariot/assembly/structure].'"

He interprets there in the *Sulam*, that "The straightness extends from the middle line, which is straight and leans neither to the right nor to the left, but squarely in the middle. But the *Sitra Achra* [other side] and the harm-doers lean to the left."

To interpret the above, we must remember the fundamental principles of the work, which is the quality of "mind" and "heart," as it is written in the book *Matan Torah*, namely that there is law, and there is judgment. "Law" means that a person must walk in it as a law, with no room for arguments, but to accept it as it was given to us from books and from authors. This is the quality of faith above reason, called "mind," and the quality of bestowal, called "heart." Those two are called "fear," and the quality of judgment is called "wisdom."

It was said about this, "Rabbi Elazar Ben Azariah says, 'If there is no wisdom, there is no fear. If there is no fear, there is no wisdom'" (*Avot*, Chapter 2). In other words, we need both law and judgment, and when the two are merged, it is called the "middle line," and this is in *Kedusha* [holiness]. It is written about this, "And their leg was a straight leg." That is, they do not lean to the left, called "wisdom," but keep the two equal.

However, if one cannot keep them equal, he must try to make the right bigger than the left. At that time, "his wisdom persists," as they said, "He would say that anyone whose deeds are more numerous than his wisdom, his wisdom persists; and anyone whose wisdom is more than his deeds, his wisdom does not persist" (*Avot*, Chapter 3:12).

"Law" means action, since there is no room there to understand and to intellectualize. Rather, it is all above reason. Hence, it is regarded as an action, meaning mind and heart, faith and bestowal, fear, action, all are considered "right," and there is nothing to argue about this. Rather, we must accept this as it is and try to seek advice to be able to take upon ourselves "as an ox to the burden and as a donkey to the load."

"Judgment" is regarded as the Torah, which we do need to understand. It is called "wisdom," meaning that one must be ready to be rewarded with the Torah, where it is actually to the contrary—the more he wants to understand, the better it is.

However, there are many discernments in the Torah. There is the revealed Torah, which is the practice, meaning that although he learns the rules, he is not obligated to follow them. That is, he learns the rules of judging although does not think that he will ever be a judge. Nevertheless, he learns the Torah [law] of the Creator, which is called "His wisdom," and this is called the "revealed Torah," since there are things that others need to do, and by learning the Torah of the Creator, he helps the *Dvekut* [adhesion] with the Creator because the whole Torah is His names, as it is written in *The Zohar*.

There is also the hidden Torah, which does not speak at all about actions, but about things that belong to the heart and to the mind, and a person must try as much as he can to have some attainment of what he is learning. This desire that yearns to achieve attainment causes the nearing of the lights, which is regarded as a prayer, where he yearns for the Creator to open his eyes in His Torah.

However, he must always see that his wisdom is not more than his deeds, as said above. This is called "And their leg was a straight leg," as explained in the *Sulam*, that the right line always leans toward *Hesed* [mercy/grace].

However, according to what is explained in the *Sulam*, "It is a commandment to give half a *Shekel* in the *Shekel* of holiness. It asks, 'What is half a *Shekel*?' It replies, 'It is like half of the *Heys*, namely the *Vav* between the two *Heys*. A stone to weigh with is the *Yod*, twenty

*Gerah* a *Shekel* is *Yod*.' 'The rich shall not give more' is the middle pillar... What is half a *Shekel*? It is like half of the *Heys*, meaning half a measure. He interprets that this *Vav* is the middle between the two *Heys*, since the *Vav* is the middle line, which is called *Mitkalah*, weighing the two lights, right and left, which are the two *Heys*, so the left is not bigger than the right" (*Ki Tissa*, Item 4).

This means that the right, too, should not be greater than the left, but rather equal, as it is written, "The rich shall not give more and the poor shall not give less than half a *Shekel*." However, there is a rule that the matter is always interpreted according to the language, yet the reality is always the same reality, except there are different languages.

# Rosh Hashanah

## 879- Good Writing and Signing

We see that a person does not need to write the letter he wants to write to his friend by himself, whether it is to let him know something or to ask him for something. It is enough if a person signs the letter for it to be considered that it is true and that he is its sender.

It is likewise to the contrary: If a person writes the letter by himself but another person signed his letter, that letter is not evidence that the letter is true, although he recognizes his friend's handwriting.

In the work of the Creator, writing means black on white. This means that what a person does in Torah and Mitzvot [commandments] means that he engraves it in his heart, meaning that the good deeds that one does are written down.

We want the writing to be for the best, meaning good deeds. Also, the signing is the intention that testifies to the letter itself, meaning that the aim testifies whose Mitzvot he is observing, whether his intention in observing the Mitzvot is for the sake of the Creator or not.

It follows that the writing, meaning the *Mitzvot* and good deeds, is called "good writing," namely that it could be the opposite, that he does bad deeds. It follows that first there must be good deeds, which are observance of Torah and *Mitzvot* in utter simplicity.

Afterward comes the matter of the intention, called "aiming" that everything will be for the sake of the Creator, for without attention, one does not know for whom and for whose purpose he observes Torah and *Mitzvot*. It is possible that his entire aim is not for the sake of the Creator. This is why we say "Good writing and signing," meaning that first there must be an act, called "body," and then an intention, called a "soul."

# 880- Judgments

Rosh Hashanah, Tishrey, Tav-Shin-Lamed-Hey, September 1974

"Judgments" means the *Kli* [vessel] of the will to receive on which a judgment was passed that it is forbidden to use it from the *Tzimtzum* [restriction] onward.

"Sweetening of the judgments" means that one can place on them *Masachim* [screens], meaning he can use the *Kelim* [pl. of *Kli*], which are regarded as judgments, in order to bestow.

*Hesed* [grace/mercy] means that one engages in acts of bestowal. A "simple voice" means that the act and the thought are similar. This is called "straight." For example, when one engages in acts of bestowal and his aim is also to bestow, it is regarded as "straight and simple."

Also, receiving in order to receive is called "simple," and the light prior to the *Tzimtzum* is called "simple light." This means that the light illuminated in the *Kelim* that are called "receiving in order to receive." Afterward, after the *Tzimtzum*, there are many calculations, meaning it is no longer straight, as in "God created man straight, but they sought many calculations."

It follows that the act of receiving and the aim should be to bestow.

ASSORTED NOTES

## 881- *Rosh Hashanah* and *Yom Kippur*

Concerning *Rosh Hashanah* [Jewish New Year's Eve] and *Yom Kippur* [Day of Atonement], we should understand the meaning of the judgments and the *Gevurot*, why good days are called "days of judgments," and why "a good day" and not "a weekday."

"Judgment" is explained (in the *Sulam* [Ladder commentary on *The Zohar*], *Emor*, Item 193), that each year, *Malchut* returns to her beginning, as she was on the fourth day of the work of creation, meaning in the diminution of the moon, when the *Hochma* in the left line of *Bina* illuminated, and *Hochma* without *Hassadim* is called "judgment."

This is regarded as "male judgments," when there is an increase of abundance, and then there is fear that they will not receive it in the manner of reception, which is hell, which was created on the second day, as in "sin crouches at the door."

## 882- *Rosh Hashanah*

Concerning the verse, "The eyes of the Lord your God are on it from the beginning of the year," sometimes favorably, sometimes unfavorably. How so? When Israel were complete wicked in the beginning of the year, they were allotted few rains, but in the end they repented. It is impossible to add, since the sentence has already been passed, but the Creator brings them down on time on the soil that needs them. Everything is according to the soil.

At times unfavorably, how so? Israel were complete righteous in the beginning of the year and were allotted many rains, but in the end they went astray. It is impossible to lessen, since the sentence has already been passed, but the Creator brings them down not in their time on a soil that does not need them (*Rosh Hashanah* 17b).

And RASHI interpreted: "Not in their time" means before sowing. Where they are not needed means in forests and in deserts.

To understand the above in ethics, we should interpret that *Rosh Hashanah* [beginning of the year] means the beginning of the creation of man. It is as our sages said that a drop is declared whether it will be wise or a fool, etc. (*Nidah* 16b). "Rains" means one's corporeal forces, whether he will have a big or a small brain, a small or a big heart, a small or a big desire, and so on.

If a person walks on the good path, when he grows, it is impossible to add, meaning to make for him a bigger brain and desire, since they were already allotted to him when he was made. However, he uses all of his brain and energy only in a place of *Kedusha* [holiness] and need. This is enough for him to achieve a degree where he can be rewarded with the revelation of the light of the Creator, truly cleave to Him, and receive his proper share in the next world.

But if a person has been allotted a big brain and a strong will when he was first created, if he does not walk on the good and straight path, he uses them not as required, which is as though the Creator brings them down not in their time on a soil that does not need them.

Thus, all the good forces he was given when he was made do not help him. He could have been proficient in Mishnah and Gemara, but he will not be awarded the desired wholeness called *Dvekut* [adhesion] with Him.

It follows that one must not complain if he is not as gifted as the rest of his friends, for this is not the deciding factor, since what matters is to be righteous. Only then does one use all his forces toward the real goal and does not waste away his strength. Instead, the powers of his labor connect and enter the *Kedusha*.

## 883- *For Man Is the Tree of the Field*

Rabbi Yochanan said, "Why is it written, 'For man is the tree of the field' (Deuteronomy 21)? Is man the tree of the field? Rather, it is because it is written, 'For you will eat from it and you will not cut it down,' and it is written 'This you shall destroy and cut down.' How so? If he is a decent wise disciple, you will eat from it and you will not cut it down. If not, this you shall destroy and cut down" (*Taanit* 7a).

We should ask what is the connection between a decent wise disciple and a tree that is for eating, and a wise disciple and a tree that is not for eating, since the verse says, "You shall not destroy its trees by swinging an axe against it, for you may eat from it. ...Only a tree that you know is not a tree for eating you shall destroy and cut down."

*The Zohar* says, "Another God is sterile and does not bear fruit" (see the "Introduction of The Book of Zohar," Item 23), and these are its words: Hence, those who fail and walk in the ways of ABYA of *Tuma'a* [impurity], their source dries up and they have no blessing of spiritual fruits. They wither away until they become completely blocked. The opposite is true for those who adhere to *Kedusha* [holiness]. Their work is blessed "as a tree planted by the streams of water, whose fruit ripens in its time and whose leaf will not wither, and all that he does will succeed" (Psalms 1).

By this we can understand the connection between a decent wise disciple and a fruit tree, of which the verse says, "You will eat from it and you will not cut it down." The fruit bearing tree is a sign of *Kedusha*, and one that does not bear fruit is a sign of *Tuma'a* and is called an "indecent wise disciple."

We also find, "These are the generations of Noah. This is as it is written, 'the fruit of a righteous, a tree of life.' What are the fruits of a righteous? *Mitzvot* [commandments] and good deeds" (*Midrash Rabbah*, Noah). By this we can interpret that if he is a decent wise disciple, meaning bears fruit, and he has *Mitzvot* and good deeds, you shall eat it. If not, "This you shall destroy and cut down."

Before these words, the Gemara brings the following words: "Tania, Rabbi Bena'a says, 'Anyone who engages in Torah *Lishma* [for Her sake], his Torah becomes a potion of life to him, as was said, 'It is a tree of life for they who hold it.' It is said, 'It shall be healing to your navel,' and it is said, 'For he who finds me finds life,' and anyone who engages in Torah *Lo Lishma* [not for Her sake], his Torah becomes a potion of death to him, as was said, 'My lesson will behead like a torrent,' and beheading means killing, as was said, 'and they beheaded it there by the stream.'" We should understand the proximity of the words to one another.

We should interpret that Rabbi Yochanan does not refer specifically to one who learns with a wise disciple, that he should see if the wise disciple is decent. Rather, this pertains to the disciple himself, in what way he is learning.

In other words, if he learns Torah but sees that the texts he is learning will not lead him to be able to eat fruits from this learning, meaning fruits of *Mitzvot* and good deeds, "This you shall destroy and from it you shall not eat." Rather, he should see that he learns Torah so that this Torah gives him strength and power to perform *Mitzvot* and good deeds, as this is called "fruits," and specifically from this you shall eat.

In this manner, we can interpret what our sages said about the verse, "The eyes of the Lord your God are on it," sometimes favorably, sometimes unfavorably.

Sometimes unfavorably, how so? When Israel were complete wicked in the beginning of the year, they were allotted few rains, but in the end they repented. It is impossible to add, since the sentence has already been given, but the Creator brings them down on time on the soil that needs them (and RASHI interpreted, "On the soil that needs them: on the fields and on the vineyards and on the gardens"), everything is according to the soil.

Sometimes unfavorably, how so? Israel were complete righteous in the beginning of the year and were sentenced many rains, but in the end they went astray. It is impossible to lessen, since the sentence has already been given, but the Creator brings them down not in their time on a soil that does not need them (and RASHI interpreted, "On a land that does not need them, in forests and in deserts") (*Rosh Hashanah* 17b).

Rains means water, and there is no water but Torah. Our sages said, "The reward for a *Mitzva*, *Mitzva*" (*Avot*, Chapter 4). That is, in the beginning of the year, a person is judged according to his actions, and he is sentenced how much Torah he will learn at this time.

Hence, if his actions in the beginning of the year were righteous, he is allotted much rain. Afterward, they reverted from their way, meaning he sinned, and then he is considered wicked. "To the wicked, God said, 'Why do you need the book of My laws?'" At that time, He gives him the rains that were allotted.

For example, he was allotted to learn eight hours a day, so He lets him learn these eight hours, but where they are not needed, meaning in forests and deserts, namely places where there can be no fruits.

In other words, he is made to learn things that will yield him no fruits, which are *Mitzvot* and good deeds. On the contrary, the learning becomes a potion of death to him, as our sages said, "He who learns *Lo Lishma*," etc.

But if he were wicked in the beginning of the year and was allotted few rains, meaning to learn only two hours a day, if he repents, he is given that little Torah in a place where it can yield fruit, which is called "vineyards and fields and gardens," meaning that the Torah will bear fruits, which are called *Mitzvot* and good deeds.

# 884- *The Rosh Hashanah Prayer*

In the *Rosh Hashanah* prayer, we say, "Happy is a man who does not forget You, and the son of man who exerts in You." We should ask what, if he does not forget about the Creator, what is the meaning of the exertion?

In the prayer "Help of Our Fathers," we say, "Happy is a man who hears Your *Mitzvot* [commandments] and places Your Torah [law] on his heart."

We should understand the meaning of obeying the *Mitzvot* of the Creator. We should say, Happy is a man who does, or observes Your *Mitzvot*, and not "hears Your *Mitzvot*." Also, what is "Your word" and what is "Your Torah"? What is the meaning of "word" and what is Torah, what is "place on his heart"? How does one place Torah and words on the heart, and why is there a need to place on the heart and not in the mind?

Also, what does it mean that in the *Rosh Hashanah* prayer we say, "*Malchuiot* [kingships], memories, *Shofarot* [pl. of *Shofar* (a festive horn)] "? Our sages said, "*Malchuiot* [kingships], so you would crown Me. Memories, so the memory of you will come up before Me. And with what? With a *Shofar*." What is the connection and what reason is there for the *Shofar* to cause kingship and memory?

Also, *Rosh Hashanah* is called "the day of judgment." Also, what is the month of *Elul*, and the matter of the repetition and the order of the prayer prior to *Rosh Hashanah*?

The thing that is the most important is not to forget about the Creator for even a moment. How can we be rewarded with this? By exerting each time more fiercely and with more power and might. By this we are rewarded with the quality of "remembering." This is why the phrasing is in the manner of an advice.

Also, "Happy is he who hears Your *Mitzvot*," meaning that there is doing and there is hearing. "Hearing" means that we are rewarded with hearing from the mouth of the Creator, which is called *Dvekut* [adhesion] of spirit with spirit. This is regarded as *Dvekut*, meaning that we hear the Giver of the Torah.

He interprets that the way to be rewarded with it is to "place Your law on his heart," and not in the brain, which is the intellect, for the intellect only serves man; it is but an external force. This is why man is called "the heart," as it is written, "For the inclination of a man's heart is evil from his youth."

"Your word" means that one must believe that all the words that one utters from his mouth are only by the power of the Creator, and this is called "Your word." If a person believes this, he will certainly not say idle words, or lie, or gossip, or slander, since the light in it reforms the bad in his heart to be good, and then he is rewarded with hearing the Torah.

Concerning "*Malchuiot* [kingships], memories, *Shofarot* [pl. of *Shofar*]," so the memory of you will come up before Me, meaning all the power of memory that is within you will be only before Me, meaning before the Creator, meaning for the Creator.

Also, there is the matter of accepting the burden of the kingdom of heaven, which is on *Rosh Hashanah*, since this day is the beginning of the month, and then we need a new arrangement, meaning accepting the burden of the kingdom of heaven, and we might forget this. This is why he says "memories," that we must always remember the acceptance of the burden of the kingdom of heaven. The way not to forget is the *Shofar*. The *Shofar* is called "the beauty of Rabbi Yochanan," *Shufra* [Aramaic: beauty] of *Adam HaRishon*, and beauty is called...

# 885- With a *Shofar* You Will Renew

Who forces the Creator so He cannot sit on the throne of mercy without blowing the *Shofar* [a festive horn], and precisely by blowing the *Shofar* He can sit on the throne of mercy?

The purpose of creation is to do good to His creations. In order not to have the bread of shame, there must be the matter of choice. After the choice, one is rewarded with the revelation.

The matter of the *Tzimtzum* [restriction] is in order to have room for choice.

The matter of devotion is because he has nothing to give to the Creator but his soul, and then he is worthy of receiving all the pleasures, since his only aim will be to bestow because he wants to annul himself before the Creator.

There is a debate above if he is already permitted to be given the pleasure. A person is given corporeal pleasures so he can exist. But he was not given spiritual pleasures, and this is called "the quality of judgment." That is, this *Tzimtzum* is called "judgment." At that time, it is called a "good day."

Man has two forces: 1) to bestow, meaning mercy, 2) to receive, which is called "judgment."

"This today, the beginning of Your works." The Creator wants to impart the revelation. There is a quality of judgment there, whether it is permitted to receive the revelation. It is called a "good day" because at that time the revelation illuminates. This is done by the Creator sitting on a throne, meaning revealing Himself to the lower ones. In order for one to be able to receive the revelation at that time, which is called "judgment" and "the quality of reception," he must evoke the quality of bestowal, called "merciful."

The Creator sits on a throne of judgment, meaning reveals Himself to the lower ones.

He is merciful, meaning that one must engage in the matter of bestowal, namely "When will I achieve the deeds of my fathers," meaning sacrifice himself to the Creator, which is completely to bestow.

Concerning having to be rewarded, the order of the work is that *Malchut* will accept the burden of the kingdom of heaven, memories, and *Shofarot* [pl. of *Shofar*], meaning that man will give the good *Kli*, as it is written, "My heart overflows with a good thing," "He who has a good eye shall be blessed." With what? With a *Shofar*, as it is written in the *Midrash*, "With a *Shofar* you will renew your deeds," meaning with a *Shofar*. A throne of judgment means it is narrow and he cannot receive, while the quality of mercy is called "broadening."

Assorted Notes

# 886- *Malchuiot*, Memories, and *Shofarot*

22 *Elul*, *Tav-Shin-Chaf*, September 14, 1960

*Rosh Hashanah* (4, 16b, 34b): "Raba said, 'The Creator said, 'Say before Me on *Rosh Hashanah*: *Malchuiot* [kingships], memories, *Shofarot* [pl. of *Shofar* (a festive horn)]. *Malchuiot*, so you would crown Me over you. Memories, so the memory of you will come before Me favorably. And with what? With a *Shofar*.''" And on page 16, it is written, "So the memory of you will come up before Me favorably."

This seems to imply that through the *Shofar* He will remember us. But the throne does not forget! And also, What does it mean that the memory should be favorable if the conduct of the Good is to do good?

Also, we should understand the words of our sages, "Rabbi Abaho said, 'Why do we blow a ram's horn [*Shofar*]?' The Creator said, 'Blow before Me with a ram's horn so I will remember for you the tying of Isaac, son of Abraham, and consider it for you as though you tied yourselves before Me.'"

We should also ask if He would forget the tying of Isaac were it not for the blowing of the lower ones, and precisely by our actions we remind Him, and then the merit of the tying counts as though we ourselves are tied before Him. And also, what does the Creator get by our tying ourselves before Him?

There are also the words of our sages, "Rabbi Yitzhak said, 'Why do we blow on *Rosh Hashanah*? Why do we blow? The Merciful one said, 'Blow!' And why do we shout? The Merciful one said, 'a reminder of the blowing.' But why do we blow and shout sitting down and blow and shout standing up? In order to confuse Satan.'

"On this month, improve your actions with a *Shofar*; on this month, improve your actions. The Creator said to them, to Israel, 'If you improve your actions, it will become for you as this *Shofar*. What is this *Shofar*? He brings it in with this one, and brings it out with that one. Just so, I move from the throne of judgment and sit on the throne of mercy, and turn for you the quality of judgment into the quality of mercy. When? On the seventh month'" (*Midrash Rabbah, Emor*, Portion 29).

It is known that the purpose of creation is to do good to His creations. For this purpose, the Creator created the will to receive pleasures existence from absence. In order not to have the bread of shame, there was the *Tzimtzum* [restriction], which is the concealment, and then there is room for work and choice to take upon ourselves the Torah and *Mitzvot* [commandments] when we do not feel the pleasure in them.

Afterward, at the end of our work, which is by adjusting to acts of bestowal, when we do not want to receive any pleasure and our only aim is to bestow upon the Creator, meaning that he is willing to give to the Creator everything he has, even his life, which is all that he cherishes, for "Man will give anything for his soul," and he is willing to give even the soul to the Creator.

This is work in devotion, and by this, the Creator can then give him all the pleasures that have been prepared for him, and there will be no flaw of shame in the King's gift.

Conversely, prior to this, before one achieves the degree of devotion, while he still has a desire to receive delight and pleasure for himself, the *Tzimtzum* and judgment lie upon him. That is, the sentence is that he cannot be given because he would receive it in the *Kelim* [vessels] of the will to receive.

However, after one acquires the vessels of bestowal, regarded as the quality of "Merciful," as our sages said, "As He is merciful, so you are merciful," the Creator can give him all the pleasures He has prepared for him.

By this we will understand that although the cow wants to nurse more than the calf wants to suckle, the Creator still does not bestow upon man, although He wants to bestow, for the above reason, since there would be a flaw in the King's present. It is like the allegory about the rich man, who indirectly imparts disgrace upon the poor.

Thus, all our prayers and work are to correct our actions so we will have the *Kelim* to receive the wholeness of the pleasures.

## 887- *I Do Swear*

*Midrash Tanchuma, VaYera*: "And he said, 'I do swear,' declares the Lord."

He said to him, "You swore, and I swore that I would not come down from the altar until I say all that I must." He said to Him, "Say, is this not what You said to me, 'Count the stars; if you can count them, so will be your descendants'?" He said to him, "Yes." He said to Him, "From whom?" He said to him, "From Isaac." He said to Him, "Just as when I had in my heart what to answer You and tell You, yesterday You said to me, 'through Isaac your descendants shall be named,' and now You tell me, 'Offer him there as a burnt offering,' and I restrained myself and did not answer You. Likewise, when Isaac's sons sin and put themselves in trouble, You will remember the tying of Isaac and will regard it as though his ashes are piled up on the altar, and You will forgive them and redeem them from their trouble."

The Creator said to him, "You said yours, and I will say Mine." Isaac's sons are destined to sin before Me and I will judge them in the beginning of the year. If they want Me to seek their merit and remember for them the tying of Isaac, let them blow before Me with a *Shofar* of one.

This means that we can extend ancestral merit only through work, which is the work in *Mitzvot* [commandments]. The meaning of *Shofar* [a festive horn] is "*Shapru* [improve] your works," and the covenant will not be broken, for through the act, "A covenant of fathers You shall remember for the sons" will be extended to them.

## 888- Good Days

We should understand that although the Ten Penitentiary Days [a.k.a., Terrible Days], which are regarded as judgment, *Gevura*, and fear, and the whole world awakens to repent, for everyone is afraid of the day of judgment, why are they called "good days," meaning days that are not regular days?

The reason is that *Rosh Hashanah* [beginning of the year] and *Yom Kippur* [Day of Atonement] are regarded as "left," meaning that then is a time of appearance of lights of *Hochma*. *Rosh Hashanah* is a returning of the situation to the time of the creation of the world, the fourth day in the work of creation, which is discerned as the "diminution of the moon."

## 889- The Quality of Mercy

The Creator sits on the throne of judgment, meaning He reveals Himself to the lower ones. "Merciful" means that a person should engage in the quality of bestowal. "Blow the *Shofar* [festive horn] of a ram," etc., meaning when will I reach the deeds of my fathers, meaning he offered himself to an authority that is completely to bestow.

The thing is that a person must be rewarded with an order of work. *Malchut*, he accepts the burden of the kingdom of heaven. "Memories," meaning one should give the good *Kli* [vessel], as it is written, "My heart overflows with a good thing," "He who has a good eye will be blessed." With what? With a *Shofar*, as it is written in the *Midrash*, "With a *Shofar* you will renew your works," meaning with a *Shofar*. "A throne of judgment" means it is narrow and he cannot receive, while the quality of mercy is called "broadening."

# Yom Kippur

## 890- The Sorrow of the Shechina – 2

"For a sin we sinned against You with the evil inclination" (from the *Yom Kippur* [Day of Atonement] prayer).

We should ask because all the transgressions come from the evil inclination. We should interpret that the sin is in saying that there is an evil inclination instead of "There is none else besides Him." If a person is unworthy, he is cast out from above. This comes by clothing in the will to receive, called the "evil inclination."

This is the meaning of "For the inclination of a man's heart is evil from his youth," meaning that the Creator created him this way, since the will to receive is the actual *Kli* [vessel], except it must be correct. By this we can interpret what is written, "He was saddened in his heart." Man feels that following the inclination gives him sadness, and this is called "the sorrow of the *Shechina* [Divinity]."

# 891- The Meaning of *Yom Kippur*

The meaning of *Yom Kippur* [Day of Atonement]. Why does *Rosh Hashanah* [beginning of the year] not atone, but specifically *Yom Kippur*?

We should say that through the *Rosh Hashanah* prayers, we see the truth, that man has iniquities, and then he can ask for atonement for the iniquities. This is why *Yom Kippur* comes after *Rosh Hashanah*.

# Sukkot

## 892- An Article for Sukkot

"You shall sit in *Sukkot* [huts] for seven days; every citizen in Israel shall sit in *Sukkot* so your generations may know that I placed the sons of Israel in *Sukkot* when I brought them out from the land of Egypt; I am the Lord your God" (Leviticus 23:42-43). Rabbi Eliezer says, "Actual *Sukkot*," and Rabbi Akiva, "Clouds of glory."

How can there be such a gap between them? One interprets a corporeal *Sukkah* [sing. for *Sukkot*], and one interprets a spiritual *Sukkah*, which is "clouds of glory." However, they are *Panim* [anterior/face] and *Achoraim* [posterior/back]. On the part of the awakening from below, the making of the *Sukkah* is an actual *Sukkah*. On the part of the awakening from above, it is the "seven clouds of glory."

"Sit" means "dwell," as in "The concealed things belong to the Lord our God." The sages of ethics interpret that the matter of "Go out from permanent residence and sit in temporary residence" is so they will know and notice that this world is like a motel and temporary lodging.

It is written in Psalms: "You hide them in concealment of the face from the conspiracies of man; You conceal them in a *Sukkah* [hut] from the strife of tongues." RASHI interpreted "the conspiracies of man" as "the connection of wicked, who connive in order to harm them."

We should understand what is "concealment of the face," since the rule is that the face is revealed, and how is the face related to the Creator? Also, what is the meaning of "You conceal them in a *Sukkah* from the strife of tongues"? What is the difference between *Sukkah* and concealment of the face? We find the words, "sitting in the upper concealment," and the meaning of "upper concealment"; what is "lower concealment"? We also find, "His concealment is straightness."

We should ask, If it is concealment, how do we know that it is straightness and not a circle (perhaps this is the meaning of *Yosher* and *Igulim* [straightness and circles, respectively], where in the quality of *Igulim* there is no concealment, but the light shines equally to the small and to the great, and this is the *Reshimot* [recollection] from the world of *Tzimtzum* [restriction])?

"Straightness" means according to the line that was done in the *Tzimtzum*. Accordingly, what we see, that there is concealment, is straight, as in "straight thinking." (The matter of *Panim* means revealing of the *Panim* and concealment of the *Panim*.) The *Sukkah* is made of four walls and a thatch, but the place of the *Sukkah* is ready, for one can build one's sukkah on the ground, which is the substance, and on this substance we make a form, the form of a *Sukkah*.

We should understand the meaning of walls and the thatch, which is waste of barn and vineyard.

It is known that there are four sides, and above and below. These are called *HGT* and *Malchut*, and *Netzah* above and *Hod* below.

In the *Shema* reading, we say "In the name of the Lord, God of Israel, *Mi-KeEl* [Michael] to my right, and *Gavri-El* [Gabriel] to my left, and *Uri-El* [Uriel] before me, and *Raf-El* [Rafael] behind, and over my head, the *Shechina* of God." Why is nothing said concerning below, which corresponds to *Hod*? Below is discerned as the ground, which is man. If he does a *Kosher* [proper] *Sukkah*, he is regarded as

*Hod*, called "the beauty of the *Sukkah*." But if not, the *Hod* [beauty] becomes *Daveh* [pain-stricken, same letters as *Hod*].

In other words, nothing should be implied concerning the place of the earth. Rather, what one extends and aims in all five *Behinot* [discernments/qualities], in this way it will appear in the earth, which is the quality of man, who extends from the root of *Malchut*, called "she has nothing of her own." In other words, she has nothing of herself except what she is given. Thus, it depends on the form of the *Sukkah*.

# 893- The Fruit of a Citrus Tree

The fruit of a citrus tree. These four kinds, some of them have taste and smell, like the citron, which corresponds to the righteous, in whom there is the spirit of Torah and the taste of good deeds.

The tree on which the palm branch grows has a taste, but no smell. This corresponds to the intermediate in Israel, in whom there is the taste of *Mitzvot* [commandments] but not the spirit of Torah.

The myrtle has a smell but no taste. It corresponds to those who have the spirit of Torah but no *Mitzvot*.

The willow has neither taste nor smell. This corresponds to the uneducated people, in whom there is neither the spirit of Torah nor the taste of *Mitzvot*.

We gather the four together, implying that the Creator does not reconcile with Israel until they are all one bundle, as was said, "Who builds His ascents in the heaven, and establishes His group on the earth." When does the Creator become ascended? When we all become one bundle.

# Simchat Torah
# [The Joy of Torah]

## 894- Simchat Torah
## [The Joy of Torah]

It is written in *Shaar HaKavanot* that Torah is called *Zeir Anpin*, and if he bestows upon *Malchut*, it means that *Malchut* is already fit to receive the abundance. Therefore, *Zeir Anpin*, who is called "Torah," is happy.

This is called "the joy of Torah." We can interpret this according to what Baal HaSulam said, that one should be happy that the Creator is happy that He can bestow upon the lower ones.

# Hanukkah

## 895- The Meaning of Hanukkah

A Hanukkah candle, its measure is "until all feet have vanished from the market."

Regel [foot/leg] comes from the word Meragel [spy]. "Market" means the public domain. When we are in the private domain, we walk in wholeness and there is no room for spies. On Hanukkah, we must extend the light of Hanukkah until all the quality of "spies" vanishes from the market, for in the place of the light, there is no room for the Sitra Achra [other side].

"The following year they were appointed as [days of] praise and gratitude." Why did they wait for the following year? It is because on the first year of their victory, because of the greatness of the miracle and the brightness, they adhered to their Maker and seemingly became one body, to the point that they did not need to appoint praise and gratitude. But the next year, they had to appoint it with praise and gratitude the way one hammers something with nails so it will not fall, so they will adhere to the Creator through gratitude (Avodat Ysrael).

The debates concerning Hanukkah were not mentioned in the Mishnah although there is a dispute between Beit Shammai and Beit Hillel, for the Mishnah is the internality of the world, but only in the Braita [Gemara], which is external, as it is written, "Go and learn it outside," for Hanukkah implies that the brightness is mainly about lowering down the *Kedusha* [holiness] so that it shines outside (idem.).

According to the view of Beit Shammai, it "wanes down" like the fruit of the festival, implying that through the external *Kedusha*, they are rejected and gradually decline. According to Beit Hillel, "it gradually increases," implying the *Kedusha*, to draw the *Kedusha* as in "increasing holiness" (idem.).

"Broke the walls of my towers." A wall means keeping strangers from entering the tower. The "tower" means *Kedusha*, called "a tower filled with abundance." Conversely, all the *Sitra Achra* has is emptiness. The wall is called "boundary that divides between *Kedusha* and *Sitra Achra*," which is faith. It is called "boundary," meaning the limit of the thought and the external mind. This is called "the seal of the token of the covenant of holiness."

We must understand why the Greeks wanted specifically to revoke the circumcision and Shabbat [Sabbath]. Circumcision is called a "token," and Shabbat is called a "token," referring to the covenant of holiness. A covenant means faith, as implied in the words, "And you shall circumcise the foreskin of your hearts." Through faith, one is rewarded with faith in the Creator. The *Klipa* [shell/peel], which is called "foreskin," parts from it, so there is room for installing *Kedusha*. All their efforts were to cancel them and admit them into the cursed philosophy, which is against faith.

This is called a "wall." To the extent that they inserted philosophy, to that extent it is considered that the wall was breached. This is the meaning of the words, "broke the walls of my towers and defiled all the oils," for "oil" means the clarity in Torah and work.

A stupor and sealing were placed on the *Kedusha*, meaning they felt no vitality in Torah and work, and found only one jar of oil that was marked with the seal of the high priest, and it had enough to burn for only one day. A miracle happened and they lit with it for eight days.

"With His mighty hand, He brought forth the *Segula* [remedy/power/virtue]."

We should understand what is this *Segula*. In the essay "Mutual Guarantee," he writes, "And you will be unto Me a *Segula* from all the nations, for all the earth is Mine." He asks what is the connection of *Segula* to "all the earth is Mine." He explains there that "You will be unto Me a *Segula*," for through you, sparks of cleansing of the body will be passed on to the all the nations, for *Segula* means a desire to bestow.

Indeed, we should understand why it is called *Segula*. It is known that something that is not confirmed by the intellect usually does not change to another state. It follows that the reason has no direct relation to the result, and this is called *Segula*.

For example, a person who needs money in order to be rich is told that there is a *Segula* that if he donates a lot of money to charity, it is a *Segula* for wealth. This is counterintuitive, for one who wants to be rich should not waste any penny on others. And yet, "Give tithing so you will become rich," this is called *Segula*.

Concerning our matter, "One who wants to live should put himself to death." That is, one who wants to lead a life of pleasure must not want and not receive anything for himself, but only to bestow. Only by this will he receive delight and pleasure. It follows that the desire to bestow is a *Segula* to thereby obtain abundance.

This is why they said, "With His mighty hand," called "the hand of *Hesed* [grace/mercy]," for *Hesed* is called "mighty," He took out the *Segula* from the people of Israel. By giving to the creatures that quality of *Hesed*, they can execute the vessels of bestowal from what one is included in.

This is the meaning of "Your right [hand] is stretched out to greet the returning." "Returning" means that when one does not want to be a receiver, but always wants to be among the returners, he returns everything he needs. Then, one who wants to be among the returners, "Your right is stretched out," meaning the quality of *Hesed* that the Creator is sending him. By this He takes out the *Segula*.

Our sages said, "What is Hanukkah? *Hanu* [parked] *Koh* [here]." It is known that *Koh* refers to *Malchut*, the name *BON*, *Aleph-Hey-Yod* with a filling of *Heys* of the filling of the filling. This means that those who had a war to take upon themselves the kingdom of heaven, because acceptance of the kingdom of heaven is built on the basis of in order to receive, there is a great war, since this is against nature. Hence, emerging from this state is called "the miracle of Hanukkah."

This is regarded as "lowers the proud to the ground, and raises the low up on high," for bestowal is low in our eyes because when one sees that this act will not yield any reward for his own benefit, he feels it as a state of lowliness.

This is the meaning of "We have no permission to use them, but only to see them" regarding Hanukkah candles. Using is with vessels of reception, and here the miracle was that they served the Creator with vessels of bestowal.

There is a difference between Hanukkah and Purim: The miracle of Hanukkah is on vessels of bestowal, whereas on Purim, the miracle was on vessels of reception. For this reason, there are feast and joy there, while on Hanukkah it is only to see them and not to use.

ASSORTED NOTES

## 896- Repel Admon in the Shadow of Tzalmon

Hanukkah, 25 *Kislev*, *Tav-Shin-Lamed-Bet*, December 13, 1971

"Repel Admon in the shadow of Tzalmon." This means repelling Esau, who is *Admoni* [red haired]. "In the shadow of Tzalmon" means *Tzalmavet*, meaning in *Tzel Mavet* [shadow of death].

We must understand this in the work. We know that there are three lines, called *Hesed*, right line; *Gevura*, left line; and *Tifferet*, middle line. The beginning of the work is in the right line, called "white" because one who walks on the right line, no deficiencies are apparent there.

Afterward, when we are rewarded with the left line, called *Gevura*, when there is the discernment of judgment, which is called "redness," since we can fall into the *Klipa* of Esau, which is the waste of Isaac, who wants to extend the quality of *Hochma*, which is the revelation of the secrets of Torah from above downward, meaning into the vessels of reception.

Yet, before the end of correction, it is impossible to draw the abundance into the vessels of reception so it will be in order to bestow. Hence, there are judgments that keep the abundance so that when we want to extend into the vessels of reception, we feel suffering.

And when we want to extend into the vessels of reception, called "from above downward," there is control to the nations of the world over the general public in Israel, since the people of Israel agree to the conduct of the nations of the world, which is the will to receive.

The miracle of Hanukkah was as it is written, "And You, with your great mercy... and to Your people, Israel, You performed a great salvation." In other words, a miracle means an awakening from above, when the middle line shines, which is called *Hassadim* that clothe the *Hochma*. That is, He bestowed the quality of "shadow," which is the opposite of "revealed," for a shadow means a place that hides the sun, where the sun does not shine because there is something there that hides the sun.

By the power of bestowal that a person discovers, he does not want to receive any attainment or knowledge. Rather, on a place where he can obtain knowledge, he extends faith, where he makes a shade on knowing. This is as our sages said, "In return for 'and Moses hid his face for he was afraid to look,' he was rewarded with 'the image of the Lord does he behold'" (*Berachot* 7a). At that time, one emerges from the judgments of the left line, which are called "red haired" and are the *Klipa* [shell/peel] of Esau, and enter the quality of "Israel."

This is the meaning of "Repel Admon," that the Creator will repel this "red" in the shadow of Tzalmon. Tzalmon means "By its *Tzel* [shade] I coveted and sat, and its fruit was sweet to my palate."

There is the quality of *Tzel Mavet* [shadow of death], when the departure of the sunlight results from a sin. That is, by wanting to receive in order to receive, there is the *Tzimtzum* [restriction] and departure of the abundance, and this is called "breaking" and "death."

There is also the quality of "shadow" when he does not want to receive the abundance due to fear of heaven, as was said about Moses, "and Moses hid his face." This is called "his shade," meaning that that shade came because of the greatness of the Creator, and he wants to be adhered to the Creator and fears that he might drift off by receiving the abundance.

This is called "By its shade I coveted and sat, and its fruit was sweet to my palate." That is, precisely by this does the middle line become revealed and there are fruits. Conversely, "Another God is sterile and does not bear fruit." This means that from the left line, regarded as "red," the abundance is blocked and the fruits are not extended.

The whole difference between Tzalmon and *Tzel Mavet* [shadow of death] is in the *Vav*. We should interpret this as it is written in *The Zohar, Beresheet*, "Thousands of *Shanaan* (*Shanaan* means ox, vulture, lion; *Nun* means *Vav* that fell into the *Klipot* [pl. of *Klipa*]). He interprets there that in the first nine, which are called "vessels of bestowal," there is *Malchut* that is called "Adam," as in "lion, ox, vulture, man." But from the *Chazeh* down, *Malchut* controls.

Prior to the end of correction, it is impossible to receive the light of *Malchut* in order to bestow. For this reason, there is a hint, *Shanaan*, meaning "ox, vulture, lion," and on the quality of man it shows only *Vav*, which expanded from the quality of man above, meaning from the *Malchut* of the first nine. But if we do not want to receive through the *Vav*, and want to extend down into *Malchut*, it becomes a *Tav*, meaning the quality of *Tzalmavet*, and about this we say, "Repel Admon in the shadow of Tzalmon."

## 897- *What Is Hanukkah*

Hanukkah, *Kislev, Tav-Shin-Chaf-Aleph*, December 1960

Our sages said, "What is Hanukkah? Our sages said, 'On the twenty-fifth of *Kislev*, the days of Hanukkah,'" etc. (*Shabbat* [Sabbath] 21a). That is, *Hanu-Koh* [parked here], for on the twenty-fifth, they parked from the war. We should understand that parking means specifically in the middle of the work. We stand and rest in order to regain strength so we can keep walking and win the war until it is finished.

We should understand what is this parking. Our sages said that at that time, the Greeks sentenced Israel not to engage in Torah. That is, the miracle was only on the redemption of spirituality, which is the needs of the soul. Conversely, on Purim, there was the redemption of the bodies.

For this reason, on Hanukkah, we were given the recognition of the miracle through praise and gratitude, whereas on Purim, it is written, "a feast and merriment," since the miracle was on the bodies. Hence, there must be recognition of the miracle through to the body, meaning with feast and merriment.

To understand all the above in the work and in ethics, we must understand what our sages said, "You shall love the Lord with all your heart—with both your inclinations, the good inclination and the evil inclination" (*Berachot* 54). We should serve the Creator with the good inclination, meaning engage in Torah and *Mitzvot* [commandments] to bestow contentment upon our Maker. But what is the meaning of the evil inclination? It is known that the evil inclination is the will to receive in us. We should understand how the will to receive can serve the Creator.

According to what is explained in the *Sulam* [Ladder commentary on *The Zohar*], when a person engages in reception of pleasures in order to bestow, there is no evil in the will to receive, as it is written, "I have created the evil inclination; I have created the Torah as a spice," for through the Torah, the evil inclination is sweetened.

The miracle of Hanukkah was only with the good inclination. This is why it is merely called "parking," since the work has not been completed, meaning that there are still more corrections on the evil inclination, which is called "body." This was only the miracle of Purim.

This is the meaning of "observed and received," thus far by force, since the evil inclination has not agreed to the work because it was still not corrected, and now that the miracle was in the redemption of the bodies, "with all your heart—with both your inclinations" comes true. This is why it is called "willingly."

Hence, on Hanukkah, there is recognition of the miracle only in praise and gratitude, which is only the needs of the soul, while on Purim, we recognize the miracle in feast and merriment, which touches through to the body.

"Greeks gathered around me, then in the days of the Hasmoneans, and broke the walls of my towers and defiled all the oils."

"Greeks" refers to a philosophy, when one wants to understand everything with the external mind. "Then in the days of the Hasmoneans" means that specifically when there are Hasmoneans, meaning servants of the Creator, we see that the Greeks have control.

*Homot* [walls] has the letters of *Techum* [zone/area] (as explained in the writings of the ARI). This means that a person limits his thought from wanting to understand the work with the external mind, but rather with faith, and faith is a wall against the external ones. "My towers" means "a tower filled with abundance." "Oils" are clarity...

# 898- What Is the Miracle of Hanukkah

Hanukkah, *Kislev-Tevet, Tav-Shin-Chaf-Vav*, December 1965

Our sages said (*Shabbat* [Sabbath] 21a): "What is Hanukkah? Our sages said, 'On the twenty-fifth of *Kislev*, the days of Hanukkah, which are eight,'" etc., when Greeks entered the hall, defiled all the oils in the hall, etc., they checked but found only one jar of oil that was sealed with the seal of the high priest. It contained only enough to light for one day. A miracle happened and they lit with it for eight days. The following year, they were appointed as [days of] praise and gratitude, and the rule is that it is forbidden to use its light.

"Greeks" means within reason, which is philosophy, meaning to adjust the *Mitzvot* [commandments] to the intellect, such as a "release" [from levirate marriage].

The "Hall" is the mind and heart, which are the hall within man.

"Oils" are the *Mitzvot* [commandments], as it is written, "oil for lighting," since the Torah is called "light" and the *Mitzvot* are called "candle," as it is written, "A candle is a *Mitzva* [sing. for *Mitzvot*], and the Torah is light." The light cannot shine without oil, for the Torah cannot shine if it has nothing on which to grip, meaning the oil.

"One jar of oil" means that after the victory and the devotion that they had with the Greeks, they found that the matter of faith is "one," as in "Hear, O Israel, the Lord our God, the Lord is one." "Of oil" means that this *Mitzva* is signed by the seal of the high priest, whose quality is the quality of *Hesed*. *Hesed* means "As He is merciful, so you are merciful," implying for the sake of the Creator.

However, this force suffices to light only one night, since the matter of faith must be renewed each time, as it is written, "New every morning; great is the faith in You." A miracle happened to them and that power of faith sufficed them for eight days.

Praise and gratitude are only a miracle for spirituality; this is why it is forbidden to use its light, implying that it is only for spirituality.

# 899- *Hanu-KoH*

Hanukkah, *Kislev-Tevet*, *Tav-Shin-Tet-Vav*, December 1954

*NeR* [candle], an acronym for *Nefesh Ruach*. We must extend light, which is the quality of *Neshama*, as in "A candle is a *Mitzva* [commandment], and the Torah is light," and this is *Hanu-Koh* [parked here].

*Koh* [here] means the quality of *Malchut*, as in the weak hand. *Hanu* [parked] comes from the verse, "the angels of the Lord *Honeh* [parks]," meaning that the *Shechina* [Divinity] must have a place in which to park within man's heart.

This is as our sages said, "What is Hanukkah? When the Greeks entered the Hall, they defiled all the oils ... they checked but found one jar of oil that was sealed with the seal of the high priest." Man's heart is called "the hall of the Creator." "Defiled all the oils" means all the sacred wisdoms.

"Finally, they found one jar of oil that was sealed with the seal of the high priest." *Pach* [jar] has the letters of *Chaf* [a spoon], meaning the unification of the *Shema* reading. "Placed" means that no one wanted to lift it.

The high priest is called "upper *Abba*," and the oil is signed and sealed, oil, as in "pure air."

Assorted Notes

## 900- *Two Degrees*

What is Hanukkah? This means that we must ask like the four questions: wise, wicked, innocent, and one who does not know how to ask.

There is a dispute concerning the Hanukkah candle: One said it was permitted to use its light, and one said it is forbidden. He said to him, "These are two degrees. One is revelation of love from the side of His goodness, meaning that by this he can praise and glorify His name, and one said it is forbidden, meaning from the side of pure air, which is only from the discernment that He is great and ruling, regarded as covered *Hassadim*."

There is an allegory about a poor man who was happy with the king's gift, who made miracles for him above nature. By nature, he is poor in knowledge and sick in the mind, and the Creator bestows upon him His light, meaning that he delights with the King's gift. This is the main thing for him, that he is serving the King, and this is all the pleasure he receives, meaning that his sole purpose is that He is great and ruling.

This is the meaning of "'If they say to me, 'What is His name?' What will I tell them?' And God said to Moses, 'I will be [Hebrew: *EKYEH*] that which I will be. Thus shall you tell the children of Israel: '*EKYEH* sent me to you.'" RASHI interpreted "I will be with you in this trouble, and I will be with you in the enslavement in the rest of the kingships."

It is written in *Berachot* (p 9): "He said before him, 'Master of the world, why am I reminding them of another trouble? They have enough with this trouble.' He said to him, 'Well said,' etc., and since then, such was the view of the Creator when He said, 'I will be that which I will be.' He said it only to Moses, and not that he would tell this to Israel."

This means that it is the degree of Moses, meaning that he is regarded as covered *Hassadim*, which is considered "The eye has not seen," meaning covered *Hassadim*, "a God besides You," meaning that all his work is in the discernment of great and ruling, and he needs no reward but God, as this is his entire vitality, that he is serving the Creator.

"I will be that which I will be." I created the world with the quality of goodness, I lead it, and I renew it, as was said, "The Lord is good to all, the Lord is good as a stronghold in the day of trouble, the Lord does good to the good." Another thing: "I will be that which I will be." I created the world with the quality of faith, and with the quality of faith am I destined to renew it. Lord, you are my God, I will exalt You, I will thank Your name for You have done wonders; counsels from afar rears into faith, a God of faith and there is no iniquity, and His faith and mercy are with Him" (*Otiot de Rabbi Akiva*, in Item 5).

# The 15th of Shevat

## 901- Rosh Hashanah for the Trees

15 Shevat, Tav-Shin-Tet-Vav, February 7, 1955

Rosh Hashanah [New Year's Eve] for the trees. Man is called "the tree of the field," and Rosh Hashanah is the time of sentencing—for judgment or for mercy. Hence, the month of Shevat is the fifth of the winter months, which is regarded as Hod, when Daveh [affliction] becomes Hod [glory/majesty].

This means that when we are rewarded with walking in the quality of Hesed, he extends from the Sefira of Hesed to Hod, and all the blessing is in the quality of Hesed [mercy/kindness], as it is written, "For I said, a world of Hesed shall be built," where through the blessing we are rewarded with fruits. It is as Baal HaSulam wrote, that this is why on the 15th of Shevat we bless on the fruits, since this is the whole distinction between Kedusha [holiness] and Klipa [shell/peel], for "Another God is sterile and does not bear fruit."

The success in the work to be rewarded with fruits is only through Hesed, since when we work with the quality of bestowal, called Hesed, we are rewarded with *Dvekut* [adhesion] with the Creator, and when we are rewarded with *Dvekut*, we are rewarded with everything. Hence, on the 15th of *Shevat*, called *Rosh Hashanah* for the trees, we must strengthen ourselves with the quality of *Hesed*, for by this we will be rewarded with fruits called "A fruit bearing tree."

# 902- Israel Are Compared to an Olive Tree

Rabbi Yehoshua Ben Levi said, "Why are Israel compared to an olive tree? To tell you that as the leaves of the olive tree do not fall during the summer or during the winter, so Israel have no rest in this world or in the next world" (*Minchot* 56b).

There are leaves and there are fruits. The leaves precede the fruits. The tree itself is man, "For man is the tree of the field." At the time of blossoming, it elicits leaves and then elicits fruits that are good for man to eat, while the leaves are good only as food for beasts.

The olive, the fruit itself, is not so important. Rather, the intention is mainly the oil extracted from the olive (so there are three things: leaves, olives, and oil).

The taste of the olive is bitter (as our sages said (*Iruvin* 18b), "I would prefer my nourishments to be as bitter as an olive and placed in Your hand than to be as sweet as honey and dependent on flesh and blood"). In other words, even though the fruit has already ripened, it is still not good for eating.

ASSORTED NOTES

# 903- Concerning the Fifteenth of Shevat

What is the reason that on the 15th of *Shevat*, which is *Rosh Hashanah* [beginning of the year] for the trees, we eat fruits? Baal HaSulam said that the whole difference between *Kedusha* [holiness] and *Klipa* [shell/peel] is in the fruits, as it is written in *The Zohar*, "Another God is sterile and does not bear fruit." For this reason, we eat fruits and imply that our joy is in the fruits.

The verse says, "And God said, 'Let the earth put forth grass, plants yielding seed, fruit trees bearing fruit after their kind."

RASHI interpreted "fruit tree, that the taste of the tree will be as that of the fruit. But she [the earth] did not do so. Rather, 'And the earth put forth... fruit bearing tree,' and not a 'fruit tree.' For this reason, when Adam was cursed for his iniquity, she, too was mentioned for hers, as it is written, 'Cursed is the earth because of you,'" and RASHI interpreted, "It will produce for you cursed things, such as flies and fleas and ants, and thorns and thistles will it grow for you, by the sweat of your brow you will eat bread."

Rabbi Yehoshua Ben Levi said, "When the Creator said to Adam, 'Thorns and thistles will it grow for you,' his eyes teared. He said to Him: 'Master of the world, will I and my donkey eat off the same manger?' When He told him 'By the sweat of your brow you will eat bread,' his mind was eased" (*Pesachim* 118a).

We should ask, 1) How can we say that the earth changed the commandment of the Creator to the point that it was punished for it? Does it have free choice? 2) If the earth should be punished for its iniquity, why was it not punished right away, and He waited for the man to sin so he would be punished together with the earth?

In ethics, it is said that "man is the tree of the field." Man was created from the ground to show him the ways of his work, how man behaves in the world. The Creator said that there would be a fruit tree, meaning that the taste of the tree and that of the fruit will be the same. The tree is the cause of the fruit, meaning that an apple tree will not yield almonds but apples, for the tree is the cause of the act.

This means that if a person does something, there should be a thought that makes him act. When a person performs a *Mitzva* [commandment], while performing the *Mitzva*, there is no telling whether it is *Lishma* [for Her sake] or to the contrary, since there is no difference in the action, but only in the thought. But the Creator wants that if a person makes a *Mitzva*, which is the fruit, the taste of the tree and that of its fruit will be the same, meaning that the aim will be *Lishma*, as well.

Just as while performing a *Mitzva* it is apparent to all that he is performing an act for the sake of the Creator, so the tree, meaning the intention, should be *Lishma*. If this is not so, it is considered that the tree is *Lo Lishma* [not for Her sake] and the fruit is *Lishma*, and this is what the Creator wants. However, the earth did not do so, showing that the man will not do so, but will engage *Lo Lishma*.

Hence, when Adam sinned and was cursed, she, too, had to suffer the curse, as well, since she must show the man the example so he will see what form he has in the work.

In other words, if his work is inappropriate, the earth is also inappropriate. For this reason, the earth was not punished right away but after Adam's sin. This matter followed the order that first he had to sin according to Adam's example that the taste of the tree and that of its fruit are not the same, and then he will be punished, and the form of the punishment that he suffered was imprinted in the earth.

It is explained that the earth did not change, meaning that she has no free choice but rather emerges in the way that the man will behave.

According to what is written about "One, Unique, and Unified," how can man and the earth be cursed by the Creator? The thing is that since the taste of the tree and that of its fruit are not the same, meaning that the aim is *Lo Lishma*, a person might stay in that state. For this reason, there was a correction of growing thorns and thistles, meaning bearing no fruits, namely that he will find no flavor in the *Mitzvot* [commandments] he performs.

This is the meaning of "The ground is cursed because of you." In other words, the earth, this foundation where he stands, will be flies to him, as it is written, "Dead flies make a perfumer's oil stink," namely foreign thoughts. And ants, which are ill wills that eat one's flesh like ants, by this he will be forced to notice and correct the intention of *Lo Lishma*, for otherwise he will suffer.

This is the meaning of the words "Will I and my donkey eat off the same manger?" meaning that his donkey and his spirituality will be of the same form—that of reception for oneself. When he was told "By the sweat of your brow," meaning through labor, "you will eat bread," which is faith, his mind was eased.

## 904- Man Is the Tree of the Field

Rabbi Elazar and Rabbi Shimon, on the first of *Tishrey*, *Rosh Hashanah* [beginning of the year] for the tithing of the beast, and on the fifteenth of *Shevat*, *Rosh Hashanah* for the trees.

"Man is the tree of the field." That is, we can discern two things in man's works: 1) A discernment of faith, called *Mitzva* [commandment], and the discernment of *Malchut* and BON, and the discernment of "beast." In *Gematria*, "beast" is BON. 2) A discernment of "Torah," called ZA, and the quality of MA, and the quality of man, for man [Adam] is MA in *Gematria*.

Concerning donations and tithing, these are given specifically from possessions, from what man has acquired and possessed, and then he gives a tithing from this. Hence, there is a tithing of the beast, which is given from the quality of "beast," which is the soul, and there is one from the fruits of the tree, which is the quality of "man."

The time of the giving of tithing begins once ripening or planting is visible, when it is certain that he has gained. With vegetables, it is done after they are collected because they are not something that remains, and with trees it is after the ripening.

With regard to the Torah, if one is rewarded with ripening then he is sure that he will have fruits. But with faith it is after the collecting because they are new every morning, meaning that faith must be renewed each time. Conversely, with regard to the Torah, Torah protects and saves even while not engaging in it.

"Torah is glorious without ugliness" (*Taanit* 7). "Faith" is called "an ugly *Kli* [vessel]" because the whole world loathes it.

A *Klipa* [shell/peel] is similar to a moist fruit that is sent inside a box. As long as it is en-route, it must be kept in a guarded place so it does not get dirty. Hence, the *Klipa* guards the *Kedusha* [holiness].

Oppositeness. On one hand, we need big vessels of reception. On the other hand, if we have big vessels of reception, we are doomed. But if we have vessels of bestowal, we cannot receive anything for lack of a *Kli* [vessel].

Two general principles: On one hand, it seems as though he is living in his own right and has his own life in nature. On the other hand, he has no life in his actual nature, but only as an artificial possession. Should he forget one day and not buy life from the outside, he will fall and die.

We should understand why if the Creator wanted to give us life, He did not give us life in our nature, and instead we must always labor and acquire life from the outside?

The reality extends from the quality of judgment. Hence, although he is alive, he is small and weak and has no persistence whatsoever because as soon as he is born he undergoes the *Tzimtzum* [restriction]. For this reason, he has no persistence.

The existence of reality is through the joining of the quality of mercy with the quality of judgment, and everything that extends through labor is through a guidance of joining the quality of mercy with the quality of judgment. This is regarded as reward and punishment.

The *Klipa* guards the fruit, meaning for the fruit to reach the recipient. Hence, until a person is fit for the work of bestowal, the *Klipa* provides him with her powers so that through her, he will receive the fruit called "reception in order to bestow." Just as when we take the fruit, the first touch of the fruit is on its peel, with the *Lishma* [for Her sake], called "the fruit," we must first receive the *Lo Lishma* [not for Her sake].

Growing accustomed to the work is through *Lo Lishma*, for otherwise we might blemish, such as "He who knows his master," etc.

## 905- *Daveh* [Afflicted] or *Hod* [Glory/Majesty]

The 15th of *Shevat* is *Rosh Hashanah* [New Year's Eve] for the trees. *Rosh Hashanah* is a time of sentencing for judgment or for mercy. The month of *Shevat* is the fifth of the winter months, which is the *Sefira Hod*, a time of sentencing, meaning that at times he is in a state of *Daveh* or *Hod*. This is the meaning of "for judgment or for mercy." Although the *Sefirot* begin with *Hesed*, as it is written, "For I said, 'A world of *Hesed* [mercy/kindness] will be built,'" we must extend the *Hesed* with the *Hod*, and then there is the completion of the work. In other words, there is no completion of *Hesed* until all five *Kelim* [vessels] are filled. Only then is there the blessing of *Hesed*, and then we are rewarded with eating the fruits.

Baal HaSulam said that we eat fruits on *Rosh Hashanah* for the trees because the whole difference between *Kedusha* [holiness] and the *Sitra Achra* [other side] is in the fruits, as it is written in *The Zohar*, "Another God is sterile and does not bear fruit," meaning that their source dries out and they do not bear fruits for blessing, which is multiplication in Torah and good deeds.

Conversely, one who walks on the path of *Kedusha* always has fruits for blessing and always has multiplication in Torah and good deeds. This is done by extending the quality of *Hesed* to the quality of *Hod*. Hence, on the fifth month, which is the quality of *Hod*, when the month is in full [moon], this is the beginning of the year for the trees, regarded as "a fruit bearing tree."

The writing says about "a fruit bearing tree," "And God said, 'Let the earth put forth grass, plants yielding seed, fruit trees.'" RASHI interpreted that the taste of the tree should be as the taste of the fruit, but she [the earth] did not do so. Rather, "And the earth put forth grass, plants yielding seed after their kind, and trees bearing fruit," rather than "fruit trees." Therefore, when Adam was cursed for his iniquity, she, too, was mentioned for her iniquity, as it is written, "Cursed is the ground because of you."

The interpreters asked, 1) How can it be said that the earth disobeyed the Creator? Can the earth choose? 2) Why was she not punished right away for disobeying the Creator, but was rather punished together with *Adam HaRishon*?

We should understand the above written in the work, the order that has been prepared for man to achieve the completion of the goal.

The earth is compared to man, as it is written in *The Zohar*, "The core of the land are the sons of man." The purpose of creation was for man to engage in Torah and *Mitzvot* [commandments] *Lishma* [for Her sake], as it is written, "All that is called by My name, I have created for My glory," meaning to engage *Lishma*, where all his actions are for the glory of the Creator.

It was interpreted in *The Zohar*, "All that is called by My name is man, whom the Creator created in His name, as it is written, 'And God created the man in His image.'" We should ask, How can we speak of the image of the Creator? However, "man" means "You are called 'man,' and not the nations of the world," for all that they do, they do for themselves.

# Shabbat [Sabbath] Zachor [Remember]

## 906- The Meaning of Amalek

"Remember what Amalek did to you along the way when you came out from Egypt." Amalek is the evil inclination, and it comes to a person only "when you came out from Egypt," meaning when a person emerges from the Egyptians who are afflicting the soul. When one takes upon himself to engage in serving the Creator, this is when he comes.

# 907- When He Let His Hand Down, Amalek Prevailed

"When he let his hand down, Amalek prevailed." The question is, Why did Moses let down his hands?

The thing is that Amalek is described in the holy books as a *Klipa* [shell/peel] against faith. Moses' hands are faith, since hands imply attainment, from the words, "For the hand attains," and all of Moses' attainment is through faith. This is why Moses is called "the loyal shepherd."

By this we can interpret that when Israel saw that Moses raised his hands, meaning that Israel exalted Moses' hands, Israel prevailed to the extent of the exaltedness of the matter, since one who despises faith cannot receive the vitality that is found in the power of faith.

This is the meaning of "Moses' hands were heavy," meaning it was heavy and hard for Israel to maintain the importance of Moses' hands. This means that they felt heaviness in faith, that the burden of faith was a burden and a toil for them.

"They took a stone and placed it under him." *Even* [stone] comes from the word *Havanah* [understanding]. This means that they took all the understandings and concepts and placed them under Moses, meaning under faith. That is, faith, which is called "Moses," rode over the mind, called "understanding" and "stone."

Aaron and Hur supported his hands, meaning the faith, helping Israel raise Moses' hands. In other words, they gave strength to the people of Israel to exalt faith. This is the meaning of "His hands were faith until the sun set." In other words, they took upon themselves the faith up to the measure of the annulment of all the power of the intellect, called "sun."

# 908- *Blotting Out Amalek*

Adar Bet, Tav-Shin-Chaf-Hey, March 1965

Why do we read the portion *Zachor* [Remember] on the Shabbat [Sabbath] before Purim? That is, we see that before Purim we must blot out Amalek. What does this imply to us?

It is known that the purpose of creation is to do good to His creations. However, in order not to have the bread of shame, we were given work in order to receive reward, so there would not be room for shame.

For this reason, we were given the evil inclination, called Amalek. During the work, it is impossible to grasp the taste of Torah and *Mitzvot* [commandments] because otherwise, this is not regarded as work. Hence, we must overcome the bad in us, regarded as the blotting out of Amalek, and then we can be rewarded with the light of redemption, as was then in the days of Mordechai, when they were rewarded with "observed and received."

Our sages said, "They observed what they had already received. Thus far by force; henceforth willingly." "By force" means compulsory, when one does something without pleasure from the act. He does it coercively, and this is called "by force," when he forces himself to observe Torah and *Mitzvot* in a compulsory manner.

However, when subjugating Amalek, we are rewarded with tasting the flavor of Torah and *Mitzvot*, where there is the actual pleasure, as in "The nations are like a drop from a bucket," meaning that in corporeality, there is nothing more than a drop of pleasure compared to a full bucket of pleasure. Naturally, he does it willingly because of the wonderful pleasure he finds in them.

This is the meaning of "'And you shall love the Lord your God with all your heart'—with both your inclinations, the good inclination and the evil inclination." How can the evil inclination agree to observe Torah and *Mitzvot*? When it feels great pleasure in them, it agrees, as well.

Hence, in order to be rewarded with the light of redemption, we first need to engage in blotting out Amalek, and then we will be rewarded with redemption, as it was then, in the days of Mordechai and Ester.

Yet, with what can we blot out Amalek? Our sages said about this, "I have created the evil inclination; I have created the Torah as a spice." Through the Torah, we can erase the bad.

But not everyone has the ability to engage in Torah. For this reason, we were given the matter of Issachar and Zebulun, namely the matter of supporters of the Torah and learners of the Torah, where by uniting into one man, they are all called "disciples." Then, when all become one bundle, we will be able to blot out Amalek and be rewarded with redemption.

# Purim

## 909- Revealing the Concealment

Ester said to Mordechai, "Go, gather all the Jews who are in Shushan, and fast over me and do not eat... And thus I will go in to the king, which is not according to the law; and if I perish, I perish." We should ask why specifically those in Shushan, since there were Jews in Persia and in Madai, as well. Why did she say "gather" specifically about Shushan?

To understand this, we need to know that Ester refers to *Malchut*, as our sages said, "Ester from the Torah, where is she from? It is as was said, and I will surely *Astir* [hide] my face" (Deuteronomy 31:18).

However, we can say that concealment pertains to where one wants to see and understand but does not see or understand. At that time, we can say that something is hidden from him. Moreover, the measure of concealment is measured by the need to know. Hence, when a person has no need for knowledge, it cannot be said about that person that he is suffering from the concealment.

For example, if a person has to work somewhere only half an hour every day and receive his salary once a month, he must believe that he will be paid although he still did not see anyone being paid. Hence, he believes in the company although it is hidden from him whether or how the company will pay the salary, since no one knows this company where he wants to work.

If he wants to work more than half an hour, he has a greater need to know that the company pays the salary on time. Thus, if he heard bad rumors about the company, he suffers more from the concealment. And if he wants to work day and night, he certainly feels a greater concealment because he has a greater need to know whether he will receive his salary as promised.

Since the kingdom of heaven is above reason, everyone suffers from the concealment. However, for those who want to work for the sake of the Creator, the concealment is greater because they have a greater need to know, since the body keeps asking "What is this work for you?" It follows that this question is always understood according to how much a person wants to work completely for the sake of the Creator.

The answer to the question is "Blunt its teeth." Baal HaSulam said that *Malchut* is called "a *Shoshanah* [lily]," as it is written, "As a lily among the thorns," and this is called Shushan.

Accordingly, we should distinguish between Jews who are in Shushan and Jews who are in Persia or Madai.

*Paras* [Persia] means *Prisa* [slicing] in half, as in sliced in the morning and sliced in the dusk, which are considered "Anyone who joins 'for the sake of the Creator' with another thing." That is, we do not need to do everything for the sake of the Creator, but half is for the evil inclination and half is for the good inclination. Madai is called *Dai* [enough], "Who said to His world, *Dai* [enough]! Spread no farther." This means that the fact that he has fear of heaven and Torah and *Mitzvot* [commandments] is enough for him and he settles for this.

To those people, Ester did not say "Gather," but only to those who are in a state of Shushan, whose work is in the state of "Blunt its teeth."

## 910- Until He Does Not Know
Purim, Tav-Shin-Lamed-Tet, March 13, 1979

"Until he does not know": There are three discernments:

1) Not knowing the distinction between cursed and blessed, meaning that knowing that the will to receive is called Haman and the desire to bestow is called "righteous Mordechai" has not been established. Rather, even when he works in order to receive, he considers it as being righteous.

2) The awareness that reception is called Haman and bestowal is called "righteous" has been established in him.

3) At the end of correction, called "very," when SAM becomes a holy angel, meaning that reception has been corrected with the aim to bestow, there will be no distinction between reception and bestowal since all of the reception has been admitted into the aim to bestow. This is the meaning of "One must be intoxicated," since all the occasions will be cancelled except for Purim, since it pertains to the end of correction.

This is why we should imply the end of correction, where intoxication implies sweetening, when all the bad has been sweetened, while in the not knowing of the first kind there is still no sweetening.

## 911- The Meal of a Wicked One

Our sages said, "Why did that generation have to be destroyed?" One said, "Because they bowed to idols," and one said, "Because they enjoyed the meal of that wicked one."

We should ask why they did not say "Because they ate from the meal of that wicked one," but rather that they "enjoyed." There are two discernments in the work: 1) Mind, which is bowing to idols. An "idol" means that one has some basis for the work. This is called "an idol." Man should work in faith, as it is written, "For you did not see any image," for an image and a similitude are bases upon which one can determine that he works for this, meaning he establishes his work on this basis, and this is the support. Conversely, when he has no support, he falls from his work. 2) Enjoying the meal of that wicked implies the heart, if a person enjoys his wicked one enjoying himself. He must eat and drink because otherwise he will not be able to live, but he must not enjoy the meal that his will to receive is doing.

For this reason, their work was compulsory, as our sages said, "observed and received," thus far by force; henceforth willingly, where by being rewarded with repentance from love, they were rewarded with their work being of their own volition.

We therefore see that even when one is at the very bottom, in the worst possible state, when one has flawed both discernments, still, afterward, they were rewarded with "observed and received," where what was compulsory has later become willingly. This is the meaning of the *Megillah* [scroll] of Ester: They are two opposites, where during the concealment, there is coercion, and during the disclosure, it is a time of goodwill.

# 912- What Is Purim

At a Purim meal, *Tav-Shin-Yod-Gimel*, March 1, 1953

Concerning Mordechai and Haman, Mordechai is regarded as "righteous," meaning that he has no need to extend light of *Hochma*, but he is rather always in a state of bestowing.

It is known that no illumination comes down without an awakening from below. Hence, when the Creator wanted to give Mordechai the great lights, He asked Haman, "What should be done with the man whom the king wishes to honor?" Afterward, the king told him, "And do so to Mordechai the Jew."

In other words, the lights of Haman must be accepted in the *Kelim* [vessels] of Mordechai and not in the *Kelim* of Haman. This is the meaning of what is written, "but they did not lay their hands on the plunder." That is, they did not extend the lights of Haman but settled for killing the *Kelim* of Haman so he does not receive the lights.

Conversely, when Saul went to Agag and received the plunder, the flock and the cattle, Samuel the prophet said in the name of the Creator that he must not accept the plunder because then it was still not the time for it.

## 913- *His Law He Contemplates*
19 *Shevat, Tav-Shin-Chaf-Vav*, February 9, 1966

"His desire is in the Torah [law] of the Lord, and His Torah law he contemplates," etc. Our sages interpreted that one is before he learns, and one is after he learns. We should ask why it is written "His desire" with regard to the Torah of the Creator.

To understand the matter in ethics, we should observe what appears to our eyes when looking at youths who attend Jewish orthodox seminaries and study day and night. What is the reason that compels them to learn Torah?

We find many reasons:

1) When he first begins to learn, the reason is that his father forces him into all the labor of engaging in Torah and *Mitzvot* [commandments]. If he disobeys him, he will punish him, so he is the obligator. Thus, at that time, he is not engaging in Torah and *Mitzvot* for the sake of the Creator, but for the sake of his father.

2) When he grows up and becomes accustomed to attending school, the teacher or the rabbi or the overseer forces him. If he disobeys them, they will punish him.

3) When he becomes a grownup, he begins to contemplate his future and sees that if he does not become a learned scholar, it will

be difficult for him to find a good wife or obtain an influential position in society, and be given the respect that Torah scholars receive. Here, too, the reasons that compel him to engage in Torah and *Mitzvot* are only people like himself.

It therefore follows that he is not learning the Torah of the Creator but the Torah of the created beings. That is, it can be said about this that even if there weren't this Torah that he is learning, the Torah of the Creator, he would still have to observe it because these elements would force him to observe or they would punish him.

However, from *Lo Lishma* [not for Her sake], we come to *Lishma* [for Her sake]. Therefore, if he is smart and contemplates what he is doing here in our world, he begins to believe that the capitol has a leader, and then he believes that the Torah that he is learning is the Torah of the Creator, and then he can observe "His desire is in the Torah [law] of the Lord," meaning the Torah of the Creator and not the Torah of the created beings.

At that time, he observes the Torah as a *Mitzva* [commandment] and not as Torah. *Mitzva* means faith, and Torah is regarded as a gift. *Mitzva* that is faith is regarded as *Tzedakah* [charity/righteousness], as it is written, "And he believed in the Lord and He regarded it for him as righteousness."

The reason that faith is called *Tzedakah* is that normally, we see that when a person does something that he does not enjoy doing, he cannot do it except for a reward such as respect or money.

If he does something for which he does not receive reward, it is called *Tzedakah* because he is not rewarded for it. Hence, since faith pertains specifically to a time of concealment, at which time he derives no pleasure from this action, for this reason, faith is called *Tzedakah*. This is not so with a gift, for then he enjoys the act itself, meaning he enjoys the gift he is receiving. If he does not enjoy the gift, it is not regarded as a gift.

Since the Torah is called "a gift," as it is written, "And from Matanah [Hebrew: gift] to Nahliel," we should know that precisely when he enjoys the Torah, the Torah is called "a gift." If he has still not been rewarded with tasting a sweet flavor in the Torah, meaning that the verse, "nicer than gold and much fine gold, and sweeter than honey and the honeycomb" has not come true in him, it cannot be said that to him the Torah is a gift. Rather, when he engages in Torah, he awaits being paid for his labor in Torah. It follows that then the Torah is regarded as a *Mitzva*. In other words, if he engages in Torah not in order to receive reward, it is regarded for him as *Tzedakah*, meaning that he is learning only as a *Mitzva*, which is called "faith."

We see that concerning giving a gift, for the joy to be complete from the perspective of both the giver and the receiver, this depends on two things: 1) The giver should appreciate the receiver, that he is worthy of such a great gift. If the receiver is an important person, he gives him an important, valuable gift. If he is not very important to him, he will not spend so much of his money to buy him a gift. 2) The receiver can be happy about the gift only to the extent of the need for it, regardless of the cost of the gift.

We see that with Bar Mitzvah boys [age thirteen], the custom is that everyone gives them gifts. But sometimes, we see that if they do not need this object very much, not only does it not please them, it even evokes unpleasantness in them to accept the gift. This is so only because he does not need the gift.

For example, if an uncle gives him a gold watch that is worth a hundred pounds, he will surely be happy with the watch, since it costs a lot of money and normally the gifts are worth five or ten or twenty pounds. Therefore, if he gives him a present that is worth a hundred pounds, he will certainly be very happy.

But then, another uncle comes and also gives him a watch that is worth a hundred pounds. Now he is not so happy, since what will he do with two watches? It is inappropriate to sell one of the watches because it is not nice to sell a gift that a friend gave him, since it is a reminder to always keep in mind that he has a friend, and he did not give it to him so he would sell it. Thus, he feels unpleasantness.

However, it is still not so bad because he can wear one watch on his right hand and the other on his left.

However, if another uncle also gives him a watch, then he really feels annoyed because he does not know what to do with the third watch. Nevertheless, he finds a solution by wearing it on Shabbat [Sabbath].

But if a fourth uncle also gives him a watch then he really becomes confused and does not know what to do. After all, it is worth a hundred pounds and he could enjoy something that is worth a hundred pounds, but now he cannot.

Thus, he is so annoyed and does not know what to do that he becomes caught up in thoughts to the point that he forgets that he is sitting at a party with distinguished guests who came to honor him and partake in his joy. But he is no longer sitting with them but is tormented and afflicted, and all this is because he has no need for the gifts he has received.

We therefore see that it is impossible to be happy with a gift if he has no need for it, even if it is valuable.

Here we see that we have two things: 1) From the perspective of the giver, a precious gift to the synagogue, the gift is not worth a hundred pounds but much more because he knows the value of the audience, that they must be given an expensive gift. 2) Although in regard to the recipients of the gift, there is a need for a book of Torah, for we cannot say that there are enough books of Torah, for each book of Torah in the synagogue adds sanctity and instills Divine spirit, adding might and glory to the intention and protects from bad things and gives life and peace and wealth and honor.

"'Fortune and wealth are in his home and his righteousness stands forever.' Rav Huna and Rav Hasda, one said, 'It is he who learns Torah and teaches it.' The other said, 'It is he who writes a Bible and lends it to others'" (*Ketubot* 50).

Here we see that we have arranged both things: the seminary, which is learning Torah and teaching it, and now also the admission of a book of Torah, called "writing a Bible and lending it to others." However, he does not lend, but gives it to the residents of the neighborhood, so the words "Fortune and wealth are in his home and his righteousness stands forever" will certainly come true for him.

We should ask, 1) What is the added merit of "fortune and wealth" to "his righteousness stands forever," since it would be enough for a person to be given fortune and wealth for his labor. Why does he need his righteousness, and what will he gain by his righteousness standing forever? 2) What is the dispute between Rav Huna and Rav Hasda?

It is known that the work is to achieve the completion of the goal for which man was created, which is called "to do good to His creations." In other words, a person should receive all the sublime pleasures.

In order to be able to achieve this goal, there must first be the correction of creation, called *Lishma* [for Her sake]. This means that all the pleasures that one contemplates receiving are only because the Creator wants it, and this will correct the flaw of the bread of shame. Hence, precisely when a person corrects himself so his intention is only to bestow for the sake of the Creator, everything will come to the end of correction.

In order for one to achieve *Lishma*, which is not in order to receive reward, we were given the work of faith, for then there is the matter of choice. In other words, even though he does not see or feel any pleasure in the work, he still works because of a *Mitzva*.

Conversely, if he felt the flavor of Torah and *Mitzvot*, there would be no room for him to work without reward since no reward is greater than feeling a good taste and elation in his work.

Only when the basis of one's work is faith is there choice, and then it can be said that he is working *Lishma*, meaning because of the commandment of the Creator. While his work is *Lishma*, the words of Rabbi Meir, that "he is rewarded with many things," come true in him.

At that time, he must renew his work so it is in the manner of faith, which the *Sulam* [Ladder commentary on *The Zohar*] calls "middle line," for only by this he will be saved from falling into self-pleasure due to the many pleasures he will be receiving by revealing the secrets of Torah with which he has been rewarded by learning *Lishma*.

It is known that faith is called *Tzedakah* [righteousness/charity], and the knowledge of Torah is called "wealth," as our sages said, "There is none who is poor except in knowledge." By this we will understand the words, "Fortune and wealth are in his home and his righteousness stands forever," meaning that one who has been rewarded with fortune and wealth, which is the knowledge of Torah, in order for them to exist in him, he needs faith, which is called *Tzedakah*.

Hence, in order for his wisdom to exist he must always try to renew the faith, and for this he needs the blessing that his righteousness, meaning faith, will stand forever, that he will always have the faith so that the wealth will be maintained.

I will conclude my letter with what I said this morning to the students. It is written in the *Megillah* [Purim scroll/Book of Ester], "After these things, the king promoted Haman." In the literal meaning, this is difficult to understand, since after the good deed that Mordechai did for the king, the king should have promoted Mordechai and not Haman.

We should interpret this in ethics: After a person does something through his engagement in Torah and *Mitzvot* [commandments], the Creator increases the evil in a person, which is called "Haman." That is, the Creator shows the person the truth that the evil within him obstructs him from receiving all the spiritual pleasures.

If the person had gone in the good path, meaning if his intention were only to bestow contentment upon his Maker, he should have been worthy of all the sublime things. This is called "the way of Judaism."

When one cannot see the true face of one's evil, meaning the form of Haman, he cannot pray to the Creator to help him be saved from the bad.

Only when one sees the greatness of Haman, that he wants to kill and destroy all the Jews, etc., meaning that Haman wants to destroy everything that has any relation to Judaism, that he does not let him do anything in *Kedusha* [holiness], then he can make an honest prayer, and then the words "the Creator helps him" come true. Hence, then the words "fasting and crying out" become pertinent, when they are praying to the Creator to be saved from this evil Haman.

When the Creator helps him, the Creator asks Haman, "What should be done with the man whom the king wishes to honor?" At that time, Haman thinks, "Whom does the king wish to honor more than me?" meaning that all the bad extends from the will to receive (as it is written in the introduction to the *Sulam* [Ladder] commentary to *The Zohar*), which is the Haman in a person, who claims that the Creator's wish is to do good to His creations, meaning that all the pleasures belong to the will to receive.

But the Creator said, "Do so to Mordechai the Jew." If He asked the good inclination, called "Mordechai the Jew," if he wanted anything, he would answer that all he wants is to bestow upon the Creator and he does not need anything. For this reason, He asked Haman, who wants to receive all the pleasures that exist in reality, and then the Creator said that all the pleasures should be given to Mordechai, meaning that the person will receive all the pleasures only in order to bestow contentment upon his Maker.

This, Baal HaSulam said, is "lights of Haman in vessels of Mordechai." This means that all the pleasures should be received only with the intention for the sake of the Creator.

# Passover

## 914- Two Opposites

There are two opposites in above reason—in mind and in heart, which is regarded as "for he desires mercy." If foreign thoughts come to a person, he should remove them from him and not listen to them at all.

This is a hard work because Pharaoh king of Egypt afflicts them and throws foreign thoughts at them in mind and in heart, as it is written, "And the children of Israel sighed from the work, and their cry went up to God." This is one side by which they are rewarded with faith, meaning the exodus from Egypt, and this is regarded as a soul of *Kedusha* [holiness].

On the other hand, "a soul without knowledge is not good, too," and we need the knowledge of *Kedusha*, which is called "wealth," for there is no wealth except in *Daat* [reason/knowledge]. When the Creator wanted to enrich them, they did not have *Kelim* [vessels] because everything was for them above reason, so the Creator gave them the advice to borrow *Kelim* from the Egyptians.

The taking of the *Kelim* was only so they would be able to receive a filling for the *Kelim*, meaning answers to their questions. But once they took the answers, they immediately returned the *Kelim* to the Egyptians. Because they are going above reason, they have no questions and they took the questions of the Egyptians only temporarily and then returned them.

## 915- I and Not a Messenger

As the ARI wrote, prior to the redemption, Israel were in forty-nine gates of *Tuma'a* [impurity] until He was revealed to them and redeemed them. That is, they were rewarded with "I and not a messenger."

Baal HaSulam said that before the redemption they thought that there are messengers, so redemption means that they were rewarded with "I and not a messenger," that there is none else besides Him. It follows that before the redemption they also believed that the Creator was helping, but there are messengers, while redemption means that they were rewarded with "I and not a messenger."

## 916- The Day after Shabbat [Sabbath]

"The day after Shabbat," meaning after Passover, since on the first day of Passover, the *Mochin* of Shabbat illuminate, called *Gadlut Bet* [Second *Gadlut* (greatness)], which are *Mochin* of *Abba* and *Ima*.

# 917- A Kept Matza [Passover Bread]

A kept *Matza* means that we must keep ourselves in a place where we are going to observe the *Mitzvot* [commandments] of the Creator so there will not be any fear of *Hametz* [leaven] there. In other words, the *Mitzvot* should lead a person toward the correction of creation, and if we do not know how to keep the *Matza*, we take what is of no significance and leave what is significant.

# 918- Concerning Passover

The King's daughter on Passover is the intellectual soul, a watch-night, a kept *Matza* [Passover bread]. The spirit that is kept opposite her is a good day, the day of *Shabbat* [Sabbath]. They are "Remember and keep," since he is *Atzilut* from *Malchut*. In the *Sulam* [Ladder commentary on *The Zohar*], a kept *Matza* and a watch-night extend from *Malchut* (*Tzav*, 64-65).

The reason we do not eat *Matzot* [pl. of *Matza*] all year long: He explains with an allegory about a king who wears his formal attire only when he is anointed. Also, each year at that same time, he wears his formal attire, but only then.

*Matzot* are regarded as "harsh judgment," which are *Mochin de Achoraim*, *GAR de Yenika*. This is the circumcision, meaning that although it is impossible to use the *Mochin* [lights], it still helps to thereby bring out the *AHP* of the *Kelim* from the *Klipa* [shell/peel]. This is why it implies the circumcision.

*Matzot* are *Mochin de Achoraim* that illuminate at the time of *Gadlut* [greatness/adulthood]. That is, during the *Gadlut*, when they have *Mochin* of *Abba* and *Ima*, the *Mochin de Achoraim* are not cancelled. On the contrary, the whole quality of *Hochma* at the time of *Gadlut* comes from this discernment.

On the night of Passover there was only cutting and not removing [stages in the circumcision], and *Gadlut* means removing, so how can there be *Gadlut* on the night of Passover? He answers that removing is awakening from below, and the *Gadlut* of the night of Passover came by an awakening from above (*The Zohar, Bo,* 49). Observing the *Mitzvot* [commandments] is the keeping of the circumcision.

"Bread of poverty"—since it is *Achoraim* and lacks *Hassadim* (there).

# 919- Concerning the Environment

"'And he took six hundred select carriages.' Whose were they? If you say that they were from Egypt, it was already said, 'All the livestock of Egypt died.' If you say that they were from Pharaoh, it was already said, 'The hand of the Lord is on your livestock.' If you say that they were from Israel, it was already said, 'Our livestock too shall go with us.' Rather, it was from those 'who fear the word of the Creator among the servants of Pharaoh.' Thus, we learn that those who fear the word of the Creator are an obstacle to Israel" (*Midrash Tanchuma, BeShalach*).

This means that the primary guard is from an environment of those who fear the Creator. They are Pharaoh's servants. Pharaoh is as the ARI said, that the exile in Egypt was that the *Daat* [reason/knowledge] of *Kedusha* [holiness] was in exile. Pharaoh would suck out the abundance, meaning he is the will to receive. They are called "working only for their own benefit" and they have no connection to the work of bestowal, for their sole intention is only to please themselves.

The keeping should mainly be from them, since on the outside, it seems as though they are working—engaging in Torah and prayer enthusiastically and making all kinds of precisions. For this reason, they are called "those who fear the Creator." Otherwise, they would not be called so.

And yet, internally, they are enslaved to Pharaoh, meaning that their only aim is to satisfy their own wishes and needs, and they have no connection to the work of bestowal.

Such an environment creates an obstacle to a servant of the Creator because he wants to walk on the path of the Creator and sees their work when they engage in fearing the Creator, and he is impressed by their zeal, since when they work as Pharaoh's servants, their bodies show no resistance because the efforts they make are also only for the body. Thus, there is no resistance here at all. On the contrary, the body agrees to give them strength.

It follows that such an environment is an obstacle to Israel, to one who wants to be "Israel" and not among Pharaoh's servants. Because a servant of the Creator is impressed by the work of the servants of Pharaoh, he likes the servitude of Pharaoh's servants and is lured after them. Thus, he absorbs their thoughts and intentions and thereby regrets all the efforts he has given in the work of bestowal.

Henceforth, he will have no strength to continue the work of bestowal.

But in an environment of unaffiliated, who are not of the type that fears the Creator, they have no connection to him because he knows that there is nothing to learn from them. At that time, there is no connection of thoughts because he knows he must not learn from the actions and thoughts of the unaffiliated. Hence, such an environment does not pose an obstacle.

Conversely, those who fear the Creator and are Pharaoh's servants do pose an obstacle for Israel, and one must run far away from them.

## 920- The Torah Spoke Regarding Four Sons

*Adar 7, Tav-Shin-Lamed-Bet, February 22, 1972, Tiberias*

"The Torah spoke regarding four sons." The whole Torah is only for the evil inclination, as our sages said, "I have created the evil inclination; I have created the Torah as a spice" (Kidushin 30b). Therefore, "He who does not know how to ask, open for him." We should understand what we should ask, and with what is it opened for him. What is the *Segula* [power/quality/virtue] with which to open for one who does not know how to ask.

The thing is that when there is an evil inclination, there is a need for the Torah. Hence, if one believes in reward and punishment, he can already observe the Torah and *Mitzvot* [commandments], since he has a reward. Thus, he is not asking the wicked one's question, "What is this work for you?" When he has no evil, he has no need for the Torah. Hence, "open for him."

If you see that a person engages in Torah and *Mitzvot* because he believes in reward and punishment, he is closed, meaning his evil is closed, concealed. For this reason, it is impossible to correct him because one corrects only that which one sees. Hence, at that time a person is taught to work in order not to receive reward.

Then the wicked one comes and asks, "What is this work for you?" That is, "What will we have if we work for the Creator without any reward? This is against our nature! We were born with a nature of delighting ourselves and not of delighting others without anything in return." At that time, a person needs the Torah, and then it can be said, "I have created the evil inclination; I have created the Torah as a spice."

But if he has no evil inclination, it means that the will to receive is not evident in him, for only this is called "evil," and nothing else.

## 921- The Need for an Act from Below

"'They are to take a lamb for themselves, according to their fathers' households.' The Creator said, 'You do the deed below, and I will break their force above. And as you make them burn in fire, as it is written, 'But roast with fire,' I, too, will take them through fire above, in a river of fire'" (*Bo*, Item 162).

We need to understand why the Creator needs the work of below, and what is the meaning of breaking and burning the power of the *Klipot* [shells/peels] above, what is the power of the *Sitra Achra* [other side].

We should also understand what is written, "Israel did not come out of Egypt until the government of all their ministers was broken above, and Israel departed their domain and came to the domain of the upper holiness in the Creator, and tied to Him, as it is written, 'For the children of Israel are Mine; they are My servants.' What is the reason 'they are My servants'? It is that, 'I brought [them] out from the land of Egypt'; I have brought them out of the other authority and brought them into My authority."

To understand all the above, it is known that the purpose of creation is to do good to His creations. For this purpose, a desire to receive pleasure has been imprinted within man, and this power controls a person. This is why the evil inclination is called "king," since it controls with this power, meaning it gives man pleasures, and because of them a person becomes enslaved to it and is as a slave, while the evil inclination is the king.

This power of giving pleasure is the governance of the evil inclination, and man is in exile under its governance. But while it has nothing to give to a person, it has no control whatsoever over a person. Also, if man could relinquish his pleasures, he would also not be enslaved to it.

Hence, in the exile in Egypt, when Pharaoh bestowed his pleasures upon them, they were enslaved to Pharaoh and could not emerge from the exile. But after they acted, meaning awakened to emerge from the exile, since this act is regarded as choosing, the Creator broke his powers above, meaning took from him the pleasures with which he enslaved the people of Israel. When he has nothing to give, it is considered that the Creator breaks his power and burns him in the river of fire. That is, He took from him all of his influence.

It follows that the *Sitra Achra* [other side] has nothing with which to control a person. For this reason, they could emerge from the exile. At that time, they entered the domain of *Kedusha* [holiness], meaning began to feel a good taste in the power of bestowal. It follows that then they became servants of the *Kedusha*.

Thus, what controls a person is pleasure, and a slave is one who is enslaved to the pleasure. When people's pleasure comes from reception, they are called "Pharaoh's servants." But if the pleasure comes from bestowal, they are called "the Creator's servants." But without pleasure, it is impossible to exist.

A person cannot break the pleasure. Only the Creator can break it by taking from it the abundance so he has nothing to give to the creatures. This is called "breaking the power of the *Sitra Achra*." All that one needs is to discover that he wants the force of bestowal, and to ask the Creator to give him that force. This is called "choice" on the part of man, and only this is regarded as "awakening from below."

# 922- The More One Speaks of the Exodus from Egypt

"The more one speaks of the exodus from Egypt, the better." We should understand why we should speak so much about the exodus from Egypt, to the point that they said, that the more one speaks of it the better. Also, we should understand what is said, "Each generation, one must see oneself as though he came out from Egypt."

It is known that there is nothing to add in the light, but rather in the *Kelim* [vessels]. Hence, "more" pertains to the *Kelim*, which pertains to the lack of sensation of exile. When one comes to feel the exile, he feels that he himself is in Egypt. In such a state, how can he praise the exodus from Egypt while he is in Egypt?

This is the meaning of "must see himself as though he came out from Egypt." It is as Baal HaSulam said, "In the future [end of correction], the righteous will sing, 'Then [Moses] will sing,'" etc.

## 923- And he said, "When You Deliver the Hebrew Women"

Shemot, Tav-Shin-Mem, January 1980

"And he said, 'When you deliver the Hebrew women, see upon the birth-stool; if it is a boy, put him to death; and if it is a girl, she shall live.'" "Pharaoh commanded all his people, saying, 'Every boy who is born, cast him in the Nile, and every girl, keep alive.'"

We should interpret this. When a person begins to walk on the path of the Creator, Pharaoh king of Egypt is the king who rules over the bodies, to keep those who work in order to bestow so that the bodies will resist and they will not be able to achieve the desired wholeness, which is that all his actions will be for the sake of the Creator.

For this reason, he said, meaning commanded that when the workers engage in Torah and *Mitzvot* [commandments], called "Hebrews," when the work in Torah and *Mitzvot* belongs to servants of the Creator, while the Egyptians are when one engages in corporeal actions in which the Egyptians engage, as well. Only when they engage in Torah and *Mitzvot*, they are called "Hebrews."

"See on the birth-stool" is the time when one says that he wants to understand what he is doing, for what purpose he engages in Torah and *Mitzvot*. "If he is a boy," meaning his work is in order to bestow, and this is his desire when he engages in Torah and *Mitzvot*, "put him to death," meaning do not give him any vitality or strength, so he will stop his work.

"If it is as girl," meaning his intention has the quality of "female," in order to receive, "she shall live," meaning you can give him strength and vitality because that person does not wish to come out of Egypt and there is no reason to fear him. Hence, you may help him, let him do whatever he wants, even if he is meticulous in all kinds of manners, since in any case, he will remain with us in Egypt and it is not worthwhile to exert for no reason, for in any case, he is one of ours.

But if he is a boy, if his aim is to come to aim for the sake of the Creator and not for his own benefit, from this he can be rewarded with "the savior of Israel," called "the quality of Moses," as our sages said, "The expansion of Moses in each and every generation."

If he is rewarded with the quality of Moses, called "the savior of Israel," who will deliver them from Egypt, we must see beforehand so as to prevent him from reaching a state where he emerges from the exile in Egypt.

However, how can they know that he is going for the aim to bestow? After all, he is still in Egypt, which is working for self-benefit and not in order to bestow. However, now he wants to be rewarded with it, and for this, he gave them as sign: "A male, his face is downward; a female, her face is upward."

He interprets face and back in the "Introduction to The Study of the Ten Sefirot," that when seeing a person from behind, we cannot know if this is truly the person of whom we are thinking. He might be another and we could be mistaken. But if we see the other's face, there are no doubts.

Hence, when we want to imply that we understand something in utter certainty, that we have no mistakes, this is called "face." Conversely, something that is not clear to the mind is called "back."

For this reason, "face" is called "knowing," that he is serving the Creator only in a manner of knowing. This is considered that his face is up in terms of importance, since what counts for him is the awareness. The "back," which is faith, since in the mind, it could be either or, he regards this as below in its importance.

For this reason, he gave them the sign: If you want to know if he is going for the goal of achieving the aim to bestow, if his face is downward, if knowing is of little importance to him, and his back is upward, meaning that faith is of high importance to him, it is a sign that he wants to achieve the quality of "boy," the aim to bestow.

Hence, "Put him to death," disrupt him however you can because he will certainly be rewarded with the quality of Moses, who is the savior of Israel, and will deliver them from the exile in Egypt and will enter the land of Israel, the palace of *Kedusha* [holiness]. This is the meaning of "And you shall see My back," meaning faith, "but My face shall not be seen," namely you will not attain Me through knowledge.

"Pharaoh commanded all his people," meaning he does not know from which nation the savior of Israel will be born, whether from Egypt or from Israel. Every person consists of corporeal actions, called "Egyptians," for the Egyptians also engage in corporeal actions. Hence, man's work in corporeal actions is called "Egypt," and when he engages in Torah and *Mitzvot*, he is called "Israel."

He says that he does not know from which discernment a person might be rewarded with the quality of Moses, called "the savior of Israel." That is, it could be that while a person engages in corporeality while all his intentions are in order to bestow, even while doing corporeal actions, he might be rewarded with the quality of the savior of Israel.

For this reason, keep an eye while they engage in corporeal actions, that if they aim in order to bestow, which is called "a male," "cast him in the Nile." That is, do not let him aim for the sake of the Creator, called "a boy," even with corporeal actions. "And every girl keep alive." Only when his aim is to receive in order to receive, you can give him vitality and strength to do corporeal deeds.

But if it is a boy, he might be rewarded with the quality of Moses, called "the savior of Israel," at that time, too, who will deliver him from the exile in Egypt and into the land of *Kedusha* [holiness].

## 924- *And God Spoke to Moses*
VaEra, Tav-Shin-Tet-Vav, January 1955

"And God spoke to Moses and said to him, 'I am the Lord.'"

We should understand what this statement means to us. It seems to refer to Moses' question that was said at the end of the portion, *Shemot* [Exodus 5:23], where it is written, "Ever since I came to Pharaoh to speak in Your name, he has done harm to this people, and You did not save Your people at all."

Moses' question was that when he told them they had to work *Lishma* [for Her sake], everyone thought that their work would be more intense and with greater force, but the truth was to the contrary—they weakened in the work.

As a result, they cried out to Moses, "What good did you do for us when you promised that we would emerge from the exile in Egypt, meaning that our mind was in exile and that by the way you are giving us, to work *Lishma*, we will be freed from the enslavement of the body, called 'Pharaoh'? In truth, we haven't any motivation! Thus, our mind is that we cannot receive your sublime goal."

To this came the answer, "And God spoke to Moses." God is nature. As far as nature is concerned, you are correct that you haven't the fuel to continue your work. "And said to him, 'I am the Lord.'" The Creator is the quality of mercy, and by His mercy they can extend forces and fuel above nature and above reason, and on this they can no longer argue because all the arguments that a person can make are only where reason affirms it. But above reason, anything might happen, except we must increase the faith that the Creator can help above nature.

In fact, it is impossible to receive something above nature before one decides that this cannot happen within nature. Only after one despairs from nature can he ask for help from above, to be given help above nature.

## 925- And I Will Take You as My People
VaEra, Tav-Shin-Mem, January 1980

"And [God] spoke ... 'I am the Lord, and I appeared to Abraham in *Shadai* [the Almighty], but My name, Lord, I did not make Myself known to them. Therefore, tell the children of Israel, 'I am the Lord.''" We should understand the connection if He was not revealed to them by the name *HaVaYaH* [Lord], and why, therefore, was He revealed to him by the name *HaVaYaH*: "Therefore, tell the children of Israel, 'I am the Lord.'"

What is the reason for sending Moses to bring them out of Egypt? "And I will take you as My people and I will be a God unto you." What does it mean that He will be a God only to the people of Israel? What is He to the nations of the world?

Also, concerning what RASHI interprets "to the fathers," he explains everything in the verse.

We should interpret that the order of revelations is from below upward, and any degree is the cause of the next degree. Thus, to the fathers, He appeared as Almighty, which is being content with little, for the smallest revelation was enough for them. *Shadai* [Almighty] means "Who said to His world, '*Dai* [enough], expand no more.'"

In that respect, this pertains only to specific individuals who can advance while in doubt but are in a state of "for he desires mercy," and whatever understanding and feeling they have in spirituality is enough for them to advance in the ways of the Creator. However, this manner cannot be given to the general public.

Therefore, now, because of cause of consequence, there is a revelation in the name *HaVaYaH*, and that revelation can be said to the general public so they will approach the Creator and emerge from the exile in Egypt. This is why the text says that since now there is revelation of the name *HaVaYaH*, "Tell the people of Israel, 'I am the Lord.'" Afterward, the text continues, and by this we can interpret what RASHI interpreted, "And I appeared to the fathers," meaning that the revelation to Abraham was the reason for the revelation for the name *HaVaYaH*, since father and son are cause and consequence, meaning that the revelation that the fathers had, in the name God *Shadai*, was later revealed as the name *HaVaYaH*.

This is the meaning of the words, "And I will take you as My people and I will be a God unto you." The writing interprets the meaning of "unto you" and not to the nations of the world. It means "and you shall know that I am the Lord your God," that I will give this knowledge only to you and not to the nations of the world.

"Who brings you out from under the afflictions of Egypt," meaning that they were enslaved to Pharaoh king of Egypt and not to the *Kedusha* [holiness]. I will bring out of this suffering and you will be rewarded with knowing that "I am the Lord your God."

This is the meaning of what we say in the songs: "All who delight in the Lord will be rewarded with much good." It means that those who delight in a manner of being content with little, called *Katnut* [smallness/infancy], and will be happy with their share, will later be rewarded with much good. "Much" means *Gadlut* [greatness/adulthood], meaning that settling for little means that although he needs much, yet settles for little, this is the reason for the *Gadlut*.

# 926- Come unto Pharaoh

Bo, Tav-Shin-Mem-Aleph, January 1981

"And the Lord said unto Moses, 'Come unto Pharaoh, for I have hardened his heart and the heart of his servants, that I may set these signs of Mine within him.'"

We should understand the following:

1) The question in *The Zohar*: Why does it not say "Go unto Pharaoh"?

2) The question people ask, Why did the Creator need Pharaoh's consent to bring out the people of Israel?

3) The question people ask, Why did He deny him the choice?

4) The reason "I will set these signs of Mine within him." If the Creator wants to make signs, why did He have to do it by afflicting Pharaoh through the plagues? He could have made signs in different ways that would not harm Pharaoh.

To explain all this, we first need to bring the words of our sages, "One should always see oneself as half guilty, half innocent. If he performs one *Mitzva* [commandment], happy is he, for he has sentenced himself to the side of merit" (*Kidushin* 40b).

This is perplexing: If he has already sentenced himself to the side of merit, how can he see himself once more as half and half? Also, we should understand, if he has committed a transgression, he has sentenced himself to the side of guilt, so how can he say afterward that he is half guilty and half innocent? We should also understand, if he knows that he has few merits, how is it that he is taught to lie and make the similitude of falsehood, which is half and half?

Also, we should understand what our sages said, "Anyone who is greater than his friend, his inclination is greater than him" (*Sukkah* 52). If he is righteous, why does he deserve the punishment of having a greater evil inclination?

We should also understand what our sages said, "Transgressed and repeated? It becomes as though permitted to him" (end of *Masechet Yoma*). Why was it done so, that it would become for him as though permitted? And we also need to understand what our sages said, "To the wicked, it seems like a hairsbreadth, and to the righteous, as a high mountain" (*Sukkah* 52). Which is the truth?

The thing is that there is an order in the work of the Creator. Because the Creator wants to prevent the bread of shame, a person has to make a choice—to choose the good and loathe the bad. Hence, the Creator can deliver the people of Israel from the exile in Egypt if He gives them only the good inclination and subdues the evil, and then a person will not be in any exile.

However, since the Creator wants man to make the choice, it is required for one to agree that the people of Israel will emerge from the exile of his individuality. This is called "by his own conscious choice." He must agree that the Pharaoh within him, who is the king of Egypt, will not govern the Israel in him.

Pharaoh comes from the words "*Parah* [Uncovered] the head," meaning revealing. That is, by wanting everything within him to be revealed, or he, the king of Egypt, controls the body with the quality of Egypt, afflicting a person when he wants to do something for the sake of the Creator, so when he wants revealing, meaning that everything will be according to his intellect, that his mind will understand that it is worthwhile to do the actions, he permits man to work. This is why Pharaoh asks, "Who is the Lord that I should obey His voice?" and "What is this work for you?" With this force, he controls the Israel in him.

Israel means *Yashar-El* [straight to the Creator], meaning that everything he does will be directly for the sake of the Creator, meaning in order to bestow. This is as our sages said, "'There shall be no foreign God within you.' Who is a foreign God within man's body? It is the evil inclination" (*Shabbat* [Sabbath] 105b). This means that if he should do something for the Creator, it is foreign to him to do such actions. This is the opposite of Israel, who wants specifically straight to the Creator [*Yashar-El*].

Hence, in order to bring Israel out of the governance of Pharaoh king of Egypt, meaning to agree to make a choice, so he can do everything in order to bestow, we need specifically the light of Torah, as our sages said, "The light in it reforms him."

By this we will understand why it is written "Come" and not "Go." "Come" means "Come, the two of us together," so that one will not think that he can submit his evil inclination by himself. Rather, as it is written, "Man's inclination overcomes him every day. Were it not for the help of the Creator, he would not overcome it." Hence, one should not say that he cannot defeat his evil, for he must believe that the Creator will help him. This is the meaning of "Come."

*The Zohar* asks about what our sages said, "He who comes to purify is aided." It asks, "With what is he aided?" and it replies, "With a holy soul. When one is born, he is given *Nefesh* [soul] from the side of a pure beast. If he is rewarded more, he is given *Ruach* [spirit]." Thus, each time a person is purified and overcomes his evil, a higher degree is revealed in him, which is called "Torah" or "the light of Torah."

By this we will understand why the hardening of the heart comes to him, and why if the Creator wants to make signs, he must suffer for no reason by the hardening of the heart. The thing is that when a person wants to walk in the ways of the Creator on the path of truth, he should not say that he is incapable because he has many iniquities, since this is not about coming before the courthouse of above when he is judged on how many merits he has. Here it is about a person himself, judging himself, and saying that he cannot make a choice, since choosing is between two equal things between which he should decide.

For this reason, they said that one should see oneself as half guilty, half innocent, since the Creator deliberately made it so that the good and the bad will always be of equal weight, so he can decide. Hence, if he performs one *Mitzva* [commandment] and has decided to the side of merit, he becomes great.

At that time, they say, "Anyone who is greater than his friend, his inclination is greater than him." In other words, the Creator deliberately hardens his heart so he would be able to make a choice once more, for in each choice, a person gains the letters of the Torah. Thus, the signs are not for the sake of the Creator but for the sake of man.

It therefore follows that the hardening of the heart is only for man's sake, for by this he will be rewarded with the letters of the Torah. Although during the fact, a person does not feel all that he is meant to feel, when he has completed his discernment, what he has done all that time is revealed to him at once.

Like the allegory that Baal HaSulam once gave, this is similar to a person earning nothing but zeros. Each time, he sees that he has earned only zero. After the first time, he has one zero. After the second time, two zeros, and after the third, three zeros, until he accumulates many zeros. But at the end of his work, he earns a one. Thus, he might have one zero with the one, which is only ten, or he might have one million, or more. It follows that each time, letters of the Torah are added in him. This is the meaning of "that I may set these signs of Mine within him."

## 927- Concerning *Hametz* and *Matza*

Said on Shabbat during Passover, *Tav-Shin-Tet-Zayin*, Fairholt, London, March 31, 1956

To explain the meaning of *Hametz* [leaven] and *Matza* [unleavened bread], and why *Matza* is called "bread of poverty."

Also, to understand the *Mishna*, "On Passover, he is judged on the crops of the grain, and on *Atzeret* [eighth day of *Sukkot*] on the fruits of the tree. Rabbi Yehuda said in the name of Rabbi Akiva, 'Why did the Torah say, 'Bring before me harvest on Passover, so that your crops in the fields will be blessed?" Also, why did the Torah say, 'Bring two loaves of bread on the *Atzeret*, since the *Atzeret* is the time of the fruits of the tree'? The Creator said, 'Bring two loaves of bread before Me on the *Atzeret* so that your fruits of the tree will be blessed'" (*Rosh Hashanah* 16). We should understand the connection between the two loaves of bread, which is wheat, from the grains of the earth, to the fruits of the tree.

RASHI brings two interpretations: "The two loaves of bread are wanted for the fruits of the tree because they permit the bringing of the first fruit, for it is forbidden to bring the first fruit prior to the *Atzeret*. I heard that Rabbi Yehuda thinks that this was the rule, as was said (Sanhedrin 70), 'The tree that *Adam HaRishon* ate was wheat [spelt here like "sin"].' There, in the Sanhedrin, Rabbi Yehuda said, 'The tree that *Adam HaRishon* ate was wheat, for an infant does not say 'Daddy' or 'Mommy' until he tastes the taste of grain.'"

We could ask, since there are five kinds of grain, what is the proof that it was specifically wheat? Also, why is the crop in the fields blessed by the sheaf, which is animal food? And also, why specifically with two loaves of bread, which is human food, and what is the connection between the wheat and the fruits of the tree?

First we need to explain who is man, that he is the will to receive, and the necessity of *Dvekut* [adhesion].

It is explained in *The Zohar* (*Bo*, Item 166) that sourdough and leaven are one degree and are all one. Another authority are the ministers appointed over the rest of the nations. We call it the "evil inclination." The Creator said, "All those years you stood in another authority and served a different people. From here on, you are free, 'But on the first day you shall remove leaven from your houses.'"

We should interpret... the will to receive is the minister of Egypt. On Passover, you were saved and emerged from that authority and came into the authority of the desire to bestow. This is regarded as being in the authority of the Creator, that the Creator is the Giver and you are liberated from the governance of the will to receive.

A *Matza* is called "bread of poverty," as *The Zohar* says, since then the moon is in diminution. What is the reason that the moon is in diminution? It is because they were not uncovered and the holy sign was not evident. This is because at that time, there was only the circumcision, and circumcision pertains to "And you will circumcise the foreskin of your heart," meaning cut, which is the removal of the will to receive when they became freed from the will to receive and were in the domain of the desire to bestow.

The Torah is called "receiving in order to bestow." This is called "removing," which is *Parah-Yod-Hey* [The Creator uncovered]. This is the *Mochin*, the light of Torah. This is the meaning of what our sages said, "There is none who is poor except in *Daat* [reason/knowledge]," for only when the *Daat* [knowledge/reason] of Torah is revealed, it is called "rich bread," meaning the food of the wealthy.

At that time, he is considered "content with his lot," as is explained (*Mishnah Avot* 6:1), "He who learns Torah *Lishma* [for Her sake] is rewarded with many things, and the whole world becomes worthwhile for him."

Before one is rewarded with the Torah, although he has taken upon himself the quality of the kingdom of heaven, which is the governance of the Creator, meaning to bestow, while he still does not have the view of Torah, at that time he is called a "holy beast," which is regarded as *Malchut*, which is *Eretz* [land/earth], as it is written in *The Zohar*, "In the beginning God created the heaven and the earth." Heaven is called "Torah" and earth is called "faith."

Hence, on Passover, when there was only circumcision, and they were rewarded with emerging from the authority of Egypt, they entered the degree of "holy beast." Hence, they bring the harvest of barley, which is animal food. By this, the crops in the fields are blessed, for a field is *Malchut*, as in "A field that the Lord has blessed."

Through the fruits of the harvest during the seven weeks, we are rewarded with receiving the Torah, which is reception in order to bestow. At that time, he is called "man" because he already has the *Daat* [knowledge/reason] of the Torah, called "heaven," and the Torah is regarded as "the tree of life," and man is called "a tree of the field." Hence, two loaves of bread are offered from the wheat, which is "human food." By this, the fruits of the tree are blessed, implied by the fact that they are blessed with the Torah.

# 928- Behold, a People Has Come Out of Egypt

"Behold, a people has come out of Egypt; behold, they covered the face of the earth."

We should say that the *Sitra Achra* [other side] says, "Behold the people of Israel, when they come out of Egypt, out of the governance of the Egyptians, they covered the face of the earth, meaning seeing the good in worldliness, in the will to receive."

Hence, the *Sitra Achra* is afraid that by the Creator helping the people of Israel, they might revoke all of our being, as our sages said, "If he performs one *Mitzva* [commandment], happy is he for he has sentenced himself and the whole world to the side of merit." Thus, they can certainly cancel all the *Klipot* [shells/peels].

# 929- The Passover Offering

"They shall eat it with *Matzot* [unleavened bread] and bitter herbs [*Maror*]." An "offering" means nearing the Creator. Passover means that he brought them closer and passed over the bad things in them, looking only at the good deeds in them. This came after they had tasted the bitter taste of the governance of the Egyptians and wanted to emerge from their control, but did not succeed, and had grievances against the Creator, which is called *Matza* [unleavened bread]; and *Meriva* [quarrel], as it is written, "When they strove with the Lord," why He created them in such lowliness.

This caused them the Passover offering, when the Creator brought them close. This is called "They shall eat it with *Matzot* and bitter herbs," that the *Matzot* and the *Maror* were the reasons they could make the Passover offering, meaning that the Creator passed over all the faults within them and they became close to Creator.

# 930- Concerning the Beginning of the Month

"This month," meaning *Nissan*, "is the head of the months." *Hodesh* [month] means *Hidush* [renewal/innovation]. "Head" means beginning. The first beginning is in the Creator delivering from Egypt, since this is above nature and a person can only go within nature. Only the Creator can do things that are unnatural.

Since man was created with a nature of having a desire to receive only for himself, he cannot do things in a manner of bestowal. But since this is all that is required of a person in this world, that his intention will be only to bestow, when a person begins the work, he sees that it is not within his power. However, a person is required to ask the Creator to help him walk in the ways of bestowal.

However, one must believe that the Creator "hears the prayer of every mouth." For this reason, a person must believe that the Creator brought us out from the land of Egypt, meaning from the will to receive for ourselves. To the extent that we have faith in this we can ask the Creator to also receive the gift of being delivered from the land of Egypt.

Only then, when we pray from the bottom of our hearts, the Creator brings us out from the land of Egypt. Hence, this is the beginning of the months, since before we come out of Egypt, it is impossible to be rewarded with any *Hidush* [renewal/innovation] in the Torah.

## 931- Peh-Sah [speaking mouth]

Rabbi Zira said, "From here, a joy for man with an answer in his mouth, and a matter in its time, how good it is. When is there joy for man? When there is an answer in his mouth." RASHI interpreted, "When is one happy with his learning? When he can answer when asked about some *Halacha* [law]" (*Iruvin* 54a).

We should interpret that when his organs ask about some *Halacha* [law], *Halacha* means *Kalah* [bride], which is the kingdom of heaven. When the mouth in *Kedusha* [holiness] is shut, a person is regretful. But when he has an answer in his mouth, this is called *Peh-Sah* [*Pesach* (Passover)/speaking mouth]. At that time, he has the joy of *Mitzva* [commandment].

## 932- The First Innovation

All the innovations begin only once a person has been rewarded with emerging from self-reception. This is the meaning of the prohibition to teach Torah to idol-worshippers, since when a person is in Egypt, he cannot be a Jew because he is enslaved to Pharaoh king of Egypt, and when he works for Pharaoh, he cannot be a servant of the Creator.

This is the meaning of "For the children of Israel are Mine; they are My servants," and not the servants of a slave. When a person is his own servant, he cannot be a servant of the Creator because it is impossible to serve two kings at once. Only once he has come out of Egypt, meaning from self-reception, can he be a servant of the Creator. At that time, he can be rewarded with the Torah. It follows that the first innovation is the exodus from Egypt.

## 933- Concerning the Exodus from Egypt

Our sages said that the story of the exodus from Egypt should be said in a manner of question and answer. One who does not have anyone to ask him asks himself "What has changed," etc.

We should interpret this. "Story" comes from the words, "the heavens tell." The exodus from Egypt means the liberation and redemption from the *Klipot* [shells/peels] and the *Sitra Achra* [other side], meaning to invoke the root of redemption and extend it. This matter is regarded as "the heavens tell," meaning that when one removes oneself from any worldliness, he can tell the praise of the Creator.

Yet, in order for one to rise to heaven, his work is in a manner of question and answer. This is the meaning of the sons asking, since *Banim* [sons] means *Havanah* [understanding] and reason and intellect, and they ask him.

One who has no sons—whose mind and reason have no questions because he is pure in his reason and qualities—must evoke the questions by himself, as Baal HaSulam interpreted the words of our sages, "I awaken the dawn, and the dawn does not awaken me."

"What has changed this night compared to all other nights?"

"Night" means the body, which is regarded as "deficiency" and "darkness." "Day" means the soul, which illuminates the body. At that time, he asks, "How has his body changed from the rest of the bodies of the nations of the world?" "For on all other nights," the bodies eat what they want without any scrutinies. Rather, whatever their hearts desire, they say is in their favor. But this night, my body is limited in both thought and desire.

The explanation is, "We were slaves... and He delivered us." That is, specifically through these limitations we will be able to emerge from exile. Precisely by seeing the changes and ascents and descents each time, by struggling, a place of prayer awakens. Then the words "And the children of Israel sighed from the work, and their cry went up" come true. If the exile is revealed in full, then begins the redemption.

This shows us the order of exile and redemption that took place in Egypt at that time, and this is the order we must extend through the end of correction.

# 934- The Duty to Tell the Story of the Exodus from Egypt

"Even if we are all wise ... we are commanded to tell the story of the exodus from Egypt."

We should say that although we have already acquired the Torah and understanding, we must still invoke the root of the emergence of the people of Israel from the exile of Pharaoh. This is so because the most important is the emergence from the *Klipa* [shell/peel] and the entry into *Kedusha* [holiness].

The rest of the degrees are considered cause and consequence. Hence, we must glorify and praise the Creator for this, and by this extend joy in all the worlds. This means that by feeling the preciousness and importance of freedom from the *Klipot*, to that extent the joy increases. To the extent that we have joy, to that extent we can glorify and praise.

This is why each year we must awaken the root, as is explained in *The Zohar*, portion *Bo*, the explanation why we do not eat *Matza* [unleavened bread] throughout the year. It explains that it is like a king who made one of his servants a minister. On that day, he wore princely attire, but later he took off his princely attire. That is, only on that day when he was anointed as a minister, he wore princely attire, so as to show his joy.

Likewise, each year on the same day, he celebrates and wears his princely attire. For this reason, we eat *Matza* specifically on Passover, and the same can be said about telling the story of the exodus from Egypt.

## 935- Concerning the *Matza* [Unleavened Bread]

*Matza* comes from "*Matza* and *Meriva* [strife]," as in "when they strove with the Lord." The rule is that as long as one works with the dough, it does not become leavened, even if it is all day long, for when one is under the governance of Pharaoh king of Egypt, he cannot do anything for the sake of the Creator.

At that time, a person makes a *Matza* and *Meriva* [strife] with the body. The body is angry with the Creator over why He does not give it all its needs, meaning to be permitted to receive for itself, and a person can work only for the sake of the Creator although his heart disagrees, meaning that his intention is wrong.

Since a person does not own the intention, only Pharaoh is the owner, if he nonetheless engages in quarreling with the body, this is still not regarded as leaven, meaning *Sitra Achra* [other side], since he is engaged with it. However, as soon as he stops his engagement with the dough, it immediately becomes leaven.

This is the meaning of "It did not become leaven until He appeared to them ... and redeemed them." That is, because they worked with it all the time until He redeemed them, and then they no longer had to engage. This is why it is called "bread," since he is still poor, without the intention, but only with the action. This is called "unknowingly." Also, "There is none who is poor except in knowledge." This is the meaning of answering it, meaning that the body sings after the fact, that he wants to work *Lishma* [for Her sake].

## 936- The Time of Redemption

"On the tenth day, a leader of the sons of Dan, Ahiezer the son of Ammishaddai."

The time of redemption is approaching and we must prepare ourselves for the light of redemption, which is the exodus from slavery to freedom. It is known that it is impossible to emerge from exile before one is in exile. It is also known that the holy Torah is eternal and applies to each and every generation. Also, we say in the Haggadah [Passover story], "Every generation, one must see oneself as though he came out of Egypt."

For this reason, we must know the meaning of the exile we are in, and what it means that each generation we must emerge from this bitter exile.

The ARI says that the exile in Egypt was that the *Daat* [reason/knowledge] was in exile, meaning the knowledge of *Kedusha* [holiness]. Also, we must explain the meaning of *Daat* of *Kedusha* in exile. The *Zohar* says that sourdough and leaven are the same degree, which we call "the evil inclination," "another authority," "foreign God," "other gods."

Baal HaSulam interprets that the *Sitra Achra* [other side] and the *Klipa* [shell/peel] and the evil inclination are all but the will to receive, and this applies in both mind and heart. That is, the rule of Pharaoh king of Egypt and of Pharaoh's servants is the rule of the will to receive over the organs, meaning that all 248 organs—when serving the will to receive—are called "slaves of Pharaoh."

It is known that the first element in the work is the *Lo Lishma* [not for Her sake]. That is, by education, called "by rote," one begins specifically relying on the will to receive, as one is made to understand that corporeal pleasures are worthless, since what are man's years in this world?

Thus, through Torah and *Mitzvot* [commandments], he will be rewarded with a spiritual pleasure in the next world, which is an eternal world. Also, winning success in corporeal pleasures in this world comes by observing Torah and *Mitzvot*, by which we will have health and salvation, abundant income and success, and we will live long.

Naturally, because of the will to receive, man has the nature of idleness. That is, some people settle for bread and water, and some need meat and fish, too. Some also need accessories and fine clothes, and some even need luxurious houses. It is all according to one's vigor, meaning they do not want to work more than is necessary for them.

Each one has his own measure of necessity, but working in order to bestow is not within man's nature, since man was created with a will to receive for himself. Because obtaining the real pleasures requires being rewarded with *Dvekut* [adhesion] first, called "equivalence of form," meaning that his aim will be for the sake of the Creator, called "in order to bestow," which is the quality of the Creator, who is called "the Giver," this is against nature.

It follows that he is placed in exile under the rule of the king of Egypt. And since the body is called will to receive, there is no point in serving the Creator against one's will, since there is no pleasure in something that is compulsory, only a sorrowful life.

But only such is the way of Torah, the way until we achieve Torah *Lishma* [for Her sake]. Until then, life is a sorrowful life, meaning compulsory.

# 937- Questions for the Exodus from Egypt

1) The wicked one's questions. We should understand the answer to the wicked one's complaint. He says, "What is this work for you?" and if he were there, he would not be redeemed. What is the reason that he could not emerge from the exile?

2) To understand why if the Creator wants to bring the people of Israel out of the hands of Pharaoh, He needs Pharaoh's consent. After all, He is almighty and can bring them out even without Pharaoh's consent.

3) Why did the Creator harden Pharaoh's heart, for it seems as though He denied him the choice?

4) It is known that it is written in the holy books that Israel in Egypt were in forty-nine gates of *Tuma'a* [impurity] until the Creator was revealed to them and redeemed them. We should understand, since after the announcement of the redemption, they must have had preparation, so why did they go into forty-nine gates of *Tuma'a*?

5) We should also understand the meaning of *Matza* [unleavened bread] and *Maror* [bitter herb], and the connection between them. It is written, "Because of it, I did not speak unless when *Matza* and *Maror* are placed before you," for then is the time to speak of the exodus from Egypt, and not at some other time.

# The *Omer* Count

## 938- Considering the *Omer* [Count]

Antwerp, *Tav-Shin-Chaf-Bet*, Jerusalem 1961-62

*Omer* comes from the words "gathering sheaves," which means connection. A person should try to make the connection between him and the Creator shine, as in a sapphire or a diamond. The world is called "the six days of action and Shabbat [Sabbath]," which are seven *Sefirot*, and there is *Hitkalelut* [mingling] of the *Sefirot*. Therefore, we must connect ourselves to the Creator on all the days of the years of our lives, which are seventy years, implying that each year comprises ten *Sefirot*.

By correcting the connection, called *Omer*, we can be rewarded with the quality of Torah, which is regarded as "freedom from the angel of death," as our sages said, "Do not call it *Harut* [carved] but rather *Herut* [freedom]," when we emerge from the enslavement to the inclination by means of the Torah.

This depends on man's connection with the Creator. When one is in separation, he is called "idol-worshipper," and the Torah was given only to the people of Israel, as it is written, "He did not do so to any nation and they did not know the ordinances," since the Torah is called "an ordinance" and "a gift," and was given only to Israel, and one is called "Israel" only when one is connected to the Creator.

# Shavuot [Feast of Weeks]

## 939- The Exodus from Egypt and the Giving of the Torah

In the exodus from Egypt, they received vessels of bestowal, which are vessels of *Hassadim* [mercies]. The tearing of the Red Sea was "seeing," which are lights of *Hochma*, received in vessels of reception. There it was through an awakening from above, as it is written, "The Lord will fight for you and you will be silent."

But the reception of the Torah was by that awakening, by an awakening from below, when they said, "We will do and we will hear." A miracle is called "an awakening from above," whereas Torah is called "for it is not in heaven," since she comes by an awakening from below. Hence, this is sustainable.

"The Torah was not given to the ministering angels, but only to people." It follows that people are a higher degree than the ministering angels, since an angel is a messenger, which is "we will do," while the Torah is called "we will hear."

## 940- *The Point in the Heart*

When the Temple was ruined, it is written, "And let them make Me a Temple and I will dwell within them." This pertains to the point in the heart, which should be a Temple where the light of the Creator dwells, as it is written, "And I will dwell within them." Hence, one should try to build his structure of *Kedusha* [holiness], and the structure should be able to contain the upper abundance called "abundance poured from the Giver to the receiver." However, according to the rule, there must be equivalence of form between the Giver and the receiver so the receiver, too, must have the aim to bestow like the Giver.

This is called "action," as it is written, "Let them make Me a Temple," where the acting applies to the *Kli* [vessel] and not the light, since the light pertains to the Creator and only the action pertains to the creatures.

The light is called "a blessing from the Creator," as it is written, "And I will bless you in all that you do." This is the meaning of "We will do and we will hear, for through our work we will be rewarded with hearing, as it is written, "And all the people were seeing the voices," meaning they heard the voice of the Creator.

Seeing means with the senses, which is a feeling in the heart, where each one, by Mount Sinai, felt that the voice of the Creator spoke to him and they had no doubt about the matter. This is called "seeing." Similarly, when a person sees something, he has no doubt about it, unlike when he hears, for perhaps he did not hear very well. Therefore, we do not rely on hearsay but only on eye witnessing.

For this reason, at the time of the giving of the Torah, when they had no doubt that this was the voice of the Creator, it is called "seeing," as it is written, "I and you shall have no [other Gods], we heard from the mouth of the Creator" (*Makkot* 24a).

# 941- Mount Sinai

"What is Mt. Sinai? A mountain on which the hatred for the nations of the world descended" (*Shabbat* [Sabbath] 89). We should understand why the Torah caused hatred specifically toward Israel, and why we do not say that there is hatred between Ishmaelites and Christians, for example. We should interpret that in ethics, the "nations of the world" are their desires, meaning corporeal lusts whose wish is only to fill their stomachs. The carrier of this is the evil inclination.

Conversely, "Israel" is called "the desire for the work of the Creator," and its carrier is the good inclination. During the work, a person has desires and yearnings for corporeal lusts. It follows that the person loves the nations of the world and has a lot of work to be able to overcome so as to change these desires. But this is possible only through the Torah, whose attribute is to hate all the corporeal lusts.

We should interpret that it is called "Mt. Sinai" because hatred descended to the nations of the world. That is, through the Torah, one is rewarded with hatred for the nations of the world, establishing in one's heart hatred for the evil inclination, as our sages said, "The light in it reforms him."

# 942- Concerning the Mind Controlling the Heart

"The mind" is regarded as *Hochma*, and the "heart" is regarded as *Bina*, which is light of *Hassadim*. The mind can control, meaning it has the ability to govern, so that specifically this will shine when he has a heart, which is the quality of *Hassadim*. Before he has *Hassadim*, the light of *Hochma* has no governance, it cannot shine, and that time is called "night."

Conversely, in the corporeal mind, Baal HaSulam said that the mind has no control over the heart, which is the will to receive, since the will to receive is the landlord and the mind is powerless to overthrow it from its governance, for "One learns only where one's heart desires." In other words, a person sees no mind but only that which the heart wants.

For example, if a person wants to steal, he asks the mind to provide him with ways and manners to carry it out. Or if he wants to do good deeds, the mind advises him how to carry this out, as well.

It follows that the mind serves the heart, which is the will to receive, just as the hands and legs and the rest of the assistants that one has. For this reason, there is no other way but to purify the heart, for which reason we pray, "Purify our hearts to serve You in truth." The mind cannot determine for man to walk on the good path or to the contrary. Rather, as was said at the time of the giving of the Torah, "We will do and we will hear."

That is, first, we will do mindlessly, and then we will be rewarded with hearing, so we can hear that what we are doing is what is good for us. Conversely, if we first want to understand that it is worthwhile for us to bestow upon the Creator and then we will do, we will never achieve this.

This is as our sages said, "'Therefore the governors said.' Rabbi Shmuel Bar Nachmani said, 'Rabbi Yonatan said, 'Why is it written, 'Therefore the governors said'? It is those who govern their inclination.' 'Come in calculation,' come let us calculate the calculation of the world for the loss of a *Mitzva* [commandment] compared to its reward, and the reward for a transgression compared to its loss. 'Build and establish,' if you do so, you will be built in this world and be established for the next world'" (*Baba Batra* 78b).

Thus, those who govern their inclination, namely by doing, which is doing above rhyme and reason, can make a mindful calculation. But without the aspect of "doing," the mind cannot calculate because one can never see the truth, for one is enslaved and partial toward the heart, the will to receive, so he takes a bribe if he sees that it might spoil the self-love.

Rather, first we must receive the Torah and *Mitzvot* [commandments] in the manner of doing above reason, which is called "doing mindlessly," and then we are rewarded with hearing, when we can make good calculations until we come to a state of hearing from heaven. As Baal HaSulam said, "The reward for the *Mitzva*—the *Metzaveh* [Commander]," meaning we are rewarded with hearing the Commander of the commandments.

# 943- Three Discernments in the Torah

6 Sivan, Tav-Shin-Lamed-Hey, May 16, 1975, Bnei Brak

There are three discernments in the Torah: 1) *Tushia*, which *Mateshet* [exhausts] a person's strength, 2) the Torah as a spice, 3) the light of Torah.

The first two discernments are regarded as a preparation to receive the Torah. Only the third discernment is called "Torah," which is the essence, in the sense of doing good to His creations. The first two are considered "corrections of creation."

# 944- The Giving of the Torah Is with Two Eyes

"You have drawn my heart with one of your eyes." Prior to the reception of the Torah, it was with "one of your eyes." After the reception of the Torah, with both your eyes.

We need to understand the difference between two eyes and one. First, we need to understand what an "eye" implies. It is written, "For they will see eye to eye when the Lord returns to Zion." This means that the eye of the created being sees the eye of the Creator, meaning Providence. This is as we explained, "A land that the eyes of the Lord are upon it from the beginning of the year to the end of the year."

When a person must believe that the eye sees, etc., since when one engages in doing but has not yet been rewarded with hearing, it is considered that the Creator sees but the person sees nothing. However, when the person is rewarded with hearing, the person sees, as well, meaning he sees the revelation of Godliness, which is called "eye to eye."

Hence, when they received the Torah, they were rewarded with hearing. At that time, it was with both eyes, the upper eye and the lower eye, as it is written, "Behold, the eye of the Lord is on those who fear Him, who crave His *Hesed* [mercy/kindness]." In other words, those who are rewarded with receiving the fear of the Creator in the form of doing are rewarded with the discernment of "the eye of the Creator." That is, they see Providence with their own eyes, how He leads the world as The Good Who Does Good.

It follows that the eye of the Creator means Providence in the form of good and doing good. When one is rewarded with seeing Providence, that it is in the form of good and doing good, this is called "man's eye."

The order of man's work should be regarded as "one eye," meaning to believe in the eye of the Creator before he has been rewarded with seeing. We can do this only through fear of heaven in the form of doing. The measure of the work in doing should be in the measure of "You have drawn my heart with one of your eyes." Once we are rewarded with hearing, it is with two eyes.

In the same manner, we should also say that "one eye" means doing, which is the quality of "right" [line], when one engages only in *Hassadim* and does not want to receive anything in return. The other eye is regarded as "left," discerned as "hearing."

The right eye is considered "learning Torah *Lishma* [for Her sake]," and the left eye is regarded as "The secrets of Torah are revealed to him," which is hearing. The reception of the Torah is doing, and the giving of the Torah is with both eyes.

# The Ninth of Av

## 945- The Ninth of Av

The Shabbat [Sabbath] after the 9th of Av

Our sages said about the verse, "And the whole congregation raised their voice and wept." "Rabbah said, 'Rabbi Yochanan said, 'That day was the night of the ninth of Av.'" The Creator said, 'They cried for nothing, and I will establish for them a cry for generations'" (*Sotah* 35).

We should understand the connection between the spies and the ruin of the Temple. Also, we should understand what is written there about the interpretation of "For they are stronger than us." "Rabbi Hanina Bar Papa said, 'The spies said a great thing at that time, 'For they are stronger than us.' Do not pronounce it as 'than us' but as 'than Him,' as though even the Landlord cannot pull out His vessels from there.'"

Also, our sages said that Caleb told them that if He says, "Make ladders and climb up to the firmament," we will not obey Him, "We shall indeed rise up and inherit it."

# Explanation of the Article, "Preface to the Wisdom of Kabbalah"

## Four Phases of Direct Light

The learning begins with a *Behina* [discernment] called "The connection between the Creator and the created beings," since we do not speak of the Creator Himself and we cannot attain Him. Instead, "By Your actions we know You," meaning all the attainment is only in the operations that extend from Him.

This connection is also called "the purpose of creation." Our sages attained that His desire and goal are to do good to His creations. Hence, the order of evolution begins from this discernment until it reaches the souls, whose root is the soul of *Adam HaRishon*, which extends from the internality of the worlds *BYA*.

Allegorically speaking, when He wished to benefit His creatures, He wanted to give them 100 kilograms of pleasure. Hence, He had to create such creations that would want to receive it. We learned that the desire to receive delight and pleasure is the very essence of the created being and after whom Creation is called "existence from absence." He created it so His thought of delighting His creations would be realized.

For the will to receive to be born, there had to be an order of development by four discernments, since one can enjoy something only according to one's yearning for it. This is why we call the *Kli* [vessel] by the name, "will to receive" or "yearning." That is, according to the measure of the need, so is the measure of the yearning to satisfy the need.

There are two conditions for the making of the yearning:

1. One should know what to yearn for. One cannot yearn for something of which one has never seen or heard.

2. One will not have the yearned for thing, since if he has already obtained his wish, he loses the yearning.

To meet these two conditions, four *Behinot* [phases/discernments, pl. of *Behina*] emerged in the will to receive, and along with their root, they are five *Behinot*. The fifth *Behina* is called a "*Kli* that is suitable for reception of delight and pleasure."

This is their order:

1) *Keter*: His desire to do good to His creations.

2) *Hochma*: His desire to do good to His creations created a deficiency existence from absence, and along with it, created the light. Thus, the abundance and the desire to receive the abundance came together. This is so because the desire still did not know what to want; hence, it was born along with the filling. However, if it has its filling, it does not have the desire for the filling, as written concerning the second condition. This *Behina* is called *Behina Aleph* [first discernment] *de Aviut* ["thickness," "desire"].

3) *Bina*: Since the Light comes from the Giver, the force of bestowal is included in this Light. Hence, at its end, *Hochma* wants equivalence of form, meaning to not be a receiver but a giver. There is a rule in spirituality: "Any generation of a new form is considered a new discernment." Hence, this discernment is given its own name—*Bina*, and this is *Behina Bet* [second discernment] of *Aviut*. We also learned that the Light that spreads while the lower one wants equivalence of form is *Ohr Hassadim* [Light of Mercy], and this is the Light that shines in *Bina*.

Question: If *Bina* yearns to bestow, why is she called *Aviut Bet* [second degree of *Aviut*]? On the contrary, she should have been finer than *Behina Aleph de Aviut* [first degree of *Aviut*].

Answer: I explained it with an allegory: A person gives his friend a gift and the friend receives it. Afterwards, he reconsiders and decides that it is not in his interest to receive, and returns the gift. In the beginning, he was under the influence and domination of the giver; hence, he received. But once he received, he felt that he was the receiver, and that sensation caused him to return the gift.

Lesson: In *Behina Aleph*, he received due to the domination of the giver, but he still did not feel like a receiver. And when he saw and felt that he was the receiver, he stopped receiving, and this is *Behina Bet*. In other words, in that state, he felt that he was the receiver, and hence wanted to bestow upon the Giver. This is why *Behina Bet* is called *Bina*, for she *Hitbonena* [examined/observed] that she is a receiver and therefore wanted to bestow. This is also why we learn that the beginning of the learning is from *Bina* down.

4) *ZA*: At its end, *Bina* received, as a kind of drive—which stems from the purpose of Creation—that she must receive since the purpose of Creation was not for the creatures to engage in bestowal. On the other hand, she also wanted equivalence of form, bestowal. Therefore, she compromised: She would receive *Hassadim* [mercy] and illumination of the *Ohr Hochma* [Light of Wisdom].

This is called *Behina Gimel de Aviut*, since she already extends *Hochma*, but there are still *Hassadim* in her. This is the reason for the name *Zeir Anpin* [small face]. *Hochma* is called *Panim* [face], as in "A man's wisdom illuminates his face," but it receives this *Ohr Hochma* in a *Zeir*, meaning a very small extent. But this discernment is still not considered a *Kli* [vessel], since if it can bestow and receive only an illumination of the *Ohr Hochma*, it is a sign that its craving to receive is incomplete, since it still has the strength to engage in bestowal, too.

5) *Malchut*: At its end, *Behina Gimel* is prompted from above to receive abundantly because of His desire to do good to His creations. After all, the purpose of Creation was not for the lower ones to receive in *Zeir Anpin*. Hence, this awakening causes *Malchut* to have a desire and craving to receive the *Ohr Hochma* as it shone in *Behina Aleph*, when she had all the *Ohr Hochma*.

But the difference between *Behina Aleph* and *Behina Dalet* is that in *Behina Aleph*, it could not be said that she enjoyed the *Ohr Hochma* since she still did not have the yearning and deficiency, since the abundance and the *Kli* came together. But *Behina Dalet* yearns for the *Ohr Hochma* while she does not have it; hence, when she receives, she feels the delight and pleasure that come with satisfying her deficiency.

Only this *Behina* is called "a *Kli*," since it wants only to receive. All the *Behinot* [pl. of *Behina*] prior to her are called "Light without a *Kli*." And when this *Behina Dalet* receives the Light, it is a state called "the world of *Ein Sof*," and also "filling the whole of reality."

Question: If we are dealing with spirituality, where there is no time and no place, what does "filling the whole of reality" mean?

Answer: Let us return to our allegory from the beginning of the explanation, the allegory that He wanted to give His creatures 100 kg of pleasure and therefore had to create 100 kg of deficiency and desire to receive in the creatures, corresponding to the pleasure. When the 100 kg of deficiency receives the 100 kg of filling, this is called "filling the whole of reality," meaning no deficiency is left unfulfilled.

Now we will explain the meaning of the name *Malchut de Ein Sof* [*Malchut* of infinity]: This *Malchut*, which yearns to receive abundance to fill her deficiency, is called "receiving in order to receive." This means that she receives in order to satisfy her lack. At a later stage, she put an end and *Tzimtzum* [restriction] on using this *Kli*. But in the initial stage, which we are dealing with, she still did not make that *Sof* [end] and *Sium* [conclusion]. Hence, this state is still called *Ein Sof* [no end].

We learned that, at its end, after receiving the abundance, a desire to bestow awakened in *Hochma*, fitting the Emanator's desire to bestow. Also, once *Malchut* received the Light, it evoked within her a desire to bestow, since this Light possesses the power of bestowal. *Bina* wished to bestow, but did not succeed because in *Bina's* way, the purpose of Creation is missing. Even her subsequent reception of illumination in *ZA* was not enough since the Creator's desire to do good to His creations was in abundance, not in *ZA*. Hence, how could *Malchut* achieve equivalence of form and obtain the purpose of Creation, too?

It is said about it that she invented something new: *Malchut* would receive everything, but unlike *Ein Sof*, where it was all in order to receive, she would do it in order to bestow. Thus, on one hand she would be realizing the purpose of Creation of doing good to His creations, since she would be receiving. On the other hand, her aim would be to bestow, which is equivalence of form.

## *Tzimtzum Aleph*

When that *Malchut* said that she did not want to receive in order to receive, it is as though she repelled the Light. That state is called *Tzimtzum* [restriction]. There is a rule in spirituality: Any appearance of a new form is considered a new discernment. Therefore, we should discern two states:

1. When *Behina Dalet* received all the Light with a *Kli* called "yearning." This is called "filling the whole of reality," as well as "the world of *Ein Sof*."

2. After she wanted equivalence of form, that state is considered a different world, called "the world of *Tzimtzum*," from which the Light departed.

Hence, as we discerned that *Hochma* received and *Bina* repelled the Light, *Malchut* remained as she was in the state of the world of *Ein Sof*— receiving all the Light—and now we discern a new *Malchut*, which repels the Light.

We should know that in the first state, called *Ein Sof*, it was "He is One and His Name are one," meaning that the Light and the *Kli* were one discernment. Only after the *Tzimtzum* was there a distinction of the four phases, or ten *Sefirot*, since the Light departed from them.

Question: With this *Tzimtzum*, the Light departed from all ten *Sefirot*. This is perplexing since the *Tzimtzum* was on reception in order to receive, which is *Behina Dalet*, and not on the rest of the *Behinot*!

Answer: The first three *Behinot* are not regarded as *Kelim*; they only prompt a procession of development, at the end of which the *Kli*, called "receiving in order to receive," is born and becomes separated from the Giver. But the first three *Behinot* are still not separated from the Giver.

After *Malchut* was born, she obtained her causes. Hence, it cannot be said that after the *Tzimtzum* the Light remained in the first nine, since they are not *Kelim*. The only *Kli* is *Malchut*, and if she does not want to receive, all the Light departs and she does not receive anything.

The Ari also says, "The *Tzimtzum* was equal," namely without distinction of degrees.

Question: If this is so, why did we say that the four *Behinot* became distinct after the *Tzimtzum*?

Answer: The distinction was made with respect to cause and consequence, but there was no distinction of Above and below.

Question: What do Above and below mean in spirituality?

Answer: Importance—whereas cause and consequence do not imply importance. For example, the Vilna Gaon was caused by his father, but who was more important, the cause or the consequence?

We need to understand why there was no distinction of Above and below. *Malchut* received the Light that "fills the whole of reality," and this is not considered a deficiency or inferiority in importance. Hence, she could have remained in that state, had she not chosen to make the *Tzimtzum*.

This is what the ARI wishes to imply when he says that the *Tzimtzum* was equal, that *Malchut* was not of inferior importance, but that the *Tzimtzum* was made through her own choice. But afterwards, when *Malchut* does not receive due to the prohibition, she becomes inferior in importance. Then, what is farther from *Malchut* becomes of Higher importance, and what is nearer to *Malchut* becomes of lower importance.

## The Ten *Sefirot de Igulim* [circles] and the Line of *Ein Sof* that Fills Them

After the *Tzimtzum*, the *Kelim* were left empty, and within them *Reshimot* [recollections/memories] of the Light they had had. They are called "the ten *Sefirot de Igulim* in the world of *Tzimtzum*." They are called *Igulim* to imply that the issue of Above and below does not apply to them, as it is in a corporeal circle.

Because *Malchut* is the operator, since she is the actual *Kli*, *Malchut de Igulim* returned and extended the Light in order to receive it in order to bestow. And here we learn a new rule: "A desire in the Upper One becomes a binding law in the lower one." Hence, now she is forbidden to receive.

I once offered an allegory about that: The eve of a new month is a time for saying the small *Yom Kippur* [Day of Atonement] prayer and for awakening to repent. Sometimes, a person debates whether or not to fast on that day, too. It is not mandatory to fast and there is no prohibition on the food itself, too. Hence, the choice is in one's own hands.

If, in the end, a person decides to fast. If he later regrets and wishes to eat, the rule is that the food is now forbidden, so "he shall not break his word," concerning the oath. Thus, we see that initially, there was no prohibition on the food, but after he had chosen to avoid eating, the food became forbidden.

Lesson: In the beginning, *Malchut* did not want to receive through her own choice. But now that she extends the Light again, it is prohibited to receive the Light. And if there is prohibition, there are Above and below in importance. Hence, this extension is called "a line that extends from *Ein Sof* from Above downwards."

We also learned that even though the *Igulim* [circles] extended the Light, they received it only from the line. We must understand why this is so: Any new form in spirituality is a new discernment. Hence, there are two kinds of *Kelim* [pl. of *Kli*]:

1. *Kelim* in which there is no prohibition on reception.

2. *Kelim* that extend now, with the extension of the Light, and whose *Malchut* is called *Malchut de Yosher* [directness], on which there is prohibition to receive, due to the rule: A desire in the Upper One becomes a binding law in the lower one.

We also learn that the *Igulim* should receive Light from what they had drawn anew. This Light is called "a line." It contains Above and below in importance, and there is no other Light. This is the meaning of the *Igulim* having no Light but from the line.

Yet, there is a big difference between *Malchut de Igulim* and *Malchut* of the line. *Malchut de Igulim* had the Light in the form of "filling the whole of reality," while *Malchut de Yosher* never had any Light, nor will it ever have Light in its *Kli*, called "receiving in order to receive."

## The Line and the *Zivug de Hakaa*

Thus far, we have discussed three states:

1. The will to receive that was created in the world of *Ein Sof* and received all the Light.

2. In the world of *Tzimtzum*, it became apparent that the will to receive must be corrected for the purpose of decoration.

3. In the line, it is apparent that the *Kli* must be corrected due to the deficiency. Otherwise, the Light does not expand to it.

Now we shall speak of the line. We have already learned that the line has Above and below in importance, since *Malchut* of the line was forbidden to receive because she is regarded as receiving in order to receive. The rule is that in all the degrees, *Malchut's* name was not changed, and it is "receiving in order to receive." And her Light is *Ohr Hozer*, meaning she wishes to bestow upon the Upper One.

When the Light extended to *Malchut*, she made a *Zivug de Hakaa*, a *Masach*, which implies ending the Light and making calculations.

For example, she assumed that she could receive only twenty percent of the Light in order to bestow. Hence, she decided to clothe only that much Light.

However, she felt that there was too much pleasure in the remaining eighty percent, and if she were to receive it, it would be in order to receive. Hence, she decided not to receive that part of the Light. So what is the difference between a *Tzimtzum* and a *Masach* [screen]?

- A *Tzimtzum* occurs through choice, as we learned that *Malchut* had all the Light and she chose to not receive it.
- A *Masach* is the domination of the Upper One on it. Thus, even if the lower one wished to receive, the Upper One would not let it.

The meaning of the term *Zivug de Hakaa* [coupling of striking] is as follows: In corporeality, it sometimes happens that when people disagree, they strike one another. In spirituality, when two things contradict one another, it is considered that they strike one another.

What is the dispute? The Upper One, who wishes to do good to His creations, awakens in the lower ones a desire to receive all the Light. But the lower one wishes the contrary, to equalize its form, and hence does not wish to receive at all. This is the striking that takes place between the Upper One and the lower one.

In the end, they equalize with one another and create a union and *Zivug* between them. In other words, the lower one receives the Light as the Upper One wishes, but only as much of it as it can receive in order to bestow, as the lower one wishes. Thus, there are two things here: 1) equivalence of form, and 2) reception of the Light.

However, the *Zivug* is possible only if a striking preceded it, since without the striking, and with the lower one's desire to receive the Light, this would be oppositeness and separation from the Creator. This process of *Zivug de Hakaa* is called *Rosh* [head]. A *Rosh* means root, a potential which needs a process of realization. The *Rosh* exists because of the existence of a *Sof*, a prohibition on reception. Hence, *Malchut* is compelled to calculate, which is called a *Rosh*, preceding the actual reception.

Accordingly, we can understand the words of the ARI in the beginning of *Talmud Eser Sefirot* [*The Study of the Ten Sefirot*]: "Behold that before the emanations were emanated and the creatures were created, etc., and there was no such part as head, or end," etc. This is so because in *Ein Sof*, there was still no prohibition on receiving; hence, it immediately received it. But now that an end was made, we should distinguish between the *Rosh*, which is the potential, and the *Guf* [body], which is the realization.

And afterwards she receives in practice, meaning the twenty percent that she receives in order to bestow are called the *Toch* [interior] of the degree, and the place of the expansion of the Light is called from *Peh* [mouth] to *Tabur* [navel]. *Malchut de* [of] *Toch* stands at the *Tabur* and says, "What I receive from here on, meaning the eighty percent, will be in order to receive. Hence, I do not want to receive, so I will not be separated." Thus, the Light departs, and this discernment is called the *Sof* of the degree.

## The *Bitush* between Internal and Surrounding in the *Partzuf*

Everything discussed here concerning the RTS [*Rosh, Toch, Sof*] concerns the first *Partzuf*, called *Galgalta*, which uses the *Aviut* of *Behina Dalet*. And we learned that *Galgalta* received the maximum it could receive in order to bestow. It could not receive more.

Yet, we learned that in the Thought of Creation, the *Kli* received everything. This is so because the *Kli* of reception in order to receive was created by the Creator, while in the *Kli* that the lower one makes, called "in order to bestow," there is a limit to the amount it can receive. It follows that there is no *Kli* that can receive the eighty percent of Light that remained outside the *Partzuf*. So what will become of them?

To correct that, a *Bitush* of internal and external was created. These are the words of the ARI concerning this issue in Part 4, Chapter 1, Item 4: "When the Inner Lights connect to the Surrounding Lights, they connect inside the *Peh*. Hence, when they emerge together outside the *Peh*, tied together, they strike and beat on each other, and their beatings engender the *Kelim*." Thus, it is through the beating that the *Kelim* are made.

We need to understand why 1) the *Ohr Pnimi* [Inner Light] and *Ohr Makif* [Surrounding Light] beat on each other, and 2) why this beating creates the *Kelim*.

Answer: We have already said that in spirituality, beating occurs when two things are in opposition to one another. But we also need to understand why the beating occurs "when they emerge together outside the *Peh*."

At the *Rosh* of the degree, 100 percent of the Light expands without a distinction of *Pnimi* [internal] and *Makif* [surrounding]. This is so because His desire to do good to His creations is complete. But the lower one, who is limited, calculates and decides, for example, that it can receive only twenty percent in order to bestow. This occurs in the *Rosh*, in potential. "When they emerge outside the *Peh*": Emergence, in spirituality, is called "revelation," when what was in potential is revealed in practice. At that time, it receives a part and repels a part to become *Ohr Makif*.

This *Ohr Makif* seemingly comes to the *Masach de Guf* and argues, "Admit that your conduct, meaning the fact that you have erected the *Masach*, is not good, since how will the purpose of Creation of doing good to His creations be implemented? Who will receive all the Light?"

On the other hand, the *Ohr Pnimi* agrees with the *Masach*, since the very expansion of the Light within is through the *Masach* and the *Ohr Hozer* [Reflected Light]. This dispute is called *Bitush* of *Ohr Makif* and *Ohr Pnimi*, or *Bitush* of *Ohr Makif* in the *Masach*.

In truth, the *Ohr Makif* is right; hence, the *Masach* agrees with it. And since it agrees, it can no longer repel and raise *Ohr Hozer*, and therefore can no longer receive in order to bestow. Consequently, the Light departs and the *Masach* is purified, meaning stops receiving. This state is called *Din* [judgment] and *Achoraim* [posterior].

Since each *Behina* [discernment] consists of four *Behinot*, the *Masach* departs gradually, beginning with *Behina Dalet* in *Behina Dalet*, then from *Behina Gimel* in *Behina Dalet*, etc., until it rises to *Peh de Rosh*, the source from which the *Masach de Guf* arrived. In other words, it stops receiving altogether.

As it rises, it uses a smaller *Aviut* each time, and thus receives smaller Light in order to bestow. For example, when it ascends to *Behina Aleph*, it can receive only the Light of *Ruach*. When it rises to *Behinat Shoresh* [root], it can receive only the Light of *Nefesh* in order to bestow. Finally, it cannot receive anything in order to bestow and thus stops receiving altogether.

Question: What is the benefit of the *Ohr Makif*, which wants to shine because of the purpose of Creation, and therefore wants the *Masach* to receive more? After all, things are unfolding in contrast to its will, meaning the *Masach* loses even what it had!

Answer: All the degrees that appeared during the departure are not residue of what it had in the beginning, since there is a rule: "There is no generation of new Light that does not extend from *Ein Sof*." This means that each discernment that appears is a new discernment. Thus, in the beginning, it could not receive anything more. But now that *Behina Dalet* has departed, it can receive more, namely from *Behina Gimel*.

This is the meaning of the *Kelim* being made through the *Bitush*. That is, prior to the *Bitush*, it did not have any more *Kelim* for reception, since it received all it could with the aim to bestow. But after the *Bitush*, when the *Masach* of *Behina Dalet* was purified, there was room to receive on *Behina Gimel*, since it departed from *Behina Dalet* and had nothing. And when it departed from *Behina Gimel*, it could receive on *Behina Bet*.

But this still leaves the question: What is the benefit if it receives less each time?

Answer: There is no absence in spirituality. This means that anything that appears remains, except he does not see it and cannot currently enjoy it, but only from the present. When the work is done, all the Lights will appear at once. Thus, in the end, he will have gained.

Baal HaSulam once said an allegory about this: Two people who were childhood friends separated as adults. One of them became a king, and the other, indigent. After many years, the poor one heard that his friend had become a king and decided to go to his friend's country and ask him for help. He packed his few belongings and went.

When they met, he told the king about his dire state, and this touched the king's heart. The king said to his friend: "I will give you a letter to my treasurer to allow you into the treasury for two hours. In those two hours, whatever you manage to collect is yours." The indigent went to the treasurer, armed with his letter, and received the longed for permit. He walked into the treasury with the box he was used to using for his beggary, and within five minutes, he filled his box to the brim and merrily stepped out of the treasury.

But the treasurer took his box from him and spilled its entire contents. The indigent started sobbing but the treasurer told him, "Take your box and fill it up again." The poor man walked into the treasury once more and filled his box. But when he stepped outside, the treasurer spilled its contents as before.

This cycle repeated itself until the two hours were through. The last time the beggar came out, he told the treasurer: "I beg you, leave me what I have collected, for my time is through and I can no longer enter the treasury." Then the treasurer told him: "The contents of this box is yours, and so is everything that I had spilled out of your box for the past two hours. I have been spilling your money every time because I wanted to do you good, since each time, you were coming with your tiny box full and you had no room to put anything more into it."

Lesson: Each reception of Light in order to bestow remains. But if the Light remained, we would not want to receive anymore, since we would not be able to receive in order to bestow on more than we had received. Hence, each degree must depart, and each time, we correct a *Kli* of will to receive with the aim to bestow until all is corrected. Then, all the Lights will shine at once.

Now let us return to explaining the purification of the *Masach*. The first expansion that emerged from the *Peh* down is called *Taamim* [flavors], from the verse, "as the palate tastes its food." After the *Bitush* of *Ohr Makif*, the *Masach* began to purify, and on its way produced a new degree each time. These degrees are called *Nekudot* [points/dots].

I have already explained the words of the ARI that the *Kelim* were made through the *Bitush*, since now he has the ability to receive more Light. But Baal HaSulam interprets the making of the *Kelim* [plural for *Kli*] differently: While the Light was in the *Kli*, the Light and the *Kli* were mingled in each other. Through the *Bitush*, the Light departed and the *Kli* became apparent.

Interpretation: While the Light shines in the *Kli*, the deficiency of the *Kli* is indistinguishable; hence, it does not merit the name *Kli*. This is because without the *Kli*, the Light cannot shine. Hence, they are of equal importance. But once the Light departs, the *Kli* is distinguished as a *Kli*, and the Light, as Light.

The *Nekuda* [point] of *Tzimtzum* is the reason why the degrees emerging during the purification are called *Nekudot*.

And what is the *Nekuda* of the *Tzimtzum*? *The Zohar* says that *Malchut* is called "a black dot without any white in it." This means that during the darkness, *Malchut* is called "a dot." When there is *Tzimtzum*, and it is forbidden to receive in order to receive, it becomes dark. In other words, the point of *Tzimtzum* is present wherever it is impossible to receive in order to bestow and there is a desire to receive in order to receive.

We should also explain the difference between *Rosh*, *Toch*, and *Sof*: *Rosh* is considered "potential," meaning there is no reception there. Two parts spread from the *Rosh*:

- One part can receive the Light, and it is called ten *Sefirot de Toch*. The Light is the abundance that enters the

*Kelim*, and it is called *Ohr Pnimi*, which is *Ohr Hochma*—the Light of doing good to His creations.

- The second part that spreads from the *Rosh* is the part of the desire to receive in order to receive, which it does not want to use. It says that it does not want to receive there, meaning it ends it. Hence, this part is called "ten *Sefirot de Sof*."

Question: We learned that the word *Sefirot* comes from the word "sapphire," meaning it shines. But if *Malchut de Guf*, called *Malchut de Tabur*, does not want to receive and puts a *Sof* on the Light, why is this part called *Sefirot*?

Answer: They are called ten *Sefirot* because, in truth, the Light did shine for them. An explanation on that matter can be found in Part 4, Chapter 5, Item 1, where he explains the difference between *Toch* and *Sof*: "From *Peh de AK* emerged ten internal *Sefirot* and ten surrounding *Sefirot*. They extend from opposite the *Panim* through opposite the *Tabur de AK*. This is the majority of the Light, but it also shines through the sides and all around that Adam," meaning not necessarily opposite the *Panim*, but also from the sides.

In Item 2, he interprets the words of the ARI as follows: "In short, we will explain that from *Tabur* up it is called *Panim*. This is because the Light of *Hochma*, considered the essential Light, spreads there, and from *Tabur* down it is called *Achor* [posterior], since it is considered receiving in order to receive. Hence, the Light of *Hochma* does not spread there, but comes through the sides."

Further down that page, it continues, "...because through the *Ohr Hozer* that *Behina Dalet* brings to the *Partzuf*, which is *Ohr Hassadim*." This means that *Malchut de Tabur* does not want to receive there, since there it is a will to receive in order to receive. Instead, it wants equivalence of form, called *Hassadim*. "Thus, she receives illumination of *Hochma*, as well, though in the form of 'female Light,' meaning only receiving and not bestowing." "Receiving and not bestowing" means that she does not want to bestow the Light upon herself, but, to the contrary, she says that she does not want to receive.

And through this *Dvekut* [adhesion], an illumination of the Light of *Hochma* shines upon her, and this is called "illumination of *Hochma*." Accordingly, the difference between *Toch* and *Sof* is that the *Ohr Hochma* shines in the *Toch* and in the *Sof*. As long as she does not want to receive for the purpose of equivalence of form, the Light that shines is *Ohr Hassadim* in illumination of *Hochma*.

We still need to explain why the names in *Ohr Hassadim* are "right" and "left," and in the *Ohr Hochma* they are called "long" and "short." When the Light shines, in *Hassadim*, it is called "right," and in *Hochma*, "long." When it does not shine, in *Hassadim*, it is called "left," and in *Hochma*, "short."

What do these names mean?

Answer: We learned that *Ohr Hochma* shines in the vessels of reception in order to bestow, of course. Hence, the measure of illumination depends on its measure of *Aviut*. This is called "above" and "below," and this is why the names in *Ohr Hochma* are "long" and "short." But *Ohr Hassadim* is not extended through *Aviut* and is not dependent on it. Hence, the names in *Ohr Hassadim* relate to width: "right" and "left," implying that they shine in the same level, and it does not matter to them if there is more *Aviut* or less *Aviut*.

## An Inner *Partzuf*

Thus far we have discussed the first *Partzuf* of AK, called *Galgalta* or the Inner *Partzuf de* AK. Now we will explain the inner *Partzuf*. There is a rule that in all the worlds, there is an inner *Partzuf* with four clothes. We will explain it in AK: *Partzuf Galgalta* has complete *HaVaYaH* within its degree, and a complete degree emerges from each letter in this *HaVaYaH*.

- Its *Rosh*, called *Keter* or "the tip of the *Yod*," is unattainble.
- From *Peh* to *Chazeh* it is called *Yod de HaVaYaH*, and from there emerges *Partzuf AB de* AK, which clothes it.

- From its first *Hey*, called *Bina*, emerges *Partzuf SAG*, from the *Chazeh* down.

Thus, the *Yod-Hey*, which are *AB* and *SAG*, clothe it from *Tabur* up. Below *Tabur*, it is *Vav-Hey de HaVaYaH*.

- The *Vav* is called the Upper third of *NHY*, called *Partzuf MA*, and from it, emerges the world of *Nekudim*, which clothes there.
- From its last *Hey*, called *Malchut*, which are the two lower thirds of *NHY de AK*, emerged *Partzuf BON*, called "the world of *Atzilut*," which works with *Aviut Shoresh*.

## The *Reshimot*

When the Light departs from *Partzuf Galgalta*, empty *Kelim* remain, and in them *Reshimot* from the Lights that shone within the *Kelim*. The meaning of *Reshimot* is as we see in corporeality: When a person eats a tasty dish or hears of something pleasant, a taste remains of what he experienced, evoking him to re-extend what he had had. Similarly, a *Reshimo* [sing. of *Reshimot*] is a yearning for what he had had.

There are two discernments in the *Reshimot*: 1) the pure Light in the *Reshimo*, and 2) the *Av* [thick] Light in the *Reshimo*.

This means that as the general *Ohr Yashar* shone in *Kelim* called "the general *Ohr Hozer*," when the *Ohr Yashar* departs, it leaves a *Reshimo* that is a part of the *Ohr Yashar*. This *Reshimo* clothes in part of the *Ohr Hozer* that was there, meaning it leaves an impression of the fact that it worked with the aim to bestow. This is called *Reshimo* from the *Ohr Hozer*.

- What remains of the *Ohr Yashar* is called "the pure Light in the *Reshimo*."
- What remains of the *Ohr Hozer* is called "the coarse Light in the *Reshimo*."

Both are clothed in the general *Ohr Hozer*, called *Kli*, and both are one *Behina*.

Explanation: When the Light shines in the *Kelim*, we say that the Light and the *Kli* are mixed in one another until the Light and the *Kli* become indistinguishable. This means that they are performing the same action, and one cannot be without the other. It is like meal and appetite: they both perform the same action, since it is impossible to eat if there is appetite but no meal, and it is also impossible to eat if there is a meal but no appetite. But afterwards, when the Light departs, we discern the *Kli*, meaning the *Ohr Hozer* receives the name *Kli*.

So it is concerning the *Reshimot*: When the fine Light and the thick Light are together, they are both called Light and they are mingled in one another. And when the fine Light is separated from the thick Light, the thick Light receives a new name: *Nitzotzin* [sparks].

We should understand why it is that when the general *Ohr Yashar* departs, the general *Ohr Hozer* is called *Kli*, but when the *Ohr Yashar* in the *Reshimo* departs, the thick Light in the *Reshimo* is called *Nitzotz* [spark], meaning a spark of Light.

Answer: We should say that when the general *Ohr Yashar* departs, it does not shine at all. But when the *Ohr Yashar* in the *Reshimo* departs, it shines from afar.

Now we can understand the matter of the root of the *Kelim* and the root of the Lights: There is a rule that all the worlds emerge in the form of seal and imprint. This means that as the discernments emerge the first time, the worlds expand from above downward by that same order. The first time that *Kelim* emerged was in *Partzuf Galgalta*. This is why it is considered "the root of the *Kelim*."

This means that when the Light shines in the *Kelim*, they are mixed. For this reason, it is impossible to distinguish the Light from the *Kli*. But after the departure of the Light, the *Kelim* appear. Also, *Reshimot* from the Light remain in the *Kelim*: a *Reshimo* of the Light of *Keter* in the *Kli* of *Keter*, a *Reshimo* of the Light of *Hochma* in the *Kli* of *Hochma*, etc. Hence, when we speak of the *Kelim*, we begin with *KHB*.

And when the second *Partzuf* emerged, called *AB*, where the Light of *Hochma* shines, following the rule that each Light that comes shines in the finest *Kli*, called *Keter*, now the Light of *Hochma* shines in the *Kli* of *Keter*. This is called "the root of the Lights," which are arranged in this order, the order of *HBD*. By this we can understand why he sometimes starts the ten *Sefirot* with *KHB* and sometimes with *HBD*.

## Tagin and Otiot

Now we shall explain the matter of *Tagin* and *Otiot*. We learned that the *Reshimot* that remained from the *Taamim* are called *Tagin*. Sometimes he calls the *Reshimot* that remain of the *Nekudot* by the name *Otiot*. The reason for it is that when the whole of *Partzuf Galgalta* purifies, which is *Behina Dalet de Aviut*, the *Masach* was included with the *Reshimot* of all the levels that departed. This *Masach* rose to the *Rosh* of the degree and asked for the powers it had lost. Since the last *Behina* is lost due to the *Bitush de Ohr Makif* that weakened the force of the *Masach*, it could not overcome *Behina Dalet*, but only *Behina Gimel*, which is similar to *Nekudot*.

We learned that two kinds of *Reshimot* remained—a *Reshimo* from the Light of *Keter* that was clothed in the *Kelim*, called *Dalet de Hitlabshut* [clothing]. However, it lost the *Reshimo* from the strength and overcoming. It is said about that, "the last *Behina* is lost," and what remains is only *Gimel de Aviut*.

It follows that when the *Masach* of *Guf de Galgalta* rose to the *Rosh de Galgalta*, it asked for the power of the *Masach* for both kinds of *Reshimot*:

1. On *Dalet*, the *Reshimo* from the level of *Taamim*.
2. On the *Aviut* of the level of *Nekudot*.

Hence, two *Zivugim* were made at the *Rosh* of the degree:

1. On *Dalet de Hitlabshut* at the level of *Keter*.
2. On *Gimel de Aviut* at the level of *Hochma*.

We also learned that *Dalet de Hitlabshut* shines only at the *Rosh* of the degree of the lower one, the *Rosh de AB*. But *Gimel de Aviut* has *Hitpashtut* in the *Guf*, as well. Since the *Guf* is called *Kelim* and *Otiot*, the *Reshimo de Aviut*, meaning the *Reshimo de Nekudot*, is called *Otiot*. This is so because afterwards, *Kelim* spread from this *Reshimo*, while the *Reshimo de Hitlabshut* remains as *Tagin*, shining only at the *Rosh* of the degree.

Orally, he explained it in this manner: *Gimel de Aviut de AB* and *Gimel de Galgalta* are not identical, since *Gimel de AB* is the *Gimel* of the general *Aviut*, while *Gimel de Galgalta* is the *Gimel* of *Dalet de Aviut*. Even so, *Gimel de AB* still extends from *Gimel de Galgalta*. Hence, here he ascribes the *Reshimo de Aviut* on which *Partzuf AB* emerged to *Reshimo de Nekudot*, whose highest *Behina* is *Gimel*.

## The Continuation of the Procession

Let us return to clarifying the continuation of the procession. Once the *Ohr Makif* canceled the *Masach de Guf de Galgalta*, the *Masach de Guf* rose to the *Rosh*. Since the last *Behina* was lost, there was a *Zivug* at the *Rosh de Galgalta* on *Reshimot Dalet Gimel* only, spreading from *Peh* to *Chazeh*.

Since the *Masach de Tabur* is included in the *Aviut de Rosh*, while it is at the *Rosh*, there are two discernments to make in it:

1. Its own *Behina*—*Masach de Tabur*;

2. *Aviut de Rosh*.

Once this *Masach* descended from *Peh* to *Chazeh*, which is *Behina Gimel*, it is considered that the Light of *AB* shines in the internality of *Kelim de Galgalta*. This means that the inner *AB* made a *Zivug* on what was included in the *Aviut de Rosh*. From *Chazeh* to *Peh de Galgalta*, a new degree emerged, called "*Rosh* of the outer *AB*," and from *Chazeh* to *Tabur* emerged the *Guf de AB*.

Question: This is perplexing. After all, there is a rule that the next degree should fill the empty *Kelim* of the previous degree. So why does *AB* not expand below *Tabur de Galgalta*?

Answer: It is because it does not have a *Masach* on *Behina Dalet*. Hence, were it to expand below and see the will to receive that is present there, it would not be able to overcome it. This is why it remained above the *Tabur*.

In *Partzuf AB*, too, there was a *Bitush* of *Ohr Makif*, and *Partzuf SAG* emerged from the *Reshimot* of *Partzuf AB*. These are still the *Reshimot* from above *Tabur de AK*, but the *Reshimot* from below *Tabur de AK* have not yet been filled.

This *Partzuf SAG* emerged on *Reshimot Gimel de Hitlabshut* and *Bet de Aviut*, as well as filled the empty *Kelim* of *Partzuf AB*. However, it could not descend below *Tabur de Galgalta* and fill the empty *Kelim* there since it has *Gimel de Hitlabshut*, which are *Kelim* for extension of *Hochma*. It follows that this discernment, called *Taamim de SAG*, expanded through *Tabur de AK*.

But *Nekudot de SAG*, considered merely *Hassadim*, since they do not have the above-mentioned *Behina Gimel*, could expand below *Tabur de Galgalta*, although there is *Behina Dalet de Aviut* there, which is a vessel of reception on which it is impossible to place a *Masach*. Still, because *Nekudot de SAG* are vessels of bestowal, they have no interest in vessels of reception. Hence, they expanded below *Tabur de Galgalta* and filled the empty *Kelim* that were there.

Yet, since they saw the will to receive that was there, they wanted to receive in order to receive, as they did not have a *Masach* on *Behina Dalet*. And since we learned that there was a *Tzimtzum* on receiving in order to receive, the Light immediately departed from them.

Question: We learned that *Nekudot de SAG* are vessels of bestowal. Thus, how were they restricted?

Answer: There is a difference between *GAR de Bina* and *ZAT de Bina*, since we learned that *ZAT de Bina* should receive *Hochma* in order to bestow upon *ZA*, but *GAR de Bina* engage solely in bestowal.

Now we can understand why *GAR de Bina*, which are *GE*, were not mixed, which left *GE* in the degree, unrestricted, while *ZAT de Bina*, called *AHP*, departed the degree because they wanted to receive in order to receive. This is called *Tzimtzum Bet* [second restriction].

It follows that in *HBD*, *HGT de Nekudot de SAG*, which are *GE*, there is no mixture of *Behina Dalet*. Hence, their place is still considered the place of *Atzilut*. Below *Tabur de Nekudot de SAG*, clothing the two bottom thirds of *NHY de AK*, the reception in order to receive governs.

When *Partzuf SAG* rose to *Peh de Rosh*, two *Zivugim* were made there at *Rosh de SAG*:

1. A *Zivug* on *Reshimot de Taamim de SAG* that did not descend below *Tabur de AK*, and from which the *Partzuf* of the upper *MA* emerged.

2. A *Zivug* on *Reshimot de Nekudot de SAG* that were restricted and mingled with *Behina Dalet* below *Tabur de AK*, from which *MA* emerged—the world of *Nekudim*. This *Zivug* took place on half a degree of *Aleph de Aviut* and on *Bet de Hitlabshut*.

Therefore, we must understand that *Malchut* does not extend Light on her own vessels of reception, but only on vessels of bestowal due to the *Tzimtzum*. Because of it, were she to use the vessels of reception, it would be in order to receive.

Here, too, we learn that the Light spreads in both the inner *Kelim de SAG*, and in the outer *Kelim de SAG*. We should know that as a rule, he does not speak of the upper *MA*, since we are speaking primarily about the association of *Midat ha Rachamim* [quality of mercy] with *Din* [judgment], which begins in *Partzuf MA*, which is the world of *Nekudim*.

We learned that there are two *Roshim* [pl. of *Rosh*] in the world of *Nekudim*: 1) from the *Aviut*, and 2) from the *Hitlabshut* [clothing]. *Keter* is called *Bet de Hitlabshut*, and *AVI* are *Aleph de Aviut*. Since *Bet de Hitlabshut* cannot extend Light, since there is no deficiency there, it needs the association with the *Aviut*, which has the power to extend Light. We also learned that the level of Light that shines there is VAK de Bina, in the form of "for He desires mercy," which frees the degree from the need for Hochma.

This Light is also called Tikkun Kavim [correction of lines]. Hence, we learned that the Tikkun Kavim shines only at the Rosh, since the Hitlabshut does not have Hitpashtut [expansion] in the Guf. But the Guf had only a small illumination, and it was not satisfied with the state of Katnut. Hence, when the Light of Gadlut came, the vessels of bestowal of the Guf broke, as well.

www.ingramcontent.com/pod-product-compliance
Lightning Source LLC
Chambersburg PA
CBHW051706160426
43209CB00004B/1047